LIKE NO
OTHER STORE...

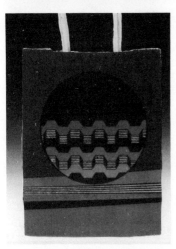

Fall 1961
L'Esprit de France, Jonah Kiningstein

Fall 1964
Johnny So Long at the Fair

Spring 1971
Tai and Rosita Missoni

Spring 1976
Michaele Vollbracht

Fall 1963
Tradition

Fall 1989
Vive la France, Geoff Kern

Spring 1988
Neville Brody

Spring 1991
Malcolm Garrett

Fall 1987
Mediterranean Odyssey, Ann

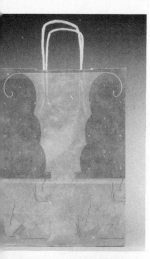

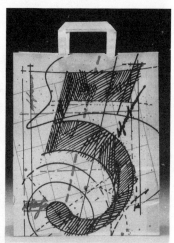

Spring 1984 *Michael Graves*	*Fall 1984 Ecco L'Italia* *Ettore Sottsass*	*Spring 1985* *Scandinavia*
Spring 1986 *Mark Kostabi*	*Fall 1990* *Palm Beach Store. Laurie Rosenwald*	*Spring 1985* *Tim Girvin*
Summer 1983 *Susan Curtis*	*Fall 1982* *America*	*Fall 1991, Tempo D'Italia* *Franco Moschino (see last page)*

LIKE NO OTHER STORE...

THE BLOOMINGDALE'S LEGEND
AND THE REVOLUTION IN AMERICAN MARKETING

MARVIN TRAUB
AND TOM TEICHOLZ

TIMES BOOKS

RANDOM HOUSE

All rights reserved under International and Pan-American Copyright
Conventions. Published in the United States by Times Books, a division of
Random House, Inc., New York, and simultaneously in Canada by Random
House of Canada Limited, Toronto.

Grateful acknowledgment is made to *The New Yorker* for permission to
reprint an excerpt from "Giving Good Value" by Holly Brubach from the
August 10, 1992 issue of *The New Yorker*. Copyright © 1992 by Holly
Brubach. Originally in *The New Yorker*. Reprinted by permission.

Library of Congress Cataloging-in-Publication Data
Traub, Marvin.
Like no other store— : the Bloomingdale's legend and the
revolution in American marketing / by Marvin Traub and Tom Teicholz.
—1st ed.
p.   cm.
Includes index.
ISBN 0-8129-1963-7
1. Bloomingdale's (Firm)—History.   2. Traub, Marvin.
I. Teicholz, Tom.   II. Title.
HF5465.U6B588   1993
381'.45'00097471—dc20   93-28035

Manufactured in the United States of America
9 8 7 6 5 4 3 2 1
First Edition

Book Design by Naomi Osnos and M. Kristen Bearse

For Lee

Contents

Part 5: Bloomingdale's and Beyond

LIKE NO
OTHER STORE...

"For me, this section of Bloomingdale's is terra incognita."

Introduction

The day after Thanksgiving in 1991, I was swimming off the Great Barrier Reef in Australia. The colors of the fish and the coral were vivid—a variety of bright greens, yellows, and iridescent blues—but my mind was not focused on them. For the first time in more than forty years I was not walking the floors of Bloomingdale's—on what is traditionally the busiest shopping day of the year. I was a whole world away. I had just left Bloomingdale's and for the first time in my professional life I was taking that all-important day off. A year later I would be back checking on my stores, embarked on a second career, but at that moment I could reflect on a lifetime of experience in retailing and on the revolution in marketing that I had helped create.

ხ

I started at Bloomingdale's in 1950 when the store was still a modest and slightly dowdy emporium—already seventy-eight years old—a place where Park Avenue maids shopped for their uniforms. Over the next forty years, my co-workers and I transformed the store: In its heyday in the 1960s, 1970s, and 1980s, Bloomies, as the store came to be called, was almost a state of mind, an institution that earned its motto, "Like No Other Store in the World." More than twenty-five of the executives running our best-known stores got their training working with me at Bloomingdale's.

We were trendsetters: We established the concept of dividing the selling floor into boutiques, and we used this setting as a showcase for the talents of such emerging designers as Yves Saint Laurent, Sonia Rykiel, Emanuel Ungaro, and the Missonis. Calvin Klein was a coat designer when he first came to Bloomingdale's and Ralph Lauren a tie salesman. Bloomingdale's was a partner to their transformation of American fashion and marketing by providing them with a launching pad.

Bloomingdale's, more than any other store, made shopping fun. We told our shoppers that we knew who they were and had what they wanted. We knew how they wanted to be perceived. No one had ever sold a store the way we did. And we received unprecedented attention from the press, tourists, movie stars, and even the Queen of England, who, on her first visit to New York in several decades, chose to visit Bloomingdale's because she viewed the store as one of the country's unique cultural institutions.

Bloomingdale's pioneered the concept of the store as a creative force, and we brought a distinctive fashion element not only to clothing but to home furnishings, housewares, and cosmetics. It was not only that our buyers went to the farthest reaches of the earth to find new products; we presented the countries themselves in such full-blown extravaganzas as "India: The Ultimate Fantasy" and "China: Heralding the Dawn of a New Era." And having established Bloomingdale's as a worldwide marketing force and a store brand, we sought to break out of our Northeast home base and establish branch stores throughout the United States.

What I could not foresee was that one day Bloomingdale's itself would become as desirable as the merchandise in its stores, that the store would be seen as a commodity, a trophy whose owner would acquire status and fame. The 1980s, and the mind-set it engendered, with its financial excesses, would forever change Bloomingdale's and end my career there.

b

Life in twentieth-century America has been shaped by the dominance of the automobile and television and by the emergence of such home appliances as the freezer and the microwave. The role of the department store in the new culture of mass consumption has been critical and yet, because shopping is so deeply rooted in habit, the great stories of the last fifty years have been largely taken for granted.

In the 1930s and 1940s, as I was growing up, shopping was, for most people, a basic function. If you needed a bed, you purchased one. You bought a suit or dress for an occasion or a specific purpose because you *needed* one. The frugality bred by the depression had a deep effect on people's shopping habits. Thus, before the Second World War, most department stores offered goods the way Henry Ford sold the Model T—you could have any color as long as it was black. Lipstick came in very few shades, and appliances and garden supplies were sold alongside cameras, radios, and religious items.

At home I was exposed to a different world. My parents were friends with some of the most glamorous retailers and celebrities of their time; through them, I saw a cachet and style that was available only to a small circle of sophisticated shoppers, people who shopped at Bonwit Teller, Bergdorf Goodman, Saks Fifth Avenue, and Neiman-Marcus. A generation later, Bloomingdale's brought that cachet and sense of fashion authority to a larger audience, a new kind of shopper created by the growing wealth of post–World War II America. To the basic concepts of good taste and good value, Bloomingdale's added entertainment and style.

The staid stores of the 1930s were right for their time. Much of this book details how Bloomingdale's created an image to fit the changing times of the sixties, seventies, and eighties. By contrast, those retailers who were unable to change were left behind. (The recent closing of the Sears catalog doesn't mean that either catalogs or discount stores are in trouble. To the contrary, catalogs are healthy, and there is great demand for mass merchandise. Sears, however, lost touch with its shoppers.)

I have nearly a half century's experience in the world of retailing. My education started, quite literally, at the knees of my parents, both of whom were in the industry. I am still immersed in business, no longer at Bloomingdale's but in exciting new projects that include both traditional retailing and marketing, as well as such growing areas as home shopping and selling through television.

b

This book is divided into several parts of unequal size. The first is autobiographical because, in many ways, my background and early work experience is representative of the generation of men and women who created the modern department store. The second part concerns the rise of Bloomingdale's and its impact on such industries as home furnishings, apparel, and cosmetics and on store display and visual merchandising. The third part is about what happened when Bloomingdale's became caught up in the frenzy of acquisition and overreaching that significantly and permanently changed the way retailing in general, and the department store in particular, will function.

Out of these sections I hope a broader canvas emerges. I want to explain how and why the revolution in American marketing matters. Shopping is a pastime as old as the medieval bazaar and as contemporary as QVC and home shopping. The best merchants have always been those who found the right mix for their times and their shoppers, and were prepared to change to meet new consumer demand. Looking back over the last fifty years, I can see that although I accomplished much at Bloomingdale's, larger forces both historical and personal were at work as well. This book places the Bloomingdale's story against the backdrop of great changes in American life-styles. Bloomingdale's has had a tremendous impact on the way goods are sold, the way we look, and even the way we live.

PART 1

The Education of a Merchant

ETERNAL TRIANGLES

ZABAR'S

BANANA
REPUBLIC

FIRE
ISLAND

JEFFERSON
MARKET

BLOOMINGDALE'S

EAST
HAMPTON

FARMERS' MARKET

MACY'S

JONES
BEACH

Stuart Leeds

CHAPTER 1

From the Bronx to Bloomingdale's

Selling has been in my blood from the start. My father, Sam Traub, was the executive vice president and sales manager of Lily of France, a manufacturer of bras and girdles, and my mother, Bea, was in charge of personal shopping for Bonwit Teller. In the 1930s, most of my friends' mothers were at home waiting for them at the end of the school day; mine was different. I knew she had an important job.

I was born in the Bronx, but we later moved to a two-bedroom apartment at 250 West 79th Street in New York City. Most nights my parents arrived home from work with barely enough time to change before they were out the door again. Their social life consisted of business dinners. As they dressed they would fill each other in on their day and I would listen.

"I spoke with Stanley Marcus today," my father would say. "He's coming to New York next week. I'm going to see if I can catch up with him."

"Fine. Mary Martin came in the store today. She's joining us at Sardi's." Sardi's was my parents' hangout and Sunday was their regular night there. They lived life as if in bold type in Walter Winchell's column, although their names rarely appeared there.

b

My father has always been something of a paradox to me. On the one hand, he led a very sophisticated life with my mother. They were a handsome couple, outgoing and very social, who enjoyed living well. They took enormous care with their appearance and their photo albums show them arm in arm like the retailing world's version of Prince Edward and Mrs. Simpson. My father's shirts were custom-ordered from Sulka or Charvet in Paris, his suits tailor-made. He was very rigid in his taste and opinions. He was concerned with status: the right clothes, the right restaurant, the right hotel, the right country club. My dad had enormous charm and people were attracted to him.

But there was another side to him. Sam Traub was a gambler who squandered huge sums at the track, who reveled in the fact that he had his hair cut by Frank Costello's barber at the Waldorf. He was a man who had little concept of family, who kept a mistress for many years, and who ran off, at one point, with a bra model. In the chasm between these two parts of his personality was his past, about which he never spoke. I never even knew whether he was born in Poland or Russia.

Over the years he let out a few cryptic comments. He was proud of the fact that he grew up on Manhattan's Lower East Side. His father died when he was in the eighth grade and he was left to support his mother and two sisters. His formal education ended and he began selling apples from a pushcart. His younger brother Joe ran off to join the navy. Joe turned up several years later in Hollywood; he changed his name from Joseph Weintraub to Joe Traub and became a scriptwriter for films, including the very successful James Cagney–Pat O'Brien movie *Here Comes the Navy*. Unfortunately, Joe died in 1937, at age thirty-seven, I gather from too much alcohol and a rather dissolute life-style. My father later changed his name to Traub as well.

In the 1920s, my father landed a job as a stock boy for a small firm called Model Brassiere, part of the fledgling bra industry. His days selling apples turned out to be an asset, for he was glib, self-assured, and a smooth talker. In no time he became a salesman for the company.

I imagine it was during these years that he transformed himself into the polished individual I came to know. He was only five feet eight inches tall and slim, but he had a commanding presence. He was perpetually tan, thanks to the sunlamp he used at home. My father was very articulate, and spoke perfect English and some French. He wore a fresh flower in his buttonhole every day, and when it was the fashion to do so, he wore spats. He walked slowly but deliberately. He spoke quickly, with gusto, but very clearly, and his subordinates feared him. "He wielded a big stick," one told me.

He never shouted when angry, his associates said; instead, he would lower his voice—a trait I don't recall, but it must be true, since I have the same habit.

He left Model Brassiere in 1936 to join Lily of France, a larger, more established company. Lily had been started at the end of the last century by a Frenchwoman who introduced French corsetry to the New York market. Her garments were so successful that by 1915 the firm owned its own eight-story building at 518 Fifth Avenue.

The bra and girdle business was run by a small group of men in their fifties, sixties, and seventies. The fitters and designers were also older. My father started as a salesman, getting to know the buyers across the country. He progressed rapidly to sales manager, then became the executive vice president in charge of sales and marketing. Lily of France catered to the top end of the market and he met with the country's leading merchandisers. As he talked with younger buyers and store principals, he saw an opportunity to appeal to younger customers. In the 1920s, the flapper had put an end to corsets, but women still needed foundations and undergarments to go with the fashions of that era.

In the 1930s and 1940s, the bra and girdle industry was big business. Compared to other garment industries, it was the closest you could get to show business. It was like being backstage at the Ziegfeld Follies. The business attracted models and actresses, and they in turn attracted businessmen. Imagine walking into showrooms where beautiful women came and went, dressed only in bras and panties. For the modest 1930s, it was sensational and my father loved it. Because, as he saw it, his wife may have known show people, but he was in show business.

At heart, Sam Traub was an idea man, always thinking of new products. At the time, bras were sold only in white or beige, but he was among the first to think that other colors would appeal to women. Sam was also always looking for new materials—lighter-weight fabric, different elastic—for a more comfortable fit. He traveled to Paris to find new colors and new designs. The buyers were his coconspirators; together they would dream up new merchandise.

The different aspects of my father's personality came together in his work. There he could be both snob and showman; there he could exercise taste and flamboyance. He could work his considerable charm in the company of the store principals, men with whom he felt at ease. They spoke the same language: marketing.

My father realized early on that, given the choice between two identical bras, people would pay a little more for a brand name they had confidence in. He realized that lingerie sold better if it appeared to be French. In the 1950s, he became the first American manufacturer to develop a license arrangement with Christian Dior. He went to Paris himself and negotiated with Dior and his business manager Jacques Rouet, both of whom became friends. Christian Dior bras and panties are strong sellers to this day.

At times we were very close. I think back fondly of when I was still a boy and he used to take me to see the great Yankee teams of the 1930s play at the stadium or to watch Tuffy Leemans and the Giants play football at the Polo Grounds. Yet as I grew older we quarreled more and more. By the time I got to college, I was happy to be on my own.

b

My parents were both in love with New York's sophisticated set. My father had assumed a personal style that seemed to the manor born. My mother was different. Though in many ways as much of a snob, she never forgot how hard she worked for her achievements.

Her parents had emigrated from Russia around the turn of the century. Bessie Bruckman (Bea came later) was one of five children; she had an older brother and three younger sisters. With only a high school education, at a time when few women held positions of importance in the American work force, she achieved a legendary position in retailing as Bonwit Teller's clothes consultant, a personal shopper for customers from all over the world. Many stores today have personal shoppers, but few give their customers the kind of attention Bea Traub provided. Mamie Eisenhower, Mrs. Ed Sullivan, Flor Trujillo, and Kate Smith treated her as a friend and relied on her sense of fashion and good taste.

My mother was an attractive woman, short, with curly blond hair and a strong resemblance to her friend Mary Martin. She dressed mostly in black and wore simple jewelry. Her great success was due to her personality. She genuinely loved people, bubbled with sparkling conversation, and had an infectious enthusiasm for fashion. She was solicitous and a good listener. She had a quality that appealed to others and her friends loved her dearly.

In the 1950s, Bonwit's salon floor had a separate area that was my mother's kingdom. It was as big as any living room. I remember large red velvet drapes and furniture inlaid with mother of pearl, comfortable couches and chairs. One whole side held lavish fitting rooms. My mother's office was off to the side, but she was rarely there. She was in the salon with her famous friends. Theater people didn't have time to browse. So they would call ahead, and by the time they arrived my mother had set aside a collection of dresses for them to consider. While they lounged in her salon, her assistants presented the outfits. Tea, coffee, sandwiches, and cakes were served. Cocktails, too. When her customers couldn't make a decision my mother made it for them.

Today, every store is trying to improve its customer relations and teach its sales staff how to woo clients. In Bea Traub's day, she had the field to herself. She kept a detailed client book listing not only her customers' preferences but also the names and birthdays of their children. Her "book" was legendary and Stanley Marcus, chairman of world-renowned Neiman-Marcus, would drop by to compare notes, and they would trade stories about the idiosyncrasies of their wealthiest customers.

Bea loved to tell our relatives about her friends, but I was her best audience. To whom else could she admit she was star-struck? Not Helen Hayes or Kate Smith. Did they care that Bea Bruckman from Brooklyn was friends with Jacqueline Kennedy and Lady Bird Johnson? My father's success grew from his love of merchandise and marketing; my mother's came from understanding her customer. My mother was very driven. Some think she was a more aggressive salesperson than my father. My mother believed that she was living proof that there was no obstacle that could not be overcome. I learned that from her.

b

In a way, my mother owes her career in retailing to me, or at least to my birth. Born on April 14, 1925, my parents named me after a business associate of my father's. At first we lived in the Bronx, in a building called the David Farragut at 1075 Grand Concourse, which, as far as I know, is still standing. In 1930, we moved to the Upper West Side of Manhattan, living first in an apartment hotel at 87th Street and Riverside Drive, then moving to 79th Street, where we lived until I went to college.

At first my mother stayed home to care for me, as was the norm then. But homemaking didn't really suit her. My father was traveling and she was lonely. She would go to her mother's for dinner, but it was not the kind of company she sought. One day she found herself telling my friend Harvey Pack's mother that she was bored and had no friends. Rose Pack suggested that she play cards with the other mothers. "I hate cards," my mother said.

"Well then," Rose suggested, "you better get a part-time job." It was the depression, and my father had no objection. She started selling dresses in a specialty store. She was very successful, and in 1935, my father introduced her to Hortense Odlum, chairwoman of Bonwit's, who hired her as a saleswoman in the designer area.

She started on the selling floor, and by 1940 she was so successful that she was given her own office. As part of the extraordinary service my mother gave, she would travel to customers' summer homes in Southampton, New York, or even to Nashville, Tennessee, armed with the latest fashions. It's hard to believe how different retailing was then. On a Friday afternoon in the summer, my mother would, on occasion, load her car's trunk with clothes and accessories from the store and head off, a scarf around her head, sunglasses on, and more clothes filling the backseat. Bonwit's was closed on summer weekends then, but mother would spend Saturday and Sunday visiting friends, bringing the season's fashions to her clients. On Monday she would report what sales she had made, and return what clothes, if any, remained. Inventory and stock control have changed a great deal since then.

My parents worked at their professional and personal relationships. For my mother, each customer was a potential resource for another. If Ed Sullivan's wife needed a favor, she asked Bea Traub. If one of her clients confessed that she was nervous about her child's private school application, mother spoke to the wife of the director of admissions and helped get a special interview. She got things done. She gave more than she got, but when my parents needed a favor they did not hesitate to ask.

People who knew my parents can see very clearly their great influence on me. My father's showmanship, his love for creating new product, and my mother's drive and enthusiasm are clearly components of my personality.

My parents believed that American democracy meant equal opportunity. My father's success entitled him, as far as he was concerned, to be more of a snob than the next guy. To my parents, the Old World, even their childhoods, were what they had worked so hard to leave behind. The trip they and their parents had taken from Eastern Europe to the United States was part of the same evolution that took them from the Lower East Side and the Bronx to Manhattan's Upper West Side.

To show how far the pendulum has now swung in the other direction, *Town & Country* magazine recently ran a feature on people whose ancestors had passed through Ellis Island, including my grandmother. My mother, whose father had worked as a translator on Ellis Island, had a distinguished pedigree that included "the Petrikover Rebbe," a legendary sage and healer in eighteenth-century Poland. How shocked Bea would have been to see her mother's picture in *Town & Country*. Today Ellis Island is chic.

Eddie's, a candy store at 2186½ Broadway between 82nd and 83rd streets, was where I met my friends after school. For kids, the Upper West Side was demarcated by candy stores. There was a 90th Street crowd—their famous alumni include tycoons Marvin Davis and Lew Rudin—that favored the candy store at 91st and Broadway. We were the 83rd Street crowd. We spent most afternoons together at Eddie's or in Central Park, and weekends in Van Cortlandt Park or at the movies.

Eddie's was a large candy and cigar store. Long and narrow, the entire left side was lined with magazines. The soda fountain and counter were in the back, as were the two pinball machines where we used to congregate. Harvey Pack and Richard Rosen were my best friends then, and we attended the local public and elementary schools: PS 9 on 83rd Street, then PS 166.

The friends with whom I grew up came from the same background: white, middle class, and mostly Jewish. It was the depression, but our part of New York seemed less affected. Our parents were all in the garment business, directly or indirectly, and we lived in a secularized world. Saturdays to us meant play group, supervised football, and baseball outings in Van Cortlandt Park in the Bronx, packing lunch and enjoying twelve-ounce bottles of that new soft drink, Pepsi.

b

In many ways, I was a typical adolescent. I was somewhat shy, a dedicated but not outstanding athlete—a good hitter but slow afoot. If I stood out among my friends in any way, it was that I wouldn't take no for an answer. One incident remains in my memory as testament to the determined qualities that would later serve me so well. I was ten, and a group of friends had gathered to play football in Central Park. We made our way to a large playing field, but no sooner had we begun to toss the ball, than a park policeman shooed us away, saying, "You can't play here."

"Why not?" I asked.

"It's not allowed."

"Where can we play, then?" I asked.

"Nowhere, you're not allowed to tear up the park."

My father always told me that if you have a problem, talk to the man at the top. The next day, after school, I went to the Arsenal, the park headquarters that sits in a red-brick fortresslike building at 64th and Fifth. I remember as though it were yesterday the insistence that fueled me.

"I want to see the head of the parks," I said. The secretary seemed surprised to see a ten-year-old boy standing before her, all dressed up in a Rogers Peet suit, with his hair slicked down.

"Just what is this about?" she asked.

I told her. She asked me to wait. Finally they brought out an assistant. I explained my problem.

"Let's see what I can do," the assistant said.

"I'll wait," I told him.

The assistant disappeared for a few minutes, but I never doubted he was coming back. He did shortly, saying that his boss agreed. We should be allowed to play football in the park.

"In Central Park?" I asked.

"Yes." He designated an area we would be allowed to play in.

"And you'll tell the police and park crew to let us play?"

"I'll tell them."

"Good. Thank you."

The next day when we went to the park to play, a park man approached us. My friends were ready to run. I told them to hold their ground.

"You boys here to play football?" he asked.

"That's right," I said, defiantly.

"Enjoy yourselves," he said, smiling.

♭

At age twelve, my parents decided to send me to Peekskill Military Academy, a traditional military school. I never fully understood why. My mother spoke of improving my posture. But I wondered if it was not because my parents fought frequently and I was in the way. My parents also believed that having a child at military school was prestigious. As a dutiful son, I went. But I was lonely, had few friends, and was uncomfortable at the mandatory weekly Christian church services. When I came home at midyear I announced I would not return next year. The following year I was enrolled in DeWitt Clinton High School, a public school in the Bronx.

It took three subways to get there. Clinton had sixteen thousand students, and its share of rough kids. But I was happy to be there, admitted as part of its twelve-hundred-student honor program, Arista. In those days, many of my friends skipped grades. I was fourteen and in tenth grade. It was not unusual to graduate at sixteen.

I went to the theater as often as I could. I didn't have a big allowance, but I could afford the five-cent trolley or subway fare down Broadway to Times Square.

I'll never forget the sense of excitement that I felt as I approached the theater district. Times Square was the center of the universe. Every way you turned there was something to catch your attention. Bill Larner was the most literate and best read of my friends, and he shared my love of theater. Tickets cost anywhere from 55 cents to $2.40. Bill and I could not afford to go as often as we wanted, so we often stole into shows after the first act, mingling with the crowds when they came out at intermission and grabbing any empty seat we could. We saw the second and third acts of many great shows that way.

The late thirties were Broadway's heyday. The four years between 1936 and 1940 alone saw productions of *You Can't Take It with You*, *Stage Door*, *Tovarich*, *Tobacco Road*, *Golden Boy*, *Pins and Needles*, *Our Town*, and *The Philadelphia Story*, among so many others. One of my favorites was *The Man Who Came to Dinner*, by George S. Kaufman and Moss Hart, which opened in October 1939 at the Music Box Theatre. I saw the second and third act five times and could almost deliver the punch lines. I saw the first act at least once.

Though among some friends the theater was our love, we also went to the movies. Times Square was only a twenty-minute express subway ride from DeWitt Clinton, so we cut afternoon classes to catch a performance at the Paramount or the Roxy. This was the day of the movie palaces with names like the Strand, the Rialto, and the Rivoli.

The Paramount, at the corner of 43rd and Broadway, was the place to go to see film premieres. The afternoon audiences consisted largely of kids cutting school. The theater was ten stories high, and the lobby and lounges were based on the chapel at Versailles. There was a blaze of chandeliers and a ceiling mural depicting the Sun King. But we didn't go there for the architecture.

The Paramount had stage shows with the big bands. As part of my extracurricular education I saw Jimmy Dorsey, Artie Shaw, Tommy Dorsey, Buddy Rich, and that hot new singer, Frank Sinatra. Kids would get up in the aisles and scream and jitterbug. A double feature would mean more than four hours of entertainment, all for thirty-five cents.

As I got older, poker and blackjack with Harvey and the guys was supplanted by dating. Mostly we went to our neighborhood theaters, the RKO 81st and Loews 83rd, where we spent many a Saturday afternoon in the balconies, sneaking cigarettes. That was where we saw *Casablanca*, and just about every single Bob Hope and Bing Crosby *Road* movie ever released.

What I didn't know at the time was that my love of entertainment would develop into the sense of spectacle we created at Bloomingdale's thirty years later. My afternoons at the Roxy and the Paramount were a great education for being a merchant. Today, 42nd Street awaits redevelopment, many of the great Broadway theaters are dark or have long since been torn down, and many of the movie houses have been multiplexed. To feel that same sense of wonder today, you no longer go to Times Square; instead, you go shopping.

b

My parents wanted me to be a doctor. Actually, I recall that all parents on the Upper West Side wanted their children to be doctors or lawyers. But they showed me a world of retailing that I ultimately found irresistible.

There was a small circle of merchants that my parents respected. At Bonwit Teller, my mother introduced me to the people who headed the store, such as Bill Holmes, who was there much of the forties, the legendary Walter Hoving, and Mildred Custin, who was close to my mother. I also got to meet Adam Gimbel of Saks, Cyril Magnin of the Magnin family, and of course Stanley Marcus.

My father was proud to have me meet his business associates. I'll never forget the time he invited me to lunch at the Empire State Club on the twenty-first floor of the Empire State Building. I was spending the summer between my junior and senior years in high school working as a shoe stock boy at Franklin Simon. Imagine my surprise when I arrived and found my father seated with Jim Storey, the head of the store. They were friends, of course. My father was one of his largest suppliers. This was the first time I had seen Mr. Storey since being hired. It still strikes me as funny: the head of the store, one of his largest suppliers, and a teenager from the shoe stockroom.

I met these men, saw the businesses they ran, and the esteem my parents held them in. I thought I might like to be them one day.

My parents did not spend much time with me, but I was a curious, eager, enthusiastic child, and ate up all they had to offer me. They instilled in me an appreciation of things well made, of fine food, and of the importance of culture that has stayed with me my whole life. If they were not the warmest or most doting parents, they did bring me up to eat and breathe retail.

Getting into Harvard was a goal I set for myself. Traditionally, only one or two students from DeWitt's four-thousand-member graduating class were admitted to Harvard, and I wanted to be chosen. I applied to Princeton, Brown, and Harvard, but was convinced that Harvard was the best. Since having a son at Harvard was also an ambition of my father's, he called one of the most prominent Harvard College graduates he knew, Stanley Marcus. My father explained that I was applying to the college and asked if Mr. Marcus would write a letter of recommendation.

Stanley Marcus would not give a recommendation, he said, unless he interviewed me. I went to see him at his office in New York. We discussed the war and politics. My father was very conservative and I was surprised to find Stanley Marcus to be a liberal. He was a very lively man and told me how much he had enjoyed Harvard. Afterward, Mr. Marcus told my father I was "bright," and agreed to call the dean of admissions to put in a good word. In those days recommendations meant more than they do today. I have no idea if it made a difference, but I was always grateful for his kindness. If there was a retailer that I later patterned myself after, it was Stanley Marcus.

b

I entered Harvard in June 1942. The college had gone on a full-year trimester program to accommodate students leaving for the service. Arriving in Cambridge was a little like being thrown into a maelstrom. Walking into Harvard Yard's Memorial Hall to register, I was besieged by a mass of students at tables soliciting me to join a host of student activities. It was like a medieval fair.

At the time, Harvard was a formal male society set up like an English university. Ivy-covered Adams House had "biddies," ladies to make the beds and clean the rooms. The House master, David Mason Little, made a point of knowing each student by his first name. Adams House also had its own kitchen and its dining room boasted the best-prepared food in the college, with elegant printed menus. Jacket and tie were required and waiter service was provided. It had its own swimming pool, which was the center of social activity during the summer of 1942.

After DeWitt Clinton, Harvard was something of a culture shock. My first impression was that everyone was extraordinarily bright, older, and more mature, more affluent, and better dressed. I had grown up in New York, with very worldly parents, but now I felt as if I'd seen very little of life. While I had been getting good grades, it seemed everyone else had been amassing vast amounts of real-life knowledge.

In the fall, I entered the competition for the business board of the Harvard *Crimson*, the college newspaper. The *Crimson* selected candidates based on several criteria including who sold the most ads.

The war was becoming increasingly important to me. So I went down to Church Street to try to enlist in the navy officer program. My eyes were not very good, though, and I did not pass the exam. In trying to sign up, however, I saw a business opportunity for the *Crimson*. Boston stores were just getting into the business of selling uniforms. Harvard was filled with servicemen and army and navy officers in training. The *Crimson* could tap this new market for the stores. I contacted the advertising manager of Filene's. I sold her on the idea of advertising for uniforms in the *Crimson*. Once Filene's was in, I went to Jordan Marsh and sold them as well. It was like a snowball. Before I knew it, uniform advertising was an important source of income for the *Crimson* and I found myself elected to the business board.

Despite my enthusiasm for the *Crimson*, throughout the spring of 1943 I found it hard to be at Harvard with the war going on. For many of my generation, the 1930s and 1940s were a time of awakened political consciousness. I was particularly influenced by Wendell Willkie and his liberal internationalist plans for building "One World." Nothing seemed more important to me than the Second World War.

My parents wanted me to finish college first, but I was as gung ho as every other eighteen-year-old. Harvard had assured us that we could return at any time and would receive credit for army instruction. In June 1943, I joined the army's Specialized Training Program (ASTP).

More than a year later, on July 21, 1944, after having done my infantry basic training at Fort Benning, Georgia, a stint at the University of Pittsburgh in the engineering program, and a transfer to the infantry, I landed in France on Utah Beach, Normandy, as part of the 379th Infantry, 95th Division, U.S. Third Army. We remained in Normandy until late September when, as part of the breakout across France, our division moved to an area of Alsace-Lorraine on the Franco-German border.

I was made acting sergeant, but as first scout I occasionally led the company. In early November, on one advance through heavy woods, we were ambushed and pinned down by German rifle fire and mortars coming from both sides of the forest. The company commander gave word for us to pull back, but I was too far up front to move back. The number two scout lay next to me and I realized he'd been wounded. We had to lie still and wait silently in place for several hours until an American barrage forced the Germans back into their foxholes and I could start to crawl back, rifle in one hand, helping the number two scout, afraid that at any moment the Germans would see us and shoot us in the back. It was terrifying. I knew we were getting close when we came upon the bodies of soldiers from our platoon. We continued to inch by, not knowing if we would soon join them.

Finally, and it seemed an eternity, we cleared the woods. I stood up, gave a great sigh, and returned to our company. The other scout was taken to an aid station. He had been shot in the stomach. I was fine and remember just feeling lucky to be alive.

On the fourteenth of November we attacked Fort Jeanne D'Arc outside Metz. Metz had been the site of the Maginot Line and the Germans were using it as a fortified position. That day the platoon leader asked me to carry the radio equipment and serve as the company's communications man. We were attacking early in the morning. We had to cross an eight-hundred-yard-long snow-covered field in heavy morning fog and descend a wooded draw before coming to our objective, two well-fortified pillboxes. I had a little notebook that I kept with me, and later I wrote down my impressions of the battle. I was nineteen, and today it still reads like the thoughts of a very young soldier, filled with the anger, horror, and passion of combat:

"Gravalotte was a mighty cold town that Wednesday morning. It had snowed the night before and was still coming down as C company spread out over the streets and moved toward the outskirts. We'd taken the town the preceding day and its few houses were pockmarked by shell holes. Shells were whistling into the ruins or just beyond them and we moved in two columns, one on each side of the street, keeping a sizable interval between men.

"I was at the head of the column that morning—right behind Lieutenant Cunningham. He had lost his runner taking the town and asked me to fill in as the platoon was in reserve and I wouldn't be needed by my squad. . . .

"We lay flat on the gentle slope that led into the field; and could hear more shells whistling overhead. Then our mortars opened up—I could hear the pop, pop, pop as mortar shell after mortar shell came out of the tubes. Then ahead of us came a steady *baruham, barahum* of the shells landing—it was too misty to see them landing. All this stopped suddenly and I looked at my watch—it was one minute to nine and Captain Carter had his whistle to his lips. At 0900 he blew and we rose up and moved ahead in a skirmish line. Every man let go a clip at once and it was a helluva racket as the mortars had resumed firing and our machine guns were plugging away, too. We still couldn't see anything in the mist, but fired straight ahead, hoping to pin Jerry down.

"We'd gone about twenty yards when we got an answer, machine guns began to yammer. . . . Somewhere to the left of us, two of our shadows fell over—I see a medic run up to one of them. We kept moving, firing at the sounds. . . . Now the fighting was getting heavy. We kept moving ahead, stopping every few steps to fire at sounds. We still couldn't make out anything. It all seemed unreal to me—I couldn't understand what was happening. Sure I saw shadowy figures pitch forward on their faces, some threw up their hands and writhed on the ground, some just lay still, but somehow it didn't seem like the real thing—it must be a movie. I couldn't realize that those figures pitching over were my friends and they were being killed and maimed right in front of me.

"The machine-gun fire seemed close now. I saw a sergeant in the first platoon pull out a grenade; a few of us followed suit and we all let loose at the MG; we bent low and heard them explode and the whirring of shrapnel. The gun was silent. We kept moving but that small-arms fire seemed to keep moving ahead of us. The field was littered with bodies, arms, and Krauts. On the right we passed a twisted machine gun with four green-clad bodies sprawled about it, one had a pistol in his hand.

"My mind seemed a kaleidoscope, filled with hundreds of different thoughts, impressions, and pictures, yet something tangible seemed missing. Off to the left, there was a medic working over a still figure, the machine guns crackled and Brad, the medic, fell over the man he was working on.

"I could make out the blurry objects ahead—most of the Krauts were dug in at the edge of the draw. We moved forward until we were only a hundred yards from the edge. Then the fire was too much; it was cutting us down, so we all threw ourselves to the ground. I lay there and bitterly recalled a speech General Patton had made before we hit combat. 'There's no such thing as being pinned down,' he said, 'when you attack I want you to keep moving ahead, don't hit the ground or you'll be lost.' Well, by God, I'd like to have seen that sonofabitch moving ahead there.

"The captain called back for more mortars, then called to each platoon to fire their bazookas. . . . The mortars and bazookas hit at about the same time and threw dirt and rocks into the air. We nosed up and found only dead and dying Germans and knocked out machine guns. As I went towards the next objective, I looked up and saw 'Mac,' the kid of the company, still 18 (I was 19), looking a little worried. Just then something went splat right between us throwing dirt into our faces—'close but no cigar,' I muttered and both of us laughed. . . . I was still close at Lt. Cunningham's heels moving down the draw . . ."

My notebook entry ends there, but we kept going. I'm convinced that peer pressure is one of the reasons soldiers in combat perform as they do—you don't want to hold back when people are moving forward on both sides, even though they're getting hit. We started down the draw. I was carrying the heavy radios on my back, and my instinct as I began to slide down the draw was to turn sideways to get better footing. There was a burst of rapid machine-gun fire and I collapsed.

At first I didn't understand what had happened; I was too stunned. But then I saw that my right leg was a bloody mess through my uniform, the bone shattered and sticking out. My first thought was terror; I was afraid my leg had been shot away. I was awake enough to take sulfa powder from my kit and sprinkle it all over the wound, which probably saved my leg if not my life. The action moved beyond me. I was lying in the draw in the snow and cold of November. I hollered "medic" and passed out, then woke only to hear others calling for medics. I felt no real pain and was in shock.

A second bullet had lodged in the upper part of my left leg but was only discovered twenty-five years later on an X-ray.

Because we had so many casualties and so many of the medics were wounded, I wasn't picked up and taken to a field hospital until three or four hours later. From there, after a diagnosis that my right femur had been partially shot away, I was sent to the American Hospital in Paris, where I was operated on and put in a body cast from chest to toe. I was to have a total of seven operations over the next year. From Paris I was dispatched to a hospital in England where I spent Christmas and where doctors tried to straighten my leg, and encased me in a new body cast. From there I was flown to Tilton General Hospital in Fort Dix, New Jersey.

The army had contacted my parents when I was wounded, and I called as soon as I arrived stateside. They drove out to the hospital immediately. I had tried to tell them that everything was all right, but when they saw me they became alarmed. I had lost a great deal of weight, and no one could say if I would ever walk again without limping. My parents were not emotional people, but they were determined to get me the best medical care possible, and went into high gear.

My parents introduced themselves to the colonel in charge of Tilton as well as Col. Al Miller, chief of orthopedics, and the medical staff. In no time they had adopted the hospital. Soon, Ed and Pegeen Fitzgerald, a famous radio couple, were broadcasting their WOR-AM show, "The Fitzgeralds," from the hospital. Ed liked to recount how I was wounded, and each time he told the story my exploits grew in heroism. Bob Considine, a columnist for the *Daily Mirror* and another of my parents' friends, published several of my letters in his column. George Selkirk of the New York Yankees came to sign baseballs for the patients. (Selkirk had replaced Babe Ruth in right field in 1934.) The hospital was theirs. While I was in the hospital, my parents and I grew close again. They visited me weekly, and were tremendously supportive.

Colonel Miller wanted to attempt a relatively new surgical procedure on me—grafting bone from my hip to replace what had been shot away in my leg, an operation made more complicated by the fact that the bone was infected. They went ahead with the procedure and I've always been grateful to Dr. Miller for saving my leg. I was put in traction to recover. The doctors inserted a metal pin, like a nail, through my knee and attached that to a system of pulleys and weights in the bed so I couldn't move while the bone graft was healing and new bone grew around it. Colonel Miller believed that I would walk, but he was not sure whether I would ever be able to bend my knee to any extent. For that, we would have to wait and see.

While I sat in the hospital, the world went on. The war ended in Europe, and then in Japan. I celebrated VE day with champagne in the ward. On the radio we listened to the joyous crowds in Times Square. I wished I was among them, but my leg had developed a new hairline fracture. I'd been at Tilton for almost a year.

Colonel Miller had been sent to the South Pacific. Colonel Brav, who was now in charge of my case, could not tell me how long it would take for my leg to heal. He recommended fusing my knee—it would be stable then but I would never be able to bend it again. I had always been quite active, and I had no intention of slowing down. My father asked for a favor: He requested a second opinion. Colonel Brav was kind enough to allow them the extraordinary privilege of getting a second opinion from Dr. Fenwick Beekman, the chief of orthopedics at Columbia University's Physicians & Surgeons. My parents then contacted Dr. Howard Rusk, a pioneer in the field of rehabilitative medicine who headed that division for the army. (Today, the preeminent rehabilitation facility in New York, the Rusk Institute, is named in his honor.) Dr. Rusk, after consulting with Dr. Beekman, suggested that I be discharged from Tilton. My leg would heal on its own, he felt, aided by a program of therapy and exercise, one that I could do while finishing my studies at Harvard. Tilton could not guarantee those results. Nonetheless, we decided to gamble on Drs. Rusk and Beekman.

b

I returned to Harvard in January of 1946 for the spring term, a sophomore with crutches and a brace. More than two and a half years had passed since I'd last set foot in Harvard Yard. I'd spent half that time in training and combat, the balance in a hospital. I had participated in a war and seen many friends killed or wounded —and on the day I was wounded my closest friend, Leonard Paulsen, was killed. I had almost lost my leg. Yet, for all the horror, I felt good about my war experience. I had been challenged, met the test, and come out a different person, more mature and with greater self-confidence. I left Harvard an eager eighteen-year-old; I found myself back in Harvard Square, now twenty, ready to meet new challenges.

Before the war I had played intramural baseball and football. Our Adams House freshman touch football team was famous: We lost to Yale, 60–0. To be back in Cambridge now with my injured leg was awkward. Dressing, washing, getting around became major inconveniences. The Harvard Athletic Department, however, had a marvelous physical therapy program directed by Dr. Norman Fradd. I went to him every afternoon, five days a week for many months and, using weights, gradually forced motion back into my right knee. It was a long, arduous, and often painful process. At first I despaired of having any motion. Yet over time I went from crutches and a brace, to a cane, and finally to walking on my own again.

That was not, however, the end of my rehabilitation. My right leg was now an inch and a half shorter than my left. I had to teach myself to walk without a limp. Walking normally again became an obsession for me. It was not easy, but by walking with the aid of a built-up shoe, I managed. I felt I had returned to the Harvard life I had left behind.

b

By 1946, Adams House was a different place. There were no longer biddies, waitresses, or printed menus at meals. Jacket and tie were no longer required at dinner; the tablecloths had disappeared and we ate cafeteria-style. The students had changed, too. Before, Harvard had run strictly by class—all freshman started in Harvard Yard —so the class had unity. During and after the war, Harvard was a total mix of people. You had students coming back from the service and a lot of my close friends, associates, and classmates were anywhere from the class of '45 to '49. My roommate turned out to be Sumner Feldberg, '45, a good friend from summer camp more than ten years before and also a war veteran. Harvard gave us credit for army courses and I graduated in 1947, having only been at the college for two and a half years. Our graduating class had no real cohesion. Ed Finkelstein, former chairman of Macy's, and I, for example, were both class of '46 and both attended the business school, but we never knew each other at Harvard (Ed was class of '48 at the business school; I was '49).

b

No problem seemed more pressing when I returned to college than getting the *Crimson* back on its feet. The last issue had been published on May 2, 1943. The *Harvard Service News* had appeared as a replacement, publishing only news with no editorials, a paper put out by civilian students and read by military and naval personnel.

The team that brought the *Crimson* back to life was a remarkable assemblage of talent that included Doug Cater, who would later write speeches for President Lyndon Johnson, future *New York Times* columnist Tony Lewis, as well as Otto Friedrich, Adam Yarmolinsky, and Burt Glynn as our photo chairman. Though students, they already looked on themselves as professional journalists. I took on the assignment as the first postwar business manager. The late hours and camaraderie, as well as the satisfaction of what we accomplished, was one of my most gratifying college experiences. Restoring the *Crimson* to health was my first true entrepreneurial venture and I found myself relishing the challenge.

We were starting from scratch. That gave us freedom, tempered by the imperative to be successful. We had to be creative, but we had to get it done. The *Crimson* receives no subsidy from the university, and my task was to set up the systems and staff that would keep the paper in good health for years to come. We published twenty-two issues that spring.

Advertising was our first priority and I made a list of the *Crimson*'s best former advertisers. Although still on crutches, I paid calls on all of them, from the manager of the Coop in Harvard Square and the people at Filene's, to Al Goro, the local manager of J. Press. Morty Sills, who ran Sills's (a store every bit as preppy as J. Press), told me that most students didn't buy before, and they wouldn't buy now. I told him that the servicemen had learned a thing or two about dressing well and would now need new suits, sportscoats, and slacks. Many of the former advertisers jumped aboard. Walking around Cambridge became a new experience: Each store was now a place where I knew someone, and I could spend days going from store manager to store manager.

The *Harvard Service News* published its last issue on March 29, 1946. Two weeks after spring vacation, on April 16, 1946, we published our first sixteen-page issue of the reborn *Crimson*. We had managed to round up a wide variety of advertisers, including clothiers great and small from Filene's, Brooks Brothers, Jordan Marsh, and J. Press to smaller stores in Harvard Square such as Leopold Morse and J. August; from Gulf Oil and Bell Telephone to Collupy & Collupy, wholesale fish merchants. We even got our printer to take out an ad.

In the almost three years since the *Crimson* had ceased publication, the college enrollment had doubled from 1,300 to 2,600. Before the war, the *Crimson* had been dubbed "Cambridge's only breakfast table daily," but initially we thought daily publication too ambitious. The *Crimson* returned with three issues a week for the spring, increasing to six in the fall.

We had to work on sales techniques and bill collecting, and we instituted a bonus system for the business manager as an incentive to make the paper profitable. It was good for the *Crimson* and lucrative for me.

b

One day during the fall of 1946, one of my classmates, Donald Rugoff, suggested I call Lee Laufer, a friend of his from home who was a senior at Smith. (Donald, whose family owned the Rugoff and Becker theaters in New York, later became well known as the man who brought the film *Z* to this country.) He told me Lee was very bright, very pretty, and then said, as if to clinch the deal, "She's a redhead." I wasn't sure what he meant by that but I imagined Rita Hayworth as Gilda, or at least the Smith version.

Strange as it may seem today, I thought it might impress Lee if, as business manager of the *Crimson*, I had my secretary, Anna Hoke, call her to set up a date. If she was impressed, she didn't let on. Lee agreed to see me, but made me wait until January when we were both home in New York on vacation.

Lee lived in Hewlett Bay Park, Long Island. We had a mutual friend, Mike Stein, and planned to double date. I stayed with Mike in Lawrence and we drove over to Hewlett together. We'd decided to take our dates to the Metropolitan Opera. I'll never forget how her mother came down to greet me with the libretto for *Tristan und Isolde*, that evening's opera. I was impressed. Lee's mother was a very charming lady.

The opera went on and on and on, for four hours, but neither of us felt comfortable enough to turn to the other and say, "Let's get out of here."

In spite of Wagner, it was a marvelous evening. Lee had magic and still does. She was bright, very pretty, and easy to be with. When I took her home that evening I made a date to see her the next day. I told Mike Stein that I felt differently about Lee than anyone I had taken out before. She was that special. We saw a great deal of each other that spring. Smith was full of tradition and visiting the ladies of Comstock House, where Lee lived, was always a treat. Rally Day at Smith, to which I was invited, was a memorable event with all the women in their white dresses and yellow ribbons. It was a sight. Lee came to my graduation, but after we both returned to New York, we drifted apart and stopped calling each other.

b

I spent the summer of 1947 working on Macy's training squad. By August I was planning to go to Harvard Business School, when out of the blue I got a call from Lee. She called, she said, to ask me about a mutual friend who was working that summer at Macy's. It was a ruse and we both knew it. We had not spoken in six weeks. I was delighted to hear from her. I felt good talking to her; she made me smile. I quickly invited her to the ballet, something I knew she would say yes to because Lee loved dance. We both knew we had let something really terrific slip through our fingers.

I saw in Lee qualities I particularly admired. While I think I am almost always diplomatic, she speaks her mind. While I am always optimistic, she is a skeptic. While I keep my feelings to myself, hers are always near the surface. But more than that I saw in Lee a partner, a person who would help me be more than I was, and with whom the sum of our personalities would create a whole greater than our parts. Lee gave me what my parents had not: a sense of family. Our love grew very quickly and she has always been my not-so-secret partner, an important ingredient in my success.

A few weeks later I left for business school. By coincidence, my two roommates were both dating Smith women whom they later married. I visited Lee and she visited me. We ran a regular shuttle service to New York. In November I asked her to come up for the Harvard/Princeton game and arranged for my roommates to stay clear of our room after the game.

Harvard lost to Princeton, 14–0, not a great game. With fall turning into winter, Lee and I hurried back to my room, Mellon D-43. Once inside, romantic that I am, I tried to light a fire in the fireplace. I lit one match, then another; the fire sputtered, then went out. Finally, I gave up. I threw the matches and kindling in the fireplace, turned to Lee, and proposed. Happily, she said yes, and we got married ten months later.

When I first told my parents that Lee and I intended to marry, they opposed it—they felt we were too young (Lee was then twenty, and I was twenty-two). With hindsight, I believe my parents were just not eager to have a married son; they thought *they* were too young.

The first time Lee met my parents, they took us to Sardi's, a restaurant they knew well. They wanted to impress her. (In those days Sardi's was a wonderful place where actors and actresses really did go after theater.) Lee always liked to sample in restaurants what she couldn't eat at home, so she looked at the menu and said, "I'd like frogs' legs." My father was very sophisticated in some ways, but he ate simply. He didn't like frogs' legs—and he could not conceive that Lee really wanted them. So he said, "You can't want frogs' legs."

"But I do, I do, that's what I want," she said. And she did. Whether they were good or not, no one can remember. But my mother never got over the fact that Lee stood up to my father; she never had.

Lee's father died in January 1948. I came down right away to be with her family; we announced our engagement shortly thereafter and her mother was very supportive of our plans. In September we got married on the lawn of Lee's home. Her brother, Jim Laufer, gave her away. Mike Stein, who had been with us on our first date, was our best man. After a week of rain, the sun came out and it was an absolutely perfect day. The best man and all of the ushers wore navy blazers and white flannels. We cherished the memory of that day and its elegance so much that forty years later, when our younger son, Jimmy, was married by the lake at our house in Connecticut, we suggested that the wedding party dress again in blazers and white flannels.

We got married without my parents' support. I had a monthly stipend from the GI bill; Lee helped put me through my second year of business school by working in an office that included such unique companies as the House of Divine Pictures and the Egyptian Chemical Company, a firm that sold embalming fluid. When we first came to New York, she took a job with pollster Elmo Roper to help support us as well.

b

But I'm getting ahead of myself. I graduated Harvard College in June 1947, magna cum laude, having majored in government. Charles Cherington, secretary of Littauer, now called the Kennedy School of Government, was my tutor for my senior honor thesis; the subject was the problems the Civil Aeronautics Boards faced in regulating the new nonscheduled freight and passenger airlines that started up after the war. But the memorable part of our graduation came when our commencement speaker, Secretary of State George C. Marshall, unveiled the Truman administration's plan to help rebuild Europe, dubbed the Marshall Plan. In those heady years, we felt there was nothing we could not accomplish if we tackled the problem with our energy, determination, and our unique American approach to problem solving.

b

Harvard's business school had been closed from 1942 to 1946 and had a large backlog of applicants. I applied and was accepted but wondered if I should go right to work instead. For advice, I sought out someone who knew both retailing and the business school: Jack Straus, chairman of Macy's and a member of the family that owned the store. Mr. Jack, as he was called, sat on the visiting committee of the business school and he agreed to see me shortly before graduation.

"What's on your mind?" he asked.

I told him I had lost over a year in the service and didn't know if two years spent at business school would be worthwhile.

If retailing was what I was interested in, he said, I would get a better education on the selling floor than I would in any classroom. With that, he sent me to be interviewed for Macy's training squad. Two days later, I was hired.

I spent the summer working at Herald Square, but much as I enjoyed Macy's, I decided it was a mistake to turn down an opportunity to go to Harvard Business School.

The Harvard Business School's class of 1949 has received much acclaim over the years. *Fortune* magazine dubbed us "the class that dollars fell on." Lawrence Shames wrote a book, *The Big Time*, profiling the members of our class, many of whom have achieved leadership positions.

At business school I roomed with Sumner Feldberg, with whom I had shared quarters in college, and Wilbur Cowett, another of my closest college friends, whom I had worked with at the *Crimson*. We shared a bathroom with our neighbors: Tom Murphy, Jim Burke, Peter McColough, and Jack Mueller.

Our "group of seven" has gone on to remarkable success: Wilbur was a senior partner of Wertheim & Co.; Sumner became chairman of Zayre, Inc.; Tom Murphy, chairman, Capital Cities-ABC; Jim Burke, chairman of Johnson & Johnson; Peter McColough, chairman of Xerox; and Jack Mueller, chairman of General Housewares. Other members of the class of '49 included Bill Hanley, president of Elizabeth Arden; Les Crown, major shareholder of General Dynamics; Jack Shad, former chairman of the Securities and Exchange Commission; and my good friend Al Kronick, who was chairman of A&S, to name but a few.

b

Georges Doriot, a slim, opinionated Frenchman, was, in my opinion, the outstanding faculty member at the business school. He lectured rather than use the case method. Of all my professors there, he had the greatest influence on me. He gave me advice that I remember to this day. "Select your accountant very carefully," he said, "for he is the person who sees you naked." He also told us to select a young lawyer, because "you will really need him twenty years from now, and you want him still to be around."

Malcolm P. McNair, the business school's professor of marketing, was the retailing guru of his day. A big burly man with a great walrus mustache, he taught the course by the Socratic method and demanded class participation. In those days, finance and banking were not growing at the rate they later would. Retailing, by contrast, was full of opportunity and 20 percent of our class enrolled in the retailing course.

Professor McNair was friendly with the major retailers of his day. Since the early 1930s he had been sounding warnings about the department store. As he saw it, in the past, stores had worked for volume rather than for profit. He theorized that downtown department stores would lose out in competition for real estate sites to office buildings, department store chains, and discount houses.

"Department stores definitely show signs of having reached at least what may be termed the maturity stage of their life cycle," he wrote in one article.

In class I disagreed with Professor McNair. He didn't seem to understand the attraction of stores that offered the customer appeals beyond price. Quality and unique merchandise had a value to the customer. I believed that with all the returning servicemen, the obvious interest in family, and the beginnings of the movement to the suburbs, the country would become more prosperous; and department stores could be the beneficiary of that prosperity.

Professor McNair, to his credit, thought the problems facing department stores could be solved. To do so, they would have to make their selling space more productive either by increasing how fast they turned over their stock, or by creating special prestige so a store could sell its goods at a substantially higher gross margin. On these points he was rather prescient: We would find ways to do both at Bloomingdale's. He was also ahead of his time in predicting the development of new forms of retail distribution through radio and television.

Finally, he was among the first to say that the orientation of the stores was wrong. "In general, I think department stores and specialty stores would do better," he once said, "if they worried less about their competitors and knew more about their customers." That is a lesson some stores still have not learned.

To Professor McNair, saving the department store was not impossible, just unlikely. The downtown department store was a dinosaur limping to its grave. With twenty/twenty hindsight, it's satisfying to note that Bloomingdale's fulfilled every step of Mc-Nair's unlikely scenario by transforming itself from the fifth-place store in New York to the neighborhood store for Manhattan's Upper East Side and an international marketing force. I smile each time someone today writes an obituary for the department store. The argument about its viability has been raging for the last half century. I know the argument will still be raging in the next century.

b

I am a great believer in planning. Shortly after graduation, I developed a series of five-year goals for myself. Lee was the only one who ever really knew about this. I wanted to be a buyer, merchan-dise manager, vice president, a general merchandise manager and president, and then chairman in defined five- to ten-year intervals. Beginning in the spring of 1949, as graduation approached, I interviewed for a permanent position in retailing, my only interest.

Both Macy's and A&S were interested in business school graduates. I had worked at Macy's before graduate school and spent the summer of 1948 on the A&S training squad. A&S, under Sidney Solomon, one of the great merchants, was a powerhouse. Both stores were prestigious, established, successful companies.

However, George Farkas of Alexander's was anxious to hire a Harvard Business School graduate. Where other companies were hiring three or four graduates, Farkas was intent on hiring only one, and he let it be known that he was prepared to pay a good deal more than the others. Alexander's was not a department store in the traditional sense—there was no home furnishings department. It concentrated on clothing for men, women, and children. Alexander's, he said, was pursuing a new direction for the future of retailing. It was a store built on a combination of fashion and price appeal.

George Farkas was short, slim, and balding. He was filled with nervous energy and yet had a certain charisma. He spoke with great conviction about his business. He took Lee and me to dinner and talked of his plans for the store and for me.

Alexander's was started in the 1930s as a small dress shop in the Bronx. During the depression, Farkas began to mark down items on the spot rather than let a customer leave the store without purchasing anything. He quickly discovered the appeal of price. As the elevated subway was extended along Third Avenue to the Bronx, Farkas expanded. In partnership with his brother-in-law, George Schwadron, his business grew from that small dress shop to a large store on the Bronx's Third Avenue, and then to a second store on the Grand Concourse. He had plans to expand into Queens and eventually Manhattan.

I was impressed by Mr. Farkas's confidence, his vision, and the huge salary he was offering: $85 a week—as compared to $75 at Macy's or $55 at Bloomingdale's. I accepted.

I began as Mr. Farkas's assistant at the Grand Concourse store, but was assigned to the selling floor to learn how Alexander's really worked. That was an education!

My first day I was stationed in one of the inexpensive dress departments when a woman asked me where the fitting rooms were. She was quite large and had a thick Bronx accent. There were none, I explained, because we provided no alterations on $5 dresses; but she would be fine as long as she knew her size. She was not happy with my answer. "*Whaddya mean no fitting rooms*," she screamed at me. With that she took off her dress right in the middle of the selling floor, and proceeded to try on the new one. Selling was a rough and, I could see, sometimes unattractive business. "Welcome to Alexander's," I told myself.

Alexander's had no training squad, but I worked as an assistant suit buyer. Six months later I became the buyer of men's casual pants and outerwear at the Third Avenue store. I had a fair notion of my responsibilities, but the merchandise manager, Milton Bogen, felt I needed further education. He was my direct superior, in charge of all menswear, and a tyrant—large, heavy, loud. If Mr. Bogen had trouble getting his calls through, he was known to rip the telephone off the wires and throw it against the wall. He took umbrage, I think, at the fact that I had gone to Harvard Business School. He was going to teach me, he said, how to deal with suppliers. What an education that was.

One time we were in our showroom looking at a line of casual pants. I liked them and was ready to write an order when Mr. Bogen came over and said, "No, no. That's not very good value." He grabbed the pants from the table and started to look closely at the details. A look of total disgust crossed his face. Then he threw them on the ground and shouted at the poor supplier, "You call these pants? I call them shit!" He jumped up and down on them, screaming, "Shit! Shit! Shit!" until the supplier lowered his price. This was a little different from what I'd learned at business school.

On one memorable occasion, Mr. Bogen's "management technique" backfired and he got what he deserved. The other buyer for menswear at the Third Avenue store was a decent young man, but Mr. Bogen made him terribly nervous. One day Mr. Bogen came into the store and began to scream at him. He berated the young man: He was a nothing, he knew nothing, and so on. As the tirade went on, this fellow's face became paler and paler. Bogen became even more abusive. "Excuse me," the young man mumbled. Bogen said there was no excusing him and continued to abuse him. "But," said the fellow . . . and there and then he threw up on Mr. Bogen. We were all speechless. It was quite a moment.

People put up with Milton Bogen if they wanted to do business with Alexander's, but it was not the way I wanted to work. I was looking for a more supportive environment. Although Mr. Farkas assured me I had a glowing future at Alexander's, I couldn't see myself dealing long term with the kind of product and atmosphere Mr. Bogen created and embodied.

After only a year, I left Alexander's and went to Stern Brothers as an assistant to its then CEO, Ben Gordon. Stern's was a step up from Alexander's but heavily in the "basement" moderate-priced business. I served as a liaison between the merchandise managers and the buyers. My particular responsibility was for the lingerie, corset, and robe departments. After only three months at Stern's, I received a call from Milton Goldberg, who had interviewed me for Alexander's. He was now at Bloomingdale's as head of the Downstairs Store, the store's separate "basement" operation.

He asked me to meet James Schoff and Jed Davidson, the president and chairman, respectively, who shared a very exciting vision of what they felt Bloomingdale's could be. Jed Davidson, he told me, wanted to make Bloomingdale's into a neighborhood store for the Upper East Side. Milton Goldberg thought it was a vision that I would want to be part of.

Growing up in New York, I had never shopped at Bloomingdale's. I knew little, if anything, about Jed Davidson. So I had no idea that I was to meet the consummate merchant who would be my mentor and friend and who, more than anyone else, would teach me about retailing; or that I was going to a store where I would spend the next forty-one years of my professional life. At Bloomingdale's, I would meet kindred spirits. Together, we would write new rules for retailing; and in our search for the cutting edge we would ultimately create a store like no other.

PART 2

Becoming
Bloomingdale's

"You've been traded to Bloomingdale's."

CHAPTER 2

The Way It Was

October 9, 1950, was my first day at Bloomingdale's. The story that best sums up the store's market position at the time is an anecdote that concerns Lawrence Lachman's first week in New York. Larry came to Bloomingdale's in 1947, went on to become its CEO, and today has his own consulting company. Shortly after he started at Bloomingdale's, he was a guest at an elegant New York dinner party. Asked by the woman seated next to him what he did, Lachman answered with great pride, "I've just been made treasurer of Bloomingdale's."

"Oh, that's a nice store," she said. "My maid shops there."

b

Before the 1950s, much as today, how people shopped was a function not only of their personal wealth but of where they lived. People in remote rural areas had little access to goods and services; so they shopped by catalog or by visiting a Sears catalog store. In suburban communities there were specialty retailers. Each small town had its men's shop where young boys were taken for their first suit and outfitted through the various stages of their lives. Dry-goods stores carried everything from lanterns and fishing tackle to blue jeans and outdoor gear. At dress shops you could buy ready-made products or the fabric and patterns to sew your own clothes. There was the hardware store where you could purchase tools as well as home appliances. Furniture was sold in separate shops. These establishments were, mostly, family-run and filled the main streets of towns across the country.

Department stores were a phenomenon of the cities, born in the post–Civil War era. Very often anchoring a downtown shopping area, department stores were emporiums, one-stop headquarters

stores where you could find basic as well as novelty items. Great
department stores were not yet part of nationwide chains, although
a few had expanded to include branch stores. Each city had its own
legendary department store: New York had Macy's; Philadelphia,
Wanamaker's; Chicago, Marshall Fields'; Dallas, Neiman-Marcus;
Atlanta, Rich's. They were great stores founded by great men, who
tried to pass the business along to their families but rarely succeeded beyond the third generation. The downtown department
store was still a sleeping giant.

Many downtown department stores came to life, it seemed, only
for the Christmas selling season. Then stores became destinations:
Suburban families would drive into the city to see the store windows
and to have their child's picture taken with Santa. At that time of
year, people would wait in line just to get inside, to see the displays,
the promotions, for their children to ride the children's train. For a
few weeks, stores became worlds of fantasy and entertainment.

b

In 1950, Bloomingdale's was seventy-eight years old. It stood, as it
does today, occupying the block between 59th and 60th streets, and
between Lexington and Third avenues. But there the similarities
end. Bloomingdale's was the number-five store in sales volume in
the city, trailing Macy's, Altman's, Gimbels, and A&S. The store's
Third Avenue side sat in the shadow of elevated subway tracks. The
street itself was dark, with pawn shops and bars on the surrounding
blocks. When the El rumbled by, every eight minutes or so, the
building shook. Bloomingdale's was showing its age and had no particular distinction as a New York retailer.

The Bloomingdale family had been involved in New York City
retailing since before the Civil War. In the late 1860s, Benjamin
Bloomingdale, with his sons Lyman and Joseph, had opened Bloomingdale's Hoopskirt and Ladies Notion shop to cash in on a fashion
fad Napoleon III's Empress Eugénie had started—wearing a hoopskirt to hide her pregnancy. Their first venture, like the fad, was
short-lived, but Lyman and Joseph were not discouraged. They were
determined to succeed in the dry-goods business in New York. Fads,
they had learned, would draw customers; to keep shoppers coming
back, you had to offer good value.

Lyman Bloomingdale was a veteran retailer. Born in 1841, at eleven he was already working in stores between school sessions. During the Civil War he was a sergeant in the First Regiment of the Kansas State Militia and ran a store in Leavenworth, Kansas. But in later years, if anyone asked him about his early days in retailing, he always mentioned the modest dry-goods store, Dettlebeck and Co., that he had briefly worked at in Newark, New Jersey, with Benjy and Abie. Benjy was Benjamin Altman, soon to open B. Altman; Abie was Abraham Abraham, who was later to be the force behind Abraham & Straus.

The center of New York's retail business at that time was Union Square on 14th Street. But Lyman thought the rents too high and the competition too steep. He preferred Manhattan's Upper East Side. By early 1872, he and Joseph were already searching for a suitable location. They walked the length of Third Avenue looking for the right spot.

They found a former shoe store at 939 Third Avenue between 56th and 57th streets. Four stories high, twenty feet wide by seventy-five deep, the store also came with large plate-glass windows that they hoped would attract customers. More important, Lyman was willing to bet on the neighborhood. Although Central Park was still four years away from completion, Frederick Law Olmsted's landscaped bridle paths were already popular. The park, he hoped, would make the neighborhood more desirable, and by being near the southern end, they would reap the benefits of increased uptown traffic.

b

On April 17, 1872, a day recorded as "cool but sunny," the Bloomingdale Brothers, as Lyman and Joseph now called themselves, opened Bloomingdale's Great East Side Bazaar. The rent was $2,400 for the first year, $3,600 for the second. It was steep, but to save money, Lyman and his wife, Hattie, moved in above the 1,500-foot store. Bloomingdale Brothers offered skirts, corsets, fancy goods, gent's furnishings, gloves, millinery, and hosiery. The opening day receipts totaled only $3.68.

Despite the disappointing first day, Lyman's confidence was soon rewarded: The first week's gross was $242.92; April's sales figures were $897.18; May's jumped to $3,119.05; and by December, monthly sales had risen to $3,816.87.

In 1879 the city continued to expand northward, extending the elevated railroad along Third Avenue. Bloomingdale Brothers also expanded, moving to buildings at 924, 926, and 928 Third Avenue. Bloomingdale's had become a department store, carrying everything from novelties and clothing to furniture. In 1880 the brothers acquired a five-story building on the southwest corner of 56th Street. But even that was too small. By the beginning of 1886, plans were under way to build a six-story store at Third Avenue and 59th Street, on the site of a former brewery. It would have a hundred feet of frontage on the avenue side and 145 feet on 59th Street.

For the new store, Lyman instructed his architect to create an unbroken line of windows at street level. He wanted not only to showcase merchandise but also to create displays in the windows that would draw attention and bring shoppers to the store. This was "window shopping" before the term even existed.

The first floor was to be eighteen feet high, creating a dramatic main floor; the second floor, fifteen feet; and the remaining top four floors were each twelve feet high. The floors were so solidly designed and built that they did not need any reinforcement when the store made additions and renovations.* To entice his customers to visit the top floors, even if they wouldn't or couldn't walk up, Lyman announced that the new store would have two "sky carriages"— elevators, as we now call them. He outfitted his steam-powered, cable-operated elevator with mirrors, mahogany walls, and little upholstered seats. Each sky carriage was a miniature parlor, way before the Hyatt hotel chain or mall developers adopted the concept.

On October 5, 1886, the 59th Street store opened. Young Sam Bloomingdale, Lyman's thirteen-year-old eldest son, couldn't attend because his father had sent him to represent the family at another city event: the unveiling of the Statue of Liberty in New York Harbor.

While Joe increasingly ran the day-to-day operations of the

---

* Today, 107 years and countless renovations later, this building, now called 1000 Third Avenue, produces more than $100 million in volume.

store, Lyman became the P. T. Barnum of retailing. He was among the first to advertise extensively in newspapers. At one point, he started his own community newspaper, the *19th Ward Gazette*, as a place for his ads. Bloomingdale's ran so many ads that this, too, became grist for his promotions: Lyman claimed he ran more lines of advertising than anyone had ever done before.

Lyman's showmanship extended to the store. Less than one year after electric arc lights began to be manufactured, Lyman had them installed outside the store. Crowds gathered to stare as two carbon pencils attached to the wall played Ping-Pong with an electric spark that shot back and forth between them. Bloomingdale's was among the first to carry the Victor talking machine, the Victrola. In 1883, seven years after the invention of the telephone, New York City had only 4,500 phones. One was at Bloomingdale's. Lyman was also the first to install an escalator in a New York department store, or as Bloomingdale's called it, an "inclined elevator."

This is all worth noting because although the store changed a great deal over the years, certain principles of retailing have always been central to its success. First and foremost, Bloomingdale's has always catered to its customer. And second, Bloomingdale's has provided entertainment for its shoppers and has been a destination for tourists and visitors since its opening day back in 1872.

b

Throughout the first half of the twentieth century, Bloomingdale's continued to turn a profit by offering quality goods at low cost: By the 1880s, it had established an international reputation, opening a Paris buying office followed by offices in Berlin, Vienna, Yokohama, and Shanghai. The key to the store's early success though was traffic, not merchandise. The subways stopped right under the store, delivering customers from all over Manhattan and the neighboring boroughs while the trolleys all used 59th Street as an important transfer point. The Queensborough Bridge, also called the 59th Street Bridge, which Joseph Bloomingdale had long lobbied for, opened in 1909, bringing an even greater flow of middle- to lower-income shoppers to Bloomingdale's doorstep. The store's fortunes were so tied to public transportation that its slogan was, "All cars transfer at Bloomingdale's."

At the turn of the century, advertisements for Bloomingdale's featured the BB—for Bloomingdale Brothers—trolley driver with his pet boxer dog Tige by his side. BB later became Buster Brown, one of the country's most beloved cartoon characters. The ads were ubiquitous. Bloomingdale's placards covered the sides of the trolley cars; the El train station at 59th Street became known as the Bloomingdale's stop because there were signs for the store everywhere you looked. At one point Bloomingdale's set bronze footprints into the sidewalk to lead the way.

A store that lives by high volume traffic, though, needs constant publicity. Sam Bloomingdale, like his father, Lyman, was a man of tremendous energy and enthusiasm. They promoted the store with abandon. They blanketed New York with advertisements for the store, even placing a giant placard across from the Ellis Island ferry landing. For many immigrants and visitors, a Bloomingdale's ad was their first image of New York.

Sam saw the store as an integral part of the life of the city, making charitable bequests, leading drives, holding benefits. Bloomingdale's promotions were tied to public transportation and public events. This was part of the store's credo, and part of what made their customers so loyal.

Bloomingdale's expanded until it occupied the entire block between 59th and 60th streets from Third to Lexington Avenue. While at the turn of the century Third Avenue was the Post road and Lexington the dingy poor relative, by 1930 the opposite was true. Park Avenue and Fifth Avenue now housed the mansions of the wealthy; while Third Avenue stood in the shadow of the El. Sam Bloomingdale decided to make Lexington the store's official entrance.

Sam's idea was to graft a whole new structure onto the Lexington side while refurbishing and renovating the rest of the store. Travertine flooring was laid on the street level, and new elevators and escalators were installed. Because the street slanted from Third downhill to Lexington, and the Third Avenue side is nine feet higher, an arcade was built on the Lexington side. The store remained open during the construction and renovation, and in 1931, when the $3 million edifice was complete, Bloomingdale's had a new entrance, complete with an art-deco facade designed by the architectural firm of Starret and Van Vleck.

The store itself, though, didn't change. Bloomingdale's continued to sell good value. It never priced itself out of the customer's reach. As a consequence, in 1932, the depth of the depression, the store sold more than $25 million worth of merchandise—more than ever before.

b

In 1929, Federated Department Stores was formed by the merger of the three department store retailing forces of its day: Lazarus, Filene's, and A&S. Bloomingdale's was asked to join a few months later. Set up as an independent holding company, each store continued to operate independently. By joining together in a consortium, each store could create great buying strength both here and abroad. By operating independently, each retained its distinct character— an important factor, as customer loyalty then was to the store, not the chain.

Fred Lazarus, Jr., head of F. R. Lazarus, became Federated's president in 1944. He was a great believer in applying modern business management practices to the retail arena. He sought out talented leaders outside his field and brought them into the Federated fold to run the operations and research side. At the same time, he recruited top merchants to improve the quality of the goods offered.

In 1944, Lazarus appointed James S. Schoff, who had been a vice president at Bamberger Bros., president of Bloomingdale's. In 1947, Lazarus decided to split the top position at Bloomingdale's in two: president and chairman. The president would be the operations and chief financial officer, while the chairman was the top merchant. That same year, J. Edward ("Jed") Davidson was hired as chairman, recruited by Mr. Schoff.

Schoff, like Lazarus, believed the key to a better department store was recruiting top professional personnel. He hired James Mitchell, later to become U.S. Secretary of Labor, to be in charge of personnel and labor relations; Harold Krensky, later president of Federated, was in charge of publicity and marketing; and Lawrence Lachman joined Bloomingdale's as treasurer in 1947—he would become CEO in 1966 and chairman in 1969. This was an extraordinary collection of retailing talent who in considerable measure would run the store for the next three decades.

By 1950, despite a premier location, Bloomingdale's was not

turning a substantial profit. The store was unionized, making the cost of labor high, and delivery and advertising costs were also great. The challenge for Schoff and Davidson was to turn the store around. As Davidson and Schoff saw it, the way to make a profit at 59th Street was to lower the expenses while raising the store's average sales check and improving the profit on each sale. In terms of fixed expenses, it cost virtually the same to sell a $5 vase as a $500 one.

Bloomingdale's had a chance to succeed because it was located on the periphery of the highest income population in the world. Fifth Avenue is to the west, and Sutton Place is to the east. The neighborhood was changing, and that would bring a potential new customer to the store. But this would not happen overnight. The greatest challenge in retailing is to change a store's image. I can't think of any store at the time that had succeeded in doing so. Few have succeeded since.

Look at the New York stores in the 1950s; many could not make the change: there was Alexander's in the Bronx, and Gertz, Namms, Loesers, and A&S in Brooklyn and Long Island. Manhattan had, at 14th Street, S. Klein's on the Square. Union Square was, by now, the low-priced retail destination. It was a giant bustling emporium of bargains that made Bloomingdale's basement look like a boutique. Across the street, there was J. W. Mays, a store with moderate-priced items.

Thirty-fourth Street was the great white way of department stores. Macy's stood on the corner of 34th Street like the Colossus of Rhodes. The giant of New York retailing, Macy's created a bargain image by promoting "Save 6% for Cash"—think of how far that would go today. Across the street was Saks 34th Street, then Gimbels, and later, for a moment, an E. J. Korvette's, the first home appliance and electronics discounter. Going east, across Herald Square, there was McCreery's, Ohrbach's, and at the corner of Fifth Avenue, B. Altman.

On Fifth Avenue there was Arnold Constable, Franklin Simon, Russeks, Jay Thorpe, and on the corner of 47th Street, E. J. Korvette's. There was also W & J Sloane, Best's, Peck & Peck, Lord & Taylor, and Stern's on 42nd Street. Abercrombie & Fitch and Brooks Brothers were over on Madison along with Rogers Peet, and on Upper Fifth Avenue there was Saks Fifth Avenue, Bonwit Teller,

Tiffany's, Bendel's, and Bergdorf Goodman. And on the periphery of the shopping district was Bloomingdale's. Back then, we took all these stores for granted. We assumed they'd be there forever. Today, the great majority are footnotes to retail history. Of the thirty-one stores I mentioned, twenty-three are gone—they did not change sufficiently to meet the shifting demands and changing lifestyles of their customers. The eight stores that remain have either been sold, gone through bankruptcy, or, as in the case of Bloomingdale's, both.

b

Few people remember the Bloomingdale's of the 1950s. At that time, it was two distinct businesses: Bloomingdale's itself, which did a solid business but had no great impact on the retailing scene, and the basement, a bargain store. Bloomingdale's had a reputation for modern furniture but lacked any other distinction.

To change, Bloomingdale's had to overcome several important obstacles, including the perceptions of the suppliers and customers and the limitations of the store's physical plant. Many suppliers would not sell to Bloomingdale's for fear it would hurt their image. Hathaway shirts insisted their labels be removed lest anyone know they were carried at Bloomingdale's. (Just before I left Bloomingdale's in 1991 we informed Hathaway that we wouldn't carry shirts that displayed *their* label.)

In 1960 we were still meeting with resistance not only from suppliers but also from the retailing community. At the time, we sold a great deal of Jean Patou fragrance, and we asked Patou's representative, Didier Grumbach, if we could display some of their fashions in our store window. He agreed. No sooner was the dress on display then he received a phone call from an incensed Andrew Goodman of Bergdorf Goodman. How could he? Goodman demanded. "It's one thing to display Patou in a Fifth Avenue store," he told Didier, "but Bloomingdale's? They are on Lexington Avenue!" A week later, with apologies, Didier withdrew the window display.

The Fifth Avenue stores had a stranglehold on the upper end of the New York market. Lord & Taylor, Saks Fifth Avenue, Bonwit's, where my mother still reigned, Henri Bendel, and Bergdorf Goodman breathed different air than we did.

They were elegant stores. Bloomingdale's was drab, a series of buildings cobbled together over the years. No two floors were exactly alike, and many tilted from east to west and from north to south. There was one set of escalators that went from the main floor through to the seventh floor and down to the first level of the basement. The escalator entrances, the most important place to put merchandise on each floor, were enclosed, obscuring vistas of the store.

The basement housed the only department store branch of a U.S. Post Office. As for the upstairs store, the Lexington Avenue entrance led into a two-story-high arcade of handbags, jewelry, and scarfs. A stairway, since replaced by an escalator, led up to the main floor where, beyond the traditional cosmetics and hosiery departments, Bloomingdale's had stationery, religious articles, notions, and a closet shop. At the back end of the main floor there was a camera shop, a pet shop selling pet supplies, and a soda fountain. And that was just the start.

The second floor housed towels, sheets, blankets, and children's and men's clothing. It was an era when our buyer was famous for being the best folder of towels in the business. Our finest apparel was on the third floor, in the Green Room, which carried line-for-line copies of European designers, as was the rage then. It was a small business; however, much larger was the shop that sold uniforms for nurses and maids—we had a separate buyer just for uniforms.

In summer we kept the Third Avenue windows open above the fourth floor—that was our "air-conditioning" for the upper floors. The seventh floor housed a very large toy department with Junglegyms, outdoor pools, and a garden shop that sold plants, shrubs, bushes, garden supplies, and bags of sand. The buying offices were tucked away all over the store, as were stockrooms, personnel, and executive offices. The store was closed Sundays, and Saturdays in the summer.

This doesn't sound much like today's Bloomingdale's, does it? The contrast between Bloomingdale's and Saks Fifth Avenue in 1950 was so great, that I daresay if you had told someone that Bloomingdale's and Saks would one day be rivals, no one would have believed you. Compete with Gimbels or Alexander's? Yes. Compete with

A&S or Macy's? Maybe. But the notion that Bloomingdale's would be fashionable seemed unlikely at best.

b

My career at Bloomingdale's literally went from the basement up. The Bloomingdale's basement, or the Downstairs Store, as it was called then, was one of the distinguishing features of the old store. It was a freewheeling place with bargain tables and was totally separate from the upstairs store. The basement was a great learning experience, a place where we had the freedom to experiment with new ways of merchandising and selling. It was where I learned the basic principles on which the new Bloomingdale's would be built.

My first day, October 9, I was twenty-five years old, married with no children, and earning $4,680 a year. I was told to report to Milton Goldberg, who had recruited me for both Alexander's and Bloomingdale's. He was a vice president and in charge of the Downstairs Store. He had only been at Bloomingdale's about six months himself. Goldberg hailed from Worcester, Massachuesetts, and was a graduate of the Harvard Business School, class of '31. He began his retailing career at Macy's as a shoe buyer before joining A. S. Beck as a vice president. From there he went to Alexander's, where we first met.

Goldberg was an unusual choice to run a basement store. His predecessor had been direct, loud, aggressive, and forceful; Goldberg was a tall, pleasant-looking, reserved New Englander with black-rimmed glasses. He was deceptively soft-spoken and appeared very gentle and reserved but actually was very excitable. When excited, he stuttered.

Jed Davidson gave Goldberg great freedom in planning the basement's future. Goldberg wanted to develop more distinctive merchandise while still providing the customer with outstanding value. He was interested in art, handicraft, and artisans of all sorts. The basement quickly became the market for his enthusiasms.

Before Goldberg's arrival, the Downstairs Store was run as a very seat-of-the-pants business. Long-range thinking then was "What are we doing this afternoon?" Davidson, however, was a great believer in planning. When I first arrived at Bloomingdale's, he and Goldberg were just beginning to draft plans several years out.

They were intent on examining and challenging every aspect of the basement's business.

The Downstairs Store generated great traffic and volume, contributing 20 percent of the store's annual sales, and was a place of constant promotional activity. We had monthly "bargain-B" storewide sales and twice-a-year basement "Miracle Week" sales. In the 1930s the upstairs store was so promotional that it was hard for the basement to distinguish itself. In 1935, for example, Bloomingdale's ran an ad featuring a man wearing a barrel, offering a complete wardrobe—a suit, shirt, tie, overcoat, hat, pants, underwear, socks, and shoes—all for $58.

The basement was several different businesses. It was home furnishings, piece goods, sportswear, menswear, infants' clothing, shoes, coats, and hosiery—all conducted on the basis of volume. To get people into the store you had to advertise, and when advertising, you had to offer a sale, so the thinking went. As a result, some items sold very close to cost.

The basement used to run over one million lines of advertising in the New York *Daily News*; that's about a thousand pages, including full-color pages advertising dresses for $2.99.

During my first week, Jed Davidson called me to his office. He asked me to undertake an assignment for him and Milton Goldberg: analyze the cost of the *Daily News* full-color ads and calculate how much we lost on those $2.99 dresses. I was surprised to hear him say the dresses *lost* money because I knew they sold very well. Bloomingdale's large-scale price promotions were part of the tradition fostered by Lyman and Sam Bloomingdale. But the question was: Did it make good business sense?

When I added up the cost of the dresses and deducted the cost of the advertising, part of which was paid by the suppliers, delivery, and returns, I was shocked. I discovered Davidson was right. The dresses lost us between twenty-five and thirty cents each! The more we sold, the more we lost.

Lesson number one: Focus not on gross sales, but on profit! We gave up advertising $2.99 dresses with full pages in the *News*.

b

I was Milton Goldberg's second assistant. His first was Melvin Jacobs, who later became vice chairman of Federated—my boss—and

then chairman of Saks Fifth Avenue. Mel had joined Bloomingdale's
in 1947, just out of college, and been part of the executive training
squad. We worked together in the merchandise office for a short
time before he was appointed assistant buyer of women's sportswear.

The Downstairs Store occupied three levels totaling eighty thousand square feet of selling space. If you came in from the subway,
as most of our customers did then, you found yourself among bargain shoe tables, carrying inexpensive lines like Enna Jettiks, and
an intimate apparel department with tables of bras and panties. Up
one level was a children's department, where the merchandise again
reflected price over quality. The major basement level housed handbags, hosiery, menswear, fabrics, and notions in addition to a series
of six bargain tables. The bargain tables, actually islands, had salespeople in the middle and offered merchandise from throughout the
basement. My first responsibility was, with Mel Jacobs, to oversee
those bargain tables.

Nothing gave off the scent of a great bargain like a crowd of
people digging their way through a pile of merchandise. But a quiet
floor is death. When things got too slow, Mel and I took matters into
our own hands—literally. We would go to our offices and put on our
coats and hats. But rather than leaving the store, we would head
straight for the bargain tables and start tossing through them as if
there was hidden gold. Once we attracted a crowd, we would quietly
slip back to our offices.

Another way to draw a large crowd was a sale of mismatched
thirty-nine-cent earings. Women, I discovered, are congenital opti-
mists. For each left shoe, they always believe there is a right. We
learned the practical effect of this with the tables. We also learned
how competitive shoppers can be. If one found a set, her neighbor
would go through the bin until she did as well.

The basement was a merchandising laboratory. We had no real
responsibility to maintain a certain assortment or price points as
other departments did. Milton was interested in going beyond that.
One of his keen interests was in developing our own brands and he
was allowed to experiment.

Our first venture with a new private label, however, was a complete disaster. Milton suggested we market our own line of cosmetics
—moisturizers, hand creams, and various lotions. Creams were

creams, right? No! We tried everything, even offering the products at a very reduced price. It didn't matter: We couldn't give them away. I ended up pouring them all into a giant vat and throwing them out. But I learned an important lesson: Cosmetics is not about creams, it's about marketing. There are no better marketers than the cosmetics companies. And as I would see many times throughout the years, cosmetics launches require major support.

I did not completely give up hope on developing a private label. Several months later, after being promoted to buyer of basement hosiery—my first buying job at Bloomingdale's at a salary increase of $25 a week!—I decided to try again by developing special packaging under the Bloomingdale's name for both first-quality and irregular hosiery. Here I was more successful. The Bloomingdale's brand name on hosiery turned out to be an effective marketing tool. The Korean War was going on and World War II was a not-so-distant memory. Many people imagined there would be a run on stockings —no pun intended. Most department store hosiery numbers were down. But the year that I was hosiery buyer, sales grew by about 30 percent.

This was one of my early successes. But my numbers owed as much to the freewheeling atmosphere of the basement as it did to the hosiery I sold. In those days, all that was recorded was how your department did; there was no real accounting for what was actually sold.

My stock of hosiery left a few extra tables at my disposal. So I called a good friend, Bob Bernstein, then vice president of Simon & Schuster, subsequently chairman of Random House, and arranged to buy close-outs of books. Pretty soon I was running a discount book business on our bargain tables. My success there helped increase my hosiery figures. I learned that I loved discovering new business opportunities and could act quickly on my instincts. I don't think I've ever stopped doing that.

b

The basement was a great learning experience, and a whole generation of very talented people were trained there, such as Mel Jacobs; Joe Schnee, who became executive vice president of Bloomingdale's; and Howard Goldfeder, who became Federated's chairman in 1981.

Many of the innovations that would help transform Bloomingdale's were first tried by Goldberg. He was the avant-garde, but he never received his due as a merchant. To compete with the upstairs store Goldberg was always developing unique merchandise. He wanted to create a clientele for the store that wasn't tied merely to price appeal.

Milton Goldberg wanted to attract brand-name merchandise, but suppliers did not see the Downstairs Store as an appropriate outlet of distribution. His response was to send buyers to Europe in search of unique, exclusive, handcrafted products—before anyone else at Bloomingdale's was doing so. For example, Hannah Mackler, fashion director for the Downstairs Store, returned from a European buying trip with Milton Goldberg in late 1952 with the decision to hold a promotion of Italy the following year. Years later, Bloomingdale's would be famous for its country promotions, but the basement was where it began.

In the spring of 1953, Goldberg opened the Capri Shop, highlighting Italian fashions and accessories. It was an immediate success and the merchandise sold out within the first few weeks. Goldberg immediately decided to plan for a London mart that same year, and a Mediterranean shop the next year. Not all the merchandise was imported; some of it was made to order in the United States, "inspired" by the foreign fashions. Much of the merchandise sold for less than $10.

Several years later, for another Italian fair, Hannah Mackler decided to present the dresses of a young Italian designer she had discovered and to sell them for $29.99—a very high price for the basement. Valentino was his name, and Bloomingdale's basement was his introduction to the United States.

b

As the basement began to do more and more importing, Abe Rubenfield, our women's shoe buyer, built an outstanding fashion shoe business by having shoes made in Italy specifically for Bloomingdale's basement. They were fashionable, of good value, and became one of the features of the Downstairs Store.

What we discovered in the basement was, in a sense, how to sell through marketing. Over time, we tried to make the basement not just a place to find bargains but a destination for fashion and value.

Customers now came to the Downstairs Store not only because of the sales but because of the merchandise. It may not sound like a big difference, but it was the start of a movement away from price appeal.

In 1966, as we examined our strategy for the coming years, we began to consider phasing out the Downstairs Store. We were opening more and more branch stores and it made no sense to duplicate the basement in the smaller physical plant of those stores. Nor did it seem a sound strategy to have only one basement location. In addition, as our business grew at 59th Street, we needed more space for many of the departments in the upstairs store.

We made the decision to close the Downstairs Store in 1967. We closed such basement departments as sheets, towels, hosiery, fabrics, and lingerie, in some cases adding lower price points to the comparable departments in the upstairs store to increase sales and broaden assortments. This decision was a bold one: The Downstairs Store was about a $20 million profitable business. But in the long run it was the right strategy. We were one of the first department stores to close our basement. Macy's followed a decade later. But by then Bloomingdale's was a different store.

b

The most important person in the transformation of Bloomingdale's from what it was to what it would become was James Edward ("Jed") Davidson. Jed transformed the store by teaching the buyers to focus on the merchandise and the Bloomingdale's level of taste.

He had a vision of a store that was defined by the merchandise it carried and the way the goods were presented. Most stores selected goods from available suppliers based on the income of their regular customers. Jed felt a store should decide what to offer based on the taste of the customers it wanted to attract. He had a vision of a buying organization that would search the world for goods that matched his exacting standards. Instead of the department store being merely a selling agent, it would become a creative force; the merchandise would be the star and the buyer would be the arbiter of taste and style. This was a revolutionary concept.

The typical department store buyer in the 1950s was a powerful, respected individual who could have been in that job for ten, fifteen, or twenty years. He knew his suppliers, his product, and his customers. Buyers were well paid and had job security; they were kings of their domains. There were few layers between the buyer and store principal. A dress buyer, for example, would go to Seventh Avenue, visit the vendors, select the dresses; figure out quantity, size range, and delivery dates; and maybe work out an arrangement to advertise them. When the goods came in, if they sold, the buyer would reorder them.

In the 1950s, Bloomingdale's was dominated by a number of world-class buyers. Lee Popell, our dress buyer, was an absolute terror and particularly autocratic in dealing with the dress industry. Madge Carroll, who bought designer apparel, was a well-known figure at the time, as was Charlotte Schiff, the handbag buyer, and Lucy Tombs in modern furniture. Jack Simon, our food buyer, was the latest word in cheeses, candies, and exotic foods. (Jed had a particular interest in gourmet food.) These buyers were famous in our industry in their time and their taste defined the store. If you knew Bloomingdale's then, you knew them. In those days stores were built around great buyers whose positions were perceived as a satisfying career.

Some buyers were equally celebrated for their personalities. *The New York Times* profiled Bill Strunck and Hy Bayer, both fifty-year veterans of the store, as "the 'Sunshine Boys' of Retailing" because they used to kid each other incessantly. Bill was the sheet buyer, Hy bought table linens. They were terrific at what they did in what is a very competitive area. They outperformed everyone half their age—both were still at Bloomingdale's in the 1980s when they did better than people a third their age. But it is their kidding I recall most.

"I'm happy to wake up every day," Hy Bayer told the *Times* reporter when asked the secret of his longevity. To which Bill Strunck one-upped, "With me, I hope that when I wake up, I know that I wake up." It went like that all day long.

Occasionally, it got out of hand. Mr. Davidson once called me to his office. "Call up Mr. Strunck," he said. "I'm having trouble reaching him." Jed had called him several times but Bill kept hanging up on him. I dialed Bill and told him Mr. Davidson wanted to see him in his office. "Really?" Bill said. "I thought all those calls were Hy pulling my leg!"

As a new trainee, I was impressed by these people. There was a

camaraderie that existed then that is lost today. When I first joined
the store, there was a fishing club and an annual golf tournament; in
the summer we held clambakes on Long Island and baseball games
in Central Park. This harkens back to an earlier era when Bloomingdale's was a family business. Sam Bloomingdale even ran a summer
hotel for his salespeople to vacation in.

Many Bloomingdale's buyers, however, were set in their ways.
They had been trained to think that the more you sold the better,
but they had no idea of the bottom-line impact. Davidson, Schoff,
and Lachman set about teaching them the concept of gross margin
and profitability, instilling the notion that the only way to build gross
margin was to develop unique merchandise. Many, like Bill Strunck
and Hy Bayer, adapted; others did not.

Today, the buyer position is often perceived as just one step-
ping-stone in a career rather than a career in itself. Accordingly, the
enormous respect and power of the buyer has diminished. In 1992
Bloomingdale's had about 120 buyers, 60 associates, and 140 assistants. There were 21 divisional merchandise managers above them,
and 3 general merchandise managers supervising the divisionals,
plus a separate organization of about 60 department managers to
supervise 59th Street. In the old days, buyers supervised the selling-
floor staff; today, they have no connection. This, too, is a major
change in retailing.

In many ways a single downtown store where a buyer selects the
merchandise, supervises the salespeople, and is on the floor with
the customer is better for the customer. Nordstrom has attempted
to find a middle ground. No single buyer is responsible for more than
three stores. This system, however, has created difficulties. Each
buyer is less powerful, and you can end up with somewhat different
assortments in various stores.

New York specialty stores like Bergdorf Goodman and Paul
Stuart have resisted the trend to open branches. Actually, Bergdorf's opened one in White Plains in 1974, but it was a failure and
they gave up soon after, closing it and converting it to a Neiman-
Marcus store. They have stayed with the system of single store
buyers. It remains one of their strengths.

The success of today's specialty retailing chains, such as Victoria's Secret or the Gap, has renewed interest in having fewer buyers

with more responsibility. Bloomingdale's has reduced the numbers of buyers and is redefining their role.

At the other end of the spectrum is the rise of "team buying," where talented buyers select assortments for entire retailing organizations—a practice already in place at companies such as the May Company or Federated. Buying teams make sense for Federated because stores like A&S, Burdine's, Rich's, Jordan Marsh, the Bon, Stern's, and Lazarus have an enormous similarity of customer and merchandise. Bloomingdale's is not part of a team system because so much of its merchandise is unique—and it was Davidson who first set Bloomingdale's on its distinctive course.

b

Jim Schoff and Jed Davidson, who ran Bloomingdale's for almost twenty years and laid the groundwork for the new Bloomingdale's, were a great team. Mr. Schoff joined Bloomingdale's in 1944 from Bamberger's and was outgoing, extroverted, warm, and possessed a sophisticated but traditional taste level. He was decisive, with a passion for people and the personnel side of the business. If there are words that summed up his point of view they are *integrity* and *character*. He expected that of people, and without that, no matter how talented, he did not want them.

Jed Davidson, who was in some ways temperamentally the opposite of Jim Schoff, shared his interest in cosmopolitan good taste. They complemented each other very well. Schoff was restructuring personnel, finance, and operations while supporting Jed in the evolving merchandise sales promotion areas.*

Jed Davidson had been Macy's youngest vice president ever and rose to become its executive vice president before leaving to become president of William Hengerer & Co. in Buffalo, and then president of McCreery's. He joined the store with the mission to create a new, upgraded Bloomingdale's.

Davidson was a formidable figure. He dressed conservatively, in dark suits, bow ties, and button-down oxford shirts, looking more

---

* Twenty-eight years later I was to select Mr. Schoff's son, Jim Schoff, Jr., to be Bloomingdale's president and take on the same responsibilities his father had.

like a business school professor than a store principal. He was not an outgoing person and many employees feared him, particularly since he was arrogant about taste. People found Jed imperious, but he was, in fact, just shy. Unless it was urgent, he was never confrontational. I picture Jed Davidson sitting in his office, puffing contemplatively on his meerschaum pipe, reviewing strategies. He did not spend a lot of time on the selling floor. He would walk through the departments and then call you to his office to tell you what he liked, what he didn't, and why. Many thought Jed a snob, but he was a snob for Bloomingdale's—that, too, was an important lesson.

Davidson had traveled widely throughout Europe but had a special love for France. He was fluent in French and served on Harvard's visiting committee for romance languages. Every spring, he spent four or five weeks traveling in the French countryside in search of the "real" France, the authentic experience. We pictured him in some small village, riding a bicycle, wearing a beret, carrying a baguette under his arm. We were not far off the mark.

What Davidson saw in the small villages formed his opinions. At Macy's, he had started as a fabric buyer before going on to head the home furnishings division. He had a special feeling for the way the French set their tables, how they displayed their food in stores, how their homes were decorated. Whenever he traveled, and when, in later years, he sent me to travel, he always counseled me to get away from the cities and search out the authentic.

Jed had his blind spots. He did not like the ready-to-wear business—neither the people who manufactured the garments nor those who sold them. But more than that he found the whole of ready-to-wear too unpredictable and changing. What he liked was design and he insisted on his standards. Once, Janina Wilner, the fashion accessories coordinator, had a plaid handbag on display. Jed turned it over and found the plaid didn't line up. He was upset. No one else noticed. But he hated it.

Jed believed that in matters of fashion, logic should prevail. One season, for example, he attempted to match the fashions to colors featured in our furniture floor. Purple was the fashion accent color that season, so Jed instructed our clothing buyers to feature purple clothes. It was quite a sight! Distinctive—and the source of large markdowns.

Jed Davidson knew more about the specifics of merchandise than anyone I ever came across. No item, no matter how potentially lucrative, was acceptable if it went against the standard of taste he was trying to present. I remember him saying, "I don't care how many cuckoo clocks we can sell, that's not what we are going to have at Bloomingdale's!"

Jed understood that shopping was about people's self-image. For example, Paul Katzman, our men's clothing buyer, knew how to tailor a suit from scratch. Katzman was very much a Brooks Brothers type, as was Davidson. Brooks was what the Bloomingdale's men's department aspired to become, but for the most part the suits were modestly priced. Nonetheless, I recall how Jed would fuss with Paul over the buttonholes on the lapels. Davidson demanded they be handsewn; he was also very particular about who printed the neckties, whether they were blocked by hand or by machine. No customer could tell the difference, only Davidson.

At first I thought Jed's perfectionism was extreme. Later I realized that this was part of his management technique, part of what he taught all of us. If you didn't care about the manufacturing of the clothes, who would? And if a principal of a store didn't care about the smallest detail, even a buttonhole, why would his subordinates?

We had a vision of how to transform Bloomingdale's merchandise. We had a vision of what kind of store we wanted to be, as well as what products did not coincide with that vision—either they did not fit with the new strategy or the new standards of taste. The makeover would have to start from the smallest detail. Over a period of years, major appliances, cameras, wallpaper, TVs, pet supplies, art needlework, and religious articles were departments that would not survive the store's makeover. Nor would the gardening department that sold fifty-pound bags of sand for children's sandboxes. They did not conform to Jed's image of Bloomingdale's. The television department, for example, made little sense: It made no money and there was no opportunity to develop unique products.

Jed's floor visits could be amusing. One spring day, as he made his way across the main floor, a woman accosted him. She wanted to know why Bloomingdale's didn't carry menorahs in their religious articles shop—we sold crucifixes and other items of interest to our Catholic customers. Jed had no particular interest in religion; I'm not even sure he knew what a menorah was. But ever suave, he motioned to Gerry Casey, Bloomingdale's very jovial Irish Catholic buyer of religious articles, to come over. Before Gerry could say a word, Jed said to the woman, "I'd like you to meet Jerry Cohen, our buyer of religious articles; he will explain why we don't carry menorahs."

From my first week at Bloomingdale's, Jed called me to his office to discuss merchandise. We had a special relationship and a good deal in common. We had both gone to Harvard, and both our wives were Smith graduates. We liked good restaurants, fine wine, and all things French, and we also shared a love of the theater, music, and dance. But Jed and I had differences as well. He was rigid in his tastes; my own taste in art and music was much more eclectic. He was a confirmed urban dweller; I wanted to raise my family in the suburbs. When I told Jed in 1953 that I had bought a house in New Rochelle, he was shocked. To Jed, leaving New York was an act of betrayal. He saw no culture in the suburbs, but I was anxious to raise our family there—I admired how Lee was brought up.

I first got to know Jed well at the time that he was planning the Stamford, Connecticut, store. "Stamford is going to be a major step forward in building suburban stores," he told me, and then said, "I'd like you to work on it with me." Stamford was to be a departure from the existing Fresh Meadows and New Rochelle stores, which were small and in moderate markets. Jed planned Stamford as a 160,000-square-foot, more complete store. At a time when department stores were first experimenting with branches, Stamford was to be the largest in the metropolitan area. I jumped at the opportunity.

For four months, as a special assignment, I assisted him in the planning of the Bloomingdale's Stamford store that was to open in 1953. My role was to meet with each of the senior merchants and review their needs. Jed's attention to detail was impressive. In planning the store's layout we had to determine not only how much square footage each department would need but how much shelf space was needed for each product. Analyzing each department and deciding how much space to allot made me scrutinize the margins in each department. I would ask myself: What are the businesses to be in? What should we emphasize or expand? And equally important:

If you condense or close one department, what should you replace it with? I watched as Jed made decision after decision. A decade later, when I was executive vice president, I would make the same decisions for the 59th Street store.

Jed had no great interest in the suburbs, but I did. Lee and I embraced the suburban life-style. We had bought our house in Wilmot Woods with a loan from Lee's mother. For several years I used to cut the lawn myself with a handmower. Finally, in the early 1960s, we decided I could afford not to. We joined Sunningdale Country Club, and I kept up my tennis and developed my golf game. In 1963 we moved to Scarsdale, again to a home we could not afford: 69 Morris Lane, a twelve-room English Tudor house on 2.5 acres. I always believed my earnings would grow to catch up. Our children were the focus of our lives. Andy was in junior high and Jimmy and Peggy were in grade school. I coached fifth-grade basketball and Lee was even a scout den mother.

What was striking about the young families who were moving out of the city, was the extent to which we continued to lead New York lives. We were in the forefront of a postwar generation who no longer wanted to raise their families in the city, yet we continued to work there. Just as I was choosing this life-style, I was also seeing its effect on the demographics of retailing.

I saw in my experience and that of my contemporaries tremendous opportunities for Bloomingdale's. A whole generation was furnishing their homes according to their tastes rather than inheriting their parents' values and furniture. In sharp contrast to our parents, we developed a passion for the new. But the new didn't necessarily mean modern: gourmet cooking, fine wines, French country style were all redefining "the good life."

At the same time, suburban life had a tremendous impact on dressing. Weekend leisure wear, casual dressing, athletic wear, slacks for women were all categories that were growing. I had great faith in Bloomingdale's branch stores not only because I was living in Westchester, but because I felt many people would be moving to the suburbs and would want the one-stop selection and taste level that Bloomingdale's planned to offer.

Jed did not share in my great enthusiasm for the opportunities in the suburbs. Within Jed's sixteen-year tenure, we opened four

branch stores totaling 600,000 square feet; during my twenty-two
years, we opened sixteen, a dozen in a ten-year period, totaling more
than 3 million square feet. But without Jed, there would never have
been a Bloomingdale's from which to fashion branch stores. What
Jed taught me, beginning with Stamford, was to think of Bloomingdale's not as a store but as a marketing concept. Bloomingdale's, he
predicted, would become a way to market new products—a channel
of distribution. What Jed was proposing was no more nor less than a
store that would influence the way people dressed, how they decorated their homes, how they served dinner—in short, a store that
would have an impact on every aspect of how people lived.

b

My education in applying Jed's principles of buying began in earnest
in January 1953, when I was promoted to buyer of rugs, broadloom,
and linoleum—my first experience in the home furnishings area.

Much of what the rug department carried then were "seconds."
Our previous buyer, Al Silverstein, had been buying much the same
styles of rugs for the previous twenty-five years. The bulk of the
business was inexpensive machine-made copies of oriental and jac-
quard rugs. We also sold scatter and bathroom rugs of dubious taste.
There was a small broadloom business with colors limited to either
taupe, green, or maroon and only two textures from which to choose:
velvet or a leaf pattern.

I knew little about rugs then. To educate myself, I talked to our
salespeople and suppliers, and I traveled to the rug mills to learn
about carpets and construction. There was tremendous innovation
occurring in the broadloom and rug business utilizing new materials.
The growing use of tufted cotton and the creation of new synthetic
fibers was causing a revolution in the domestic carpet business. For
the first time, we could produce great colors inexpensively for wall-
to-wall or area rugs.

Today it seems commonplace to talk about designing new carpets, but no one at Bloomingdale's had ever done it before. So I
made several trips to carpet manufacturers in North Carolina and
Georgia to get more of a feel for developing new products and
worked closely with them. At my suggestion, Wunda Weave hired
radio and news personality Dorothy Kilgallen to promote the new

rugs. They became a sponsor of her radio show and one morning she broadcast live from the rug department at Bloomingdale's. It created great excitement. We received tremendous press attention and drew many customers.

In a matter of months the rug department was carrying a wide range of new colors and patterns. At the same time, in my first six months, I discontinued linoleum, broadloom seconds, and two thirds of our inexpensive imitation oriental rugs—totally changing the look of our department. They were replaced by better-quality cotton and synthetic fiber rugs in a broad range of contemporary colors and higher-quality oriental reproduction rugs. Our customers were delighted and our sales rose accordingly.

Once I felt the domestic rug programs were on course, I approached my then boss, Frank Chase, the merchandise vice president in charge of men's and home furnishings, and proposed I travel to Europe to study the import rug business. The Downstairs Store was having great success with European goods, we were beginning to import in tabletop and gifts, and I felt there was an opportunity as well for the rug department.

Jed Davidson approved wholeheartedly. Scandinavian design was the rage in home furnishings then, and Jed had a list of museums and factories he wanted me to visit. He felt the trip would be good for my education and suggested I take Lee.

In the 1950s, overseas buying was done at a much more leisurely pace. I was given five weeks to travel to Denmark, Sweden, and Spain. It was a twenty-hour flight to Scandinavia then, in planes complete with berths.

In Denmark, I had my first experience in overseas product development. Our Danish representative took me to Wittrup, a manufacturer who had developed a form of flat weave rug not known in America. The Danish carpets had beautiful patterns but were manufactured in muted tones of beige and brown. I felt New Yorkers wanted something bolder; so we asked them to add accents in bright primary colors, making them much more contemporary.

It was exciting. Developing a new product overseas from a new resource is a high-risk adventure for any young buyer. But there I was, in Denmark, looking at a product that Bloomingdale's had never sold. To visualize what colors could be purchased, at what

price, then to place an order is like standing at the craps table with
dice in your hands and money on the table. I felt my instincts were
right and that the new products would sell. But at that point no one
knew for sure.

You could also see the explosion in home furnishings design
talent in such shops as Ilums Bolihus or Georg Jensen, which featured the work of Danish architects (the Danish name for what we
call a furniture designer) such as Finn Juhl and Arne Voder—all of
whom were emerging as major influences on 1950s style.

From Denmark and Sweden, we went to Spain, traveling from
Valencia to Granada, the center of the Spanish rug industry. We
traveled to Murcia, a small town where we heard they wove interesting sisal and seagrass carpets. But to get there, we had to navigate
small, winding dirt roads.

In 1953 the visit of an American buyer to this town of no more
than a hundred people was a state occasion. They had never had
any visitors from the United States and the idea that a store from
New York was interested in them was big news. The mayor, dressed
in a dark suit with a red sash, welcomed Lee and me and led us into
his home. I think the whole town was there. There were speeches
and toasts. They served local wine and some terrible-looking hors
d'oeuvres. Lee could not get them down. I did, with great gusto,
eating seconds and thirds. Later we learned that the crunchy ones
were grasshoppers; I did not ask what the others were.

At Jed's suggestion, Lee and I visited the Alhambra as well as
the Gypsy caves of Granada to see flamenco performed. The Alhambra, with its fifteenth-century Moorish architecture, gleaming tiles
and colorful floors, beautiful vistas and gardens, was an education
in Spanish design and an inspiration for the products I was developing. I now knew why Jed had made these visits mandatory. You
understand the products of a foreign culture so much better when
you see them presented in context. Doing so opened my eyes to the
depth and variety of Spanish culture, and in their traditions I found
much inspiration for developing new products for Bloomingdale's.

One of my discoveries on that trip was a colorful open-work
woven throw called a manta that the Spaniards use as a bedspread.
I was struck by how the colorful patterns would work well with so
many decorating styles. I decided to bring them in as rugs. Another

was a Spanish loop carpet called an alpujarra. The designs were bold, fresh, and rendered in intense colors. I knew that no New York department store was selling them, so I put in a substantial order.

My greatest challenge, however, was in getting the staff behind me and motivating them to sell the new products I'd bought in Europe. I was replacing a buyer of long standing and managing a selling staff who were all much older than I. Finally, Bloomingdale's did not have great union relations in those days. I was now management, the enemy.

What I set out to do, from the first, was to make clear that we had a common interest: the improved performance of the department. I decided that I wanted the selling staff to go on commission as soon as possible, although the change could not happen immediately. I was fortunate, however, that my office adjoined that of Vin Brennan, who worked in personnel and was ultimately senior executive vice president of the store. Vin and I worked out a plan to gradually change the way the salesmen were paid and offer them the opportunity to earn more.

I wanted to have a good relationship with my coworkers, so I met immediately with the shop steward and made it clear that I was there to talk but, more importantly, to listen. I set up weekly meetings with the sales staff. Slowly, we got to know each other, and their initial resentment disappeared. Our relationship grew, eventually, into mutual respect and, later, friendship.

By dropping several products, such as linoleum, and by adding new and exclusive merchandise plus a motivated selling staff, it was no surprise our sales increased dramatically. Even so, it was an extraordinary year. We sold more rugs in some months than were sold in entire years past.

Bringing in new products created excitement in the department: People came to see what was new. New Yorkers loved the rugs because they were well made, reasonably priced, and unique. As we had discovered in the basement, imported unique goods often sold out quickly, with greater profit for the store. We had transformed a sleepy department by developing new sources and introducing colors and textures. We learned that we could exercise more control, gain distinction for Bloomingdale's, and build new businesses at very good margins. The success of the rug department was the foundation for the Bloomingdale's furniture and home furnishings programs to follow.

b

By February 1956, I had held seven different jobs in the six years I'd been at the store, and managed to raise profits in each department. For a year after being a rug buyer, I worked as an assistant to Frank Chase, who ran the men's and home furnishings division. Then Jed Davidson and Jim Schoff wanted to create a new position for me. At that time Bloomingdale's had three merchandise vice presidents to whom the buyers reported, but Jed and Jim decided to make me their first divisional merchandise manager, reporting to Frank Chase. I would oversee a portion of home furnishings with direct responsibility for furniture, rugs, curtains, draperies, toys, cameras, and stationery.

Jed Davidson's own background, as I mentioned, was in home furnishings. It was the area he knew best and loved most. His idea of repositioning the store was meeting with resistance in the apparel market, but he felt Bloomingdale's could compete for better customers in home furnishings. In the 1940s, Bloomingdale's had held a design show with the Museum of Modern Art and already had a respectable modern furniture business. Jed decided the best place to implement the changes he sought was in home furnishings. If we failed there, the whole plan was in jeopardy.

Drawing by Lorenz; © 1979 The New Yorker Magazine, Inc.

CHAPTER 3

The Way We Live

There's a chair in my office that I value dearly. It is a copy of an Empire chair with a Biedermeier-style back that I found in Italy in the 1950s. Elegant but comfortable, it works as well in a dining room as behind a desk. It's a hybrid, and was the piece that launched the Bloomingdale's furniture import program. You may own several or know someone who does. We sold thousands of that chair for $79.95 at the time. For the last thirty years, it has been a constant seller for Bloomingdale's, and the last time I checked they were still selling strongly. If you bought it back then, you were lucky. Today, it retails for $500. That chair was the start of the transformation of Bloomingdale's from a store with little distinction to a trendsetter. Home furnishings was where we, as a store, first found our voice.

b

In the early 1950s, the Bloomingdale's furniture department didn't carry much Italian furniture. Henriette Granville, the fashion coordinator for home furnishings, preferred American manufacturers such as Baker, Widdicomb and Kindel. She was a well-educated, elegant woman with a particular interest in modern American collections such as Paul McCobb. Modern furniture in 1950 was still all wood and it was several years before chrome and glass tables were popular.

Most home furnishings departments displayed furniture by lining up their sofas back to back, and chairs the same way. But Miss Granville, as everyone called her, was already doing some well-coordinated furniture presentations or, in decorator parlance, vignettes. Her decorator rooms in January 1951, for example, presented wrought-iron tables with milk-glass tops, iron chairs with foam-rubber cushions—foam rubber was a new product then, and all the rage—all very influenced by Scandinavian design. The floors were bare parquet with a single shaggy white polar bear throw. Very fifties.

I took over the furniture division on February 15, 1956, as a divisional merchandise manager—the first in home furnishings. Henriette Granville and I did not hit it off too well, I believe, because she felt I was trying to instill a more commercial approach among our buyers. Our main competitors then were Macy's and W. & J. Sloane, but their displays showed less taste than Miss Granville's. However, for all the discrimination her rooms displayed, her choices were essentially conservative. She had raised the taste level for expensive merchandise, but designer sales were only a small part of a furniture floor that carried moderate-priced bedrooms and bunk beds. The challenge was to build up the mid-price business for which Miss Granville had little interest. Miss Granville might entice Park Avenue and Sutton Place matrons to shop at Bloomingdale's, but I was interested in attracting their daughters and the flood of young people who were beginning to populate the East Side.

On August 1, 1955, the Third Avenue El made its last trip. When the tracks came down, the street below was revealed as a wide, sunny avenue. Giant apartment buildings seemed to sprout overnight, along with restaurants, bars, and boutiques. Advertising agencies, design and decorator firms rushed into the new office space created along the avenue. Suddenly, Bloomingdale's was in the center of a boom.

Miss Granville and I seemed destined not to get along. Her job was to recommend; I had the power to order the merchandise. She wanted to have the last word, but, in fact, I did. This tension between buyer and fashion coordinator exists to this day. Actually, it's healthy. The fashion coordinator fights to keep the store's standards high; the buyer helps edit the fashion coordinator's recommendations. That's how it's supposed to work.

In the early 1940s, before Miss Granville's or my time, the Bloomingdale's furniture business was very different. The furniture department used to regularly hold Thursday surprise sales. All through the week a selected item of merchandise would be displayed on the floor concealed by a sheet. Thursday evening at six, a whistle was blown, the sheet was withdrawn, and for that evening the item was on sale. A far cry from today's elegant model rooms.

My first promotions were pretty conservative, but when I organized a sale of tables that Miss Granville considered inferior quality, she went over my head to Frank Chase.

"Why are we selling these?" Miss Granville asked in disgust.

"Marvin tells me he can sell a lot of them," Frank answered, "that's why!"

More often than not, Frank stood up for me, but Miss Granville and I were locked in battle. A few months later she ordered the entire new season's samples of upholstered furniture in bright orange fabric. The collection was lined up on the center aisle, acting as a barrier to the rest of the department, as if to say: "Buy orange, or don't buy at all." It made a fashion statement, but not many of our customers wanted it in their homes.

I responded by requesting that Miss Granville accompany me to the furniture show at High Point, North Carolina. Today, North Carolina is the center for furniture of all qualities, but back then it was the starting price point of the business, with the better furnishings to be found in Grand Rapids, Michigan. I doubt if Miss Granville had been there before.

I remember, at one point, showing Miss Granville a chest that had such a commercial finish you could see your face in it. Back then, the cheaper the case piece the more it shone. "What do you think?" I asked. I can't remember what she answered, but I'll never forget the look of disgust on her face.

After our first full season together, Miss Granville decided that she would prefer to work more closely with designers in the furniture industry and announced her resignation. To my surprise, she strongly recommended as her replacement one of her assistants, Barbara D'Arcy, whom I already held in great esteem.

If Barbara D'Arcy isn't a household name, she certainly should be: Her style has influenced the taste and decorating ideas of Americans throughout the country. Her model rooms at Bloomingdale's have been featured in many magazines, including *Life, House Beautiful, McCall's,* and *House & Garden,* and her *Bloomingdale's Book of Home Decorating* was so influential that a whole generation has adopted her style, whether they know it or not.

b

Barbara grew up a few blocks from Bloomingdale's and her decorating education began as a child. On weekends her parents would walk her along Madison Avenue and down the side streets of the sixties and seventies looking in the windows of the antique stores, discussing French bureaus and chairs. Barbara developed a unique sense of style, one I could relate to, that is not school-taught but city-bred.

Barbara attended the college of New Rochelle, and in May 1952, after a short stint as an "Alexander Smith Carpet Lady," she joined Bloomingdale's as a junior decorator in the fabric department. She is very lively, with vivid red hair and a theatrical manner—she can be serious but also has a great sense of humor.

The fabrics Bloomingdale's sold then were not terribly stylish—brocades and unattractive multicolored wovens. Barbara's job, as far as the public was concerned, was to answer questions about fabrics and make decorating suggestions. From the store's point of view, she was there to help consummate sales. What immediately distinguished Barbara was her talent at performing both functions so well.

One day a South American couple whose beach home Henriette Granville had decorated came to Barbara to have everything slipcovered. Mattress ticking as a decorative fabric had just become very chic and Barbara was enthusiastic about it. She sold the couple on using brown and white ticking for the slipcovers. They were delighted. Next, she suggested that they also use ticking for their draperies to pull the whole look together. They liked that, too. But Barbara wasn't finished. In no time, the couple had committed to using ticking throughout the house, and Barbara had made the biggest fabric sale in the history of Bloomingdale's. Needless to say, she was quickly promoted to the fifth floor as a decorating consultant.

b

As I watched Barbara at work on the fifth floor I was aware of her great talent. Bloomingdale's wanted to be the neighborhood store for the Upper East Side and Barbara knew our ideal customer, her tastes, her ambitions—she had grown up with her. Identifying our new shopper was not so much a matter of geography or demographics; it was more about attracting a new generation who had a certain state of mind. We were looking for customers with curiosity, with a sense of adventure and fun.

Barbara was unafraid to mix and match: new with old; foreign with American. Her eclecticism was the essence of New York, and exactly the image I wanted to project. Barbara never had to ask herself: Is it right for our customer? If Barbara liked it, there was a good chance it would sell.

b

A few months after Miss Granville's departure, I invited Barbara on a trip to Grand Rapids, Michigan, our most important market, home of Baker, Widdicomb and Kindel. Barbara assumed that I had no one else to go with me. But I had another agenda.

High above the ground, strapped into our seats, I asked Barbara if she would take over Miss Granville's responsibility. "Oh no," she said. "How could I?" Barbara was afraid she didn't have enough experience. "I haven't studied, I don't know, I'm not ready yet," she protested.

If we hadn't been on a plane, I think Barbara would have run out of the room. But I was so confident of her ability that I suggested she try the position on a temporary basis. Barbara would only commit to a year. Fine, I said. Barbara held that "temporary" job for sixteen years before we promoted her to head of store design.

To round out our management team, I promoted Carl Levine, a young furniture buyer. Carl, who was to become one of the country's greatest furniture and rug merchants, was born, prophetically enough, in Bloomingdale, New Jersey. He was a third-generation home furnishings merchant.

Carl joined the Bloomingdale's executive training program in 1955. He expressed a preference for furniture, so Bloomingdale's assigned him to the women's dress department. He stuck it out there until an assistant position came up in mattresses.

When Carl and I first got to know each other in 1956, he was studying seventeenth- and eighteenth-century furniture in his spare time, and was teaching himself how to distinguish one wood from another. I was attending night courses at the Metropolitan Museum of Art to learn about furniture, so I used to quiz him. Together, we learned the difference between Louis Quinze (XV) and Louis Seize (XVI) furniture. (Louis Quinze is very rococo with rampant decoration and is, perhaps, the most popular of French styles; Louis Seize is more severe and straight-lined. Not that you *have* to know the difference—it's just useful when you're head of home furnishings.)

We wanted the home furnishings buying staff to be as knowledgeable as possible about merchandise and to heighten their taste level, so I hired the curator of the Frick Collection to hold evening classes. The curator would line up six different chairs from the Bloomingdale's floor and ask the buyers to rate each as to good taste. It was a great teaching technique and inspired heated debates that increased the education and perception of taste and quality in our buyers.

Jed was as much an educator as a merchant, and he believed that the store was a means to further knowledge for both the consumer and the staff. (Today, young executives barely have time to learn about merchandise.) As Jed set the tone, I set out to train Carl. Carl was used to making gut decisions, but I asked him to translate those feelings onto paper and develop planning skills. We were learning to work together, and I was assembling a formidable and enthusiastic team.

Which brings us back to the chair in my office. As a rug buyer, I had traveled to Scandinavia and Spain. What I had seen in Europe was no more or less than the future of Bloomingdale's: that by finding and manufacturing goods abroad, Bloomingdale's could create excitement for our store—at a substantial profit.

My success with rugs now led me to the north of Italy to develop an import program for furniture as well. Franco ("Nap") Napolatani, Bloomingdale's Italian representative, and I drove through the Venice region, to Bassano Del Grappa, which had a history of making both furniture and ceramics. We pulled up to the farmhouse of Guido Zichele. At first, I didn't make much of the roosters running around his backyard. But then we walked by the chicken coops and Nap whispered to me, "Mr. Zichele makes his living as a chicken farmer." Furniture, aparently, was a sideline. He led us across the street to his so-called factory, a former barn turned garage that housed his workshop.

I walked around inside and found I didn't like most of what I saw. He led me up to the attic. I was about to leave when an unusual piece caught my eye. It was a chair with only three legs—one was missing—but it was stylish and had a strong clean look. I took a long hard stare at it, imagining it standing on our showroom floor, and in an American home. This, I thought, is exactly what I was looking for. Without hesitating I asked Mr. Zichele if he could reproduce the chair. He said he could, and I ordered four, as samples, to be sent to my office in New York.

Up the road was Count Alessandro Bussandri. In sharp contrast to Guido Zichele's simple surroundings, Bussandri lived in a walled castle, part of which was devoted to his home and part to antiques and antique reproductions that he sold internationally even then. We sat in his ornate drawing room as liveried servants carried in beautiful pieces. I saw a small table that I liked as well as other pieces, and ordered several samples.

Several months later, my sample orders arrived. I arranged the chairs and tables in my office and called in Barbara and Carl. Casually, I asked them what they thought. "Fan-tastic!" Barbara exclaimed.

I told them where I had found the chairs and tables and what they cost and both Carl and Barbara became very excited. What we saw in those first pieces was a look, something new, that no other department store was offering. Most American furniture manufacturers were using mass-production techniques. With these few items, we saw the beginning of a new Bloomingdale's.

But first, there was a lot of research and planning to do. Our decision had to be based on business as well as aesthetics. We investigated the cost of having the furniture manufactured here. It was about twice as expensive. Next, I asked Carl and Barbara to study what was selling in the interior designer showrooms in New York.

Yale Burge, David Barrett, and Rosalynd Rosier were the big names then. Barbara and Carl visited them and confirmed that many decorators were acquiring French country antiques or expensive reproductions. Most original pieces were not, we felt, appropriate for the wear and tear of New York families. Based on what I had seen in Italy, I felt Bloomingdale's could offer reproduction pieces that were more stylish than those from any department store and far better priced than what any decorator offered. The combination of fashion and value was bound to be a winner.

Jed had led us away from Paris to the provincial museums, and as Barbara, Carl, and I discussed it, we found ourselves leaning toward a style that would incorporate the elements of fine French furniture but had a more rugged construction with a more rustic feel to it.

The plan was to go back to Italy and search out appropriate pieces, expanding our experiment if successful by several items a season. If we found the right items, fine; if not, we would have them manufactured in Italy to our specifications, at a cost that would be affordable yet earn us a larger profit than having them made domestically.

We called the look "French Country." We took a little from here and a little from there. A French back, Italian legs. If the Italians didn't carve enough, we showed them what the French did; if the French legs were too ornate, we showed them how the Italians did it.

The following year I went back to Italy and this time Carl came along. Although he was still an associate buyer, the full buyer sent him because he thought the business would never amount to much. Carl was elated. Barbara joined us the next year. This was the start of our European buying trips.

Barbara recalls that the first thing she ever saw in Bassano, before she even arrived at Zichele's house, was a donkey making its way up the road with a two-drawer commode strapped to its side. As the commode approached Barbara realized it was one that she had designed. During that visit, we placed a second order with Mr. Zichele, and then a third for over $50,000. He gave up chicken farming soon after.

Italian reproduction furniture had a deep, shiny finish then, but we wanted to produce pieces that had an antique look. Mr. Zichele and his workers didn't understand what we meant by an antique finish. So we went out to Mr. Zichele's garage. Carl had a rock in his hands, Nap held some chains. And we took a delicate end table and began to hammer it all over.

The Italians thought we were stark raving mad. Punching holes in beautiful furniture? Rubbing ash into a fine finish to scratch it up?

We tried to show them how a pastry crimper could be used to good effect creating cuts in the surface, but it was beyond them.

Our Italian friends couldn't understand why anyone would want something old for the same price as new. Imagine being able to buy a shiny new car and, instead, insisting that you wanted a rusty, dented one. Crazy Americans, they said. But we were paying; so they hammered away. In no time they became quite proficient in the art of antiquing, developing a variety of effects and finishes, and even lining the drawers with antique-looking wallpaper.

Since we were making it up as we went along, we felt free to borrow where we wanted. Barbara, Carl, and I pored over art books looking for new inspiration. We visited museums and villas. Once, while visiting the Villa Pisani in the Venice region, we found a set of chairs we loved. The villa was too dark to photograph in, so Carl asked the guards if, for a small fee, we might take the chairs outside. They agreed. And so the guards carried these priceless antiques and set them on the grass for us to photograph.

Barbara's special gift was to see new uses for old products. Take the armoire, for instance. Europeans had been using furniture for storage since before homes had closets, yet the closest thing in the United States was a hope chest, sitting at the end of a bed. On our trips we had gone to museums, seen how armoires were used, and loved them. Because she was so in touch with our customers' lives, Barbara knew that New York apartments were only getting smaller and storage would come at a premium. We imported a few, and from the first shipments, armoires sold out. Barbara has used them to hold clothes, linens, office equipment, liquor, stereos, and TVs.

Over the years Barbara has championed the use of English campaign chests as end tables, coffee tables, or stacked up one atop the other; African masks on walls; elkhorn chairs; draperies hung on poles; tented dressing rooms; and giant Japanese paper lamps. One of my personal favorites was a special porcelain planter one of our buyers discovered in the south of France. It was actually an antique bidet and Bloomingdale's sold them in great quantity.

Looking back, it is remarkable how few mistakes we made. We had the confidence—the arrogance—of youth, but we also had checks and balances: Carl and Barbara both had to like an item, and if they wanted to order twelve, I probably said six. Our chemistry produced unique results. What we had, really, was the freedom to fail because, in pure numbers and dollars, the investment was not so great.

b

Jed Davidson had given us lists of museums and places of interest, as well as great restaurants with specific dishes to order and wines to select. To see the sights and do our work made for eighteen-hour days beginning at 5:30 in the morning.

One time when we were working with Pompellio Zavenella, a craftsman outside Florence, the sample he made for us had some problems that we had to solve that night. This was our only chance to discuss details of the designs before they arrived in New York six months later, so we needed to go over every detail and carving, often doing full-scale drawings to explain what we wanted.

At mid-morning he served us coffee. A few hours later, his wife served some pasta and wine for lunch. There was coffee at the end of the afternoon, and a little something in the evening. We worked on and on, until at three in the morning his wife appeared in her nightgown with a candle and said, "Basta! Enough!" and threw us out. But we got it done.

That was the rule rather than the exception. The dedication showed then was the spirit that would come to infect all of Bloomingdale's. We had high standards and "whatever it takes" was our modus operandi. Working such long hours together increased our camaraderie. At Bloomingdale's I was very serious, but in Europe we all got to know each other, and learned to appreciate each other's sense of humor.

No one knew who we were: We were seen simply as American buyers whose checks were good. "Bloomeen-dollies," they called us. Once we were better known we had to develop our own code to judge merchandise on the spot without the owner's understanding us. Barbara came up with the word *stratz* for terrible. However, so the owner wouldn't be insulted, we had to use the word as if it were a compliment. We would rave, "How stratz! Very stratz!" We stood in many a showroom biting our lips to keep from laughing.

b

Finding the merchandise was only half the battle; the other half was presenting it to best advantage. Barbara, Carl, and I discussed what changes we should bring to the furniture floor to accommodate our new products and new image.

First, we cut the ad budget. The $2.99 basement dresses had taught me how inefficient advertising could be. Our new merchandise represented so dramatic a departure that I believed our money was better spent on display than advertising. We created space on the furniture floor that was then designated for permanent "installations," a series of designer rooms that would change four times a year—major shows in the fall and spring, as well as the less important January and summer sales. Henriette Granville's rooms featured designer furniture collections; Barbara's were filled with our own creations that would reflect the new Bloomingdale's sense of style.

Barbara, Carl, and I had visualized how the entire furniture floor would look. We decided to display fewer items but make the space look more attractive by extending the concept of the model rooms to the entire floor. Most furniture departments displayed all bedrooms in one place, all living rooms in another, all lamps in another. We pulled them together in one fluid, constantly changing floor. We developed the concept of planning a floor by piece and color; nothing could be added unless another piece was dropped. Each area was color coordinated. The business grew and grew because we got rid of the $19 tables and put $100 tables in their place. We got rid of the $200 sofas and put in $600 ones. We were merchandising for the new affluent neighborhood as well as younger suburbanites decorating their own homes.

As we discovered, it's easier for the consumer to buy when she sees a total home furnishings presentation. Couches were now presented with rugs, side tables, lamps, bookcases, and armoires. The new displays were warmer, and put the customer at ease by showing the pieces as they might appear in her own home. At the same time, Bloomingdale's was sending out a message that home furnishings were a fashion decision: choices abounded.

The work of our fashion coordinators became even more critical. We were creating new products in every area of home furnishings— rugs, lamps, furniture—so I believed we needed specialists in each.

We appointed three different fashion coordinators, each with the title of vice president. Barbara D'Arcy was responsible for all furniture presentation including model rooms as well as new furniture development. Elaine McAllister became fashion director for rugs and home textiles, and Mary Trainor Rice was in charge of housewares, food, and tabletop. Back then stores did not make fashion coordinators vice presidents. This was a significant statement, not only within the store but to the entire retailing and manufacturing community, that Bloomingdale's was reorganizing and putting a major emphasis on home furnishings style and fashion.

b

Bloomingdale's had held an exhibition of Scandinavian design in 1957. "At Home with Scandinavia" had not been a financial success, but it had garnered a great deal of press attention. Two years later, Jed Davidson proposed that we organize a merchandising event to display all our new Italian home furnishings. We scheduled it for the fall of 1960; it was to be called, simply, "Casa Bella," beautiful home.

Neiman-Marcus had been doing import fairs for many years. The "Fortnights," as Stanley Marcus called them, were only in the Dallas store and lasted two weeks, but they brought great cultural events to the store and created traffic for the traditional October retailing slump. Jed, however, wanted the merchandise itself to be the star.

Until then not more than a handful of Bloomingdale's executives had visited Europe. Now, more than a dozen buyers, decorators, and other home furnishings executives crisscrossed Italy searching out new sources of unusual glass, china, linens, pictures, mirrors, furniture, and antiques.

Virginia White, the picture and mirror buyer, spent days hunting through the cellars of old country houses and churches for exciting bits of architecture that sold out almost immediately when the show opened. Elaine McAllister found an Italian dealer who led her to a barn filled with antique silver church candle holders. She decided they would make beautiful lamps. To show you the lengths Elaine went to, one glass bottle with a flowered top required four or five steps for assembly and each was in a different Italian city. But she did it.

A preview cocktail party for "Casa Bella" was held in late September 1960 on the fifth floor. Italian murals and statues were recreated for the entrance and Italian food and wine were served. But most important, the merchandise took center stage. "Casa Bella" announced that the home furnishings department was adding traditional furnishings while maintaining the contemporary. To emphasize that this was truly a Bloomingdale's look, each item carried a red tag with a drawing of a cherub holding a candle encircled by the words *Made in Italy for Bloomingdale's*.

The stars were the seven model rooms Barbara designed. I recall one room where Barbara displayed the furnishings of an entire villa in a space the size of a New York studio apartment. The room was split into two levels. On a raised platform stood a wood canopy bed that looked more like a carriage. Nearby was a formal desk that had begun life as a table before we raised it to American proportions. Behind the table, two double-cane ladder-back chairs were surrounded by bookcases copied from the designs of large Venetian armoires. Down a few steps was the living room, decorated in the Louis-Quinze-by-way-of-the-Italian-provinces style we had invented. There were low overstuffed couches and armchairs with high backs, both with finely carved legs. Barbara used a small commode as a side table, and there were silver lamps. It was breathtaking—old world luxury at department store prices.

We invited the press and some of our manufacturers, along with store executives and members of the Italian consulate. The party and the show received tremendous attention. *Look* magazine even did a story. But more important, the customers came and bought all our unique items. Sales were extraordinary and Carl went back to Italy to reorder.

I was relieved, I confess. Our budget for "Casa Bella" had been $6,000. With the cost of construction, we had spent slightly more than $21,000. Had the show been a failure, I might still be trying to pay back the difference. That was, however, probably the last time Bloomingdale's covered the entire cost of a promotion itself. In the fall of 1991, we would mount "Tempo d'Italia," the largest Italian promotion in the store's history, for a cost of almost a million dollars; but Bloomingdale's would share the cost with corporate sponsors and the Italian government.

I can't tell you how often I have been invited to people's homes in New York and seen items that were first displayed as part of "Casa Bella." The double-cane chairs from Zavenella, which sold for little more than $100, became an instant classic, and were for two decades among our most popular chairs. Lee and I still use a set for our dining table in Connecticut.

"Casa Bella" was successful not only because of the merchandise but because of the times. The postwar generation thought differently from their parents. Carl, Barbara, and I were all of a generation that desired a freer way of living than our parents had known. The depression had dominated the 1930s; World War II, the 1940s. We were the first generation that could turn its attention to quality-of-life standards. Where to buy a home and how to furnish it were central concerns in the 1950s. No longer would a young couple strive to inherit their parents' grand piano, oriental rugs, and sterling silver. They wanted their own.

b

After the success of "Casa Bella," Jed wanted to expand the concept of an imported promotion to the whole store. For him, Italy was just the warm-up. Now, in the fall of 1961, we were to go to heaven, or Jed Davidson's version of it: France.

The fashion coordinators, decorators, and buyers spent a year selecting imports from France to appear in more than fifty-five departments throughout the store. Some forty buyers covered more than 300,000 miles in France to gather merchandise for "L'Esprit de France," as we named our first storewide import promotion.

On September 26, 1961, after the store had closed, Bloomingdale's held a party for the press and selected guests sponsored by the French consul as a benefit for Entraide Française, an organzation that helps destitute French persons and Americans of French descent. More than eight hundred guests sipped champagne, ate steak au poivre, and wandered through a transformed Bloomingdale's.

Paris's famous shopping street, the Faubourg St. Honoré, was re-created on the third floor with small shops. (They were not called boutiques yet.) The Town & Country shop carried an exclusive knit collection designed by Lanvin, Jacques Heim, and Guy Laroche, among others. Ready-to-wear fashions were created for the chil-

dren's department with French knits and berets. There was a millinery shop—women still wore hats—and the main floor perfumery
shop offered a varied selection of French perfumes, all specially
packaged in France for this occasion. The model rooms embraced
Davidson's philosophy of searching out the authentic. Bloomingdale's re-created an eighteenth-century French provincial kitchen,
complete with a Normandy fireplace, a caldron blackened by smoke,
beamed ceilings, and an alcove bed with a feather mattress.

The single modern item in the kitchen was an electric range at
which Georges Pesquet, chef of the French ocean liner *Flandre*,
performed French cooking demonstrations twice daily during the
first week of October.

What drew the greatest attention, however, was not any special
event, or even any special item of merchandise, but the wrapping
paper and shopping bags created for the event. Their design was
based on old French tarot cards, contained no mention of the store,
and for reasons known only to the gods of retailing, having a tarot
card shopping bag became a status symbol. Before we knew it the
bags started appearing all over town, swinging from the arms of
people who never would have admitted to shopping at Bloomingdale's.

b

The import fairs became annual events throughout the sixties. Having featured Italy and France, the two countries that Jed most cared
for, the fairs took on more metaphoric concepts, such as "Romance," "Tradition," and "Symphony in B." The import fairs were
suspended in 1970—we had other priorities, such as opening new
stores—but were revived in 1978 as country promotions.

Jed made it clear that the purpose of the fairs was to develop
new merchandise. Many stores do fairs for publicity, with banners,
celebrities, and special events. Our promotions generated great
press for Bloomingdale's but our primary purpose was to motivate
buyers to search out and develop new merchandise. We were re-
making the store, department by department, item by item.

The fairs were another way for Jed to teach the virtues of planning. Before one import fair ended, we began planning the next, a
year in advance. At the same time we had to manage our day-to-day

responsibilities. This may not sound like a big deal, but at the time it was a radical change from the way department store merchants worked and thought. Our belief was that since we spent less time on sales and advertising, we had more for planning and product development.

Barbara D'Arcy's model rooms continued to be the heart of every import fair, but they also took on a life of their own. Barbara created not just rooms but environments that no one could ever have imagined appearing in a department store. She re-created an authentic Japanese farmhouse she had visited for one fair, and on another occasion a Spanish bullfighters' tavern.

I was conscious of the entertainment value of the model rooms. People now came to Bloomingdale's and took home ideas. What other store offered that?

Each year we returned to Europe to develop additional pieces and new resources. In England, we found a manufacturer named Kennedy whose firm had made oak sailing ships in the seventeenth century. He looked like Colonel Blimp, and his factory was a warren of cottages, but he made the most incredible oak furniture. In France, in Orléans, there was Claude Amos, one of the finest furniture makers we ever used—it was difficult to distinguish which of his pieces were reproductions and which were antiques. Claude was the third generation to run the factory and gave up teaching economics at Princeton's Woodrow Wilson Institute to take over. In Provence, we worked with the Demery family of Souleiado fabrics, who had the finest hand-blocked paisley and provincial prints and were to become lifelong friends. You may also know Souleiado as the fabric supplier for Pierre Deux.

We never forgot our Italian friends, and have continued to work with the Zicheles. Today, the third generation runs the now $10 million business. I last saw the Zicheles a few weeks before I left Bloomingdale's. Franco, Guido's son-in-law, had come to see a model room completely furnished with Zichele furniture created for the 1991 "Tempo d'Italia" promotion. More than forty years had passed since I found the chair in Guido's attic that had been the spark for the transformation of the entire store. It's no wonder I value the copy in my office so much!

It was an extraordinary period. We were building a bigger and bigger business. The import fairs were a draw not only for new customers but also for the merchandising elite of Europe. Their high opinion of our goods spread to other manufacturers in the United States, and the word-of-mouth meant a great deal. "You have to go to Bloomingdale's and see what they're doing" was a common refrain. Decorators and designers began to visit the store regularly to see the model rooms, the fairs, and found the merchandise, which they now bought, a source of ideas and inspiration.

Our own enthusiasm was raging like brushfire throughout the whole store. As Vin Brennan, our personnel director then, once described the feeling by saying, "Bloomingdale's wasn't a store, it was a cause."

*"Look, lady, if it's trendy you want, Bloomie's is at
Fifty-ninth and Lex."*

Drawing by Geo. Price; © 1982 The New Yorker Magazine, Inc.

CHAPTER 4

The Way We Look

T he clothing business is, in many ways, the lifeblood of a department store. Almost 75 percent of department store shoppers are women, and clothing and accessories account for two thirds of a store's business, with women's apparel making up the lion's share. So it made sense that fashion was to be the second pillar of our rebuilt Bloomingdale's.

♭

As Bloomingdale's emerged from the 1950s, the store was still grappling to find a niche for itself in apparel. The American designer business was dominated by the Fifth Avenue stores. At the same time, Ohrbach's and Alexander's had found leadership roles by offering line-for-line copies of French couture fashions, so much so that when Ohrbach's sold copies of a $1,250 Balenciaga dress for $59.99, fashion writers dubbed it "the miracle on 34th Street."

Bloomingdale's had its Green Room for designer clothes and opened the Sutton Shop in 1959, but neither clearly defined the store's fashion role. We had not yet given chic women a reason to shop at Bloomingdale's for clothes.

The key to our success was in realizing that there was a younger shopper who was looking as much for style as for function. Just as we did in home furnishings, we wanted to develop our own products. So rather than select from what was currently being offered by American manufacturers, we sought out designers who were creating the fashions that we felt our customers would appreciate—clothes with flair.

At the beginning of the sixties, our ready-to-wear business was very different than it is today. Many Sundays our first ad in *The New York Times* featured dresses retailing anywhere from $14.95 to

$26.00. One of our better sportswear buyers told me she thought any woman who spent more than $25.00 for a skirt was out of her mind. Hard to believe that less than a decade later our Paradox shop would offer $200 sweaters that women couldn't live without.

b

Bloomingdale's underwent major organizational changes in the sixties. By 1960, Jim Schoff, sixty, and Jed Davidson, fifty-nine, decided Bloomingdale's needed a clear line of succession for the day when they would step down, and they began planning their replacements over time so as to prepare the next team. They selected Larry Lachman, who had been executive vice president since 1958, and me. In June 1962, Jed relinquished his day-to-day responsibilities as chairman of the board to devote all his time to working on our import program, then retired the following year. Jim Schoff became chairman and, in 1963, Larry Lachman became president.

Without Jed the store needed a merchandising head; so in 1962, at age thirty-seven, I was promoted from vice president of home furnishings to executive vice president and general merchandise manager for the entire store. Until then, Jed held the title of general merchandise manager.

In December 1965, Jim Schoff retired as CEO and Larry Lachman succeeded him. The board felt that at forty I was still too young to be president and appointed Harold Krensky chairman of the board and managing director. I reported directly to Harold until 1969, when he left to become a group president of Federated (he became president of all Federated in 1973).

I became president of Bloomingdale's in 1969, at age forty-four, and Harold announced that there really had been no need for him to come back to Bloomingdale's. But I had found Harold incredibly helpful in completing my education in apparel. This long, carefully planned-out transition and support of one generation of leadership to the next was intended to ensure, as Ralph Lazarus put it at the time, "increased depth and continuity of management."*

---

* When Larry Lachman retired as chairman in 1978, I succeeded him and Jim Schoff, Jr., became president. Once more we put in place a team groomed inside Bloomingdale's to take over.

b

In 1967 Howard Goldfeder, then our vice president for ready-to-wear, announced that he was leaving the store to join the May Company in St. Louis. Howard was forthright with me and over lunch said that with my promotion he felt it appropriate to move on. I understood. I took advantage of the opening to learn the fashion business. For six months I kept two offices, one on the seventh floor in the executive offices and one on the third as general merchandise manager of ready-to-wear with the merchandise managers reporting directly to me.

I spent time in the ready-to-wear markets with our fashion coordinators to learn more about the apparel business. We were beginning to develop businesses out of Europe and I traveled to Paris as well. It was a great introduction, and after six months, Mel Jacobs, my good friend from the bargain tables who had gone on to supervise the entire Downstairs Store, was appointed the new vice president for ready-to-wear and fashion accessories.

Harold Krensky at this point took on an important role in my training and development. Harold is a genial Bostonian with a career focusing on fashion. He was first hired by Jed and Jim in 1947 for merchandising and publicity, a position he held until 1959 when he went to Filene's in Boston, rising to chairman, leaving in 1966 to rejoin Bloomingdale's.

Harold is good-looking, articulate, with a marvelous personality and has to be one of the best-loved people in the retail industry. It was very easy for me to work with him. We had adjacent offices and would meet every morning at 8:30 so I could keep him informed; after that he totally left me free to direct the business. Harold had an encyclopedic knowledge of the apparel business and was a great teacher.*

b

---

* Harold and I continued to be very close. When he went to Federated I reported directly to him and we continued to have a very supportive relationship. Harold, like Ralph, believed in strong management in the divisions with the corporate office only in a supportive role. This was a major contrast to the future management of Federated.

The prototypical fashion director of a department store then was a woman who wore long gloves and a big hat. She was often mistrusted by the buyers and thought to be frivolous. When I first joined ready-to-wear, Margaret de Mille, Agnes de Mille's sister and Cecil B. deMille's niece, was the fashion personage of long standing. Margaret was a serious businessperson—no big hats or gloves for her. Her main function was to select windows and coordinate interior displays and fashion presentations. Throughout the sixties, one of our fashion buyers was Doris Salinger. People always wanted to know about her brother, J.D.

My experience in home furnishings, however, had taught me the importance of having fashion directors as full partners in product development. Barbara D'Arcy had become one of the great assets of the store. We hoped the fashion director for ready-to-wear would do the same. In Katie Murphy, whom we hired in May 1967, we found someone who was to become the heart and soul of our apparel division.

b

Katherine Murphy Grout—or Katie Murphy as everyone called her, usually in one breath—was a tall, attractive, enthusiastic woman with an engaging personality and a ready smile. The entire fashion community admired Katie, who started her career in the Macy's training program after attending Pembroke College and the Rhode Island School of Design. She worked at Bergdorf Goodman, Lord & Taylor, and Bonwit Teller, where she had been the merchandise manager of accessories. Katie had manufacturing training as well: She had worked on Seventh Avenue for Ellen Brooke, a blouse manufacturer. Her business instincts allowed her to move easily among all the players in the clothing world and made her a valuable partner in our ready-to-wear business. The buyers would turn to her for advice, as would designers, and as did I.

After a few years at Bloomingdale's, Katie became a vice presi-

---

In 1974, Harold and I had lunch and he sounded me out on going to Cincinnati for a major position in the corporate office. I declined and told Harold that running Bloomingdale's was far more satisfying and I would never move to Cincinnati. He understood, and ten years later told me what a sound decision I had made.

dent of the store, giving the ready-to-wear and fashion accessories coordinator a status it never had before. It was critical to let the retail community know the emphasis we placed on fashion, and the trust we had in Katie.

The youth culture dominated the 1960s. The decade began with the inauguration of forty-three-year-old John F. Kennedy as President and his thirty-one-year-old wife as First Lady. Suddenly, fashion was dictated by the culture not the couture. Astronauts, the Beatles, all influenced how people dressed. The baby boom had driven many of us into the suburbs, but it was the baby boomers who drove the culture in the sixties. Youth became anti-fashion, and started buying their clothes at army-navy stores and Salvation Army thrift shops. Designers took note. André Courrèges gave us boots worn indoors or out. Yves Saint Laurent came to New York and bought a pea coat in Times Square. The next year pea coats turned up in his collection, creating an uproar.

Ford launched the Mustang at the 1964 World's Fair as a car for those who think young. Youth culture could mean dressing like your grandmother or a Native American, in bell-bottom jeans or overalls. The truth was that most of our shoppers were not so youthful, or so fashion forward, but they wanted to feel young. We set out to offer a great variety of fashions that were casual but chic. Bloomingdale's became a store for young people, whatever their age.

Bloomingdale's was the right store at the right time, and we had a very talented team to lead us in ready-to-wear. With Harold Krensky at the helm, Katie Murphy as our fashion director, Mel Jacobs as merchandise vice president, and a strong trio of divisional merchandise managers, we had the players that would shape our fashion identity. And a team it was: Harold and I would meet first thing; and as Katie and I lived in Westchester, we would commute together and work out strategy on the way home. We were ready to take on the world. Or at least France.

b

You may wonder why Paris has always been the center of fashion. It is not necessarily because the French have any greater talent for design. In fact, many of the greatest couturiers of the last century were not French. Worth was an Englishman, Balenciaga was from

Spain, Schiaparelli was an Italian, and Mainbocher, the famous designer of the 1940s, hailed from Chicago, of all places. Even today, the House of Chanel has the talented Karl Lagerfeld, born in Germany, as its designer.

Paris is the fashion center for three reasons. First, and most important, is the support the government gives the industry. In the seventeenth century, Louis XIV and his prime minister Jean-Baptiste Colbert set up guilds to raise the quality of French artisanship. Second are the French suppliers themselves. Fabric companies are willing to experiment and to run up small samples for designers. Button, pearl, and lace makers are all available to help with custom work to an extent that exists in no other country. Finally, there is the French woman. Since the end of World War II and Christian Dior's New Look of 1947, fashion directors have always asked: "What are the fashions this summer in Saint-Tropez? What are women wearing on the streets of Paris?" The reason is that the chic of the poorest shopgirl on the metro still inspires fashion directors and editors all over the world.

b

At the same time, in the mid-sixties, dramatic changes were occurring in the French fashion industry, and it was Bloomingdale's and my good fortune to be part of that revolution.

Foreign fashion producers fall into three categories: haute couture, ready-to-wear, and mass-produced garments, usually manufactured at low cost in low-wage countries, primarily in the Orient.

The word *couture* derives from the French verb *coudre*, to sew, and implies handsewn, made-to-measure garments. Couture is governed by the Chambre Syndicale de la Couture Parisienne, a French trade organization founded in 1868. Membership is limited to designers who meet certain specified qualifications.

The Chambre Syndicale rules with an iron hand. Just as bubbly from any region other than Champagne is just sparkling wine, the Chambre Syndicale does not consider every designer a couturier. Couture must operate in a residential building in Paris rather than a commercial one, hence the phrase "the house of . . ." The head of the house is the designer, the couturier, and he need not be the owner. Twice a year, in January and July, on dates set by the

Chambre Syndicale, a couturier must create a collection of seventy-five or more original garments of his own, made to order and presented on live models. He must employ three models on a year-round basis, and employ a minimum of twenty workers in the firm's couture-production workrooms. This is an expensive enterprise.

A 1965 *New York Times Magazine* article gave these figures for Dior's show that year: "In a collection of 174 models, $200,000 is invested in labor and materials. Then each model is reproduced, one by one, to a client's measurements, with three fittings according to haute couture traditions. Each dress represents an average of 135 working hours—$470 just in labor costs—plus the material, $80—plus general overhead." And those were in 1965 dollars! Today, a couture collection can cost over a million dollars, and the show itself can cost another half a million.

So why do it? In part because couture is the arena where the designer can express himself most purely as an artist working in a tradition. There is, of course, a sound financial reason as well. Although a couture collection is rarely profitable, it is just one business of a house that may include ready-to-wear, accessories, licenses, franchise shops, and fragrances. The couture collection is the flagship, providing prestige and publicity. It establishes the designer's reputation within the trade, permits him his creativity, and allows the designer to cater to a private clientele who bring the designer attention by wearing his fashions.

Couture creates prestige and, increasingly, is publicity for the perfume. Often the perfume licensee picks up the cost of the couture fashion show, in whole or in part. The cost of a show, however great, is still small compared to the average fragrance company television ad budget, and you cannot buy the press attention couture receives. Not all designers have fragrances, but most do license their names for products of one kind or another.

The future of couture has been debated every decade for the last half century. Currently, the Chambre Syndicale has commissioned a major report on the subject. Rumor has it changes will be recommended to make couture more economically feasible and allow many ready-to-wear designers to become couturiers. Whatever the outcome, couture will continue.

Ready-to-wear implies factory-made clothing or sportswear. The firm of Mendes-France is credited with having started the industry in 1903. For the first half of the century, ready-to-wear was not considered fashionable in and of itself. In the 1960s, however, changing life-styles created a greater demand for sportswear among the couture crowd, where, until then, the focus had been on dresses and suits. Eventually the Chambre Syndicale created an organization for ready-to-wear designers as well.

Department stores in the United States were on two tracks: American designers or line-for-line copies of French designers. Harold Krensky and Katie Murphy thought European ready-to-wear from established as well as up-and-coming designers presented a great opportunity. Krensky referred to the couture business as "pheasant under glass," his way of saying that the high-end businesses set a tone, but the big opportunity was in sportswear.

As our apparel vice president, Mel Jacobs began to visit sportswear fairs in Paris, London, Milan, and Munich, looking at the work of young designers. Bloomingdale's had success commissioning work in children's wear, and decided to try the same with sportswear, then move into coats and, finally, dresses.

At the time competition was nothing like it is today. The only other executives we would regularly see at the European ready-to-wear fairs buying the same merchandise were Geraldine Stutz of Henri Bendel and Joan Burstyn of Brown's of London. As we covered the fairs, we got to know European designers and manufacturers, and more important, they quickly got to know us. The first step to fashion leadership was raising the profile of the Bloomingdale's name in European circles.

b

Shortly before his death in 1957, Christian Dior visited the United States with Jacques Rouet, his business manager and a friend of my parents. Several years earlier, Monsieur Dior had graciously received Lee and me at his atelier in Paris. Now they called on me at Bloomingdale's, and I showed them our home furnishings department. Monsieur Dior later confided to Jacques Rouet that he felt Bloomingdale's would succeed in fashion *because* of its home furnishings department. "No other store has both. Women will come to each," he predicted, "and shop at both." He was right, of course, but it would take us over a decade to realize it.

Emanuel Ungaro came to New York for the first time in the late sixties. Ungaro was born in 1933 in Aix-en-Provence, France, to Italian parents. His father was a tailor and had trained him to join the family business, but Ungaro went instead to Paris where, in 1955, he joined Balenciaga and learned the couture business. Balenciaga was his mentor, and to this day Ungaro keeps a picture of him on his office bookshelf. After a brief stint at Courrèges, Ungaro opened his own couture house in 1965, and three years later produced his first ready-to-wear collection.

My mother sold his clothing at Bonwit's, and he had been visiting her when she told him all about her son and Bloomingdale's. "Go there and see what's going on," she counseled.

Ungaro walked over and found the main floor crowded and filled with the decor of our most recent international fair. While there he ran into Rose Wells, a former Ohrbach's executive who later worked at Federated and is one of the most extroverted people in the world.

"Emanuel! What are you doing here?" she shouted—everything Rose did was at full volume. "Come along," she ordered and led him up the escalator. They went up to the second floor and then up to the third, when suddenly they heard, "Rose! Rose! They won't take my American Express card!" (Bloomingdale's only accepted its own credit card then.) Rose motioned the tall, thin young man—his name was Halston—to join them and then called someone over to help him. Then she turned to Ungaro, "Well, if you're here, you really should meet Mel Jacobs." So they went to find Mel. And then Mel, in turn, brought Ungaro to meet me. Ungaro thought Bloomingdale's was one giant party.

The import fairs had given us dramatic license. There was always something going on: cooking demonstrations, mimes performing, banners unfurling; we were a store in a state of joyous flux and constant renovation.

The model rooms taught us that a Spanish bullfighters' tavern or a houseboat in Srinagar could inspire shoppers to purchase decorative goods. The more dramatic, the better. I began to think we could have the same fun with fashion. First, though, as in home furnishings, we needed European resources.

On my next trip to Paris, I called on Emanuel Ungaro at his couture house on the Avenue Montaigne. He gave me a tour of his studio and a preview of the collection he was to show the following week. I invited him and his staff to join the Bloomingdale's buyers for a meal at the Petit Montmorency restaurant. And in that way we developed a habit that became a tradition. Every season, usually on the Sunday before he presented his collection, I would go with Lee and Katie for a glass of champagne to preview his work, and we would always share a meal with both our "families," his staff and mine.*

Sonia Rykiel is another designer with whom I am very close. Sonia's first success was as a window dresser at a Paris store. Henri Matisse saw her display of colorful scarves, bought them all, and asked to meet her. She began designing maternity clothes when she was pregnant in 1961. In the late sixties she started designing sweaters, just for fun. She opened a little shop outside Paris proper on the Boulevard General LeClerc. At the time, everyone told her she was crazy not to have a shop in Paris. Sonia's shop, however, was on the road to Orly Airport, and people would stop there on their way to the plane. When Audrey Hepburn appeared in one of her sweaters, everyone wanted to know where she bought it. Sonia Rykiel was a name one started to hear a lot.

Today, neither Sonia nor I can recall the first time we met, but we know it was love at first sight. Sonia had designed a sweater that we thought was unique. It was a ribbed sweater with elbow-length sleeves and a shallow boat-shaped neckline that ran from one side to the other and was the same depth front and back. It was dubbed "the Poor Boy sweater." It could be worn with pants or skirts or over blouses. I knew immediately that we wanted a Sonia Rykiel boutique. At the time, Sonia was selling a few items at Bendel's, but she gladly added Bloomingdale's. We have been working together ever since.

Sonia is a person of far-ranging interests. She has written poetry, novels, and children's stories. She has designed hotel rooms, restaurants, sheets, china, writing paper, and even chocolates.†

* Emanuel Ungaro recently celebrated the twenty-fifth anniversary of his couture house. His success lies in his training as a tailor; like his mentor Balenciaga, his love of fabric and his respect for detail show through in every collection. Today I still regard Emanuel as one of my close personal friends. He is an incredibly sensitive and perceptive person, and I have enjoyed every minute of knowing him.
† Sonia has a passion for chocolate and serves on a committee that each year selects the best new chocolate products in France. That's a meeting that must be fun to attend.

Being a designer is very demanding, and designers are often misunderstood. "The problem with being a designer," Sonia once told me, "is that you have to come up with something new twice a year, but not too new."

In my friendships with designers I made it clear that I always had time to listen. No matter how busy I was in Paris or New York, I would make the time to visit Sonia, Emanuel, or other friends. It was not about me or Bloomingdale's. I was not looking at my watch or who else was in the room. I was there for them.

b

The boutique concept is usually thought of as an invention of the sixties. However, Janina Wilner, our fashion coordinator for accessories, actually opened the first boutique at Bloomingdale's, Place Elegante, in 1950. It was a Christmas shop of accessories from all over the store. Bloomingdale's was probably the first major store to have Christmas shops, and since then the store has continued to use small shops that change frequently around the store.

In the late sixties, when fashion became more volatile, seeming to change from one moment to the next, being a fashion buyer became an even more difficult position. There was more at risk. We wanted to be a fashion-forward store and stock the trendiest clothes, but because we were a business, we hoped to limit our risk and exposure. The first time we bought miniskirts, we discovered that not everyone was ready for them. We flopped in a major way.

Boutiques made good business sense. You could experiment with new fashions, but in small amounts. You could display the most fashion-forward designs that would give you the image, while still selling more mainstream items. This was the same strategy that worked so well in home furnishings.

At the same time, Bloomingdale's continued to carry traditional fashions. I remember asking one customer why she bought her Kimberly dress, a very conservative line, at our store. "I feel more fashionable buying it here," she said. And that was exactly what we were after.

b

People still talk about the maxi skirt, or midi, as one of the great fashion failures. The magazines promoted them, the designers all endorsed them, but women didn't buy. But by then Bloomingdale's had learned its lesson. We purchased a few hundred, sold them, and didn't reorder. For us the midi was a success. But by then our buyers had learned how to use our boutiques to their advantage.

Fashion is nearly impossible to analyze or predict. Selecting a certain dress, at a certain length, is a very personal decision. At the same time, we know that people follow fashion, so there is an element of the group in any fashion decision. The trick for a merchant is to present enough of an assortment to appeal to the individual while having sufficient stock of any current trend.

Before the sixties, fashion designers and magazine editors proclaimed what the look was—and there wasn't much choice. By the sixties, women could choose between a peasant blouse, a cowboy jacket with fringes, or mini and micromini skirts. There was a great variety of choices that were best highlighted in a series of boutiques.

To this day, women often ask why all jackets or all skirts can't be shown together. This would eliminate selection by life-style and attitude as well as by designer. Choice would actually be lessened not increased. Boutiques allowed us to have all the choices under one roof and that was good for business. Traffic increased as women who were shopping for their own look came to find it at our store. We had finally given women a reason to shop at Bloomingdale's.

Our ability to jump on new fashion trends became apparent with one of our early successes: the Mic Mac boutique. Mic Mac was a small shop of designers in Saint-Tropez. The fact that Gunther Sachs, a socialite playboy, was listed as both an investor and designer enhanced their notoriety. Katie Murphy visited Michel and Chantal Faure and designer Tan Guidecelli in the south of France. Most of their clothes left her cold, but they had a giant coat that swept the floor. The image of a long coat open to reveal a woman in a mini skirt was arresting. Katie gave them a large order.

The press dubbed it "the Maxi coat" and Bloomingdale's was the first to carry it. We sold out our initial order immediately, and Bruce Morrison, our talented coat buyer, flew to France to order five hundred more. The fashion press went wild over it. We then asked our American coat suppliers to make Maxi coats. The Maxi coat represented the first time that Bloomingdale's had created a fashion trend that others quickly followed. It was a landmark because

Bloomingdale's was now setting the fashion agenda. There was no turning back.

b

Once Bloomingdale's was firmly entrenched in the boutique and French ready-to-wear business, I knew that having an Yves Saint Laurent boutique would be a coup, and could set us apart from every other department store. The story of how Bloomingdale's won, lost, and eventually opened the Yves Saint Laurent Rive Gauche boutique is a good one, because it illustrates the lengths we were willing to go for a designer, and how concerned the designer is about his image.

Yves Saint Laurent was born Henri Donat Mathieu in 1936 in Oran, Algeria, then a French colony. At seventeen, while studying fashion in Paris, he won first prize for a cocktail dress design in a competition sponsored by the International Wool Secretariat. Shortly afterward, he was hired by the House of Dior, and when Christian Dior died in 1957, Saint Laurent took over. He was twenty-one. In 1960, however, he was drafted for service in the Algerian war. Discharged a few months later, he returned to Paris to find Marc Bohan in charge of design at Dior.* Saint Laurent resigned, uncertain of what to do next, but Pierre Bergé, a friend of Dior's who had been artist Bernard Buffet's business manager and a former impresario of the Ballets Russes, encouraged him to open his own house, which he did in 1961. Bergé has been more than a partner to Saint Laurent. He is the defender of the faith, his watchdog, and pit bull—there is no one more gentle in Yves's care and no one more fierce in his defense.

At the same time, Mack Robinson, a banker in Atlanta, Georgia, was scouting investments for a Swiss insurance company and heard about Saint Laurent. Although he concluded that a couture house was an inappropriate investment for an insurance company, he decided to put up his own funds. How much he invested at the time is not known, but a *Wall Street Journal* article reported that in 1967 he

---

* Rumor has it that Dior's owner, Marcel Boussac, arranged for Saint Laurent to be drafted, after a disappointing collection, so he could replace him with Bohan.

sold his 80 percent interest in Yves Saint Laurent to my good friend
Dick Salomon at Charles of the Ritz for $1 million. "My biggest
mistake was in ever selling him," Robinson said in 1984. "Yves
makes more in a month now than I made on the entire transaction." *

Charles of the Ritz was in the cosmetics and fragrance business
and had such lines as Jean Naté and Lanvin. Dick saw publicity
value in Yves's couture business and in strengthening the name
Yves Saint Laurent so that they could better license fragrance, sunglasses, handbags, and sheets.

Yves, however, approached them with an idea. He wanted to
design ready-to-wear: clothes that the daughters of his couture customers would wear. Yves told his idea to Didier Grumbach—the
grandson of Mendes France, the founder of France's ready-to-wear
industry—who had the resources and the know-how to enter the
field. Like Yves, Didier was very young at the time, still in his late
twenties, very idealistic, and he had already had success working
with other designers such as Jean Patou. Didier loved the idea. He
suggested that Yves open his own shop near the student quarter on
the Left Bank and call it Yves Saint Laurent Rive Gauche. Yves
appointed Didier head of Rive Gauche. They opened the first boutique near the Luxembourg Gardens. It was a residential block with
a small hotel but without any other commercial establishments.

From the day Rive Gauche opened in 1966, it was mobbed—the
publicity was terrific and it was a great financial success. Yves had
created a whole new market, a veritable revolution in fashion merchandising. What Yves discovered was that everyone wanted to be
fashionable—even people who proclaimed themselves antifashion,
much as the Gap today has successfully exploited this same senti-
ment. Suddenly every couturier wanted to do ready-to-wear—and
everyone in retailing wanted to open a Rive Gauche shop.

---

* Charles of the Ritz was acquired in 1971 by the Squibb Corporation. In 1973, Squibb
allowed Saint Laurent and Bergé to repurchase the company over time at its book value,
with Charles of the Ritz retaining the perfume license. Most recently, in 1993, Bergé and
Saint Laurent sold their company to French conglomerate Elf Sanofi while still retaining
control of the couture and licensing areas until 2001. In twenty-six years the selling price
went from $1 million, in 1967, to $650 million. Such is the value of a great designer
business.

Lord & Taylor, among others, came after Yves. Didier, however, didn't want to sell Rive Gauche in American department
stores. Undeterred, I set up a meeting with Dick Salomon, then
president of Charles of the Ritz, with whom we did a significant
cosmetics business. Dick told me that Yves loved Bloomingdale's
because of all the excitement the store generated. But, he said, and
this was a big but, Didier and Yves's strategy so far had been to
open Rive Gauche boutiques themselves, where they could afford
to; where they couldn't, they would enlist a licensee to pay a royalty
to Saint Laurent on its retail sales and carry Rive Gauche exclusively. In the year since they opened their first shop, ten more had
been launched throughout France, Italy, and Monaco. In each case
the store was an independent Rive Gauche shop, usually on a good
street near the student area. They had been very successful. The
next stage for them, he said, was the United States.

"The fact is," Dick said, "it doesn't make sense to distribute
Rive Gauche through department stores. Up until now, every one of
the shops we've opened is a shop with its own address."

On the spot, I had an idea. "That's no problem," I said. "We
can do it for you." I explained: "It's simple. We'll open a space for
you on the 59th Street side of the store. It'll be your own shop with
your own street address. And in every way it will be a freestanding
store, just as you would create anywhere else in the world. Except
for one thing: There'll be a back entrance to Bloomingdale's." I had
come up with a completely new concept. Instead of a shop inside a
store (the boutique), it was a store within the store.

Dick paused for a long few seconds before saying, "Marvin,
that's a hell of an idea." Yves, Pierre, and Didier all agreed.

We were very excited at the prospect of opening the first Rive
Gauche boutique in the United States. Dick was going to Paris soon
and agreed to set up a lunch there for Katie Murphy, Didier, and
Pierre at his suite in the Ritz. By that time Dick and I had worked
out most of the details, and they had samples of the previous collection ready for Katie to study. We would then finalize all the other
issues.

The lunch went off without a hitch, or so it seemed. Yves did
not speak much. Katie and Didier, however, had gotten along well.
And everyone was enthusiastic about the clothes. All the prices and

shipping dates were decided; every detail was covered. Afterward, Katie took her notes, and Didier and Yves took their clothes, and everybody shook hands.

When Dick returned he asked to see me. I assumed he wanted to firm up what the boutique would look like, or even to renegotiate the markup, but I was completely unprepared for what he had to tell me.

"The deal is off," he announced.

"*What?*" I was stunned, and angry. "We had a done deal!"

"Hear me out," Dick said. "Let me tell you everything, every word, exactly as it happened."

Dick explained that the meeting in Paris had gone well. During lunch, however, conversation had turned to their plans in the United States. In doing so, they discussed other American stores. Whereupon Katie said, "You know you've made no mistake coming to Bloomingdale's. I used to be the merchandise manager of better ready-to-wear at Lord & Taylor and I would have two good months when the summer collection came in spring, April and March; and two good months when the winter collection came in, September and October. For the rest of the year, you could shoot a cannonball down the aisle and not hit anyone.

"Bloomingdale's would never let a thing like that happen," Katie told them. "They make the store come alive and stay alive. If one thing doesn't work, they try another." Everybody thought it was great that Bloomingdale's was like that.

"After everyone left," Dick recounted, "Yves spoke up. At that time he spoke very little English. But he could understand fairly well."

"Dick," Yves said, "I would never ask a favor of you, and I never have, but if I understood that woman correctly, if our first collection is a bust, they will move us and the noise will be heard around the United States and our whole future in that country will be dead."

Bergé sometimes likes to give the impression that Yves is an artist uninvolved with the business. Not true. Yves has very good business instincts.

Dick told me that Yves said to him, "Please do me a favor. Let me open my own store, put it anywhere you want, but let's do it our own way—as we did in Paris. That way, if we make mistakes the first year, nobody will know but us."

"But Yves," Dick said he told him, "those people have left, believing we made a deal. We shook hands on it."

"Dick," Yves said, "I beg of you, please let me do it this way."

"And so I'm here now." Dick told me. "It's not that Katie Murphy did anything wrong. But Yves is right, Marvin. We can't gamble the whole future on how well our Bloomingdale's boutique does. If we have a bad first year at Bloomingdale's, even if we keep the lease, people will know, and it would be death."

I was still listening.

"So now, I will make a new proposal," Dick said. "We will open our own Rive Gauche boutique in New York, but we won't open it in this area. It will not compete with you. And if we ever open a department store boutique in New York or anywhere else, you get the first one. And you can place it wherever you want in the store. We will no longer require you to have a shop on the street."

I thought it over. Dick had come to me, and been upfront and honest. And it was at some risk. We did a great deal of cosmetics business, and Dick knew I could make life difficult for him. Yves was a young man, clearly one of the most important designers of our time, who had every chance of having a long career. So after what, to Dick, must have been an annoyingly long silence, I said:

"Okay. I'll let it ride, along the conditions you've laid out." Opening a Rive Gauche boutique at that time would have been a major coup, but if Yves was not comfortable, it made no sense. The fact that no other department store would get a Rive Gauche boutique before us was some consolation—not much, but some. So I told Katie and Mel and the buyers. It was a disappointment, but the next day we set about working on a boutique with Hubert de Givenchy, which we opened the following year.

There are few other punch lines to this story: Yves Saint Laurent did open his Rive Gauche boutique in 1968 on Madison Avenue and 70th Street and I made a point of attending the opening. Many other department store heads did not. Andrew Goodman called Dick and told him that he "considered anyone who sells expensive ready-to-wear in New York someone he hates," that they were now in competition and he "liked to knock the competition dead."

That was not my way. As a result, Bloomingdale's had tremendous success over the years with Yves Saint Laurent fragrance and accessories. We did open a Rive Gauche boutique in 1972 on our newly renovated third floor, and it was the jewel of our ready-to-wear boutiques. In the 1980s, when the boutique was not doing as well, we wanted to move it. Yves felt his initial fears were justified and he and Pierre pulled the boutique out of the store.

My concept for the original Rive Gauche boutique did not go to waste. In 1991 we persuaded Armani to open its largest department store menswear boutique by offering them their own shop on 59th Street with its own entrance and address. Armani thought it was a great idea. We did too, but we waited over twenty years for the right customer, and that customer today has a $5 million shop.

b

Missoni is another fabulous story. In the early 1960s, Dick Hauser, our vice president of ready-to-wear, was in Milan with our sweater buyer and he asked our foreign office whether anyone worked in Lurex (a metallic fiber yarn woven or knitted with cotton, nylon, rayon, silk, or wool fibers). Dick was taken to a supplier who made a turtleneck sweater. It was expensive and we bought a few. The supplier told us the sweaters were knit by a talented couple named Missoni. In 1968, Katie was in Milan scouting the boutiques with Leonard Rosenberg, who was in charge of the sportswear division, when she discovered that the Missonis were now making exquisite sweaters under their own label. The sweaters were absolutely wonderful, but Missoni had a deal with a small boutique on Madison Avenue. They didn't want to sell to us.

At the same time, Diana Vreeland, *Vogue*'s fashion doyenne, had discovered the Missonis and invited them to come to the United States. They were staying at the Plaza, and Mrs. Vreeland sent the Missonis all over New York and invited Katie Murphy to meet them in their hotel room. The Missonis showed Katie their knits, and she fell in love with them. The Missonis were making, and are still making, incredibly intricate knits of unparalleled craftsmanship. What they do is unique; no one has been able to combine colors the way they do. They were among the first to bring a couture level of craft to distinctive sweater designs.

Katie returned the next day with Leonard Rosenberg, the day after with Mel Jacobs, and finally they brought me to see the knits. I was struck as much by the Missonis as by their work. Tai and Rosita met in London at the 1948 Olympic Games where Tai was competing as a long-distance runner. He is tall, thin, and has a very dry sense of humor. Rosita is small, intense, and very lively. Tai had owned a company that made track suits and Rosita's family made bedding. Together they made for a winning combination and decided to open their own company, at first designing sweaters for other designers. By the time I met them, they were marketing their own designs. I was very impressed by them, but they were headed home. They hoped we could meet again, perhaps in Europe. I agreed, and they left that night.

I dispatched Leonard Rosenberg that Friday on a plane to Milan. By Sunday, we had a Missoni boutique. Missoni became a cornerstone of our designer boutiques. It was not a volume business, because the Missonis never manufactured in large quantity. It was the image.

b

By decade's end, Bloomingdale's became known as the fashion laboratory, where new designers wanted to show their clothing. We no longer had to seek out talent. In 1970, for example, Bloomingdale's got a call from Dupont about a Japanese company that had invented a new synthetic fiber, and asked Bloomingdale's to look at the work they had commissioned from a young Japanese designer. Issey Miyake was his name, and Bloomingdale's was the first to carry his designs.

One day in 1969, Mel Jacobs got a call from a young man named Halston. He had just had a fight with Bergdorf's and asked if he could come over to talk about an idea he had. Halston, up to that point, had been a hat designer. He told Mel that he intended to design clothes for everyone, sportswear, shoes, hats—everything in one boutique. Harold Krensky was called in. He believed in Halston and felt he had talent. Mel said, "Wonderful. Now when can you show us clothes?"

"Clothes?" Halston said. "I don't have any clothes yet. When do you need them by?"

"We should open in August," Mel answered.

Halston agreed so we put him together with a team. Halston wanted to be involved in every detail of his shop down to the shelving. But the night before the shop was to open the drapes were not ready. So Halston, the great designer, stayed up all night and sewed them himself.

The Halston shop was a tremendous success. Halston, in turn, introduced me to one of his models, Elsa Peretti, who was designing accessories. We loved them and Bloomingdale's was the first to carry Elsa Perettti jewelry and accessories. She built an empire on her signature "bean" design and her odd-shaped hearts. Later, Tiffany's offered her a deal that we couldn't match. They were right to do it because in 1992, rumor has it, Elsa Peretti accounted for about 20 percent of their U.S. business, and a substantial portion of their international business. In Japan, Elsa Peretti was responsible for almost one third of their sales.

b

One day Bruce Morrison, our highly respected buyer of women's coats, told me about a very talented young coat designer and suggested I join him in his showroom—and that was my first meeting with Calvin Klein. I was enormously impressed with his talent and we began to work closely together, first in coats, then in ready-to-wear. He then joined forces with Maurice Bidermann (I helped put them together) to do a Men's Collection that became a feature of our Men's Store.

I also became very friendly with Barry Schwartz, who remains Calvin's partner to this day and who helped develop the strategies that built their enormous business. I counseled against their starting their own cosmetics fragrance company—it was very high risk and required enormous capital. When it did not succeed, we helped locate Dr. Robert Taylor, who bought them out, then made it a much more successful cosmetics venture.

Calvin is a great designer and over the years has had tremendous impact on American style and marketing. His sensuous approach to advertising has had a great influence on the content and look of contemporary advertising.

b

As Bloomingdale's changed, so did our shopper. Dick Hauser recalls looking at a shipment of Sonia Rykiel sweaters that arrived one day in our store. They were oversized sweaters decorated with a large red apple, and he wondered: Who will pay $250 for this? But sure enough, they sold out. Dick then went to the selling floor and approached a young woman who had just purchased one, asking her about the sweater and the price.

"I don't care if I don't go out to lunch for a year, I have to own it," she said. And that became the reason the new shopper purchased at our store. What Bloomingdale's carried, she had to have. We developed a hard-core cadre of devotees who referred to themselves as "Bloomie's Groupies." Lois Gould wrote a piece for *New York Magazine* called "Confessions of a Bloomingdale's Addict." Another writer, Blair Sabol, confessed on national television that she had to leave Los Angeles and return to New York, because there were two things she couldn't live without: "her gynecologist and Bloomingdale's."

Bloomingdale's came to be perceived as a young place. And as sportswear exploded across America and in New York, we were lucky to be the place to go for sportswear. Before the 1960s, department stores were in the dress business. Sportswear was a small but not very important area of the store. Suddenly in the 1960s, every woman was wearing a skirt or pants.

Bloomingdale's catered to a 1960s woman who was redefining herself by what she wore. If you thought you were a Sonia Rykiel customer, there was a boutique for you; and if you thought you were a Mic Mac customer, we had a place for you. The same for Halston, Missoni, and so on.

Our buyers, though, kept finding wonderful, extreme merchandise that fit no department. Katie said we should create a swing shop for all this outrageous merchandise. Mel Jacobs loved the idea. A shop for everything that didn't fit into a shop; a place for goods that were so far out, they were in; a boutique where items cost so much that no one could afford them but that someone wouldn't be able to live without.

"A paradox," Mel said. And Paradox is what we named the shop. Paradox was the place for all the people who marched to the beat of a different drummer. Paradox opened in January 1970 with a collection of unique imported knits and went on to become the home of the newest, most avant-garde fashions. Over the years, Paradox has been the place to first feature such talented designers as Cacharel, Issey Miyake, Henry Lehr, Romeo Gigli, Jean Paul Gaultier, and Thierry Mugler.

When a designer had grown sufficiently to merit his own shop, we moved him out of Paradox and other designers moved in. Back then you didn't have the pressure you have today for each designer to have his own boutique. We had swing shops that were seasonally related and even one on the second floor that was the avant-garde for juniors—throw-away chic was how we referred to it. Everything we did seemed to generate tremendous publicity, but this was Harold Krensky's genius. He knew that any store could offer a designer selling space; we, on the other hand, could offer publicity that would be heard around the world.

You could be well known as a designer in Europe, but if you were in Bloomingdale's, your reputation increased. For a designer to have a shop in Japan can be very lucrative, but only the Japanese know about it. For a European designer to have a boutique in Bloomingdale's and have the store feature his or her fashions in the windows, even for only a week, means that suddenly the whole world knows about it. In the late sixties, when *The New York Times* was not covering Italian ready-to-wear, no one had heard of Missoni. But when we featured their sweaters in every window on Lexington Avenue, the *Times* wrote them up. That was the power we came to have.

During the sixties and into the early seventies, we continued to find new European designers. The first time I visited Kenzo, he was a struggling designer from Japan who had moved to Paris in 1964 and was creating freelance collections and selling designs to Louis Feraud. He really didn't know the American stores. He had very little money and was showing in an old warehouse. There were a few old packing crates outside, and Katie Murphy, Dick Hauser, and I sat and waited while he saw another American store because we thought Kenzo had talent. When, finally, we went in to see him we found out the store he had been busy with was Gimbels.

Gimbels was appealing to the mass market, much as a J. C. Penney does today. Kenzo was interested in the fashion stores but thought it would be prestigious if any American department store carried his clothes. He is a quick study and he soon learned to discriminate among stores.

At the time of our first visit, Kenzo was making a sweater with huge lips on the front that Katie knew would fly out of the store. It did, and we opened one of the first boutiques for Kenzo in the United States. In 1970 he opened his own shop, Jungle Jap (an ugly name, in my opinion), that was immensely successful, later expanding from ready-to-wear to menswear to children's wear to perfume.

b

For most of the 1960s the American press didn't cover the European ready-to-wear collections, but as more buyers started to attend, the press caught up. Intimate shows in the designer's ateliers were no longer possible. The collections became media events. Fashion became part circus and part rock-and-roll concert with each designer trying to outdo the other by showing in a more exotic location. During the 1970s, I attended Paris fashion shows at the Bourse, at the Museum of Modern Art, in circus tents, and in a slaughterhouse. Crowds shoving to get inside became commonplace. Stranger still, students waited outside for autographs from the designers. You had the whole phenomenon of fashion groupies and fashion victims.

b

Even before all the craziness exploded, Katie Murphy saw the need for the Bloomingdale's team to have an informal meeting in Paris during the collections. The idea was to assemble in one place merchandise managers and buyers from accessories, ready-to-wear, and shoes as well as people from display and advertising to catch the spirit of the collections. Katie wanted to let the fashion office give their impressions of what was most important that season. At the same time, buyers who had been to England or Italy would give reports on what was happening there, what Zandra Rhodes or Armani was up to.

The fashion shows started at nine o'clock, and our people would meet in the lobby at ten of to go to the first shows. We scheduled the meetings very early, at 7:00 A.M., in my hotel room, in order not to interfere with anyone's workday. Many jokes have been made about those early morning meetings, mostly at my expense, but it was the only time we could all gather. Over the years, the Paris morning meetings have become more formal affairs. Nonetheless, they have always been fun and instructive, and have had a great bonding effect. I believe that it was those morning meetings that, more than anything else, transformed us from a group of store buyers into the Bloomingdale's team.

Of course, once we started having twenty-five buyers come to Paris, we had to move the meetings to a larger place. Most recently they've been held at the Crillon or the Meurice, in one of the hotel's private rooms. Over time, a legend developed about our early morning Paris meetings. Rumor had it that it was then and there that Bloomingdale's decided the next season's fashion trends. We were doing no such thing, but the idea that people believed Bloomingdale's had the power to dictate fashion proved just how far we had come.

Sonia Rykiel used to tease me about the meetings. She couldn't believe we really worked at seven in the morning. She assumed it was just some special gourmet breakfast. She needled me so much that one year I invited her to attend. She was surprised: the croissants were tough, and the coffee watery. She sat in the back and listened as Katie and other members of the fashion office outlined what they saw happening at the shows and on the streets of Paris. Models were brought in to demonstrate how to accessorize the latest fashions, and Katie was very vocal in expressing her opinions: what worked that year, and what didn't.

Sonia came up to me afterward and said, "I had no idea it was so professional!" adding with a wink, "And I learned quite a few things."

The morning meetings also had another effect. Remember that in an earlier era, the role of the Bloomingdale's fashion buyer counted for very little. The notion that thirty-five people met at seven in the morning while the rest of Paris and the retail community slept said a lot for us. We were hungrier, we worked harder, and we were not afraid to tell the designer what our customers would like. We wanted to be first.

Katie Murphy played a tremendous role in training our young and sometimes inexperienced buyers. She was right so often about fashion and trends that the buyers put enormous faith in her. She taught them that each item of clothing did not stand alone. They needed to be coordinated to form an outfit.

Just as Barbara D'Arcy and Carl Levine rethought the furniture floor and the home furnishings business to integrate sofas with lamps and rugs, so Katie integrated blouses, skirts, handbags, and shoes as part of a total fashion look. At the same time, we learned that a customer would pay a premium for just the right item that would be the finishing touch to a wardrobe. Seen in that light, a $100 belt no longer seemed so crazy.

More than anything Katie Murphy was an incredibly perceptive student of popular culture. *Women's Wear Daily* once described her as having "a sense of history about fashion as well as an open-mindedness toward it. She not only could recognize forward design talent but had an appreciation of the jeans and T-shirt look of the young." She interpreted fashion for us, sometimes no easy task. She was wise, mature, and very persuasive.

As I mentioned earlier, Katie and I used to commute home together regularly. But on Friday, March 14, 1975, there was a problem with the trains, so I decided to rent a car. Katie, Joe Schnee, our ready-to-wear and fashion accessories general merchandise manager, and I went together after work to the Hertz offices.

As we were standing in the waiting area, Katie suddenly collapsed. I desperately tried to resuscitate her, but she didn't respond. The ambulance came a few minutes later and the paramedics tried as well, but she died of a heart attack shortly after arrival at New York Hospital. She was fifty-eight years old.

We were all in shock. Over the weekend I called Dick Hauser and Mel and others. It was hard to believe that she was with us one moment and gone the next. A memorial service was held the following Tuesday. More than five hundred people attended, but we all wanted to do something more, so that she would be remembered.

A few months later, more than twelve hundred people gathered in the ballroom of the Waldorf-Astoria for "A Very Special Tribute to Katie Murphy." Geraldine Stutz helped organize a fashion retrospective. Michel and Chantal Faure, Sonia Rykiel, Ungaro, Didier Grumbach, and Regine flew in from Paris; Tai and Rosita Missoni came from Italy; and Issey Miyake arrived from Tokyo. Retailers, manufacturers, everyone wanted to be there. Katie's mother, Eliza-

beth Murphy, Katie's husband, Joe Grout, and her son were there
as well, to see the esteem in which a whole industry held her. We
raised a quarter of a million dollars to pay for the construction of the
Katherine Murphy Amphitheater at the Fashion Institute of Technology, where today, appropriately enough, many fashion shows and
important industry meetings are held.

Harold Krensky may have said it best when he told a reporter
from *Women's Wear Daily*, "the overall thing about Katie is that she
was a fine human being. You can't give greater praise than that. She
helped so many." *

b

Katie's death was a great loss to the fashion community. At
Bloomingdale's, we realized that no one could replace her. Over the
next two years, we tried to manage without her—I think the store
was on automatic pilot. With time, I began to think that Katie had
transformed the role of fashion coordinator, and my task was not to
find her replacement so much as her successor.

Part of being a good manager is always keeping your eyes open
for talented people. When you're in the market you listen and, of
course, you always watch the competition. I had been watching Kal
Ruttenstein's career for many years. I first asked Kal to come to
Bloomingdale's when he was a suit buyer at Lord & Taylor. I approached him again when he was at Saks Fifth Avenue. Kal, however, was very ambitious, and when he was offered the presidency
of Bonwit Teller, he took it. Unfortunately, it was a job at which he
could not succeed—not because he lacked the talent, Kal was and
is a great merchant, but because of Bonwit's inherent problems. In
1977, when I read in the paper that Kal was leaving Bonwit's, I
called him immediately and set up a breakfast.

"Kal," I said, "I've always wanted you to join Bloomingdale's."
I told him that he had every right to be happy, and that I thought he

---

* Joe Schnee, who had been with me when Katie had her heart attack, fell ill shortly
afterward. I accompanied him to New York Hospital and was with him when he was told
he had inoperable cancer. He took this with extraordinary bravery, and continued to work
daily, helping me to find his successor. He passed away less than a year after Katie's
death. Shortly thereafter, Joe's wife, Caroline, and I dedicated the Joe Schnee Cancer
Immunology Center at the City of Hope in Los Angeles.

was not happy as a store president, but that as fashion director of Bloomingdale's, he would have a great time. "You are the only person," I said, "who can take over for Katie Murphy." I hired him on the spot.

b

The best merchants are those who see several steps ahead, and I frequently suggested new ways for designers to expand their businesses. One of the most challenging and gratifying parts of my job has always been to sit down with designers and talk about their business and what their next steps might be. Bloomingdale's has helped many a designer move from one area to the next, whether from men's to women's, as in the case of Ralph Lauren; or vice versa, as with Calvin Klein; or from clothing design to a collection of sheets and bath towels, as with Perry Ellis, Missoni, and Fendi; or swimwear, as with Norma Kamali; or into fragrance—the list goes on and on. Many designers have received their greatest financial rewards from licensing their name.

Not that I was always listened to. In the 1970s, I suggested the Missonis produce a line of designer jeans, with special Missoni embroidery, colors, and designs. This was before the heyday of the designer jeans business. I promised to put them together with Levi-Strauss and help them create the business. Tai and Rosita were hesitant, however, and decided to stick to what they knew, and not venture into products for which they would exercise so little control over so great a volume. Today they do not regret their decision, but acknowledge that had they done so they would have realized a tremendous profit.

On the other hand, many years ago, when Lester Gribetz, then a Bloomingdale's vice president, and I visited the Missonis' home in Sumirago outside Milan and saw how they used their fabric to cover floors, walls, and furniture, we saw a tremendous opportunity to develop a collection for the home. I introduced the Missonis to David Tracy, the chairman of Fieldcrest. Starting in 1975, they did four extraordinarily beautiful sheet-and-towel collections for Fieldcrest. The Missonis won awards for their sheets and they sold very well. So much so, that they purchased an apartment in Venice with the first year's proceeds, and invited us there.

By the end of the seventies, Bloomingdale's was operating at full throttle. It was a very special time to be a Bloomingdale's buyer. A typical day at the Paris Prêt-à-Porter would start early and end late. The buying appointments would start at nine and finish around seven. There was barely enough time to run back to the hotel, shower, and change to go out. There were always dinners, and I invited buyers along to meet with the various people that Lee and I dined with. The dinners would go until midnight, and then there would be several hours of work waiting for them in the hotel room.

Being a Bloomingdale's buyer meant special treatment from our suppliers. There were certain houses that would let Bloomingdale's see the collection and order early. In those days, there was a Mercedes stretch limo in Paris that was used to shuttle all of us around. People referred to it as the Traubmobile. It had a jump seat and, at night, after dinner, Lee and I and our buyers would talk business on the way home. It was our way of touching base.

It was a time when we rarely took no for an answer. If a buyer wanted to get something, she called, and kept calling until she got what she wanted. If the head of the house was in London, she tracked him down. We sneaked as many of our people into shows as we could. By the late 1970s, being a Bloomingdale's buyer meant you were special. You were the best. Our people believed that, and I had great faith in them. They could do it all. And they did. Over and over again.

PART 3

Let's Go to Bloomingdale's

"Bessie, it's them—the Bloomingdale couple."

CHAPTER 5

Selling the Store

People often ask me, how did Bloomingdale's become Bloomingdale's? There is no easy answer. Clearly the changes in home furnishings and fashion; the leadership of Jed Davidson, James Schoff, Lawrence Lachman, and Harold Krensky; the contributions of many, including Barbara D'Arcy, Carl Levine, Lester Gribetz, and Katie Murphy all played important parts. But if you ask me how Bloomingdale's became Bloomie's, not just a store but a state of mind, for that I have an easy answer: our merchandise, our customer, our public relations, and our advertising.

Bloomingdale's devoted more of its resources to public relations than any modern department store ever had. We made our customers the focus of our campaigns, something that is commonplace today but was novel then. We gave the store a personality. In the process I came to be identified with the store as well, a strategy that today permeates marketing with recognizable figures as Lee Iacocca and Frank Perdue.

The high point of all our efforts was, without question, the 1976 visit of Queen Elizabeth II and Prince Philip. That was our show-stopper, the event that validated Bloomingdale's as a must-see destination in New York. My instincts told me that the Queen's visit would be an event on which all our publicity would pivot. For if the Queen came to Bloomingdale's, clearly we would be the king of department stores.

When there are many stores to choose from, why do you pick one? After all, 60 to 70 percent of the goods at any department store, including Bloomingdale's, are the same. And when you walk into a store and there are many items to select from, why pick one over another? In part, the human eye and the human mind need a focus. There is a sea of items, you notice one—you may buy another, but one draws you in. The sharper the focus, the easier the sale.

Bloomingdale's success has been to find ways to distinguish itself, by its merchandise and in the consumer's mind. One of my
strengths is my instinct, my ability to find a pivot—something that a
whole promotion can turn on. It may be a single item that focuses a
boutique, or the chair that began our furniture import program, or
Saturday's Generation, as a handle for customers. We needed to
bring the same creative spirit to the store's image that we had to its
merchandise.

b

The sixties were the decade in which advertising really came of age.
Whether it was "You don't have to be Jewish to love Levy's Jewish
rye," a campaign that seemed to express the hopes and dreams of a
nonracial society, or Volkswagen's "think small," an idea that offered comfort and community to an increasingly fragmented group
of consumers, advertising was the cutting edge.

These two campaigns were created by Doyle Dane Bernbach, an
advertising agency that prided itself on spotting trends. They used
to send reports twice a year to their clients to keep them current,
and I was impressed by how well written and informative they were.
Joan Glynn, a senior vice president at the agency, I learned, was
responsible for the reports. She had a broad range of marketing
responsibilities and headed the product/styling department.

Joan had begun in retailing as a trainee at B. Altman & Co.,
then as a stylist for Simplicity Pattern Company. She was a market
editor for Tobe Associates, a trade publication, and merchandise
editor for eight years at *Glamour*.

Joan had recently approached Bloomingdale's with the idea of
doing a series of shops to coincide with a promotion Doyle Dane was
organizing for the Italian government. The centerpiece was "Orlando Furioso," a full-blown medieval fair with horsemen, sword
fights, jugglers, and acrobats staged in Bryant Park behind the New
York Public Library.

Bloomingdale's never did the shops, but I went to see "Orlando
Furioso." It was ambitious and audacious, a larger-than-life, once-
in-a-lifetime multimedia happening. As I wandered through the
maelstrom, I was delighted. This, I thought, was my idea of a Bloomingdale's event. At that moment a hunch formed that the person who
organized it must be a kindred spirit, so I invited Joan to lunch.

Joan is attractive, thin, intense, and very animated—she seems to sparkle with energy and ideas. We didn't talk long before I asked her to join Bloomingdale's.

"As what?" she asked.

"Public relations, sales promotion, advertising, special events, everything."

I think Joan liked the last word best: everything. She liked me to keep her informed about everything that happened at the store. Her official title was vice president of advertising and sales promotion, but her responsibilities extended far beyond traditional public relations; she later became vice president of communications.

b

In the Davidson era, Louise Langdon directed public relations. She was a slightly severe, thin, elegant lady who had excellent contacts among the New York social set and press—very much the model of a 1950s department store publicist. Ruth Strauss was the sales promotion director then. Ruth upgraded our image as the store changed, publicizing our import fairs, and first developing our reputation for exclusive imported merchandise. One of Ruth's major contributions was the shopping bag.

Over the years, our shopping bags have brought the store distinction. The first was a paper bag for merchandise that was created for Bloomingdale's fiftieth anniversary in 1922. But it wasn't until 1954 that the shopping bag, as we know it, was introduced. Bloomingdale's first bags featured a gloved hand, an umbrella, a rose, and a sheet of paper with a crimson script *B*. Very ladylike.

For the "L'Esprit de France" promotion, Ruth turned to her son-in-law, Jonah Kiningstein, an architect and artist, to design a new bag. Jonah selected the image of a French tarot card from among the many themes Jed had chosen for the promotion, and created a design for a shopping bag that was controversial because the Bloomingdale's name was nowhere to be found on it. The tarot card shopping bag became immensely popular. The ultimate was when Jonah went to Jamaica for Christmas vacation the following winter. He was sunning on the beach when he saw a native woman walk by, with two dead fish in her hand and the tarot bag filled with groceries on her head. He was so charmed by the sight that he made a painting of it that now hangs in my home.

b

But I digress. When Ruth Strauss retired in 1970, I wanted to look outside the world of department store advertising—a specialty in itself—to break with tradition. Joan Glynn was the perfect partner. She joined Bloomingdale's in April of 1971.

Because of the store's need for a distinctive image, I placed great importance on our advertising, publicity, and sales promotion executives. Where other stores frequently promote a merchant to the sales promotion position, I often recruited people from outside the field of retailing. Over the years I have hired such diverse talents as Doris Shaw from Saks, Cathy Cash Spellman from Revlon (she is today a best-selling novelist), journalists Carrie Donovan and Nina Hyde, Gordon Cooke from Macy's and the Bon, and John Jay, a unique talent in the sales promotion field who joined us from *MBA* magazine. Joan was the first of this new generation at Bloomingdale's.

Joan and I spent a lot of time talking about the future of the store, and what we wanted the image of Bloomingdale's to be. We began by considering what makes a store's image. For the last two decades Bloomingdale's had been concentrating on its merchandise; Joan wanted to take a more conceptual approach. First, I said, we need to crystallize and communicate what the store had become. Joan's experience in product development taught her that the best way to tell people the product had changed was to redesign it.

"Do you mean redesign the store?" I asked, because there were already plans to renovate certain departments.

"No, I'm talking about something more immediate, and far simpler." Joan proposed to redesign Bloomingdale's graphics and packaging: the logo, the signs, the boxes, all in a way that would express how the store had changed.

We also needed, Joan said, a unifying theme. It was spring of 1971 and we were planning to renovate the designer shops, but doing so would take about a year's time. We needed a major event for fall 1972 and I had just the idea. The following year would mark Bloomingdale's hundredth anniversary. What better occasion for a storewide celebration? "A centennial campaign." Joan loved it. A perfect excuse for renovation, for redesign, and a large-scale store promotion. There was just one little detail: Bloomingdale's actual birthday was April 17, and our annual events were traditionally held in the fall as a lead-in to Christmas. No matter. As Larry Lachman later told *Women's Wear Daily*: "When you're a hundred years old you can take the privilege of celebrating it when you like."

b

For the graphics and packaging redesign we hired Massimo Vignelli. A handsome, intense-looking man with a penetrating gaze, he was an internationally known graphics and product designer whose work was part of the permanent collection of the Museum of Modern Art.

For the logo we wanted something clean, classic, and youthful. Joan and Massimo felt that only stripped-down type was acceptable. The typeface had to be balanced and not too gimmicky. We surveyed the existing typefaces: Massimo liked one called Avant-garde, but it was too slanted. We all liked Bodoni, but it was too thick. Massimo decided instead to design a new typeface. What he created was absolutely pure and simple: Bloomingdale's all in thin lowercase letters with the "o"s looped together.

bloomingdale's

Subliminally, the numerals "100" appear incorporated subtly into the type. Joan dubbed it "bloomingtype." The new logo was used throughout the store on all displays and labels.

Joan and Massimo took on our advertising, attacking not only the contents of the ads but their visual and technical aspects as well. Massimo overhauled the advertising into a grid, and Joan insisted that our ads use photographs rather than illustrations, as was the style. Again, this may not seem earth-shaking today, but it was then. Many people in the ad department were against it. They were afraid our ads would lose their allure, and that, logistically, it would never work because, for example, no one wanted to hire photographers. But it worked brilliantly and still does.

b

Joan and I thought it was great the customers referred to the store as Bloomie's.

"How many stores have a nickname?" she asked.

I thought that was a unique selling point and Joan agreed. She then had the idea of making the store's uniquely loyal customers part of our sales pitch. In reviewing the advertising plan, she had noticed that the store didn't advertise on Saturdays. Joan asked me why.

"No one looks at the advertisements on Saturday," I answered. The circulation of *The New York Times* is a third less.

"Don't you read the papers Saturday?"

"Of course, but . . ."

"No buts," Joan said. "There's a whole generation out there that works hard all week, and the weekend is their time to relax. Saturdays, they drink their coffee, read the papers, and then come to cruise Bloomingdale's."

Joan was right, of course. In the fifteen years since the El stopped running, the neighborhood had indeed changed. At the time, we had predicted the influx of higher-income residents. What we didn't foresee was the singles scene.

The neighborhood around Bloomingdale's had become an amalgam of renovated tenements and luxury high rises. Rents were cheap and when they were not, people shared apartments. The Upper East Side neighborhood had the highest per capita number of young single people with disposable income. And they wanted to meet each other.

It was a time of liberation and experimentation, of birth control and women's lib, of the *Playboy* philosophy, of gay liberation, and of pickup bars. Over on 64th Street and First Avenue, Warner Leroy opened Maxwell's Plum. (His father was the legendary Hollywood producer Mervyn Leroy, producer of the *Wizard of Oz*.) Maxwell's Plum was a production number itself: a virtual Noah's ark of porcelain animals hung from the ceiling; there were stained-glass windows, a waterfall, gas lamps, and a long bar.

Whether they were bankers or account executives, stewardesses or actors, everybody checked in there. And when it was too crowded at Maxwell's Plum, they wandered down the street to T.G.I. (Thank God It's) Friday's or Adam's Apple, or Daly's Daffodil just across the street from the store.

Wherever they went in the evening, on Saturday they all came to Bloomingdale's. The fashions drew the young women, the young women drew the young men. Women who would never ask a man out found themselves lingering in the men's department to answer the inevitable ice-breaker: "What do you think of this tie?"

The main floor of Bloomingdale's also became a place where gays would meet. The store did not cater to them, but Bloomingdale's emphasis on style, visuals, and its own sense of the dramatic attracted a new generation of young homosexuals, many of whom lived and worked in the neighborhood. Many people believed that gays were at the cutting edge of fashion and style, and their presence only enhanced our reputation.

Straight or gay, young or old, they all came to Bloomingdale's on Saturday to find the other. I think Joan put it this way: "They were shopping . . . for each other." And that, Joan said, was an ad theme. She wanted to test what effect a Saturday advertisement would have on this crowd. Home furnishings was still where we tested our new ideas, so Joan met with Carl Levine. They produced an ad for a chair. The headline: "Saturday's Generation." "They'll know who they are," she predicted.

The chairs flew out of the store. Saturday's Generation was, at first, just a home furnishings concept for young apartment dwellers, but I understood immediately that Joan was onto something bigger. Before the age of psychodemographics, Joan had identified ours. Did we create them or did they discover us? It's hard to say, but once we invented the concept, we ran with it.

By 1974, Saturday's Generation was a well-priced, unisex, fashion-forward shop located at what we then called the metro level. The irony, of course, was that the store's most trendy shop was where the basement used to be.

b

For the centennial, Bill Berta, our creative director, created a handsomely stylized portrait of Janus, the ancient Roman threshold god, to serve as Bloomingdale's overall centennial symbol. "The medallion-like rendering," the store's publicity materials at the time said, "symbolizes the store's perspective on two centuries . . . looking back, fondly, to a history of growth as a major department store . . . and looking forward, eagerly, to a future of continuing growth and involvement within and beyond the city."

We planned a series of events to mark the centennial year beginning in May at both 59th Street and our branch stores. Each event would increase in importance, and the celebration would culminate in our October gala "Party of the Century."

What was so brilliant about the centennial promotion was that everything, and anything, became cause for celebration. As more and more people entered the store from Third Avenue, we realized we needed an escalator that would take them directly to the other shopping floors, and the increased traffic in the men's shop made us realize that it, too, needed renovation. This new construction had long been planned, but now it became part of our centennial celebration.

On Wednesday, September 6, we held a ribbon cutting ceremony for the new escalator. At the time of the fiftieth anniversary, a commemorative staircase had been installed; now a new escalator seemed appropriate for the up-beat pace of the seventies. Larry Lachman announced this as our "centennial escalator" and I said it was the perfect symbol that everything at Bloomingdale's was headed "up, up, up." We also used the occasion to unveil the new centennial graphics Joan, Massimo, and Bill Berta had designed.

Two weeks later we held a press preview of our newly renovated designer collections on the third floor featuring shops for Missoni, Sonia Rykiel, Ungaro, Saint Laurent Rive Gauche, and Ralph Lauren. The year before, Ralph had done his first "Polo by Ralph Lauren" shirts for women; now for Bloomingdale's hundredth anniversary he was launching his first Ralph Lauren women's collection. The following week, we held receptions for the model rooms and furniture floor, which had been redesigned to feature a "centennial" Paris flea market; and on Wednesday, September 27, we held a benefit for Odyssey House, a drug rehabilitation center for the introduction of the new Men's Store, as well as the new entrance at 60th Street and Third Avenue.

Bloomingdale's has been under construction ever since, but from the 1972 centennial on, whenever we completed a new shop, it became an event. We were not alone in tooting our horn. Our neighbor across Lexington Avenue, the Dry Dock Savings Bank, threw us a block party on Friday, September 29. The public was invited and three thousand people showed up on a rainy day—the party was moved inside the bank—and waltzed and polkaed to German music.

New York's mayor John Lindsay cut the birthday cake while a hurdy-gurdy man played and soft drinks, beer, pretzels, and popcorn were served. Douglas Elton, Dry Dock's chairman, presented the store with a bicycle rack as the "only thing Bloomingdale needs." But the big event was our own centennial gala.

The evening of October 3, 1972, klieg lights lit up the store. Bars were at the ready on the lower level in part of the new men's shop, on our renovated third floor where we unveiled the new designer boutiques, and on the fifth floor, the home of the model rooms—our intention was for partygoers to see our new space before they'd even had so much as a drink. We cleared out the seventh floor as our dance floor and the eighth floor was set up to accommodate a sit-down dinner for thirteen hundred of our nearest and dearest extended family.

Festivities began with cocktails at 6:00 P.M. followed by dinner and dancing. Just before dinner we summoned everyone to the seventh floor where Larry Lachman presented a gift of $150,000 to Mayor Lindsay and Parks Commissioner August Heckscher. Bloomingdale's scrolls were presented to twenty-five civic leaders including Mayor John Lindsay, His Eminence Terence Cardinal Cooke, consumer advocate Bess Myerson, and Dr. Howard Rusk—the man who had saved my leg twenty-five years earlier—among others. The mayor declared a city-wide "Bloomingdale's Week."

Dinner was served on white and silver tablecloths with white flowers as a centerpiece. The menu was artichoke cups stuffed with baby shrimp, roast baby pheasant with grape clusters, and birthday cake, one to a table—all created by Restaurant Associates.

The Forest Perrin Orchestra, which had been split into smaller groups during the cocktail hour, reassembled to play the music of the last hundred years, from waltzes to the twist. After the main course, a fashion show from FIT's collection was modeled by Bloomingdale's employees.

Who was there? Lyman Bloomingdale, of course, having a grand time. There were people ranging from mayor's office officials to the Odyssey House choir to Ralph and Ricki Lauren and Calvin Klein and his first wife, Jane. Mollie Parnis, Kasper, and John Fairchild mingled with Edward Durrell Stone, Grace Mirabella, Pauline Trigere, Mala Rubinstein, Charles Revson, Leonard and Evelyn Lauder, as well as Ronald and Jo-Carol Lauder, Emanuel Ungaro, Egon and Diane Von Furstenberg, John Kloss, Andrew Goodman, Bruce Gimbel, Oscar and Francoise de la Renta, Angelo Donghia, Kenneth Jay Lane, and, of course, along with the other important retailing figures, Bea Traub.

Bloomingdale's had arrived.

b

Bloomingdale's advertising continued to focus on our customer. We developed a whole series of ads based on "The Bloomingdale's Man" and "The Bloomingdale's Woman." They were young, good-looking, sophisticated, and internationally traveled. The press picked up on this and Ed Koren at *The New Yorker* drew a now famous cartoon about "The Bloomingdale's Couple."

b

I became Bloomingdale's sixth president in 1969. My promotion was duly noted in the press, and from then on my name started to appear regularly in the trade publications.

In retailing, it was not considered good taste to be more important than your store, though there were exceptions, of course. Walter Hoving was a larger-than-life figure at Tiffany's, Dorothy Shaver *was* Lord & Taylor's in the 1940s, and Stanley Marcus had pioneered using publicity to enhance Neiman-Marcus's image. Stanley believed that an editorial mention was always better value than an ad because it carried more weight with customers. Stanley was the first in our business to realize that reporters were always in need of good stories, and when working on stories, they always needed good quotes. By writing columns, and making himself media available, Stanley became a prime source for how merchandise was selling outside of New York. Not coincidentally, Neiman-Marcus came to be perceived nationally as a leading retailer. Their influence with suppliers and European resources grew accordingly.

What Stanley Marcus realized has become commonplace today: Reporters tend to rely on the same sources over and over, and the public will see you as the press sees you. If you have an image to convey, whether it is as the arbiter of fashion or as the place for best bargains, the media is your partner in creating that image. And a store must work to build that partnership.

When I became president of Bloomingdale's I gave great thought to what Stanley Marcus had accomplished. Taking a page from his book, Joan and I started to develop a strategy for working with the press. We created our own "expert" sources: Barbara D'Arcy for model rooms and home furnishings, Katie Murphy for fashion. I was to represent the store.

It was a gradual process. You need only look at the Bloomingdale's clippings from those times. The article that says it best, I suppose, appeared in the November 1974 issue of *Esquire*. The headline read, "Who Is Marvin Traub?"

"Okay, people watchers," the feature began, "did you know that Marvin Traub is one of the ninety-two most publicized persons in the world? Well, neither did we." *Esquire* had compiled a list of who had been mentioned most in *The New York Times* and other publications during the past year, using their own scoring system—points were awarded for where in the paper you appeared. I was number ninety-two.

Esquire imagined a gala dinner party for its honorees, "the Great Celebrity Ball," and had Nicki Zann draw a cartoon of everyone seated at tables based on their point tally. Henry Kissinger and Jackie Kennedy Onassis were king and queen. I was seated at the last table along with Anwar Sadat, Nelson Rockefeller, Jack Nicholson, Joe Namath, and Barbra Streisand among others—not so bad, after all. To rub in the fact of my anonymity, the article concluded with, "And in case you were wondering, Marvin Traub is the President of Bloomingdale's."

As Bloomingdale's became better known, more and more people from all walks of life wanted to attend our events. Joan invited them. They reciprocated by inviting Lee, Joan, and me. There is no shortage of events in New York. My personality is such that I always try to add one more thing into a day than can possibly be scheduled. Suddenly I was attending two or three events a week, sometimes two or three a night. Once I became Bloomingdale's president, my comings and goings suddenly became newsworthy. I became a public figure of sorts.

There was a purpose to all this frenzy. Each time the press called, it was an opportunity to put forward our version of Bloomingdale's. Our strategy was to make Bloomingdale's into a "hot spot," a place where people went to see and be seen. Celebrity attracts, sex sells. It was this one-two punch—the famous shopping at Bloom-ingdale's, and the Saturday shoppers looking for a date—that was the winning pitch.

As I looked over the clips from these years, I was struck by how often we succeeded. Our efforts paid off in a major way when on Tuesday, September 24, 1974, *The Wall Street Journal* had a front-page feature article headlined: "Shopping Spree: To Many in New York, a Trip to Bloomingdale's Is a Major Happening." The subhead read: "The store is a favorite spot for meeting, browsing and, of course, buying."

The article began, "On Saturdays, Bloomingdale's is the biggest party in town. It's a place," says Marvin Traub, "where the young make dates for the night."

The Wall Street Journal's reporter found my description re-strained. On a Saturday, the reporter wrote, the store's floors were "a jam-packed frenetic carnival where Murray Hill matrons rub shoulders with East Village transvestites; where the wares of the world are to be had at the flick of a credit card. . . . [Bloomingdale's is] in a class by itself; the quintessence of fashionable New York; with all the positive and negative attributes that such quintessential status entails." One negative cited was that we were "overstored, over-boutiqued, overdisplayed and overwhelming." To me, that was no negative: We had brought the excitement of the bazaar back to shopping, and doing so was bringing us national attention.

What we were doing was making Bloomingdale's into a brand. I don't think anyone had ever sold a store the way we did. Stanley Marcus had sold Neiman's, its store, its merchandise, its chairman. But we sold a life-style. Today, such marketing is commonplace, whether it's L. L. Bean or Armani, but it seems to me that no one had ever made a department store into a brand the way we did.

During this era, *Women's Wear Daily* became something more than a trade paper. John Fairchild and Michael Cody expanded the paper's coverage so that *WWD* was transformed into a social arbiter, as well as a serious business publication, the chronicler of who or what's in and who or what's out. This unique combination of infor-mation, all critical to the very trend-conscious fashion industry, made the newspaper very influential. *WWD* played a major role in building the image of Bloomingdale's because the paper found what we were doing interesting. Sometimes it criticized us, sometimes it applauded us—but Women's Wear almost always wrote about us.

Joan and I once calculated that in a typical year if we had to pay for all the space devoted to Bloomingdale's in articles and on TV, it would have been worth more than $15 million. Over the years, people have charged Bloomingdale's with being publicity hungry. That's just envy. The reason Bloomingdale's received more publicity than other stores was that we worked at it.

b

Joan Glynn left Bloomingdale's in 1974 to become president of the Simplicity Pattern Company. By then, Bloomingdale's was nationally known, with the culmination of our publicity efforts occurring when we made the cover of *Time* magazine.

The cover of *Time*'s December 1, 1975, issue read: "U.S. Shopping Surge . . . Trendy Bloomingdale's." Here's how the story began:

"On any given day, Dr. Spock might be glimpsed there selecting towels, Walter Matthau trying on suits. Jacqueline Kennedy Onassis recently passed through to order presents to be sent to her daughter, Caroline, in London. Singer Diana Ross outfits herself and her children there—by long distance from California. Basketball star Earl Monroe may drop in to pick up some after-shave lotion—and, he says, to 'see how people with money act.'

"What is this emporium? It is Bloomingdale's, the flashy department store on Manhattan's East Side. Now, as Christmas approaches, more than 300,000 shoppers weekly—some 60,000 on a Saturday alone—surge through the store's eleven floors. While ogling the merchandise, they also eye each other. For Bloomingdale's is both a neighborhood center and a celebrity hangout, a place where the next person a shopper bumps into (literally) may be either an acquaintance or someone familiar from a thousand newspaper photographs. . . . But the big attraction is the merchandise—thousands upon thousands of items chosen in part for high style and displayed with show business flair. . . ."

I remember holding that issue in my hands. It was, without doubt, one of the high points of my career to date.

"How do you top the cover of *Time* magazine?" Lee asked me.

I had no answer. But then there was the visit of the Queen, the ultimate event in selling the store.

b

In late fall 1975, the Queen of England announced that she was going to visit the United States the following spring. It was to be her first visit to New York in several decades and she would be there for only one day. You can't imagine what excitement and anticipation this news created. Today, the House of Windsor may be tarnished, but back then Elizabeth II was probably the most famous woman in the world. Wouldn't it be marvelous, I immediately thought, if she came to visit Bloomingdale's?

I was friendly with the British consul, Gordon Booth. One night over dinner at his River House apartment, I asked, "How does one go about having the Queen visit Bloomingdale's?"

"That's very simple," he said. "You invite her."

So we did.

It wasn't *quite* that easy. The invitation had to be made, Gordon informed us, through the British ambassador to the United States, Sir Peter Ramsbotham. I traveled to Washington to meet Sir Peter. Like Gordon, he was a very easygoing fellow. He knew Bloomingdale's and the idea of Her Royal Majesty touring our store piqued his interest. So he asked me to put my request in writing.

Gordon helped me compose a letter that would satisfy all the formalities of diplomacy. We sent it off, fingers crossed. A month went by before I received a phone call from the ambassador's office. It was not a yes or a no. We were informed that the Queen herself would make the final decision about her schedule. However, if the Queen came to Bloomingdale's, the embassy asked, what would she do? The process had begun.

To answer the embassy's question, I set up a meeting with Larry Lachman and our senior merchants—Carl Levine, who was responsible for furniture; Lester Gribetz, who was involved with both cosmetics and home furnishings; and Jack Shultz, who was responsible for men's, women's, and children's apparel. We decided that for the Queen, Bloomingdale's would assemble a combination of a tribute to British products with a survey of what was current in American design. There would be a series of model rooms commemorating the bicentennial, an exhibit of British and American ready-to-wear with the opportunity to meet American designers, a show of American children's clothes modeled by American youngsters, and finally, a tour of the Men's Store highlighting fine British menswear products —all in under an hour.

In January of 1976 we submitted our invitation and plan, and then waited. We had reason to be optimistic. Bloomingdale's was not an unknown quantity even to the Royal family. On the occasion of Elizabeth's coronation in 1953, our windows had displayed her picture for a week, and Bloomingdale's had received national attention for it. Prince Philip had visited the store in 1963 during our "Tradition" import fair. The past summer, Lee and I, among several hundred others, had been invited to tea with the Queen at Buckingham Palace.

We also had the enthusiastic support of the British ambassador and the British consul general. I called our British suppliers to make them aware of the project, including Sir Arthur Bryan, then chairman of Wedgewood and a director of the committee to encourage British exports. They in turn communicated their support to the British authorities.

On the other hand, every attraction in New York was competing for the Queen's very limited time. When it was announced that instead of a full day in New York, the Queen would only spend half a day we became discouraged.

b

In April, I received a phone call from Peter Ramsbotham. I expected him to tell us to wait a little longer. But all he said was, "You've got it." I didn't understand for a second and then I said, "Oh my God, that's terrific. What else do I need to know?"

The Queen would be visiting New York on July 9, he said. We should expect her in the afternoon, for no more than an hour. They would be in touch with us concerning matters of protocol and security.

b

Sometimes it was hard to believe that months of planning, hundreds of meetings, fifteen different rehearsals, and the dozens of security agents from the FBI, the Secret Service, the British embassy, and the New York Police Department who inspected our plans over and over again, all led up to a single half-hour tour of the store.

It was even more mind-boggling when you considered that for the Queen, the Bloomingdale's visit was just one small stop in a whole day of activities. Considering the logistics involved, it's probably best that the royal couple decided to spend only a limited time in New York. I don't know if the city could have survived more.

Queen Elizabeth and Prince Philip began the day of the visit, Friday, July 9, 1976, in Washington, D.C. To get to New York they flew to Newark and were driven to the naval base at Bayonne. There they boarded the royal yacht *Britannia*, which was to be their home base for their stay, and sailed into New York harbor. They docked at the Battery in Lower Manhattan.

Once in New York the Queen was taken to Federal Hall, the place where one of her ancestors turned over the Colonies to Washington. Mayor Abraham Beame, who had been born in London, then presented Her Majesty with a proclamation making her an honorary New Yorker. This was followed by lunch at the Waldorf and a visit to the Morris Jumel mansion in Harlem, which had been Washington's headquarters in 1776. Then Bloomingdale's. After Bloomie's there was to be a reception at Lincoln Center, and then another reception and dinner that night aboard the *Britannia*. Sounds like a typical New Yorker's day.

b

That afternoon I kept walking through the store, making sure everything was perfect. A little before four o'clock, I walked out on Lexington Avenue. No one was prepared for the enormous crowds, both inside the store and out, behind barricades on the street and leaning out windows. Security people with binoculars were posted on the top of every single building.

Everyone who was to meet the Queen was asked to arrive two hours early. Even so, there were a few personal crises. Donna Karan, then half of the Anne Klein design team, was one of the young designers selected to meet the Queen. She had her own dilemma. How to get from her office on 39th Street and Seventh Avenue to Bloomingdale's without wrinkling her dress. Traffic was so congested that taking a cab and sitting in a car was out of the

question. So, like a true New Yorker, she decided to take the subway. At least she would be standing the whole time. As she looked
around the BMT in her large hat, she thought it was a very funny
way to go to greet the Queen of England.

We had decided to keep the store open throughout the Queen's
visit, so it would appear as if she and Prince Philip were seeing the
store under normal operating conditions. Besides, to close the store
on the day the Queen visits . . . we hoped this would be a record
day in more ways than one.

b

We did, however, make some changes to accommodate Her Royal
Highness. The Queen of England always exits a car from the right.
The Lexington Avenue entrance to Bloomingdale's is on the left. No
problem. For Her Majesty, Lexington was closed off so she could
drive against traffic and pull up from the right. We had the Queen's
portrait in our windows so she could see them when she came up
Lexington Avenue if she glanced up.

Larry Lachman and I took our positions on the sidewalk to greet
the royal couple, followed by our wives. We had been instructed that
in meeting royalty, the husband goes first and the wife second. As I
stood on the sidewalk next to the red carpet waiting to greet the
Queen of England, I had a sudden thought I had come a very long
way from selling forty-nine-cent irregular hosiery in the basement.
In all my dreams, I never quite thought I'd see the day when I would
welcome the Queen of England to our store.

The limousine arrived. The Queen alighted from the car first,
followed by Prince Philip. As prearranged, she and Prince Philip
were presented to Larry Lachman by Henry Catto, Jr., then U.S.
chief of protocol and later our ambassador to Britain. I stood alongside. She acknowledged both of us with a very warm and friendly
smile. She was then presented to Judy Lachman and Lee Traub,
who both dipped their heads slightly. (Lee had threatened to curtsy
like the third act of *Swan Lake*.) Larry then took Her Highness up
the steps and I escorted Prince Philip. Each of the other members
of the party was assigned a key Bloomingdale's executive. Mrs.
Lachman accompanied the Duchess of Grafton, Mistress of the
Robes; Lee escorted Lady Ramsbotham.

The red carpet led the Queen through the Bloomingdale's arcade up the steps to the elevator bank where we had blocked off Elevators 1, 2, and 3 to take the Queen and her party to the fifth floor. Carl Levine joined us there and led the group, by now a large crowd, to see the model rooms.

The fifth-floor exhibit was called red, white, and Bloomingdale's. The model rooms celebrated the U.S. Bicentennial, displaying American reproductions of English antiques, and an oriental room with Chippendale-style chairs—adapted, as always, for the American market.

"What wide chairs," Her Highness exclaimed.

"The English are very disciplined," Carl explained. "They sit in small tiny spaces. We like to spread out."

We proceeded to the fourth floor, where we had assembled an exhibit of Wedgewood products and created a special presentation area. We had spent a long time trying to select an appropriate gift. Should it be British, typically American, or of historic value? We finally decided it should be American, and of historic value, but most important, it should somehow be a symbol of the peace and friendship between our two countries. After searching through many antique dealers, we came up with a genuine Sioux Indian peace pipe, authenticated by the American Museum of Natural History as dating between 1850 and 1870. Equally important, protocol authorities on both sides of the Atlantic approved of the gift. After the presentation of the peace pipe, Prince Philip whispered to me, "Let's put the good stuff in and light up."

We were inundated with requests for press coverage. The TV crews agreed to pool their coverage. ABC was on the fifth floor, NBC on the fourth, CBS on the third. Reporters and photographers had also been assigned specific viewing perches.

I led the Queen to our third-floor designer area. We had prepared a collection of American sportswear designed by Ralph Lauren, Calvin Klein, and Donna Karan and Louis Dell'Olio for Anne Klein. They had been asked to design special fashions for that day using British woolens. The Queen toured a room full of fifteen mannequins wearing the designers' clothes. Suddenly three came to life (they were real-life models) and twirled around in the fashions.

After the show, Calvin, Donna, Ralph, and Louis were each presented to the Queen. The Americans were honored, but felt that the Queen could have used some fashion advice herself. This was way before Lady Di's fashion triumphs. Her Majesty on this occasion was wearing a sleeveless dress of lime green dotted swiss with a matching turban, pearl earrings, a triple strand of pearls, and her white gloves and handbag. It was attractive but matronly; nothing that would have made Seventh Avenue or Norman Hartnell, the Queen's favorite designer, proud.

b

The Queen maintained her composure and concentration throughout the event, occasionally giving her famous one-handed wave. Prince Philip, by contrast, enjoyed the circus of it all. At one point, he reportedly turned to a group of onlookers and with a smile said, "Are all of you really here to buy shoes?"

As protocol had suggested, we were told to say goodbye inside the store. Security did not want the Royal couple to linger on the sidewalk. So the Lachmans and the Traubs said goodbye to the Queen and Prince Philip in the vestibule of Third Avenue, under our centennial digital clock. Then they hurried out of the store and into their limousine to head for their next stop. The tour had taken twenty-five minutes. I, for one, heaved a long sigh, felt elated, and went back to work.

Though everything went off without a hitch, there were a few who complained of the event. As Blair Sabol put it in *The Village Voice*: "[The Queen] saw nothing of the real Bloomingdale's. She didn't dine on their frozen yogurt in their 40 Carrots cafeteria; she didn't stand in line with a number in her hand at the cheese counter; she didn't tool around the Jap-designed line in the avant-garde paradox boutique; she didn't hit the cheapy lingerie and blue jeans in the basement. . . . But worst of all she wasn't even welcomed at the Lexington Avenue and 59th Street entrance by the spastic man selling comic books . . . a city trademark."

Now *that* would have been some tour!

Lee and I were invited to dinner that night on the royal yacht, the *Britannia*. Lee commented that at a length of 412 feet and with a crew of 250, it looked more like an ocean liner. The guest list was impressive: David Rockefeller, Arthur Schlesinger, Dorothy Schiff, Barbara Walters, Walter Cronkite. There was a small band. The

Queen spoke with her guests, and the Prince strolled around glass in hand, like any host at a party.

That night, the Queen commented again on how much she had enjoyed her visit to Bloomingdale's. I saw Prince Philip and asked him: Why did the Queen select Bloomingdale's? She had many invitations in New York and a very limited amount of time, he said. In the end they had to chose between the Metropolitan Museum and Bloomingdale's. And according to Prince Philip, the Queen said, "I can visit a museum anytime, let's go to Bloomingdale's."

"I met my first husband at Bloomingdale's and my second
husband at Banana Republic."

CHAPTER 6

What You See

"Marvin, you have to see these windows," Lee said. By the 1970s, those Saturday mornings when I wasn't playing golf were spent in the office working. Lee would join me in the city, and we would spend the late afternoon window shopping and checking up on the competition. On this day, we were at the corner of 57th Street and Fifth Avenue.

There were several stores at that intersection: Bergdorf's, Bonwit's, Tiffany's, and I. Miller shoes (today, only Bergdorf's and Tiffany's are there). Lee, however, led me down the west side of Fifth Avenue, past the Doubleday Book Shop, and Hallmark Cards (now Fendi), past Harry Winston and the Rizzoli Bookstore (now Bendel's). All had window displays, but the crowds were gathered at the corner of 55th Street and Fifth Avenue in front of Charles Jourdan, a shoe store. There, in the window, was an old-fashioned toilet with a pull chain, pristine like a work of art. Next to it were two beautiful yellow pumps, and in the corner a mess of other shoes. "It was as if Holly Golightly had just run out of her bathroom to get the phone," was how one person later described it.

The window was shocking. No one had ever displayed a toilet in a Fifth Avenue window—or in any New York store window for that matter. Even toilet manufacturers displayed their wares indoors then. You looked to the toilet, bang! Then to the shoes, bang! You never forgot it. I'm not sure I completely understood the display, but I appreciated the crowds gathered to look at it. Lee said she had been hearing about the Jourdan windows for some time.

The next day I learned that those windows were the work of a twenty-five-year-old woman, Candy Pratts. I called and asked if we might meet. The timing couldn't have been better. The Bloomingdale's display director had recently announced his intention to step down and I was on the lookout for someone new.

When I first started at Bloomingdale's in the fifties, the display director, Edward Von Castleburg, had been with the store for many years. He was a tall, elegant man who struck me, even then, as out of another era. He seemed to have walked out of a play by Noël Coward. He was very sophisticated but the windows had no personality of their own. He was followed by Jack Lindsay and Gordon Ryan, each of whom represented the store well—today, Gordon is display director of the Daimuru department store in Melbourne, Australia. Now I was looking for someone who would create the same drama for the windows that Bloomingdale's was creating inside the store.

Retailers often don't give visual display its due. That's understandable. A merchant can say, "Last year I sold $50,000 worth of coats, and this year I'm up 20 percent." The connection between the windows and the bottom line is not always directly evident. Visual display rarely has such tangible results. But the windows are important because they set a tone for the whole store.

Bloomingdale's was selling entertainment. The windows could provide it all—glamour, beauty, movement, mystery, humor. One factor that separates merchants from marketers is a keen sense of how to use visual display to focus the customer's interest. If Bloomingdale's was going to be *the* store to shop at, we would have to distinguish ourselves in every area of visual display, from our windows to the look of every department to the visual material we sent out to our customers. Each was to be an ambassador for our cause.

By the time I approached Candy to come to Bloomingdale's, she had been at Jourdan for three years and was their director of public relations. At that time, she and Robert Currie of Bendel's were the two most famous window designers in New York. I liked her immediately.

Candy was a graduate of the Fashion Institute of Technology, where she had studied merchandising. She had worked at Bergdorf Goodman while at school and was a favorite of Nena Goodman, wife of the store's chairman, who offered her a job after graduation. She had also worked briefly for Bachrach, styling photo shoots. When Jourdan opened in New York, Candy fell in love with the shoes and began to frequent the store. She realized that the French executives had no idea how to run a store in New York and told them so. They offered her a job as a salesperson. That was not what Candy had in mind, but in no time she was their star salesperson.

Candy then asked if she could decorate Jourdan's five huge windows, two on Fifth Avenue and three on 55th Street. To this day, Candy is not sure why she asked: She had never done windows before and couldn't sketch. The Charles Jourdan executives at first said no. "Give me three months and if everyone in New York isn't talking about your windows, I'll quit," Candy counterproposed. They agreed.

For her first windows, Candy went over to the Museum of Modern Art on West 53rd Street. The museum has a long-standing art lending program, and Candy brought back huge artworks by Frank Stella to hang in the windows, placed with a few pairs of shoes. That was her display and it worked. Crowds gathered. It stopped traffic on Fifth Avenue. You have to understand that many of the people walking down Fifth Avenue had never been to the Museum of Modern Art. They had never seen much contemporary art. The paintings were overwhelming. Candy had brought the museum to the street. She won her bet with her boss.

Bloomingdale's represented an offer that was hard to refuse. We had thirty-nine windows, and a whole staff of carpenters and electricians ready to carry out her vision. Candy was interested. But first I asked Barbara D'Arcy, who supervised visual display, to meet her.

b

Throughout the 1960s, Barbara continued to oversee the model rooms. With each import fair, Barbara grew in stature and self-confidence; she also became more fanciful in her designs. Barbara once confided to me that whenever she designed a model room, she always had someone specific in mind. Out of the blue I asked her: "Who would you like to design rooms for?"

"Creative people," Barbara answered.

"Such as?"

"Truman Capote, Leonard Bernstein, Balanchine," Barbara answered. That conversation became the basis for a set of model rooms Barbara designed called "the Creators," part of a storewide promotion of the same name. But along with the other "creators," I suggested Barbara design a room for herself. "Me?" she said. I insisted. She's one of the most creative people I know.

The result of Barbara's efforts, the Barbara D'Arcy room, combined the elements she loved most. It was a multileveled environment with beamed ceilings; strong, brilliant colors, including her favorites, orange and purple; and her signature eclectic mix of furniture: French antiques, a modern Plexiglas table, African sculptures, baskets galore. The white plaster walls, painted beamed ceiling, and fireplace presaged the Sante Fe look. But then Barbara was always ahead of her time.

Barbara's most innovative creation, however, was the Cave Room. Her inspiration was the work of a French architect named Jacques Couellé, who designed homes in the South of France and on the Mediterranean coast. Barbara was intrigued by the free-form architectural shapes of white stucco . . . very Mediterranean yet very contemporary. She felt the look—a series of free-form levels— could be duplicated utilizing a sprayed-on material.

She contacted the American manufacturers, who assured her that yes, a room of sprayed-on polyurethane could be fabricated to her specifications. She then spoke with Bloomingdale's own construction manager, who told her they would have to build a special housing for the room, otherwise they'd never be able to remove it from the store. So there was Barbara a few months later in overalls and gas mask, overseeing the workmen spraying layers of polyurethane on a chicken-wire grid.

In its finished form, the Cave Room was a series of shaped white walls and a ceiling. A set of steps divided the space into living, dining and bedroom, while round holes served as windows between the rooms. The living area resembled an Arctic lair, complete with fireplace and conversation pit piled high with purple cushions. The dining area had a free-form Plexiglas table with columns lit from within. The floor was made of quarter-inch mirrors that reflected the light and made the rooms feel airy. The Cave Room received more attention than any room Barbara had ever designed. It remains, to this day, one of her personal favorites.

Shortly afterward, in February 1973, we promoted Barbara to head of store design and visual display for all stores, and two years later she became a vice president. During her sixteen years, we once counted, she had created 632 rooms! There were some who wondered if, without Barbara, people would stop coming to the model rooms. But we left them in the talented hands of Richard Knapple. Today, almost twenty years later, Richard is still creating show-stopping model rooms.

At the same time, the Blooming-style that Barbara had been developing since our first trips to Europe in the 1950s was applied to the entire store. When people think of Bloomingdale's, they expect to be surprised, never to know what they'll find around the corner, what new item, what exclusive product. She modulates the cozy with the modern, the overstuffed with the stark, all in a manner that keeps the consumer's interest, and yet is a distinct style. Over the years, Barbara and I have worked very hard to make Bloomingdale's unique visual style appear natural and effortless.

The first place we present the store's personality is with our windows and display, or as many stores call it, "visual merchandising." That's one reason why I treated display with such importance. Which brings us back to Candy.

b

Barbara thought she was terrific. Candy saw the windows as a theatrical tool to tell a story. I had her meet Larry Lachman and Vin Brennan. Vin was, I recall, a little shocked by her. Candy dressed downtown—the shortest mini skirts—and always on the cutting edge of fashion. But he said, "If she's who you want, I'll be supportive." So we hired Candy.

Candy could not trim a window and didn't sketch that well. She was an idea person. Buddy Hoskins, who now teaches display at FIT, was the one who translated her dreams. Remember, Bloomingdale's was unionized. Candy couldn't pick up a hammer and she was barely allowed to move a mannequin. So she would stand outside on Lexington Avenue and direct: "Move that there, turn her arm that way."

Candy had a habit of placing the mannequins in poses no mannequins had ever been in before. When the mannequins' arms wouldn't bend the way Candy wanted them to, she broke them and taped them back in positions she liked better.

Adel Rootstein in London was the most famous mannequin man-

ufacturer. She would get calls all the time, "Can we have a mannequin just like the one in Bloomingdale's window?" More often than
not, she couldn't satisfy their request. In 1978, however, Candy gave
Rootstein a call to commission the first mannequin based on a black
woman. Not a "white mannequin" with dark skin tones, but one
based on an actual African-American model, Toukie Smith. (Toukie,
the sister of the late designer Willi Smith, later starred in the television series "222." Today she is president of the Smith Family
Fund, a charity that benefits children with AIDS.)

Rootstein gave Bloomingdale's a three-month exclusive and then
sold the mannequin around the world in various shades of Toukie.
"Toukie" went out on tour to all the Bloomingdale's branches. People noticed; they liked that our mannequins represented "real"
women and not some homogenized android.

Candy next commissioned mannequins in what she called the
"bisque" complexion of a Latin woman. They, too, attracted much
attention. For Bloomingdale's, this wasn't civil rights; it was Candy's
World.

Candy brought a tremendous energy to her work. Like Barbara,
she had a strong sense of personal style that had "New York" written all over it. She mixed uptown with downtown, avant-garde with
mainstream. The store's thirty-nine windows were her personal canvas.

Candy's windows often captured a moment. She did a series in
which you were looking in on a group of women who might have
been in a bathroom, fixing their hair, putting on lipstick. They were
seated at makeup tables and vanities but instead of mirrors, they
just looked out into the street. It was almost as if you were a voyeur,
looking through a two-way mirror into a powder room.

For the introduction of a Sonia Rykiel collection, Candy created
a Paris hotel room—that was Candy's description, others preferred
the term *brothel*—with a group of models in various stages of dress,
some putting on and others taking off the latest Rykiel fashions.
There were cigarette butts everywhere, in the ashtrays, on the floor,
in the potted plants.

Candy was always pushing the limits. Then again we gave her a
lot of leeway. One of the more outrageous incidents concerns a
promotion we did of Philippine briefcases and luggage. Candy's Lex-

ington Avenue windows showed a group of men and women traveling. There was a conveyor belt and their luggage sat on it open—there was even a little sign that said, "Customs." Under it was a second sign that read: "Out to Lunch." Inside the attaché cases were glacine bags.

Jim Schoff, the store's president, came to me distraught. "What are those packets of white powder?" He was very worried. There had been a few calls from the press, and he had visions of a public relations fiasco. I decided to ask Candy directly.

"Candy, what's in the bag?"

"Maybe it's rice?" Candy said. I looked at her skeptically.

"It's the Philippines, isn't it?" she continued, improvising. "They export a lot of rice." Finally, she said, "Who knows? Doesn't everyone take pills when they travel?" I let them stay in.

To understand what Candy was doing, you also had to understand something of the times. Candy came to Bloomingdale's at a moment when a whole new level of theater transformed visual display. New York was experiencing a downtown cultural renaissance. At galleries in SoHo, at music clubs on the Bowery, at performance spaces in TriBeCa, a new generation of artists was converging on New York. Manhattan at night took on a whole new excitement.

On the West Side, Studio 54 became the epicenter of New York nightlife. The former television studio–turned–disco promoted itself through a combination of fantasy, special effects, theme parties, and a steady stream of celebrities. Although the club could hold thousands, it promoted an air of exclusivity by having doormen stand behind a velvet rope with one of the owners often signaling who could enter. On any number of evenings, Halston, Liza Minelli, Bianca Jagger, Andy Warhol, and Calvin Klein could be found inside. You could be sure to find their names the next day in bold type in several gossip columns. Studio 54 delivered a voyeuristic mix of romance, mystery, and celebrity with a touch of decadence that seemed to represent New York at the end of the seventies.

Back in the daylight hours, Candy created windows that reflected this same sense of fantasy. What Candy did was take the Bloomingdale's couple through the looking glass, down to Studio 54, and back to the East Side. The windows were our loudspeakers. They beckoned.

Department stores have always had someone in charge of visual display, but in most stores that person has been low in the store's hierarchy. It was my belief that what makes a great store, much like what makes a great restaurant, is the total experience: how you are greeted when you arrive, the decor and ambience, the selection and assortment, the presentation, the service. Consequently, we made our visual display director a key member of the marketing staff. Candy was a vice president and we raised the pay scale for the staff.

For Candy, the windows advertised the spirit and sense of adventure that made Bloomingdale's different. During the day, it was what the shoppers saw first. At night the windows were all they could see of the store; it was what made them want to come back the next day. Many came just to see what Candy would do next.

b

To make Bloomingdale's a national institution, the quality brand for the mobile upper class, we had to extend the way we merchandised fashion and home furnishings to every business in the store. It was also of critical importance that we turn our attention back to the home, to housewares and food, areas that touched people's lives all over the country.

Housewares at Bloomingdale's had never been very profitable; its importance was as a destination, as a way to draw customers to the store. Going back to Davidson's own love of sophisticated cuisine, and the days of our Au Gourmet shop where a young Craig Claiborne gave cooking demonstrations for our shoppers, the housewares department of Bloomingdale's was a place for events. At Bloomingdale's, shoppers could have a learning experience, a shopping experience, a food experience. It stood to reason that if there was ever a department naturally suited to drama, it was housewares.

b

For years, housewares had been an undistinguished area with open bins carrying utensils, aprons, and knives. Almost half of the business in most housewares departments was in toasters, coffeemakers, irons, steamers—"small electrics" as we call them. They were the easiest to sell but traditionally not an area of uniqueness and distinction. It was also the area with the greatest discounting and, therefore, the lowerst margin for stores.

I noticed, however, that when I visited friends' homes, they loved to show off their kitchens. They always had to have the latest gadgets. It didn't matter if they never cooked, they still had to own the best pots and pans.

Our notion was to treat housewares like fashion, with boutiques, designers, and celebrity appearances. To carry out this new strategy, Jim Schoff and I called upon the genius of one of my most trusted and talented associates, Lester Gribetz, who was then merchandise vice president for home furnishings.

Lester joined Bloomingdale's in 1953 directly out of NYU and was assigned to me as a trainee. I was working for Frank Chase at the time. Frank was a very staid New Englander who was an aggressive merchant and a good manager and later became chairman of G. Fox. Lester and I both had energy to spare, and as our offices were on opposite sides of Frank's, everyone imagined the day would come when Frank would call us, and we would both explode out of our offices and collide with each other. It never happened, but Lester and I hit it off from the start.

Lester recalls the first assignment I ever gave him: I sent him to our warehouse to check on our latest shipment of bicycles—Bloomingdale's had a pretty good bicycle business then—they were late and we needed them immediately. I gave Lester no other guidance than that I expected the bicycles to be in the store as soon as possible. At the warehouse, Lester discovered that no one could assemble the bikes because a piece was missing. Union rules didn't allow him to touch the bicycles and the problem seemed insoluble, but Lester just ordered a worker to manufacture the missing part on the spot. The next day, he delivered the bicycles and came to my office.

"Mr. Traub," he said, "I've completed the assignment. But how could you ask a nice Jewish boy to go assemble bicycles in a warehouse?" What can I say? It was the start of a beautiful friendship. Lester Gribetz always had an uncanny ability to sense the potential, be it of a Pet Rock, Dancing Flower, or Dancing Coke Bottle, each of which added millions of dollars to our sales and heightened our image for unique, imaginative, and fun products. For almost forty years now, I have asked Lester to do the impossible. He has never disappointed me and we have had a great time in the process—and we are still having great fun together at Marvin Traub Associates.

The redesign and display was carried out by Fred Palatinus, then assistant director of store design, reporting to Barbara D'Arcy, with input from Lester and me. Fred brought an almost stage-set quality to his designs. Our conceptual breakthrough was in organizing the various components of housewares by activity rather than product. For example, instead of having all the plates in one area and cutlery and glassware in another, we created a shop, "That's Entertainment," that carried everything you need for serving cocktails, dinner, or a late-night snack.

Each shop had its own name and a customer could wander from one to the next with a salesperson. We trained all the salespeople to sell from shop to shop, but each shop had its own "expert" to answer any specific question.

We had been planning the Main Course since 1975. However, before we opened in 1977, Macy's San Francisco unveiled their Cellar, a very similar concept. That made it all the more important for the Main Course to be distinctive in every respect, from the merchandise to its visual design. I wanted the space to be stunning. And it was.

White marble was laid for the floor, and a green neon strip along the ceiling led the customers down the center aisle, past the series of specialized boutiques, such as the Real Pros, which featured professional cooking equipment, and the Cook's Kitchen, a collection of famous chef's personally recommended cooking implements.

We kept the housewares department open during the construction, as was second nature to us now, closing it off section by section. Each closed section became an advertisement for the new redesign and we built up excitement all the while. Only at Bloomingdale's is renovation a promotional event.

When completed, the housewares department was 25 percent larger, covered almost fifty thousand square feet, and cost more than $2 million. We raised the roof on the Third Avenue side an additional eighteen feet and constructed a giant skylight to illuminate our demonstration kitchen designed in consultation with master chef James Beard and designers Milton Glaser and Burt Wolf. We had guest appearances by Julia Child and classes by Marcella Hazan.

The Main Course was dramatic. It sparkled with an energy all its own. Traffic on the sixth floor surged dramatically. What's more, we transformed how people thought about kitchen items.

For example, Bloomingdale's was not about to sell a food processor, but a Cuisinart. That was perfect for us. At $200 each, Cuisinarts were a good business for us to be in. They made their first appearance at the Bloomingdale's Stamford store. Carl Sontheimer, Cuisinart's founder, had shown them to Larry Hurd, our housewares buyer, who bought twelve. Carl, who lived nearby, came into the store on a Saturday and demonstrated them. He sold all twelve. We ordered more and more. In no time Bloomingdale's was closely identified with Cuisinart.

We sold kitchen items as status symbols: Calphalon cookware, Sabatier knives, Braun electronics. The newest, the best, the trendiest, Bloomingdale's had it first. Chinese woks, bread machines, ice cream makers.

One of the successful items we carried, over my initial objections, was a unique apron called "Cleansleeves" marketed by Lee Traub. In the late 1970s, Lee decided she wanted to start a business and had an idea to market an apron of her own invention. The problem with most aprons, Lee observed, was that they offered no protection for the sleeves of a woman's dress or blouse. She had seen a design in Japan for a kimono-like long-sleeved apron. Inspired by that, she created her own version and started a company from her desk in our apartment to market what she called "Cleansleeves."

The business was very successful. At first I advised her not to sell to Federated stores, so there would be no conflict of interest. Her aprons were launched at Macy's and stores across the country. They grew to be such a success that one day I got a call from Howard Goldfeder asking why Lee's aprons were available everywhere but in Federated stores. I explained my concerns, but Howard overruled me. "Cleansleeves" were soon selling out at Bloomingdale's, A&S, and Rich's.*

---

* At a certain point, the business had grown to such a degree that Lee either had to hire a staff and work at it full time or close it. She decided to close it, which she did, ending her business career with a small profit.

From the moment it opened, the Main Course became one of the most popular areas of the store. In no time, Saturday afternoons at the Main Course became the place for singles to go, much as the main floor had been a few years earlier. Since then, whenever we have held focus groups to study our customers' attitudes, they have always reported that housewares was high on the list of why people shopped at Bloomie's. Housewares—and food.

b

Food and restaurants, in the eyes of Bloomingdale's, became a status symbol. Around the time of Saturday's Generation we created 40 Carrots, a health food–type restaurant. I was inspired by a small health food stall I found at Harrod's food hall in the early 1970s. The timing for a health-conscious snack bar was just right. An in-store contest came up with the name 40 Carrots. The design was done in natural wood and we featured a new product that had just come on the market, frozen yogurt.

Forty Carrots was a success from day one, and we opened them in several branch stores, where they were also immensely popular, and even licensed the name to a Florida restaurateur.

We also opened the Espresso Bar on the metro level, Bloomingdale's most profitable restaurant. It was smoky, bustling, and continental, with a clientele similar to what one would find in SoHo. The menu heavily favors pasta and espresso, two very popular and profitable items, and it's busy all day.

At the time we redesigned the Main Course, we thought of creating a sophisticated continental restaurant offering good service and elegant atmosphere, comparable to a fine restaurant in New York. Most department store restaurants featured counter service or a snack bar as an amenity to shoppers. B. Altman had its Charleston Gardens and Lord & Taylor its Soup Kitchen. Only Neiman Marcus, however, had a fine restaurant. I thought Bloomingdale's should have one, too, one that would become a destination in and of itself. I refused, however, to give up any selling space.

The Bloomingdale's building is actually nine different structures. Since housewares is on the top floor of the Third Avenue building, we could take advantage of the roof right above us. That was how we created the skylight in the center area for the demonstration kitchen.

At the same time, we discovered that if we broke through the wall of our sixth-floor stockroom, we would find ouselves on the roof of the original 1886 Bloomingdale's building. The roof was a beautiful, long, narrow space from 59th Street to 60th facing the East River and the Queensborough Bridge. We could build a new restaurant there with a stairway leading up from the Main Course. It would provide our shoppers with an oasis from the store.

The notion of transporting shoppers to a quieter place gave me an idea. The space was long and narrow. I had recently returned from Europe where I enjoyed several wonderful business luncheons aboard trains. Why not re-create a train on the roof of Bloomingdale's? That would be unique.

Our first thought was of buying an actual railroad car, but the roof could not support the weight. Next we looked to re-creating one. Fred Palatinus researched the subject extensively. My favorite was Le Train Bleu, a train that ran between Paris and the Riviera. We reproduced the car down to the smallest details: the mahogany panels and green velvet walls, brass lamps on the tables, the brass luggage racks. There was one important difference, however: Our car was fourteen feet wide to make waiter service easier.

Le Train Bleu at 59th Street became a popular lunch spot. Although the restaurant has little to do with housewares, its success has added tremendously to the prestige of those departments. Most people do not realize the extent to which Bloomingdale's is in the restaurant business. We actually run a chain of restaurants: By 1992, we had twenty-two restaurants in our stores doing more than $12 million annually.

The importance of the Main Course cannot be overstated: Bloomingdale's invaded the kitchen and the home. Doing so, making fashion out of the kitchen, provided the entrée to homes all over the country. The Main Course was a marketing concept that created another strong foundation for our national expansion.

At the same time, I was interested in taking the excitement of Bloomingdale's directly into people's homes. For that we would have to remake our catalogs in the Bloomingdale's image.

b

In 1976, as part of the ongoing renovation of the store, we planned to move the intimate apparel department from the second floor to the lower level—the former basement. No one had ever sold high-priced lingerie in a basement. I decided that we needed a promotional vehicle to highlight the move. In the 1960s and 1970s, Bloomingdale's strategy was to use catalogs both to sell products and to enhance our business. Our Christmas catalog, for example, was more a way to increase the sales of specific products and lure customers to our stores than to do business by mail.

I asked Arthur Cohen, our senior vice president of marketing, to take responsibility for the project. I gave him one guideline:

"Arthur," I said, "I want it to be amazing!"

Arthur Cohen was not your traditional retail marketer. We had hired him from General Foods. As with Joan Glynn, I had looked outside the traditional retail arena to find someone who could market Bloomingdale's as a total merchandising concept, more like a brand than a department store. Visiting art galleries on the weekend was his favorite activity, and Arthur owned an outstanding collection of contemporary art. He was very tuned in to the creative world. He had a very strong sense of what sells, and today he is president of worldwide marketing for Paramount.

To photograph the catalog, Arthur wanted to hire Guy Bourdin, a French surrealist photographer. Guy was well known in Europe but little known in the States, where his principal commercial work had been for Charles Jourdan shoes. But Arthur considered Guy to be one of the world's great artists and asked him to do our catalog.

Guy demanded complete autonomy: We would only see the photos when he turned them in. He would deliver thirty-six photos for thirty-six pages, with no reshoots. Those were his terms. It was all or nothing. Arthur accepted—doing so was a very gutsy move.

Guy arrived in New York with his girlfriend, his assistant, and two dogs. His only requirement was that we book adjoining rooms for his entourage, and that the accommodations include a kitchen so they could cook and eat together. We put him up in the Surrey Hotel, a residential apartment hotel on East 76th street near Central Park.

Guy began by meeting with more than sixty top models in New York. He asked each to pose and then undress. None were to his taste. So he stalked the city and cruised the clubs, recruiting a half dozen women, some of whom had never modeled professionally before, and all of whom were very young.

Guy gathered the models, had them heavily made-up, and then photographed them as if they lived together in some boarding school for wayward girls. He used several locations around Manhattan. His favorite, though, was his hotel room because, he told Arthur, he loved the wallpaper.

Guy continued to call with surprising requests: He needed a grand piano, immediately! We sent one. He wanted to photograph the girls breaking into Bloomingdale's, smashing the Lexington Avenue windows—to that, we said no. What, we wondered, would the completed photos look like?

Finally, Guy gave Arthur the slides. Arthur was stunned. The photos were startling. Traditionally, photographers used one model to a shot. Guy bunched them together, shooting three, or even all six, in one shot. In some of the shots, the women had wild, big hair, teased and blown—it was not a look you saw in *Vogue*. At the same time, the photos were suggestive, sexy, and bound to create a sensation.

"These are either brilliant," Arthur said, "or a disaster."

Arthur had not shown me the photos yet. Our schedule was such, however, that we had committed to printing 500,000 copies of the catalog. Arthur was concerned. He asked Carrie Donovan, who was then our senior vice president for sales promotions, what to do.

Carrie suggested he get a second opinion. When it comes to judging sexy photos, one name came to mind. She called Calvin Klein and asked if he would look at them. Calvin created a huge success with his Brooke Shields jeans ads, "Nothing comes between me and my Calvins," and was to create an even greater success with his controversial Obsession ads. His 1993 campaign with Marky Mark and Kate Moss shows he hasn't lost his touch for the provocative.

Calvin invited Arthur and Carrie over to his apartment, two blocks from Bloomingdale's. He pored over the photos, and then said, "These are fantastic!"

Armed with Calvin's approval, Arthur came to see me. He showed me the photos and told me of Calvin's support.

"Marvin," he said, finally, "what should we do?"

"What are our options?" I asked.

"We can burn them," Arthur said, "you can fire me, or we can send them out."

I looked at the photos. The models were so young, and so made-up. But they were compelling. No one had ever sold lingerie like this. Victoria's Secret was more than a decade away. Frederick's of Hollywood was the only comparable publication, but it was aimed at a completely different audience. By using a European photographer we had created a completely different feeling. The models had an air of mystery about them. The settings left a great deal to the viewer's imagination.

The cover, for example, showed a girl in her undergarments, her wedding dress thrown over a nearby chair. She is looking off to the right where a hand beckons. Is the photo taken moments before her wedding, or moments after? Is the hand that of her groom, or some-one else? They were the kind of photos that, today, could get your National Endowment grant dropped. The taste level was so high, however, that it convinced me.

"Run it," I said.

We called the catalog "Sighs and Whispers." And contrary to our fears, we received very few complaints.

Each photo in "Sighs and Whispers" appeared on a black bor-dered page, looking more like a photography art book than a sales vehicle. The news media seemed to agree. Articles "reviewing" the catalog appeared in publications in New York, Los Angeles, Wash-ington, D.C., and even abroad—that, too, was a first.

"Sighs and Whispers" became an instant classic. People were selling them, we heard, for $20. That turned out to be a good buy. A few years ago, Lee and I found a copy being offered in the Meisel Gallery in SoHo for $500.

I can think of no other department store catalog that had ever received that treatment—or any that has since. Bloomingdale's re-ceived a tremendous amount of publicity, and a great many people came to see our new lingerie department.

The surge in our business convinced us to repeat the experi-ment. The next year we hired David Hamilton, a photographer who has since made a reputation—a career, some would say—of his romantic photos. At the same time, Richard Avedon was shooting our Christmas catalog.

Over the next few seasons, Arthur hired Richard Avedon, Horst, Francesco Scavullo—photographers who were not associated with department stores—to give Bloomingdale's a more distinctive look. John Jay would continue this tradition by employing Helmut Newton, Sheila Metzner, and Steven Meisel.

But the forum in which all the various visual aspects of the store came together, where store display, visual merchandising, and catalogs found their ultimate expression, was in our mega-events, the country promotions.

*"Before we decide on our next expansion of the people's
industry, shouldn't we check with Bloomingdale's?"*

Drawing by Stevenson; © 1980 The New Yorker Magazine, Inc.

CHAPTER 7

The Ultimate Fantasy

hroughout the 1970s, Bloomingdale's increased sales by creating such marketing concepts as Saturday's Generation that made Bloomingdale's a destination. And with every event we extended the notion of Christmas year-round and brought drama to the store. By the end of the decade, however, we were in the position of having to top ourselves. Shoppers expected excitement at Bloomingdale's and we always had to give them more. To do that I proposed we return to the seven-week themed promotions that Jed had used in the 1960s to transform the store, and reinvent them for our times as full-blown extravaganzas. We would take our customers to places they had never been before, and offer them unique and exclusive merchandise that our buyers selected or created. We would do what we did best, but this time on a larger, international scale.

By staging promotions of foreign merchandise we were able to unite three separate strengths the store developed over the past two decades: our aggressive, creative buying organization; our innovative store display and visual merchandising; and our high-profile public relations and advertising. Bringing these talents together for an event would transform the entire store for a limited time—and simultaneously raise the perception of Bloomingdale's as a worldwide marketer.

From 1978, when we revived the country promotion, to 1991, my last year at Bloomingdale's, we took our shoppers around the world. A list of the promotions by year is revealing: In 1978 we staged "India, the Ultimate Fantasy"; in 1979, "Israel, the Dream"; 1980, "China: Heralding the Dawn of a New Era"; 1981, "Ireland—That Special Place." In 1982 we did two: "America the Beautiful" and "The Philippines"; 1983, "Fête de France"; 1984, "Ecco l'Italia";

1985, "Japan"; 1986, "The South China Seas"; 1987, "Mediterranean Odyssey"; 1988, "Year of the Dragon—Hong Kong, China, and Macau"; 1989, "Vive la France" and "Hooray for Hollywood"; 1990, "Spain: Europe's Rising Star," and "Broadway Ninety"; 1991, "Tempo d'Italia."

Each one was an adventure, and each was a story in itself. I'll never forget the surprise Imelda Marcos gave me during our Philippine promotion. On April 14, 1983, during an in-store celebration, she took the microphone to sing "Happy Birthday" to me. (It was in fact my birthday. We had celebrated hers the day before in Washington.) Then, she motioned to her ladies-in-waiting to join her. As the band struck up "Hava Nagilah," she started to dance the hora and invited me to join her; I couldn't refuse. It was a night to remember.

But it was in the first projects that we learned our way. With India we learned the logistics of how to do a country promotion; with Israel we discovered how exhibits could enhance a promotion; and with China, everything came together—it was Bloomingdale's at its best.

b

By the mid-sixties Bloomingdale's had mounted several promotions of European merchandise, so I felt it was time we explored the Orient. In 1966 I organized a team to travel to Hong Kong, Thailand, and India. My hope was that we would find the goods around which to plan a theme promotion. When we did, the result was our festival of goods from the Far East called "The Colors of Asia."

The designer Adele Simpson had first urged Lee and me to visit India in the mid-1960s. She was passionate about the country, its art and culture, and her enthusiasm was infectious. We had also become friendly with M. Vardarajan ("Varad"), managing director of India's export corporation for marketing handicrafts. Soon, we found ourselves among a group who shared a love for India that included textile designer Boris Kroll, filmmaker Ismail Merchant, and conductor Zubin Mehta and his wife, Nancy. It made us all the more eager to visit India.

The Indian government was anxious to cooperate with a Bloomingdale's visit, so I suggested and they agreed that Varad accompany us and arrange our itinerary. This was both good and bad. In

January 1966, I organized a team of a dozen Bloomingdale's merchants to visit Delhi, Bombay, and Rajastan. Varad arranged so many lunches, dinners, and official galas that we barely had time to look for products. But he also introduced us to an India that we might not have otherwise seen. (Varad, who has remained a close personal friend, later became India's secretary of culture.)

India was a paradox. While many of the cities were overcrowded and vast numbers of people surged through the streets, it was also one of the most romantic places Lee and I had ever visited.

India is "colorful" in every sense of the word. It is a country of awesome splendor, of music, art, and tradition. The architecture is spellbinding. The majority of women still dressed in traditional saris and wherever we walked, no matter how bleak the surroundings, we were surrounded by a sea of brightly colored fabrics. There was a mystery and mysticism to the country that held us enthralled, but there was also intense poverty.

We found unique products for Bloomingdale's everywhere. The carvings, brassworks, and weavings were extraordinarily beautiful. The craftsmanship, whether woodcarving, jewelry, or hand-blocked prints, was unmatched. I knew a thing or two about carpet weaving from my days as a rug buyer, but to visit the carpet looms of Kashmir was to see masters at work—and the prices were very attractive, too.

Even after we returned to the United States, India remained a strong part of our lives. Lee studied classical Indian dance, Bharata Natyam, and became accomplished in Indian cuisine. I became entranced by the art and culture of India, and we developed a whole circle of Indian friends, both in India and the United States.* I was convinced that Indian goods had a place at Bloomingdale's, so beginning with the 1966 "Colors" import fair, we began to import Indian rugs and furnishings. The business grew steadily and by the late seventies we were doing more than $1 million a year in direct import business with India.

When I suggested, in 1977, that we do an India promotion, how-

* One highlight was when we took our good friends, then Indian ambassador to the U.S. Ali Java Jung and his wife, the Begum, to see *"Oh Calcutta!"* even after we explained it was not about India. They loved it. "Good for the inhibitions" was how he described it in his Oxford English.

ever, there was some concern that production was not up to Western standards. I decided that we would travel again to India to see if there was enough merchandise that could be manufactured to our specifications and delivered on time.

From March 24 to April 17 we visited Delhi, Jaipur, Udaipur, Bombay, Aurangabad, Bangalore, Madras, and Cochin. We had with us eight of the original twelve who had traveled to India in 1966, among them Lee, Barbara D'Arcy, and Carl Levine, and we were astounded by the progress. In 1966, India was a patchwork of cottage industries. In a decade's time, Indian manufacturers—some of whom had been trained by Bloomingdale's buyers—had become far more sophisticated and more accustomed to dealing with the U.S. market and its requirements.

I felt the same excitement that I had in the late 1950s when I first visited Italy. Here was a whole world of goods unknown to most Americans, another opportunity to introduce exclusive imported merchandise with the winning combination of superb craftsmanship at prices that made for excellent value.

The challenge was to explain India to our shoppers. It would not be enough just to present merchandise with backdrops of the Taj Mahal and other tourist sites; we had to bring to Bloomingdale's those things we loved: the sights and smells, the spectacle and mystery. To succeed, I felt we had to take Jed Davidson's theory of searching out the authentic one step further. We would have to bring the authentic India itself to Bloomingdale's. Not the whole country, just the best of it, the part that we missed when away, the part we dreamed about. We decided to call the promotion "India, the Ultimate Fantasy."

To succeed we needed a partner, both to help with the costs and to guide us in Indian cultural matters. In Air India we found both. Over the next year sixty-five buyers made over one hundred trips. Planning also involved eight vice presidents and merchandise managers, plus our display and sales promotion teams. Chota Chudasma, director of public relations for Air India, and Pallavi Shah, his counterpart in New York, helped us assemble the almost thirty dancers, craftsmen, musicians, and artists who performed in the United States as part of the promotion.

In November 1977, I held a press conference to announce that we would be holding our largest promotion to date: We would be selling more than $7 million worth of Indian goods, the largest offering to date of Indian consumer goods in the United States. After that, there was no turning back.

Bloomingdale's traditionally held its import fairs in the fall to lead in to Christmas, but India was announced for spring 1978. This was no accident. We decided that the products, particularly Indian cloths, such as madras and other colorful lightweight fabrics, were better suited to American spring and summer fashions. By holding the promotion in April, we hoped to sell more apparel and seasonal merchandise.

Barbara D'Arcy, skilled at scouting Europe, took Candy Pratts under her wing to merchandise the entire Indian subcontinent. "Bloomingdale's buys India" is how Candy recalls her adventure. The more they traveled, the more inspired they became. The more inspired, the more they had to buy. No Indian artifact was too small, or for that matter too large, for their attention.

As a way to further involve the Indian business community in our project, Bloomingdale's and Air India jointly sponsored a poster competition among Indian ad agencies and artists. The prize went to Annad Zaveri, whose silhouette of a flying elephant surrounded by a brightly colored border became our symbol throughout the store. The flying elephant decorated over half a million shopping bags, our catalog, and mailers.

As we toured the country we had more and more ideas. The colors of India lent themselves to pillows, throws, carpets, Indian furniture. We visited Ahmedabad, the weaving center of India, and had them create special fabrics for us. Everywhere we went, our Indian friends always answered, "Yes, yes." Manufacture? Deliver on time? "Yes, yes." We prayed they understood us.

In India we were also privileged to see a very luxurious world, whether it was staying at Roosevelt House, the American embassy in New Delhi, the palace of the Maharanee of Jaipur or Raj Bhavan, or at the palace of our friend Ali Java Jung, the former ambassador to the United States, now governor of Maharastra province, which includes Bombay. I took note of everything, much as Jed had taught me: the settings, the costumes, the way things were displayed and served. I conferred with Barbara and Candy, with Carl and Lester, with our merchandise managers and buyers. Nothing went to waste.

Because we had decided to put the storewide theme promotions on hold in 1971 to concentrate on other challenges facing the store, we had to return with a large splash. To do "India, the Ultimate Fantasy" in our twelve stores required a larger merchandise commitment and hence a greater financial risk. By 1978 there were Bloomingdale's branches in White Plains, Garden City, and two in Washington, D.C., as well as our home furnishings stores. The stakes were higher in every way.

As we were now promoting a whole country, we decided to launch our promotion with parties in both New York and Washington, the seat of all foreign embassies. I had spent a good deal of time in Washington planning and opening our stores in Tyson's Corner, Virginia, and White Flint, Maryland. Over the years, Lee and I had become friendly with the ambassadors from France, Italy, England, Thailand, Japan, and now India, so we had good friends there.

I learned firsthand that Washington is a town where you have to watch what you say. A few years before, in 1976, as we were about to open the Tyson's Corner store, I was interviewed by the *Washington Star*. They asked a number of good questions about why Bloomingdale's was coming to Washington, about the competition, and what our hopes were. I was evenhanded in my answers. As a parting shot, the reporter asked: "If you were not running Bloomingdale's, what would you like to do?" After making sure I would not offend anyone, I answered that I imagined I would enjoy being ambassador to India. Soon after, the *Star*'s main competitor, *The Washington Post*, ran a blind item that implied that the Traubs were spending all their time hobnobbing around Washington seeking the ambassadorship to India. Lee and I denied it, but the rumor would not die and surfaced a few years later in *The Wall Street Journal*.

S. Dillon Ripley, the Smithsonian's director, shared our love of India and was delighted to work on our promotion. He arranged to exhibit a major collection of Indian costumes, and we decided that the Smithsonian was the perfect beneficiary of our opening night party. We planned a second benefit the following week at the White Flint store for the Capital Children's Museum. It soon became the most involved event we had done. We had a dinner there with Indian ambassador Nani Arheshir Palkhivala and the American ambassador to India, Ken Keating.

Part of my philosophy—part of the Bloomingdale's philosophy

—was to give something back to the community through benefits. So this was an opportunity to help the Smithsonian, an established favorite, and the Children's Museum, a new organization that could never afford to organize the kind of gala we did. Many people take for granted that a Bloomingdale's opening will be a charity benefit, but the beneficiaries never do. Washington was not used to department stores throwing black-tie events; that was more the style of Embassy Row.

While working with the Children's Museum, I met Ann Stock, who had volunteered to organize their public relations and raise funds for them. She is bright, attractive, and extremely well organized. She impressed me immediately. Ann went on to serve as deputy press secretary to Vice President Walter Mondale, after which I hired her to direct Bloomingdale's public relations—first for the Washington area and then as a vice president for all the stores. She worked very closely and traveled extensively with me, and helped to create many memorable promotions. Ann survived the highs and lows of the Campeau era, an enormously demanding time. She now has a new job as White House social secretary.

♭

"India, the Ultimate Fantasy" opened in Washington on April 17. The following evening we launched our 59th Street event. More than a dozen Indian performers and craftsmen demonstrated their talents, including the shadow puppets of Meher Contractor. There was dancing by Mrinalini Sarabhai, whom *The New York Times* called the Martha Graham of India, and Mallika, her Oxford-educated daughter. The first Asian Awareness award was presented to Henry Kissinger. Madame Pandit, Jawaharlal Nehru's sister, was there as well.

We had turned the 59th Street store into a dramatic Indian spectacle. As you entered, you came upon what *The New York Times* called a "musk-scented slice of India." There were life-size papier-mâche camels painted in bright primary colors and covered with small reflecting mirrors. Thirteen new boutiques were set up throughout the store to look like mini-bazaars, one of which was called Shalimar. Everyone got into the act: Our lingerie boutique called itself Intimate India.

For the India promotion, our fashion staff worked with designers such as Donna Karan, Kenzo, and Willi Smith to create exclusive designs using Indian fabrics. Our home furnishings staff imported a collection of new dhurrie and sisal rugs, which we had adapted for the American market. Ralph Lauren created an exclusive Indian menswear collection.

The model rooms were exceptional. Richard Knapple designed seven, each named after a different Indian city and each reflecting a different region. There was the all-white Udaipur room that had to be assembled in pieces in India and reassembled here; the navy blue Delhi room, with the largest bronze Shiva in North America; and the Goa beach house, with rattan furnishing. There was even a solid-silver three-piece seating group for $80,000.

"India, the Ultimate Fantasy" exceeded our wildest expectations. Bloomingdale's was again offering its customers goods they could not purchase elsewhere. Customers who bought Indian relics at Bloomingdale's were as lucky as they were smart: A few years after the promotion, India passed new regulations concerning antiquities. Many of the items we sold would no longer be allowed out of the country.

We did, despite everything, receive some rebukes in the press for celebrating a third-world country plagued by poverty. I understood the criticism but felt it was misplaced. Our promotion was a tremendous benefit to India. The Indian community in the United States, and the Indian business community at home, were very appreciative. We raised their profile, and introduced many of their goods to the American public for the first time.

The India promotion created several new businesses at Bloomingdale's that were to be successful for many years to come. For example, Hy Bayer, our linen buyer, discovered that the round brass ring that Indians use decoratively on the toes of elephants made an ideal napkin ring. We sold them for years. The Indians carved marvelous toy elephants that we mounted on wheels and made into a popular children's toy. One of our greatest successes was in discovering that Indian brass water jugs made great lamp bases.

The Indian government was so appreciative that then prime minister Morarji Desai contacted us to say that he wanted to visit our promotion and convey his thanks personally. He had already scheduled a state visit for June, and asked that we extend our promotion until then. Originally scheduled to close on May 20, we were already planning to extend it, and so decided to prolong it until mid-June.

Prime Minister Desai arrived at Bloomingdale's on June 12, 1978. Although already in his eighties, he brimmed with energy and self-confidence. He often boasted of his continued sexual prowess, the secret of which he said was that he drank a small portion of his own urine daily. A few years earlier in India he had walked away from a terrible plane crash and had since come to believe in his own immortality. Yet for all his grandeur, he toured the store wearing the simplest of Indian cloth, more a mystic than a government leader.

b

We had every reason to believe that a storewide Bloomingdale's promotion of Israel would also be successful. A few years before, in 1973, Bloomingdale's had held a small show of Israeli crafts and goods called "Israel Passage" that was very popular. Bloomingdale's continued afterward to have an ongoing interest in Israel, particularly for knitwear, and we regularly sent our buyers there.

In 1977, shortly after we announced our India promotion, I received a call from Zvi Dinstein, Israel's economic minister, suggesting we mount a promotion of Israeli goods. I thought it was a good idea but said I would first send someone to assess the viability of the promotion. I couldn't go: I was still in the midst of planning the final touches of the Indian promotion. Barbara D'Arcy, for her part, was very involved in the design of our branch stores. So we sent Candy to scout Israel.

When she returned, her report was not favorable.

"It's an awe-inspiring place," Candy said, "but there's nothing to buy there!"

We talked about what made the country so special. Candy had been impressed by the archaeology and the sense of history. She had also been struck, in marked contrast to the timeless scenery, by the cutting-edge quality of Israeli medical and scientific research, as exemplified by facilities like the Weizman Institute.

"Fine," I said. "Now, you're ready to head back to Israel."

"For what?"

"Everything you told me about. That's the Israel we'll promote. Everything you liked, we'll exhibit."

Israel was the most pragmatic nation Bloomingdale's ever

worked with. There was nothing they could not do. They were eager
to develop their tourism and trade and have their products internationally recognized.

I admired the informality of the country. In the United States,
trying to meet with the head of state is no easy task. It is much
simpler in Israel: You call him. His secretary puts you through and
suddenly, it's President Yitzhak Navon asking you to "drop by." Or
—and this I'll never forget—I was on the phone in my room at the
King David Hotel in Jerusalem when the phone operator interrupted:
"Excuse me, it's Teddy calling," she said. Not the mayor or Teddy
Kollek—just Teddy. It's hard to imagine another mayor with such a
personal relationship with his constituents.

I met several times with Israel's then prime minister Menachem
Begin. In sharp contrast to most Israelis, who went about in short-
sleeved open-necked shirts, Begin wore a jacket and tie. Although
formal, he had a very warm side. Our visit coincided with Begin and
Egyptian president Anwar Sadat being awarded the Nobel Peace
Prize. The Bloomingdale's contingent—Peggy Healy from our public relations staff, Lee, Peggy Traub (who was spending a college
year abroad studying at the Hebrew University of Jerusalem),
Candy, and I—were all invited to an impromptu party at his home
the next evening.

Begin's home was simple, filled with knickknacks and pictures
of his children and grandchildren. As the evening wore on, people
drifted in. It was like a family barbecue—simple, friendly, yet an
emotional occasion. Guests started to sing songs from their days as
partisans during World War II, and from the Irgun, the Israeli underground freedom fighters. I was introduced to one of Begin's
friends, a short, vigorous fellow who looked liked a bulldog. That
was Yitzhak Shamir and he was singing, too.

The phone rang. At first, no one went to get it. Finally it was
answered. It was Anwar Sadat on the line calling congratulations. It
was amazing to think of the two great world leaders sharing a cele-
bratory phone call—more amazing still was being in the room when
it occurred.

We photographed all of our advertising in Israel, which gave it a
very authentic look. We also did a catalog there. Dan Reisenger, the
head of an Israeli advertising agency, designed a poster and shop-

ping bag, as well as special tags. His design—a dove and rainbow in the colors of the State of Israel—conveyed the mood of what we called "Israel, the Dream."

As I toured Israel, I became confident that we could develop a wide assortment of both traditional and modern merchandise. My instincts told me that the prices were right, the locale was exotic enough, and the connection for our customers would be so strong that they would each want to leave the store with a souvenir.

With the strength of Gottex, Israel's internationally known swimsuit manufacturer, and Diva, a less well known swimsuit company, we created a beach shop that we dubbed "Elat Shores." We created several other shops: "Jaffa Gate," which carried Beged-Or, the well-known leather goods manufacturer, and "Haifa Port O'Call," a men's shop.

Kal Ruttenstein, our fashion director, felt that we needed a world-class ready-wear designer. In truth, there was none then. However, Kal had seen the work of a local Israeli designer, Ricki Ben Ari, that he admired. Kal went to see her, saying: "You're going to be our world-famous Israeli designer."

Over the course of several months Kal and his team worked closely with Ricki Ben Ari to create a whole line of brightly colored sportswear and separates in lightweight polished cotton. The clothes were manufactured in Israel and shipped to us.

We talked up Ricki to the fashion press and our customers and the excitement started to build. We set a date for her in-store appearance at 59th Street and flew her over. She arrived at Bloomingdale's with great anticipation, but there was one problem: She couldn't find any of her clothes.

She became very nervous. "What's happened?" she asked Kal. "Was there a problem with the manufacturer? Or the shipping?"

"The only problem," Kal told her, "is that your clothes have already sold out!" Ultimately we obtained more from the other stores.

That was the Israel promotion: everything sold out.

The opening was a benefit for the American Friends of the Israel Museum and the American Israeli Cultural Foundation. The Lexington Avenue windows displayed Israeli fashions against a background of Agam lithographs. The turnout was extraordinary: Israeli minister of commerce Gideon Pratt, Israel U.N. ambassador Yehuda Blum, Counsel General Yosef Kedar, and Chaim Herzog. Also in attendance were former New York mayor Abe Beame, former New York State attorney general Louis Lefkowitz, Isaac Stern, and Zubin and Nancy Mehta—Zubin was conductor of the Israeli Philharmonic and the Mehtas were close friends from our India days, as well as good customers.

Our exhibits presented a broad spectrum of Israel's achievement and culture: from the contemporary artworks of Agam to a collection of biblical coins. We had a large display of costumes from the various regions and tribes that once inhabited Israel, from Yemen, Morocco, Bukhara, and Byelorussia. Our exhibit "Synagogues of the Centuries" featured superbly crafted scale models of synagogues throughout the world, including China and South America. We displayed beautiful antique Yemenite jewelry as well as the most modern designs—Israel is one of the world's leading centers for fine jewelry.

People were captivated by the computer display from the Diaspora Museum, an interactive program for learning about Jewish history. There were photo exhibits of the Camp David summit conference as well as an exhibit called "Israel, As She Was." Finally, we had a display of children's paintings of Jerusalem.

The centerpiece of our Israel promotion was, without a doubt, the sarcophagi. While visiting the Israel Museum in Jerusalem I became fascinated with the display of clay sarcophagi, elaborate ancient burial containers from the thirteenth century that had been unearthed at various archaeological sites. We approached the Israel Museum and asked if they would reproduce the clay sarcophagi for us. We worked out a price and they reproduced several that we then had flown over and exhibited in a special presentation reminiscent of the desert where the originals were found. We sold them after the show, and to this day I wonder what even our customers are doing with a six-foot clay sarcophagus.

I was confident that we would sell Israel through exhibits. It was a radical approach—Bloomingdale's never likes to give up selling space—but I was convinced that the more unique the displays, the more visitors we would attract. The increased traffic, I wagered, would stimulate sales and make up for any lost selling space. To hedge my bet, we purchased a smaller amount of merchandise for the Israel promotion than for India—$5 million as opposed to $7 million.

We need not have worried. The exhibit was so popular that we extended it for two weeks beyond its run. We had over 2 million visitors, and the sell-through was very healthy.

All this is, of course, with the benefit of hindsight. At the time, I was already deeply involved in planning what, in many ways, was the most far-ranging country promotion we ever did: China.

b

Bloomingdale's had a long-standing relationship with the Chinese, having opened a Shanghai buying office at the turn of the century that closed in 1947 when the Communists came to power. I thought: What if Bloomingdale's was the first to create a boutique for China? Now that would set us apart. And what if Bloomingdale's unveiled its shop on the same day that the United Nations recognized the People's Republic? That, too, would be a first.

In the summer of 1971, I read that the United Nations was debating the entry of the People's Republic of China into the United Nations, and I saw a great opportunity. The United States did not have trade relations with the People's Republic, but I was well aware that the French did. There were stores on Paris's left bank called Companie Française de L'Orient et de la Chine that sold all manner of Chinese merchandise, from Mao jackets to coolie hats. Bob Meyers, our merchandise manager of housewares, served as a liaison to the owner, François Dautresme. I asked him to find out if François had some Chinese goods we could purchase.

"As a matter of fact," Bob said, "Francois has a ship with a container of goods from China on its way to Marseille."

I was interested. Could he reroute the ship to New York?

Bob said he could, but on one condition: that we buy the whole container.

"Sight unseen?"

That was his condition. All or nothing.

"Done," I said. Then we set about haggling over price.

b

We had just about put the finishing touches on the plans for our shop when we heard that the Chinese delegation was en route to the U.N. to present its credentials. Accordingly, we announced that we would open our Chinese boutique on the same day as the vote.

"China Passage" opened on October 6, 1971. Our boutique was a mélange of merchandise: baskets, brooms, whisks, trays and straw objects, fish tanks and back scratchers. We carried blue Mao suits and caps. We realized that the blue dye bled when worn; but even that we turned into an asset: We advertised that the suits were "guaranteed to bleed."

Now that the Chinese delegation had finally come to New York, I invited them, of course, to do as many foreign dignitaries before them had done: come to Bloomingdale's. We invited them to have lunch at the store and view the new shop. What a thought: Chinese Communists at Bloomingdale's! Devoted Maoists lunching in the very cathedral of consumerism. China, once called "the sleeping giant," had been cut off from the world. There was great curiosity about its people, politics, and culture. And they, in turn, were very cautious toward the West. The U.N. vote, their shop, their presence —all created tremendous excitement at Bloomingdale's.

U.S. and Chinese relations proceeded apace, with President Nixon's visit to China soon after. The following year the United States and China resumed trade relations. However, not everyone could do business in the People's Republic—you had to be invited. We asked, and the People's Republic sent an invitation for Bloomingdale's to attend the Canton Trade Fair.

I sent Carl Levine to make the initial contacts. We knew that China would be very strong in rug-making and porcelains, but we hoped to have merchandise made-to-order. Although the Canton Fair offered everyone the same products, Bloomingdale's prided itself on developing goods that best suited our customers, and on garnering exclusives. That, we knew, would take time.

The Chinese, interestingly enough, also believed trade status was relationship-driven. During one of his first visits, Carl tried to buy some lacquered bamboo at the Canton Fair. They wouldn't sell him any. "That's for our special friends," Carl was told politely. "We haven't known you long enough." Beginning in 1975, however, merchants from Bloomingdale's were allowed to explore beyond

Canton, to Shanghai and Beijing. Throughout the 1970s we sent our key merchants to buy furniture, gifts, and jewelry.

In the mid-seventies we first approached the Chinese about doing an event with the participation of the People's Republic. They declined politely. I had the sense, however, that with the Chinese "no" was just the first step toward "yes." So I continued to approach them from the highest diplomatic levels to those contacts we made at the Canton Fair. All to no avail.

In 1978, however, Ralph Lazarus, Federated's chairman, was invited to visit China. He, too, was impressed by what he saw. He knew I had been negotiating with China for several years, and he again raised the subject of Bloomingdale's doing a China event. Much to Ralph's surprise, not only were they familiar with Bloomingdale's, but they expressed interest in exhibiting their goods in the United States.

By 1978, I had become chairman of Bloomingdale's, succeeding Larry Lachman. I invited the Chinese to our promotions of India and Israel. They did not accept officially, but I learned later that they did visit, because they showed themselves to be very familiar with the store and its promotions. In early 1979 they invited me to bring a group to China to discuss the possibility of a joint promotion.

Julian Tomchin, fashion director for home furnishings; Dennis Wong, head of our Hong Kong buying office, and his wife; Lee; and I traveled that spring to Beijing. We were met there by Woo Shu Dong, from Chinatex, the Chinese National Textile Export Corporation, who was to be our official host. We toured many of the major cities, including Soochow and Hangchow. Julian was the official chronicler of the trip, taking photos and sketching all we saw that might inspire a promotion. By the trip's end, I was convinced that we could mount an extraordinary promotion.

b

During the first week of July, I negotiated an official agreement with the Ministry of Foreign Trade for a merchandise fair. I insisted the agreement be in writing. This appealed to the Chinese officials, who liked fanfare and formal documents, but doing so added several days to the negotiations. Some of the Chinese representatives were reluctant to sign their names to the document. There was a general feeling that Beijing officials had signed too many contracts already with the West, and that some already needed to be renegotiated or delayed. We continued, however, to meet over banquets and toast with Mao-tais, the fiery Chinese liqueur. Finally, I think we agreed that it was better to sign the agreement before either side passed out. We concluded our negotiations on the Fourth of July 1979, and our joint document is dated as such. The actual signing, however, was postponed until the following evening at, what else, a banquet.

On the evening of July 5, 1979, we gathered in one of Beijing's formal banquet halls. I signed as chairman for Bloomingdale's. Chairman Marvin had a particularly nice ring to it in China. The agreement stated quite boldly that "Bloomingdale's will endeavor to mount the largest exhibition ever done in the United States of China, its merchandise, its products and its people," and went on to say that Bloomingdale's would do so in all its branch stores, detailing the various types of merchandise, and our commitment to advertising as well as direct-mail promotions.

For their part, the Chinese agreed to cooperate with the buyers and adhere strictly to delivery dates for both samples and final shipments, notifying our Hong Kong office should there be any delays. Keeping close tabs on shipments was something we learned from our promotion of India.

The signing was followed by an eight-course banquet that featured white fungus soup and Peking duck. After many more Mao-tai-fueled toasts, we got down to the business of making it all happen.

Fox Butterfield, writing from Beijing for *The New York Times*, did a major story about the agreement and that launched our publicity efforts. What made our agreement singularly newsworthy was that it was signed a few days before the United States concluded its trade negotiations. The U.S. agreement granted China "most favored nation" status and a significant reduction in tariff barriers on its imports to the United States.

Again, we were first. That we were negotiating ahead of the U.S. government led me to make the now oft-repeated claim that "Bloomingdale's may be the only store anywhere with an independent foreign policy."

I have always felt that business is a bridge between countries, and that even though the Chinese were Communists, as we built ties we were promoting international understanding. Bloomingdale's, as I saw it, was an agent for developing greater understanding between the Chinese Communists and the United States. It's easier for businessmen to talk about a common problem—for example, making a great-looking sweater—than for countries to discuss their bilateral relations. A successful business enterprise can become a bond between two nations.

To prepare for the promotion, I organized a group of thirty Bloomingdale's buyers, merchandise managers, and fashion directors to travel, en masse, to China. Our large group of eager, curious, and demanding executives went into the workrooms, factories, warehouses, and export corporations and saw an incredible array of merchandise. We visited stores geared for export and the People's Stores, where the Chinese themselves shopped.

We were taken to see the No. 1 department store in Shanghai, which is almost half the size of the Bloomingdale's 59th Street store, but very spartan. In its pre-Communist heyday it must have been very impressive, but it was now more functional than glorious. There were escalators, but they hadn't run in years. No display, only racks. When we entered everybody froze and stared at us. Many of the products represented enormous skill, but they were not in very good taste. I was convinced, however, that given the opportunity to work together with the Chinese, we could create the most extraordinary collection of merchandise Bloomingdale's had ever shown.

In 1979 the streets of Beijing were jammed with bicycles and most of the women wore gray Mao suits. As in India, we discovered that our hosts were more interested in banquets than work. In Beijing and Shanghai, people worked from nine to twelve. We would then have a two-hour break for lunch. I introduced the concept of the working lunch to our friends. It quickly became a working banquet, after which work would resume until five, when we would adjourn for another meal. We never really knew what we were eating at these feasts, and we preferred not to know. An orangelike soda was the drink of choice, unless we were toasting, and then we had to down large quantities of Mao-tais.

We learned that doing business in China was different from anything we had ever experienced before. Not only did we have to deal with the manufacturers, but there were also the various levels of the Chinese Communist bureaucracy. There was no actual plant owner. Each factory was run by government-controlled committees, and each committee reported to a government-controlled corporation, which in turn had its own leading representative.

Compared to China, our promotions of India and Israel were nothing but dry runs. During 1979 and 1980, Bloomingdale's merchants took more than 150 trips to China. All the while, our senior management, fashion offices' executives, and key buyers worked extensively with the corporations in China to bring this full-scale promotion into commercial reality.

b

One of the real heroes of the China promotion was Julian Tomchin. Julian, who at that point had been associated with the store for almost a decade, had just been appointed fashion director for home furnishings (today he is senior vice president at Fieldcrest). He was our eyes and ears, traveling around the country sketching ideas, finding the sources and working to execute our plans.

The real test, however, was educating the Chinese to our taste. Many of their products, while beautifully made, would never sell to our customers, so we had to educate them painstakingly about our needs. China has a very old culture. At the same time, because of the revolution, the Chinese saw themselves as a new country, one with great conflicts about its past. This worked to our advantage, making them more receptive to developing new products.

We sought out existing merchandise that reflected the diverse life of the people of China. Combing the People's Stores we bought the flap-eared fur and leather caps that are worn at rakish angles or with solemn precision by the bicycling workers; the quilted and padded worker coats in somber blues and greens and browns; the ponchos; the vivid jogging suits; the bright long underwear; the Shanghai, Canton, and Beijing T-shirts.

We searched out traditional products as well. Silk brocades and embroideries in jackets and robes and skirts were translated into American evening apparel. Fabrics were re-created into ready-to-wear for day and evening: cashmere for sweaters; silk for evening and intimate wear; corduroy for sportswear and menswear.

Goose down was on many buyers' lists. The bedding group

looked for comforters, the apparel division searched out jackets and coats made in both practical and new elegant editions. One buyer, Amy Wall, whose trips established a healthy rapport with the Chinese, handed one of her factory workers a sketch of a quilted down bootie that soon landed on six thousand American feet. Amy was nicknamed "the Great Wall" by her new Chinese friends.

Clearly, what was going to help sell much of our goods was the pricing. The Chinese, with 900 million skilled hands, could produce quality goods that were always priced below market. We showed them catalogs, including our provocative 1976 lingerie catalog "Sighs and Whispers." They were a bit shocked at first, but very quickly they picked up the ideas. We developed a beautiful silk nightgown that retailed for $130; had we produced it in Europe it would have sold for $300.

As we were learning the Chinese market, we helped our Chinese friends to understand the desires of the vast American market—far different from the markets in which they had been trading. The Chinese were used to working with importers who shipped large quantities at a low price. We demanded a higher standard. In doing so, we opened the routes for many of our retail colleagues.

For example, we commissioned wonderful home furnishings of bamboo and rattan at very reasonable prices. Until then, rattan had been used primarily for outdoor furniture. Bloomingdale's led the way in designing rattan couches, chairs, beds, and side tables for the home. Our oversized bamboo couches were a huge best-seller for years to come.

Some other great successes were in snapping up a batch of Beijing Hotel laundry bags and shocking pink satin baseball jackets for boys. They ended up selling very well. At higher price points, we came across an exquisite cache of freshwater pearls, jade adornments, antique boxes and bibelots, cutwork lace table accoutrements, cloisonné objects, porcelains, fans, and scrolls. Not to mention chocolate and ginger crisp candies and crunchy chocolate biscuits.

b

One day I was taken with Lester and Barbara to the Palace Museum in Beijing, also known as the Forbidden City. The Palace Museum is the former palace of the emperors of the Ming and Qing dynasties.

The palace occupies 250 acres of land in the heart of Beijing. It is the largest and best preserved group of ancient buildings in China today, with a total of more than nine thousand rooms. Surrounding it is a wall more than thirty-five feet high and a moat more than 150 feet wide. In the center stand the three Great Halls where the emperors performed official ceremonies and held audiences with their officials. It was there we met a man who would be very important to the Bloomingdale's China promotion, Mr. Peng Yei.

Mr. Peng (pronounced Pung), a very old and wizened gentleman, was the curator of the museum. He led us to the Queen's apartment where he served us tea. It was a very large room, filled with dark lacquered Chinese furniture, beautiful screens, and a sofa covered with dark silk damask cushions.

At one point, to impress us, he brought out some of the Imperial robes of China. These were breathtaking creations worn by emperors and empresses that had rarely been seen in China and never exhibited outside the country. We were, Mr. Peng told us, very privileged to see them.

After our meeting, I turned to Lester and said, "Let's see if we can get those robes for Bloomingdale's."

"But they'd never let them leave the country," Lester said.

"I'm sure that if you speak to Mr. Peng, they'll do it," I said and left the project in Lester and Barbara's capable hands.

What followed was an elaborate ritual that involved Lester and Barbara drinking large quantities of tea over several days with Mr. Peng. The first day they spoke about everything but the costumes. Mr. Peng was fascinated by what Barbara and Lester did and the way they ran their businesses. The next day, Lester mentioned that they would really love to display the robes at Bloomingdale's. Mr. Peng said that would be impossible as the robes never left their vaults. The day after he revealed that, in fact, we had never been shown the real robes—the ones we had seen were the display ones. The true Imperial robes were in the vault, and had not been out for years. Mr. Peng then stood and motioned to Barbara and Lester to follow him. Shrugging to each other, they hurried after their host.

Mr. Peng led them down to the rooms where the costumes were kept in a very advanced temperature-controlled, humidified room. The robes themselves were housed in individual coffinlike structures, folded in tissue with nonglare paper. They were in pristine condition and were exquisite.

Mr. Peng was in a playful mood. He moved excitedly about the room, lecturing at the same time. Then he did something quite extraordinary. He selected one of the robes and motioned for Barbara to try it on, which she did—this was a rare honor. Then he encouraged Barbara to strut about in it. Barbara did, like a fashion model, and everyone suddenly erupted in laughter.

Mr. Peng then led Barbara and Lester back to the Queen's apartment for more tea. By this time Lester's bladder was about to burst, but it had been worth it. Mr. Peng came across the room, shook hands with Barbara and Lester, and said, "I would be very honored for Bloomingdale's to exhibit these priceless treasures from China's Forbidden City." Therefore he would loan Bloomingdale's twenty of the Imperial robes. Of course, we would have to protect the robes as a national treasure. Lester agreed immediately—and then ran for the nearest rest room.

When I met Lester that evening at the hotel in Beijing, I asked about his progress on the robes. "We got them!" he said, smiling.

"Great!" I said. I never doubted it.

We agreed to a unique set of arrangements for the robes. A representative of the Palace Museum would accompany the robes at all times. Guards would meet them at the airport, accompany the robes to Bloomingdale's, and watch them twenty-four hours a day. We agreed to build individual hermetically sealed temperature-controlled display cases for the costumes. We made arrangements for the lighting, as well as the room temperature. In every respect, we promised museum-quality standards. Now all I had to do, as chairman of Bloomingdale's, was find a way to pay for it.

b

The China promotion was our most complex ever. Early on, I realized that just dealing with the technical aspects of the promotions, finding underwriters, making arrangements for the exhibits and cultural performers, was a full-time job in itself. I needed someone I could trust to carry out some of the complicated negotiations involved. I also needed someone I felt comfortable with, someone I could bounce ideas off of and then trust to execute them. What

I needed, I realized, was someone like Joan Glynn. Better yet, I needed Joan herself.

After leaving Bloomingdale's in 1974, Joan had gone to Simplicity, and from there back to advertising at Wells Rich and Greene, and then to *Esquire*. In 1979, *Esquire* was sold to Chris Whittle and Philip Moffit. I understood that her future there was uncertain; I called her.

"Joan, come home," I said. And she did, rejoining us as vice president for public relations and special events. Bloomingdale's had grown since she had left. As there were extraordinary costs to this promotion, among Joan's duties was to find sponsors and underwriters for the event—not the traditional work of a department store public relations executive.

Joan delivered, as always, rounding up an impressive list of partners. Mobil underwrote the costs of exhibiting the costumes, around $250,000; sponsored our Washington gala; and helped with advertising and promotion. Pan American provided air transportation and advertising. Murjani sponsored several of the craftsmen. American Express, Revlon, Eastman Kodak, and Tsingtao Beer all helped underwrite cultural exhibits from museums.

We still needed to come up with a theme for the China promotion. "Bloomingdale's" had been translated phonetically into Chinese as "Boo Ming Dai." The Chinese translation consisted of three letters. When we discovered that the pictograph of the symbols could be roughly translated as "Heralding the Dawn of a New Era," Joan seized upon that as the theme for the China promotion. We were entering the eighties; the Chinese were joining the West. It was the right slogan.

We then held a poster competition among Chinese ad agencies, just as we had in India and Israel. Our prize-winning poster, designed by an artist from a Shanghai advertising agency, incorporated a bold representation of China's Great Wall. The fall 1980 shopping bag was also based on the design. Joan and I agreed that the Great Wall, stretching fifteen hundred miles across the north of China, had come to symbolize this vast land.

b

Now we had to recast Bloomingdale's and all its branch stores as Chinese emporiums. We created a Chinese marketplace. Saturday's

Generation, our metro level shop for casual men and women's clothes, became "The People's Store," selling Beijing T-shirts and down vests; the men's shop became "Warriors of Sian" with cashmere and knits; lingerie became "The Palace of Eternal Spring"; Young World became "The Children's Palace." "Three Pools That Mirror the Moon," inspired by the garden city of Hangzhou, was the name for one shop filled with elegant accoutrements, from handknit cashmere to antique embroidered robes and jewelry. "Liulichang Street" on the fifth floor was a re-creation of Beijing's famous street of antiques and was filled with unique procelains, paintings, and scrolls.

Two gigantic Foo dogs flanked the entrance to our model rooms, called "The Six Worlds of China." The rooms included a farmhouse in Canton with bamboo ladders and brooms leaning against the walls and giant baskets everywhere; a traditional bedroom, inspired by Beijing, with intricately carved chairs and side tables and a canopy bed and a beautiful chinoiserie armoire; a striking black bedroom with gold accents inspired by Shanghai; a modern library with a view of the harbor in Hong Kong; a glitzy Chinatown loft; and a dramatic scarlet room inspired by Beijing's Forbidden City.

We exhibited Ming and Tang dynasty scrolls from the Shanghai Museum of Art and History; antiques on loan from the Brooklyn Museum included a twelfth-century bronze ritual vessel from the Shang dynasty, an intricately carved seventeenth-century jade mountain, a Ming-dynasty jade gong, and an eighth-century glazed pottery tomb horse from the Tang dynasty. Throughout the store were exhibits of double embroidery, calligraphy, basket weaving, and demonstrations by lace makers and rug weavers. The faces and people of China were reflected in twelve photo exhibits on display throughout the store.

I was right about the robes: They were the centerpiece of the promotion. We installed the twenty ceremonial robes of Beijing's imperial court, spanning the period from 1795 to 1908, on the fifth floor. People lined up to weave their way through the exhibit. Again we were presenting at 59th Street something that our customers had never seen before. That the Imperial robes had never left China, and that when the Chinese decided to let the West view them they chose Bloomingdale's, signaled, once again, that Bloomingdale's was unique. The Imperial robes created such a sensation that they prompted Grace Mirabella to call me "the Sol Hurok of retailing."

b

And of course, there was an opening event. On September 24, 1980, a Chinese banquet was held to benefit UNICEF. Leonard Woodcock, the U.S. ambassador to China, flew in for the event, as did Chai Zemin, the Chinese ambassador to the United States. Hugh Downs was there in his capacity as chairman of the U.S. Committee for UNICEF; there was an unscheduled speech by Senator Jacob Javits, who was running hard for reelection on the liberal ticket (he lost). New York's most famous Chinese food aficionado, Mayor Ed Koch, was present along with Tom Brokaw, Zandra Rhodes, Hermione Gingold, Marc Bohan, Letitia Baldridge in a silk kimono, Adele Simpson in gold embroidery and about twelve hundred others.

We had a marching band on Third Avenue playing John Philip Sousa, and a choir of Chinese children, the Seward Park High School Chinese Culture Club Chorus, serenading the arrivals. Many of our friends from China flew in for the event including Mr. Wang Mingjun, director of Chinatex, and China's finance minister Wang Binquian, and Peng Yei, our friend from the Palace Museum. A member of the Chinese dance company did a ribbon dance on one shirt counter, a three-piece orchestra played in the men's department, and dancers performed throughout the cosmetics department. The evening raised $60,000 for UNICEF.

The China promotion was carried by all fifteen of our stores. We had major openings in New York, Washington, and Boston, each benefiting a different Chinese-American group. The White Plains store had an actual Chinese junk on display. The Imperial robes traveled from New York to Washington, where they were exhibited in our White Flint store.

More than anything, it was the merchandise that made the event, the ability of our buyers to see new markets for goods that made the difference. For example, the ginger jar with the double happiness sign sold only in the People's Stores, but we recognized that priced at $25 we could sell thousands of them. We sold thousands more by using them as lamp bases. They're still selling today. The jar wasn't designed by us—its grace and beauty owe everything to the Chinese—but it was our eye that saw in it the marketing opportunity and the way to merchandise it.

Our original agreement with the Chinese stipulated that we would help the Chinese organize a comprehensive exhibit of their goods. We did so at the New York Coliseum, creating and stocking our own shop of made-to-order merchandise. The exhibition became the grand finale of our promotion of Chinese goods.

The China festival cost $2.5 million, and we filled our stores with $14 million worth of merchandise. In our agreement with the Chinese, we had predicted that 4 million people would visit the stores during the promotion. When it was over, we estimated that more than 11 million people had come to Bloomingdale's. Consequently, we also had good financial news to report. Sales for the season were up 13.5 percent over the previous year.

The China promotion was widely covered by the news media, receiving more than 415 pages of news and feature stories in newspapers and magazines, plus some key television coverage on local and national news and CNN. The *Times* ran several features about the merchandise and the promotion. Many magazines did features on the merchandise we carried. *New York* magazine, for example, had us in their "best bets" column. We received 210,823 lines of publicity, or more than two hundred pages, for the branch stores alone, and 237,514 for the New York store.

For Bloomingdale's, China was more than a country promotion. We had no way of knowing the tremendous appetite that Americans would have for China, its goods and culture, but once again, we were in the right place at the right time. The message we were sending to our customers was that so much coincidence was no accident. We would send our buyers and executives to the ends of the earth to provide distinctive goods for our stores; that when it comes to merchandising and visual display, when it comes to generating traffic, no one could outdo us. Finally, China, underlined that, as I told *People* magazine, "From time to time, it's appropriate to do something that demonstrates that Bloomingdale's is more than a store."

*"By the authority vested in me by Bloomingdale's,
how may I help you?"*

Drawing by P. Steiner; © 1989 The New Yorker Magazine, Inc.

CHAPTER 8

The Dream Factory

N o space in a department store produces more dollars per square foot than the cosmetics department. Cosmetics, including fragrance, is an area where packaging, positioning, and advertising are paramount—it is pure marketing. As Charles Revson once said, "In the factory we make cosmetics; in the store we sell hope."

In the apparel or home furnishings departments, the buyer is a creative force in product development. In cosmetics, it is the vendors who provide the products. Yet the cosmetics companies still need the department stores to provide the customers and the proper selling environment to reach their target audience.

Cosmetics and fragrance first came of age in the 1960s. The freedom of the sixties—the sexual revolution—created an atmosphere of experimentation. People tried new hairdos, new clothes, and some even tried drugs, and this search for self carried over into the seventies and eighties. Customers were willing to try new things, including new creams and fragrances. By the 1980s, the cosmetics industry was booming. Coupled with the maturation of cosmetics companies into sophisticated marketing forces, once-small companies became million- and billion-dollar ventures.

Does a woman buy cosmetics because she's in the store, or does she go to the store to buy cosmetics? It all depends on whether you ask the department stores or the cosmetics companies. Each would like to believe that they are the motivating factor. And at various points in the history of the cosmetics industry, one or the other has had the upper hand. But the truth is that they each need the other. At Bloomingdale's, we sought to give customers a reason to buy their favorite brands at our store, and we sought to give the cosmetics companies a reason to view Bloomingdale's as the best environment in which to sell their product. If cosmetics companies sold fantasy, we set out to be the dream factory. To do this, we developed relationships with the cosmetic and fragrance company presidents, many of whom were larger-than-life figures.

When I became executive vice president in 1962, I quickly saw the growth potential in cosmetics. The demographics were in our favor. In 1950, less than 20 percent of our female customers worked. Over the next four decades that number would almost quadruple. As women joined the work force, the issue of how they looked during the day and at night, at business lunches and dinners, boosted the cosmetics industry to exponential growth in sales and earnings. I was convinced that cosmetics would soon be one of the most important businesses in the store.

Cosmetics operate like no other business in a department store. Because we can return cosmetics that do not sell, our gross margin is very close to our initial mark-up—40 percent. Cosmetics companies participate with the store in almost every aspect of the selling process: They contribute to the costs of the space, they often use their own selling specialists, and they pay a portion of the salaries of the salespeople. They also usually share in the cost of advertising and promotion. Cosmetics offer lower overhead. Although the margins are lower than for other goods, the profits are often much greater and the productivity per foot is very high.

To give you some idea of the costs involved, take, for example, a lipstick that retails for $15.00: the cost of the raw materials is around $1.20; with labor and overhead, the expense rises to $1.60; and the store buys it for $9.00. The cosmetic company receives $7.40, which can be divided among the cost of selling, advertising, marketing, displaying, et cetera, plus profit; the department store receives $6.00 as its share, which covers distribution, their share of advertising and selling expenses, as well as salaries, overhead, and profit.

Over the years, productivity has improved, and so has cosmetics' share of a store's total business. In the fifties, cosmetics, including fragrance, was probably 5 percent of a store's business. Today, in a well-run operation, cosmetics can represent 9 or 10 percent of a store's entire business while it probably occupies roughly 5 percent of the store's selling space.

b

When I was growing up, the grande dame of American cosmetics was Helena Rubinstein—or Madame Rubinstein, as she was called. Born in Poland, she had already found success in Australia and England before arriving in the United States in 1915 with her home-made creams. Helena Rubinstein had opened the London branch of her Salon de Beauté Valaze in 1908, and announced herself as the World's Greatest Beauty Culturist. As far as cosmetics were con-cerned, Madame claimed the wisdom of the ages. In her 1930 book, *The Art of Feminine Beauty*, Madame Rubinstein explained that to create her rouges and lipsticks, "I haunted the art galleries of Lon-don to study the various shades of coloring in the portraits. . . . I also went to France, Spain, and Italy, and, finally, India, Egypt, and other tropical countries to learn more about the preparation and use of decorative cosmetics."

Madame Rubinstein was a terrific saleswoman and a great copywriter. There was something of the poet and artist about her that, together with her business sense, made for a formidable com-bination.

By the 1940s, Madame had over six hundred items in her line— 78 powders, 62 creams, 69 lotions, 115 lipsticks, 46 perfumes and toilet waters, and a variety of rouges, eyeshadows, and mascaras, including Aquadade foundation and Town and Country face powder.

Long before anyone else, Madame Rubinstein knew the value of dramatic department store events. For her perfume Heaven Sent, five hundred wicker baskets with a vial of the cologne, held aloft by five hundred balloons decorated with pink and blue angels, were dropped from the roof of Bonwit Teller.

By the early sixties, when I first became responsible for the cosmetics department, Helena Rubinstein was no longer a major factor at the store. However, one day in 1964, I received a phone call from Madame herself. She had seen the model rooms a number of times and very much admired Bloomingdale's. She wanted to meet Barbara D'Arcy and me. Would we come to lunch at her apart-ment? Would we? Barbara couldn't be more excited. Madame Ru-binstein's apartment was legendary.

The story goes that in 1941, when Madame first tried to rent the eight-bath, twenty-six-room penthouse triplex at Park Avenue and 64th Street, she was refused because she was Jewish. So she bought the building and installed herself in the penthouse. After her death, the building converted to cooperative ownership.

Barbara and I were shown into the living room by a butler; Madame awaited us there with her nephew Oscar Kolin at her side. She sat in the center of the room surrounded by Picassos and African art as we entered, and she rose to greet us. She was dressed in a bright muumuu, and was wearing heavy bracelets. Her hair was pulled back away from her face and combed into a chignon. The total effect was quite dramatic.

We were served cocktails, then out of the blue, she turned to me and said, "What do you think of my complexion?"

I was startled. It was an unusual way to start a conversation.

"I think it's very special," was all I could say on the spot. Looking closely at her, however, it was true her complexion was beautiful.

"I'm ninety-one years old," she said, "and it's only because I use the special skin treatment that I developed in Australia. Isn't that so, Oscar?"

Miss Rubinstein used her nephew to punctuate all of her remarks. Throughout the rest of her conversation, outlining all of her various projects, she would turn to her nephew and say, "Isn't that so, Oscar?" To which he would nod.

We never got around to talking about the model rooms. But she gave us the impression that she thought the model rooms showed a certain level of taste, and that, perhaps, executives with taste might understand her products better than others—and therefore make a greater commitment to her products.

Madame was very competitive. Throughout most of her career her great rival was Elizabeth Arden. According to one story, the extent of their competition was such that in 1938 Arden hired away Rubinstein's sales manager. The following year Madame hired Miss Arden's ex-husband and general manager. In the 1960s, though, Revlon was the dominant force, and Madame Rubinstein was interested in finding out as much as she could about his business and what she could do to compete.

We were served an elegant luncheon in her dining room decorated with Italian baroque furniture. Then she took us on a tour of the apartment. On the main floor were the public rooms filled with French antiques; one floor below were the bedrooms. Madame's own bedroom featured a Lucite bed that she had had designed and built by Ladislas Medgyes, her package designer. The bed was lit by hidden fluorescent bulbs, giving the effect of a heavenly sleigh. If this was not unusual enough, she showed us one room and said, "This was the bedroom of my late husband, Prince Gourielli [Artchil Gourielli-Tchkonia was a prince of Russian Georgia]. He died ten years ago, but I have maintained it just as when he lived."

We reached the third floor by a spiral staircase. The ceiling was vaulted, and gold spiral Spanish columns framed one window. The walls were lined with paintings, including works by Modigliani, Picasso, and Braque. African icons were lined across the fireplace mantel.

Madame was famous for always speaking her mind. One example occurred when I admired the art in the penthouse.

"This isn't great art," she said dismissively. "I keep the really good art in my home in Israel. This," she said with a flip of her thin wrist, "is dreck."

She was an outrageous character with a tremendous force of personality. Barbara and I returned to the store, saying we would never forget that lunch. Within the year, Helena Rubinstein was dead and her company fell into disarray. It was owned briefly by Max Factor, then purchased in the late 1980s by L'Oreal, which has plans to relaunch Helena Rubinstein products in the United States and Europe.

b

Before the 1950s, most retailers bought directly from a factory and there were few branded cosmetics in any store. To the consumer, the name of the store was important, not the manufacturer. In 1960, for example, the largest cosmetic brand in Macy's was Macy's Own, made in the store's cosmetics factory by their own chemists. Back then, Scruggs Vandervort and Barney, a St. Louis store, sold the best-selling hand cream in the United States, and one of the most popular toiletries was John Wanamaker's hard-water soap. As for Bloomingdale's, our largest revenues in the cosmetics department then came not from creams but from our own brand of facial and toilet tissue. That was what women came to the Bloomingdale's cosmetics department for.

The cosmetic industry of the 1950s was a small world. There were many small independent cosmetic makers, each with only one brand and little control over their customer. Their business depended almost exclusively on their relationship with the store. The two exceptions were the great marketing forces of their day: Revlon, under the direction of Charles Revson, and Lanvin, under the direction of Edward Counard.* They were the only ones who could control the distribution of their products. All the others had to depend very much on personal relationships. Cosmetic companies then did not deal with store principals, but with the buyers, most of whom had been in their jobs for twenty or thirty years.

Slowly, however, individual brands began to gain consumer acceptance. And the day the first customer came in asking for a specific brand of cream was the day the business changed. Power began to move out of the hands of the stores and into those of the cosmetics manufacturers. Companies that could create customer loyalty such as a Revlon or an Estée Lauder came to dominate the market. They had the power—the customer. At the same time, those cosmetic companies that served small regional stores were edged out by national marketers. In the 1950s, there were probably thirty cosmetic companies; two decades later there were less than a dozen. Only the strongest would survive and when I started to learn the cosmetic business, the strongest was Charles Revson's Revlon.

b

Charles Revson was once quoted as saying he didn't meet competition, he crushed it.

In the early sixties, Revlon and Lauder tried to dominate the department store business. Each would have liked to have the whole

---

* Lanvin had become famous as a fragrance company under the direction of Counard, who invented the phrase "Promise her anything but give her Arpege"; in 1961, when they merged with Charles of the Ritz, under the direction of Dick Salomon, they became a powerful cosmetics-fragrance company and strengthened their position in department stores.

field to themselves, or at least 50 percent with the other excluded. I set a goal that Revlon *and* Lauder should not represent, combined, more that 50 percent of our business. That put pressure on our buyers to make other lines keep pace with the growth of Revlon and Lauder.

Charles Revson did not care for our policy, and the message was passed along by his sales force, but I stayed the course. Still, Mr. Revson came to the store for special events. One day in around 1963, I got a call to come to his offices for a luncheon. Being summoned for a private lunch with Charles Revson was considered an honor for a young merchant.

The Revlon offices were then at 666 Fifth Avenue—they moved to the General Motors building later. The whole setting was out of a movie version of an executive office—all dark paneling and classic English furniture. Mr. Revson had a very opulent dining room with a beautiful dining table. There was even a gold telephone on a table just to his right.

Charles Revson sat at one end of the table. He was handsome with dark features, tightly drawn, as if he might at any moment explode. I sat at the other end. In the middle sat Mike Blumenfeld, our cosmetics buyer, and Joe Anderer, Revlon's then president.

Mr. Revson began by telling me that he had hired one of the world's finest chefs from one of the better-known New York restaurants to prepare our lunch. We were having steak, he said, and I settled back in anticipation.

The meal came. Mr. Revson was smiling a thin smile. "Go on, please," he said. I cut in with great expectation. The meat was tasteless. Mr. Revson explained, as he ate his meal with gusto, that he believed, for health reasons, that steak should be well done without any seasoning.

Although the food was bland, the conversation was anything but. Over lunch, he took me back over his career. How he had sold nail enamel for another firm. How in 1932, along with his brother and a friend named Charles Lachman, he had started Revlon in the back room of an office on West 45th Street. Their initial outlay was $300 for a batch of nail enamel. Three years later, Revlon was grossing $68,000. After the war he had begun making lipsticks using shell casings for containers.

At that time lipsticks came in a limited selection of shades. Revson introduced color. The company's great success came in the early 1950s when he convinced women to match their nail enamel to their lipstick. Charles Revson's great talent was what is called "sell-in"—that is, creating the need for a new product.

In early 1952, Revson sensed that American women, constrained by postwar America, wanted a sense of glamour and passion. Revlon decided to launch a lush and deep-red lipstick that suggested, in the immortal words of their advertising copy, "the rich red of rubies and the expensive glamour of diamonds," or, as they named it, "Fire and Ice."

In November 1952, window displays for the new product appeared in nine thousand department stores, drugstores, and beauty salons. Simultaneously, newspaper advertisements appeared with the "Fire and Ice girl," a dark-haired model named Suzy Parker in a silver sequin dress with a scarlet wrap, "the 1952 American Beauty with a foolproof formula for melting a male." The result was the largest sales volume Revlon had ever achieved for a single color. *Business Week* estimated that in 1952 Revlon's product line grossed $25 million in seventy three countries.

Throughout the 1950s and into the sixties, Revlon color promotions dominated the cosmetics industry. Its sales were never dependent on department stores, which were only a small and not very profitable part of their business. But it had prestige, and that was important to Revlon and Charles Revson.

"Now that you understand everything about me and Revlon," Charles said, "you should understand my demands for more space on the Bloomingdale's floor. It is important to me. Personally."

I can no longer recall the specifics of his demands. I only remember that I thought they were unreasonable and told him so. It was a poor choice of words. Because Revson, who until that moment had been genial, started shouting at me.

I stood my ground—and I learned an important lesson. I learned that the best way to deal with Mr. Revson was to shout back. We argued for the rest of the meeting. At its conclusion, we both agreed we had important mutual interests and called a truce, and were on far more cordial terms from then on.

b

Meanwhile, Estée Lauder was coming into her own. Estée's success owes something to the fact that Revson never thought much of her, and by the time he should have, it was too late. I always enjoyed Estée. She's a brilliant businesswoman who lives in two worlds: the business world, where she has been a formidable success, and a society world that she also enjoys, be it in Palm Beach, the French Riviera, or entertaining in her double town house in New York.

In Estée you see the first generation original. Her determination and dedication is unparalleled; she is a salesperson par excellence. Her son Leonard may be a more successful marketer and international corporate businessman and her grandson William may be better schooled in management, but put Estée in front of a crowd and she will sell, sell, sell. I have always admired her, and her drive reminds me of my mother. She treated Lee and me very warmly, like her children.

Estée, though, was no pushover—she was an extremely effective negotiator. Where Charles Revson bullied, Estée pleaded. One incident in particular comes to mind. When we were redoing our cosmetics department in the early sixties, Estée was concerned about her location. Department store cosmetics is all about real estate.

We fought and fought and couldn't settle it. Estée was sailing to Europe with her husband, Joe. As was the custom then, Lee and I went to see her off. We went down to her spacious cabin, which was filled with flowers. We were there to wish her well, but all Estée wanted to talk about was where the Lauder counter would be located.

"How can you say no to me?" she asked. Spontaneously, she burst into tears. "How could you!" she said and started to cry. The ship was preparing to leave its berth and we were being asked to leave. I confess I was not used to bargaining under such conditions. We compromised—I gave in—and Estée left for Europe. By the way, the space worked so well that today, thirty years later, the Lauder counter is in the same location.

Estée's great contribution to the industry is sampling. At a time when no one gave anything away, Estée encouraged women to try her products by handing out a generous free sample. Once women had tried her products they came back for more. She followed up sampling with her innovative "gift with purchase." There is even the further wrinkle (no pun intended) of "purchase with purchase": Buy $25 worth of products today, and get a $50 item for only $15.

Estée revolutionized the industry. Today, many cosmetic companies have giveaways and gifts, but she started it. In the struggle between cosmetic companies and retailers for control of the consumer, Estée Lauder's innovative marketing techniques changed the balance of power. Where Revson was great at the sell-in, Estée was queen of the sell-through. She got women to try, and then use, her products. They came to the stores for Estée Lauder gifts, for her products, and they were devoted. Estée was always her best advertisement. According to her, Revson was telling women what a man thought was beauty. *She* knew what a woman had to do to attract and keep a man.

At a certain point, Lauder eclipsed Revlon in the department store field, and the fact is she worked harder at it. After Charles Revson's death, Revlon continued to focus where its greatest strength had been—in the chain stores; and today, Revlon's total sales still outpace Lauder's. But Estée became queen of the department store, while Revlon remained king of the drugstore.

Estée created the company. But it was her son Leonard who took Estée Lauder, Inc., to the next level. Leonard Lauder and I became close friends in the early sixties. Leonard is tall, thin, animated, and enthusiastic—always thinking. He's very outgoing and possesses an extraordinary curiosity about everything. He wears a wide range of suits, as long as they're blue, and a broad range of ties, as long as they're red. We have much in common, and would often discuss business, as well as designers and executives we both knew and admired or disliked. As we grew more comfortable we would bounce ideas off each other about our businesses. We were both at a stage of our careers where our business was growing and we had each started to take on more responsibility.

Estée Lauder had two lines with a common sales force: Estée Lauder for women, and Aramis for men. They were talking about launching a new line, Clinique.

It was at one of our lunches that Leonard said, "Marvin, I've been thinking about something . . . General Motors sells a lot more cars, because they have four competing divisions. No one has ever organized a cosmetic company with separate divisions." Traditionally, Revlon sold one line named Revlon, Rubinstein sold Rubinstein, Arden sold only Arden. Even when these companies had several product lines, they still maintained one selling force, with a single management and promotional staff. At the time, everyone thought that was the most cost-efficient way to proceed. But Leonard saw the wisdom in what GM was doing. One has to remember that at the time, GM was the single strongest industrial force in the world.

"The way to get really big," he said, "is to set up each brand as a separate company, let them compete with each other and fund them as separate businesses." I thought it was a brilliant idea and I told him so. After his family agreed, he went ahead. Aramis was spun off, and when Clinique was introduced, it was a separate venture. Later, when other brands were created, such as Prescriptives, they were set up as independent entities.

Leonard's idea was the beginning of the growth of the Lauder business. Now every department store has not only a Lauder counter, but one for Clinique and another for Prescriptives. In the battle between stores and the cosmetic companies, Leonard's innovation gave Estée Lauder the upper hand. Even if a store chose to limit Estée Lauder, they had the other brands. The actual real estate of Estée Lauder, Inc., doubled and tripled.

Estée Lauder was smart to move into new market segments with each new company. Leonard wanted his family's company to have a preeminent role in the development of new ideas in the cosmetics world. Accordingly, he has gone into hypoallergenic cosmetics (Clinique), custom color (Prescriptives), and natural products (Origins).

Each has a distinct marketing approach and a unique position in the marketplace based on real and perceived differences in product. Clinique was created in consultation with a dermatologist and conveys an atmosphere of freshness and laboratory purity. Prescriptives has tapped into color blending and custom color with its sensual approach to makeup. Origins has all natural packaging; everything about it says "green." Having several lines did not detract from the business of any one brand; rather it appeared to increase the business of all.

Leonard has a very intellectual approach to business. At any given moment, he is planning several years ahead. I recall one occasion in particular when Lee and I were on safari with Leonard and his wife, Evelyn. (Evelyn is a very active Senior corporate vice president and plays an increasingly important role in the company.) Leonard and I were sitting on top of a Land Rover looking over the Serengeti Plain when he asked me: "Where do you think the cosmetic industry will be in five years?"

But back to the sixties. In 1962, when I first became involved with cosmetics, Mike Blumenfeld, Bloomingdale's cosmetic buyer, was the absolute dean of the industry. Mike was very boisterous and knew every salesperson intimately. He would boom, "Marion, how are the sales today?" and the salespeople loved that because he was a cheerleader. He brought a sense of theater to the department and understood that selling cosmetics at Bloomingdale's was not just putting lipsticks out over the counter. You had to make it into an event.

Yet Mike could occasionally be a little off the wall. I remember one time when we had promised Estée Lauder an exclusive promotion and Estée discovered that another company's promotion overlapped hers by a few days. She was furious.

She came to my office with Leonard. "How can you do this to me?" she said. I called Mike to my office and Estée immediately started in on him: He had betrayed her; he had broken his word.

"Mike," I said, "what do you have to say?"

Mike seemed nonplussed. "I have no idea what this is about, but if you wait a second, I'll get *my* mother and we'll work it out." Leonard looked at Estée and they both broke out laughing. That was Mike. To him, it was all freewheeling.

In the June 28, 1993, *Fortune* list of the World's 101 Richest People, the Lauder family ranks 48th—ahead of Rupert Murdoch and Ross Perot. A real tribute to Leonard's business acumen—but Estée has never been willing to give him appropriate credit.

I care about details, though. So in the 1980s I added cosmetics to Lester Gribetz's responsibilities and he then supervised Mike. They made a great team. When Mike retired, the whole industry turned out for an immense tribute. It was very touching. Today, he teaches at FIT.

In the 1960s, however, most stores treated cosmetics as a single commodity without much fanfare. Bloomingdale's was the first to recognize that cosmetics was a separate division, like ready-to-wear. We were the first department store to have a separate merchandise manager for cosmetics and separate buyers for each major line.

As I mentioned, relationships between cosmetic companies and stores had traditionally been handled between the salesmen and the buyers. It didn't take long to recognize that cosmetic company presidents prefer to deal with store principals, so I set out to woo them. Whenever there was a store event we invited the cosmetic company presidents, and treated them like major celebrities, which, in time, they became.

I carried this strategy over into our business planning. We developed the practice of sitting down with every major cosmetics company once a year to review their business. We compared their current year's performance to the last three, then set goals and planned strategy. We customized our plans so that what we did for Lancôme in Boston was different than in Washington; and different from what we did for Chanel in Chicago. It made perfect sense, because we were partners with the cosmetics companies, more so than with other vendors.

Cosmetic companies are not supposed to favor one store over another in their pricing (to do so would be considered an illegal restraint of trade). However, every store makes its separate arrangements with the cosmetic companies as to the attendant marketing costs. The net result is a casbahlike negotiation at the end of which each store feels they have very special deals.

I realized that we had to provide the cosmetic companies with more ways to increase their volume at our stores. A very profitable area for cosmetics companies is skin care, or treatment. So Bloomingdale's, with the help of the cosmetic companies, developed that business with appealing marketing concepts. For example, Bloomingdale's ran a week's promotion during which Adrien Arpel came to Chicago for private treatment consultations and makeovers. We took over several hotel rooms and she did more than $100,000 worth of business. Another example was the promotion we did with Georgette Mosbacher for La Prairie Cosmetics. Georgette, the wife of the former secretary of commerce, appeared at the 59th Street store. We took over Le Train Bleu and gave a cocktail reception for Georgette and her customers. She then personally escorted her custom-

ers down to an area where we created treatment rooms and the La
Prairie experts gave the ladies individual consultations, selling each
$100 to $200 worth of product.

b

By the late seventies we wanted to launch a major offensive in cosmetics; it had grown to be such an important business that it was
critical that we establish our preeminence in the field. That was not
easy. Since cosmetic companies control the customers and have
their own selling specialists, what's left for the stores? The answer
was that we had the real estate, and we had the Bloomingdale's
magic and mystique, and we had to leverage them all in such a way
that the cosmetics companies would need us as much as we needed
them.

New York is the mecca for cosmetics. Stores and shoppers from
all over the country, and from all over the world, look to New York
for their lead. I realized that if Bloomingdale's was going to be the
leader in cosmetics launches, we had to have the most exciting
selling floor.

The main floor had not been renovated in twenty-five years. We
needed a bold, striking concept, one that would communicate the
energy and romance of New York, and would be instantly understandable anywhere in the country. We held a meeting of our most
creative executives and decided upon B-way—a double entendre
meant to suggest both the Broadway theater and Bloomingdale's
way. I called upon Barbara D'Arcy to interpret our idea, and told
her to throw out the rule book.

Barbara wanted a design that tied in with the glory days of the
theater—the thirties—to create an opulent dramatic environment.
We talked about New York at night, the sparkle and the glamour.
Barbara wanted to add art-deco elements, in some ways reminiscent
of Radio City Music Hall.

Barbara was fearless—and smart. She created a black ceiling
that was recessed in several levels to make the space seem more
airy, and the black was complemented by gold and lighting that
created the effect of an expensive gift box. Finally, just as in housewares, where we used green neon on the ceiling to tie the area
together and direct the customers, here we used a white and black

marble floor to guide consumers through the area. The total package was dazzling.

As Barbara went about creating B'way, she had many naysayers. The black ceiling shocked many people. Black had always been anathema to selling and was considered "too down." I remember one shopper, watching the renovation in progress, who came up to Barbara and said, "I hope you have lots of white paint to redo this."

When B'way was launched, however, Bloomingdale's and Barbara D'Arcy received major acclaim. Paul Goldberger in *The New York Times* called the renovation "perhaps the most daring piece of large-scale design in a decade." And he described the experience of walking through the main floor "as if one were shopping in the Rainbow Room."

b

Of course, the redesign also had a business strategy animating it. Just as we had with apparel and housewares, we created boutiques and islands for vendors. Each piece of real estate was part of our plan to make Bloomingdale's the most important cosmetics floor in the country.

It was in our interest to help new companies. Having our success tied to any one vendor was just too dangerous. If that vendor failed in any of their promotions, the whole division could be hurt. We gave important pieces of real estate to small or growing companies like La Prairie, Clarins, or Erno Laszlo—choices that were not necessarily part of everybody's coterie of vendors.

Chanel has a very special approach in all they do, from pricing to the look of their stores. For example, the price of their lipstick is $18.50 as opposed to many of the other brands, which are anywhere from $8.00 to $15.00. Their people are very well trained, their packaging is superb, and they are sold in a limited number of stores, all of which creates a feeling of quality for the entire company.

Most recently, in 1989, when we moved our perfume department, a very desirable space opened up on the main floor. Many cosmetic companies wanted the space, and we asked each to make a proposal. In the end, we selected Chanel because they had limited distribution, a more up-scale product that represented a very important business for Bloomingdale's, and could generate substantial volume in that location.

Arie Kopelman, Chanel's president and chief operating officer, joined the company in 1986. His background was in marketing, having been at Procter & Gamble after Columbia business school, and then at Doyle Dane Bernbach, the same agency as Joan Glynn, where he rose to vice chairman and general manager. At Chanel, it was thought a good omen that his wife's name is Coco. Arie and I hit it off immediately. He did not, initially, know a great deal about department store retailing. But he is very intelligent and a quick study, and early on we saw eye to eye on marketing Chanel at Bloomingdale's. By the time this opportunity came up on the main floor, we were both eager to do something unique, something that would move both our businesses forward in a major way.

Arie wanted the new shop to be distinctive. It was important that Chanel not only stand out among the other cosmetic vendors, but that, in some way, the shop further the Chanel image. We agreed to do two things Chanel had never done in any other store in America. First, we would create a section to sell jewelry, watches, and scarves along with the cosmetics. And second, they could use the upstairs space to create the first Chanel treatment room, where a customer could have color consultations and skin treatments.

Arie's concept was to add elements of the signature Chanel shop in Paris. Part of the elegance, classicism, and design of the company is expressed simply by the distinctive curving marble staircase that greets one when entering their shops, whether it is the original in Paris or their stores in New York or Tokyo. We decided to re-create the feeling of that staircase in Bloomingdale's and have it lead to the treatment rooms. When completed, we had created a little Chanel oasis in the midst of Bloomie's traffic, and found a way to increase all our business at the same time.

b

Cosmetics, however, is only half the story. Fragrance is the other half, and over the years it has become a giant industry. To give you some perspective, in 1991 alone, Bloomingdale's launched fifteen new fragrances and discontinued thirty others.

The proliferation of fragrances, however, is a rather recent phenomenon. During the 1950s and 1960s, fragrance was a rather staid industry dominated by such standbys as Joy or Chanel No. 5. It used to be that a woman received a bottle of perfume only on a special occasion, a birthday or an anniversary, and used it sparingly. Today, most women use scent as an essential part of their daily routine. As marketing became increasingly more sophisticated, a whole new generation of fragrances emerged, based on aggressive promotion and more selective distribution.

Perhaps the most flamboyant launch of this first new wave was the 1978 launch of Yves Saint Laurent's Opium.

Yves had already had success with fragrances such as YSL. When he announced that he was preparing to launch a new fragrance called Opium, the very name created something of a scandal. Mike Blumenfeld had a feeling about this fragrance, and I trusted Mike's hunches.

We wanted the launch; so did Bob Suslow at Saks Fifth Avenue. Each store wanted an exclusive. The Saint Laurent organization decided that the best of both worlds was for us to share it. In the meantime the controversy was growing over the "decadence" inherent in naming a perfume Opium. To us, this meant only more press attention, and more business. We agreed. It was the first time we had ever shared an "exclusive" with another store, much less a close competitor like Saks. But we were right to do it.

For the opening launch and press party, Saint Laurent took over a Chinese junk, moored in the East River at 23rd Street, adorned it with Japanese lanterns, and played disco music for the celebrity-filled crowd. There was an air of fantasy to the whole evening that suited the launch of Opium perfectly. Bloomingdale's sold more than half a million dollars' worth in three months. That was a record then, and Opium is still selling well today. According to *Adweek*, 1991 sales were an estimated $35 million, making Opium the fourth prestige fragrance (after Red, Giorgio, and Obsession).

The best sellers at Bloomingdale's were most often those perfumes we launched or sold exclusively. Market research told us that the Bloomingdale's perfume shopper was a woman who wanted to be the first to wear a new scent. We discovered that, for us, the more exclusive the better. This was particularly true of designer fragrances, where women were buying a little piece of an imaginary world. We found that if a woman couldn't afford a Chanel suit or handbag, she would buy the fragrance. The more out of reach the image, the more successful the fragrance was at Bloomingdale's.

Another reason for our success with fragrance was that Bloomingdale's was best at providing the physical setting and excitement for launching fragrances. We provided the drama by having a talented display person, Rolando Seinheart, who worked full time on cosmetics displays. Rolando helped create the strategies and would often present his display concepts to the cosmetic companies who, in most cases, underwrote his creations.

We also had such creative executives as Robin Burns. At one time, Robin was a shy, reserved woman from Colorado who was our bedspread buyer. Lester brought her to cosmetics, which she understood innately. At the time we were discussing launching Calvin Klein's first fragrance, a men's fragrance called Calvin—Robin, I recall, had an idea.

"Wouldn't it be terrific," she said, "if we had fifty hot-looking guys on the floor spraying the fragrance wearing an outfit that Calvin Klein designed."

"Where are you going to get fifty guys?" Lester asked. Robin said not to worry. She went out in the street, stopped great-looking men, and asked them "How'd you like to work for a week at Bloomingdale's?" They were actors, dancers, and models, and Robin got them into the store. It was the most successful fragrance launch we'd had to date. It was extraordinary. Every inch of space was covered with people, mingling with all these great-looking models and actors.

So it was no surprise that several years later, Robin was recruited by Bob Taylor, the president of the company that was marketing Obsession; or that Estée Lauder recruited her from that position. Today, Robin is president of Estée Lauder U.S.A. She is no longer shy.

b

We were always trying to expand the reach of the cosmetics and fragrance department beyond its actual real estate. At the time of a launch, you would find displays in the windows, signs in the elevators, and transparencies along the escalators. We have displays on several floors; when it is a designer fragrance, we also do a tie-in to their fashions. The demonstrators, who were so effective for the Calvin Klein launch, appear throughout the store, asking shoppers to try the new fragrance.

Now a few words about Bloomingdale's and spritzing, those short bursts of fragrance directed at customers. Lester will admit that he is responsible for tripling or even quadrupling the number of sprayers in Bloomingdale's. I'll admit that Bloomingdale's in the eighties went overboard. Friends would complain, "We can't walk through your main floor without getting five different kinds of fragrance sprayed on us."

Russell Stravitz, who at the time was in charge of stores, said, "We've got to stop spraying." I asked Lester what he thought. "You stop spritzing," he said, "and you stop selling." We argued it back and forth. Should we lessen it? If so, by how much? Finally, Lester said: "Let's just stop for a week and see what happens." I agreed.

The following week, we suspended spraying. Business did not tumble, it plummeted. It was remarkable—and frightening. That was how I learned that although many dislike being sprayed, there are many more who want to experience a scent and we are always trying to find new ways to sample the product.

The fragrance companies also caught on to the impact of spritzing. And why not? Suddenly they had ten new outposts to sell their product. We had a sprayer at every entrance to a department. And they would sell $200 or $300 a day, not only on the main floor—I decreed that only one cosmetics company at a time could spray on the main floor.

We did, however, instruct the demonstrators not to spray the customer unless she agreed. One woman was sprayed without her consent, suffered an allergic reaction and sued.

With the extraordinary traffic throughout Bloomingdale's 59th Street, we created cosmetic outposts on many floors that became valuable pieces of real estate. The fragrance and cosmetic companies would fight for these counters where customer service was sometimes less pressured than the overcrowded main floor. The cosmetics companies wanted even more space all over the store. The third-floor Clinique outpost, for example, does almost one million dollars a year—found money for Lauder—and Lancôme has opened a second-floor outpost that is expected to produce a million dollars.

b

Successful launches come at a premium and cost a fortune. Bloomingdale's asked the cosmetic and fragrance vendors to share in the costs for the sales, marketing, promotion, and launches of their products. Since Bloomingdale's was the hottest place to launch a fragrance, we developed a commensurate arrogance. People in the industry say that Bloomingdale's pressed its advantage very hard. But tough bargaining is a two-way street. Bloomingdale's was on the receiving end for many years, and when we could play from strength, we did so. We didn't negotiate, we tried to set terms. This was particularly true in the 1970s when we had little competition. However, by the 1980s, there were more players in the field, and accordingly we shared more costs.

But the truth is, in all our negotiations, nobody forced the cosmetic and fragrance companies to agree. For our terms, however onerous, we gave those companies the best piece of real estate in America. I suspect that if you asked them if their presentation on 59th Street was worth the investment, they would agree it was.

b

Intelligent executives used Bloomingdale's as a marketing and advertising tool. Bloomingdale's had the advantage; its launches got attention. And once the product was successfully launched, that attention was worth more than advertising. It's true, for example, that Fendi was a $200,000 launch. But Fendi was a smash hit. So if you ask Joe Ronchetti, then CEO of Elizabeth Arden, whether he thought Bloomingdale's was responsible for the Fendi success, I think he would agree that Bloomingdale's made it happen.

The Fendi launch is a good example of the lengths we will go to. The week before the launch, Carla Fendi arrived to inspect our installation. She walked in, and began to shriek: The carpeting we had installed throughout the main floor was not the correct shade of purple! Carla had a particular shade that was the theme of her fragrance packaging. Ours, she claimed, was all wrong. Our design team told me that they could not find the exact shade, and that on such short notice they could not replace the carpet. I went downstairs to look. Carla showed me her packaging. I looked at the carpet. Ours was slightly different. Close, but not the same. Most people would not care. But Carla did. I told our staff to replace it. And, miraculously, they did.

The Fendi launch, in the end, was theatrically and visually one of the most exciting we ever had. The five Fendi sisters flew in from Rome. They all arrived in flamboyant floor-length sable and mink coats. Fendi carpeted the main floor, took over all our windows. We trimmed the center aisle with larger-than-life Roman torsos made at Cinecitta, the famous Italian movie studio complex. Fendi also created a romantic television commercial that was shown in the store and on TV. The night of the opening Arden gave an elegant black-tie dinner for the Fendi sisters and *le tout* New York was there.

Giorgio is another success story. At first, the fragrance was only available at a small shop in Beverly Hills called Giorgio of Beverly Hills. In the early 1980s, Margot Rogoff, our public relations director, was in Los Angeles and visited the store with its bright yellow-and-white striped awning. The fragrance came in a similar package. Margot felt Beverly Hills had a marvelous cachet, and "Giorgio Beverly Hills" was even better. We made an arrangement that Bloomingdale's would carry Giorgio exclusively on the East Coast while Fred and Gayle Hayman, who owned the Giorgio shop, would have it on the West Coast.

Giorgio is an extremely strong, recognizable, floral fragrance. Some people find it offensive, but no one can ignore it. In 1982 Giorgio began its mail-order campaign, advertising its product with scent strips in national magazines and providing a toll-free number for potential customers. Sales boomed and magazines have never smelled the same since. By 1984, Bloomingdale's was doing $8 million in sales out of Giorgio's annual $60 million. Remember purchase with purchase? In 1984, Giorgio was offering a Giorgio bath towel with the slogan, "You know who wears it," for $18.50 with any purchase.

Giorgio sold extremely well at Bloomingdale's and they soon began to open up many more stores. In 1987, the Haymans sold Giorgio Beverly Hills to Avon for $165 million. Not bad for the Haymans and not bad for Avon, which has expanded Giorgio into a diversified company whose volume for 1991 alone was $165 million.

We attempted, without success, to persuade Giorgio management to maintain a narrow distribution. The expansion strategy may have made sense for Giorgio, but not for us. At its height the key Giorgio demonstrator was earning more than $150,000 a year at Bloomingdale's. But the business in Bloomingdale's shrunk from $10 million to $2 million. The problem with major launches is that although they can be a huge success the year of the launch, that volume is difficult to maintain. You must invest to maintain the excitement, otherwise, what was thought to be a success quickly turns into a failure.

b

The world is littered with failed fragrances. Sometimes the problem is the packaging, sometimes the scent itself, sometimes the marketing. In my opinion, the women's fragrances from Valentino and Armani suffered from all three. Ultimately neither succeeded in the American market, although Armani has now been successfully relaunched by Cosmair. A famous name does not, in and of itself, guarantee success. There have been many occasions where the fragrance's name did not garner enough attention. For example, Bloomingdale's helped launch the Claude Montana fragrance. We thought Montana was a powerful designer name for fragrance. The public did not seem to agree.

The biggest example of a launch that went terribly wrong was Lacroix. Christian Lacroix is a very talented French designer whom I consider a good friend. Bloomingdale's fully expected to launch his fragrance C'est la Vie. He wanted us to, but the Lacroix people in France wanted us to spend what we thought was an inappropriate amount of money advertising the launch, and we refused. Lacroix's C'est la Vie was launched at Saks Fifth Avenue and by an A&S television campaign. This created very mixed signals in the consumer's mind. She didn't know whether the fragrance was an exclusive or a mass scent.

Fragrance can be positioned as exclusive and launched in a limited number of stores—most typically Saks, Bloomingdale's, and/or Neiman-Marcus—or it can be positioned as a mass fragrance such as a Liz Claiborne, Gloria Vanderbilt, or Charlie. Then you launch in many, many stores. Either way, you must send a very clear message.

With Lacroix, who is a prestige designer, it did not make sense to have a mass launch. And the executives at Lacroix did not realize this until after the perfume was launched. Consequently, a year later, C'est la Vie was withdrawn from every store but Saks Fifth Avenue. We heard the estimated worldwide loss was $30 to $40 million.

b

In the postwar era, with changing life-styles and new marketing techniques, the men's fragrance business shifted from mass market drugstores to a major opportunity for department stores. In the fifties most men used Old Spice or Aqua Velva, commercial after-shaves available in drugstores (I used Old Spice). In the sixties, marketing changed all that. The first popular men's fragrance, called Jade East, portrayed a James Bond–type figure being bathed by an Asian beauty, and was followed by the high-impact ads for Hai-Karate. On the prestige side, Estée Lauder introduced Aramis. Aramis's advertising breakthrough came when they showed a woman getting turned on by the Aramis man—Ted Danson, of "Cheers" fame. Men got the message. It was sexy to smell good.

Aramis, being an Estée Lauder company, knew how to market that feeling. Not surprisingly, Aramis was also the first men's fragrance to offer a gift with purchase. They had great gifts—Aramis watches and umbrellas—that often seemed worth more than the fragrance. Estée Lauder is one of the largest consumers of umbrellas in the United States. In the 1970s, we gave away an absolutely phenomenal number of portable hair dryers tied in with Aramis. This gives some idea of the change in men's grooming habits, as well.

In 1978 we launched Ralph Lauren's Polo, which quickly became our second most important business. We knew that 75 percent of men's fragrance was bought by women as gifts. We started to build around that, using both Father's Day and Christmas as times to really expand the men's fragrance business.

At the same time, the men's business was growing beyond after-shave. Suddenly companies were introducing body lotion and a proliferation of grooming products. The men's market had also branched into skin care. Aramis even developed a new division called Lab Series aimed at skin care and treatment. The product line includes, for example, a shaving cream made in Switzerland that I use and believe to be the best. Clinique also developed a series of men's products from moisturizer to razor-burn cream that now represents 10 percent of their business.

The most spectacular men's launch in recent memory was Chanel's Egoiste. Most people recall their spectacular TV commercial, directed by Jean-Paul Goode, in which a dozen women stand at different balconies of a building shouting "Egoiste." Shot in Brazil, Chanel invested over a million dollars in it. The launch was successful, but as I indicated earlier, it will be several years before anyone knows how profitable it will be. Right now my guess is that for every dollar of Egoiste we sold, either Chanel or Bloomingdale's spent somewhere between $2 and $3.

To create a proper selling environment, in the early 1960s Bloomingdale's pioneered "Harry's Bar," which was meant to suggest Hemingway and drinking and men who were macho enough to use cologne. We were among the first to create an environment where men felt comfortable sampling colognes. By doing so we set the standard for others to follow. In 1979, at the same time we created B'way, we renovated the men's space into "The Board Room," looking to tap into the image of the successful American businessman. For the 1980s man I wanted scent to be another status symbol. The sales area, as I saw it, should look and feel like a corporate boardroom. I called Leonard Lauder and asked if we could send our design team over to his office for inspiration. For many years to follow, what you saw in the Bloomingdale's "Board Room" selling area was a photograph of the view from Leonard's office on the thirty-seventh floor of the General Motors building.

b

The growth areas in cosmetics for the future, as I see it, all have to do with the changing nature of our population, life-style, and the ozone layer. People are concerned about exposure to the sun and stores now heavily promote sun care products. The cosmetics companies are all following that lead, creating their own products. Sun care has become an enormous business. Nonetheless, people are vain and still want to look tanned, even if they stay indoors. For that reason, there has been tremendous growth in tanning products. Almost every cosmetic line now has self-tanning products, and they are improving all the time.

Another high growth area is products targeted for individual parts of the body. The best recent example is cellulite treatment creams, where French companies including Elancyl have been the leaders. Cellulite is a good example, I think, of how the cosmetics industry continues to invent problems for women and then develop products to deal with these problems. Then there are products to enhance various portions of the body, whether it's the bottoms or the tops, the buttocks or the breasts, in which Clarins and other firms deal. There are hand creams, face creams, eye creams. The new hot area is neck creams. And to counter all of that, there is a growing market for all-in-one creams.

Another emerging growth area is cosmetics aimed at women of color. As our population demographics change and the percentage of nonwhites increases, there will be increasing demand for products specifically dedicated to women of color.

In addition, the population is aging, while a great emphasis remains on having a youthful appearance. There will continue to be great growth in anti-aging products. Retin-A, for example, is a substance with reported anti-aging properties that many believe will receive FDA approval, and become a big business.

At the same time, concern for the environment has spurred tremendous interest in natural products. Origins, a natural cosmetics line launched by Estée Lauder, Inc., is probably the best-conceived new company that I've seen in the cosmetic industry. They have face and hand creams, and also aroma therapy products. In fact, one of their best-selling items is called Peace of Mind. Imagine, you can buy "peace of mind" for only $10. The packaging is all recyclable, the bottles are refillable, and the products are priced very attractively. A combination that will appeal to the consumer of the nineties.

b

But in the beginning of the 1980s, Bloomies and the cosmetics companies were on a giddy wild climb. Everything we did seemed to take us even higher. And there was one designer, Ralph Lauren, who more than any other shared in our success.

*"The shirt, kerchief, and pants—all Ralph Lauren. The belt and
my undergarments—Calvin Klein."*

CHAPTER 9

The Ralph Lauren No One Knows

O ver the years Bloomingdale's taste and style have been defined by our identification with designers. For us, the designer was the vehicle that brought the merchandise and the marketing together. Whether in home furnishings, housewares, apparel, or cosmetics, Bloomingdale's promoted designers and used them to establish our image in the minds of our customers.

But Ralph Lauren stands out because he, more than any other designer, represents the Bloomingdale's-ization of American life. Ralph Lauren is the quintessence of that certain taste that Jed Davidson and my parents aspired to, and more important, the notion Bloomingdale's advanced that good taste was available to anyone who embraced its standard.

This cartoon of September 25, 1980, best defines the extent to which Ralph Lauren has become part of the American Landscape. Everyone knows what people wear in Ralph Lauren country.

Drawing by Lorenz; © 1989 The New Yorker Magazine, Inc.

Ralph Lauren has built his business step by step, side by side, and hand in hand with Bloomingdale's. Ralph's story, as I see it, is representative of the way in which one designer has carried the marketing principles that Bloomingdale's championed, with regard to merchandise, publicity and advertising, to levels even we never imagined.

b

I'm not sure when I first met Ralph Lauren, but it was probably in 1967 when Ralph, then a tie designer for Beau Brummel, would come to Bloomingdale's to straighten his tie cases. Ralph was fastidious, passionate about every detail. It was clear, even then, that he had "it": a vision, and the enthusiasm and dedication to carry it out. Among the many relationships that I developed during my forty-one years at Bloomingdale's, my relationship with Ralph has been one of the closest as well as most important.

Ralph is fourteen years younger than I am. He, too, was born in the Bronx—in 1939; the third son of Russian immigrants. His father, a painter, changed their family name from Lifshitz to Lauren. Like me, he attended DeWitt Clinton, but Ralph's dream as a young man was to be an athlete.

Nonetheless, he found himself drawn to retailing. In high school he worked part-time at Alexander's, and at eighteen spent Christmas week selling sweaters at Bloomingdale's. In 1958, at nineteen, he joined Allied Stores as an assistant buyer in menswear. A few years later, he worked for Brooks Brothers for six months before joining the army.

By 1964, Ralph Lauren was a road salesman covering New England for A. Rivetz of Boston, a men's neckwear manufacturer. They sold a very traditional line of solid and rep ties. Ralph, however, wanted to sell something with a little more flair.

The Rivetz executives in Boston, Ralph felt, were too conservative. He was in his early twenties and living in Manhattan; Ralph told them that he was more in touch with new trends in the men's field. But they didn't have to take Ralph's word alone. They could turn to the pages of the *Daily News Record*, the trade newspaper of the menswear business. In May 1964, *DNR* ran an "everybody's talking about" feature about this well-dressed Rivetz tie salesman named Ralph Lauren. Ralph, according to the article, was a very stylish fellow: he drove a Morgan; he had definite opinions about clothes. He wore fitted jackets with broad lapels and riding pants. Ralph hung out with the custom tailors at Paul Stuart and Meledandri, who made his clothes to his exacting specifications, though he could barely afford them on his salary. Ralph Lauren was someone to watch.

Ralph yearned to apply some of his personal style to the necktie field. At the time, ties were dark and narrow. Ralph had an idea for a wide tie that he wanted Rivetz to carry. They refused, so Ralph left Rivetz in 1967 to join Beau Brummel and start a neckwear division. Most ties then were 2⅞ to 3 inches wide. Ralph designed ties that were 3½ and sometimes 4 inches wide. A four-inch tie has a totally different look; it was the most important change in men's fashion in many years.

Ralph's ties were handmade from unusual fabrics. He had the shell and lining stitched so the tie could stretch but would always pull back to its original shape. He found exotic fabrics, Indian silks, and old remnants. And they were expensive. Many ties sold for $2.00, the more expensive ones for $5.00; Ralph's retailed for $7.50 to $15.00. His ties cost more to make, and he wanted to send a message to shoppers that they were worth it. Ralph always believed consumers were willing to spend more for a superior, well-made garment or for an important new fashion. He called his tie division Polo.

Why Polo? Ralph has explained over the years that as a sports fan, he wanted a name that conveyed a national image. "I couldn't call it basketball or baseball," he has said, so he chose Polo. Ralph's press materials say he chose the name Polo "because the sport represented to him a life-style mood of athletic grace and discreet elegance, an image of men who wore well-tailored, classic clothes and wore them with style."

Many people who don't know Ralph, and know little of his business history, assume that Polo was Ralph's attempt, in some way, to assimilate. People occasionally pontificate on how all Ralph did was copy WASP style and sell it to everyone including the WASPs (as if that was no accomplishment in itself). And that Ralph's success can somehow be dismissed as the desire of a Jewish boy from the Bronx to create the very same non-Jewish world that would not readily accept him. To think that way, however, shows no understanding of Ralph or his fashions.

Style does not belong to any class, nationality, or religion. In Ralph's case, I am sure, his sense of style was formed in childhood and influenced by the movies, by the Hollywood visions of style embodied by Cary Grant, Gary Cooper, and Fred Astaire.

Ralph Lauren is someone who has a very clear vision. He closes his eyes and knows how he would like every last detail to look. He knows what the shirt should look like, what the collar should feel like, what the buttons should be made of. He thinks in images, and those images tell the story of a life-style. Ralph sees it all very clearly, all at once. This is what led him, before he could afford it, to have his clothes custom made.

And what of those glamorous movie stars who inspired Ralph? Fred Astaire was not born to the upper classes, nor was Cary Grant. Their sense of style was innate. Even Edward, Duke of Windsor, often cited as the best-dressed man of the century, had style that was as independent of his birth as Cary Grant's was of his. Ralph's style is American and entirely his own.

Ralph had definite notions about which stores he wanted to carry his ties. He had a strong image of his customer and wanted to be in a fashionable men's store. In those days, most stores held to a very conservative line. There were few choices if you wanted something with a little more dash. In New York, there were a few specialty shops with exacting tailors at their disposal. Ralph knew most, and succeeded in getting Paul Stuart and Meledandri to carry his ties.

Roland Meledandri had a small store making custom clothes and selling shirts, ties, and accessories. Meledandri, who wore a bushy mustache and cut quite a figure himself, had great style. He was, in Ralph's words, "almost a cult." There is no equivalent today. Back then custom tailors were only the province of the rich. It was not a big business, but it was where someone like a David Susskind would come to find clothes that told people he was a businessman who traveled in a more sophisticated world. That was the world Ralph wanted to be in.

As for department stores, Ralph had one choice: Bloomingdale's. He understood what we were doing; we had the right taste level. He knew, almost instinctively, that his customer—the man

Lee and I leaving for our honeymoon aboard the S.S. *Santa Rosa*, September 3, 1948. Skirts were long then and hats and gloves de rigueur.

Right: My grandmother, Lila Bruckman, as she appeared in *Town & Country*. She was the granddaughter of the Petrikover Rebbe.

My parents, Bea and Sam Traub, made a handsome couple. This was taken in the 1950s, as they were sailing to spend August at La Reserve in the South of France.

I was six and my mother saw me as a young fashion plate with a beret and Buster Brown collar.

Below: On maneuvers in West Virginia, as a first scout in the 379th Infantry, 95th Division, with a B.A.R., shortly before leaving for England and Normandy.

I was wounded November 15, 1944, at Metz and spent fifteen months in Army hospitals in France, England and the United States. Here I'm in traction at Tilton General, Fort Dix, New Jersey.

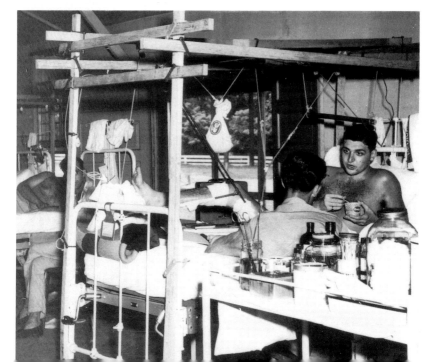

Right: April 17, 1872, Lyman and Joseph Bloomingdale opened Bloomingdale's Great East Side Bazaar at Third Avenue and 56th Street. First day's receipts were $3.68, first week's $292.92. *Below*: With growing sales and a need for more space, in 1885 Lyman and Joseph expanded, acquiring an adjoining five-story building on the southeast corner. The store's catalog for that year modestly proclaimed "the lowest prices anywhere in the United States."

Despite the Depression, in 1931 Bloomingdale's completed construction of a totally new Lexington avenue facade. The store now occupied the entire block from 59th Street to 60th Street, Lexington to Third Avenue. The store was, and still is, an amalgam of nine separate buildings.

Below left: The Bloomingdale's era began on October 5, 1886, with an ambitious move to a six-story building at Third Avenue and 59th Street. The main floor was an impressive eighteen feet high.

The Men Who Built Bloomingdale's

Lyman Bloomingdale

Joseph Bloomingdale

Jim Schoff, Sr.

Jed Davidson

Larry Lachman

Harold Krensky

This portrait of Lyman Bloomingdale hangs in our boardroom—the classic portrait of "our founder." Lyman was the merchant and creative partner, and his younger brother Joseph focused on organizing the stock and inventory. Sam Bloomingdale, Lyman's son, succeeded him as chairman and in 1929 merged Bloomingdale's with three other stores to create Federated.

In 1944, Jim Schoff, Sr., became president, and began to plan Bloomingdale's modern era. In 1947 he recruited Jed Davidson, who became chairman of the board. Jed was the creative genius who transformed Bloomingdale's into a chic neighborhood store and was my mentor.

Schoff and Davidson laid the groundwork for the Bloomingdale's of the 1970s and '80s. They trained their talented successors, Larry Lachman, who became president in 1964 and chairman in 1969, as well as Harold Krensky, who was chairman and managing director from 1966 to 1969. Harold was my second mentor, a true genius in the apparel business and totally beloved by the industry.

On September 26, 1961, we opened our first storewide country promotion, L'Esprit de France. In a year of preparation, forty merchants traveled 250,000 miles in France creating unique and exclusive merchandise. Our windows highlighted an extraordinary variety of French products. Much of the furniture was French Provincial style, but like this armoire, was made in Italy.

Bloomingdale's was a highly promotional store. This Depression era ad offered a complete men's wardrobe including suit, shirt, tie, underwear, shoes, overcoat, hat and gloves (a $100 value) for $58.

The 1969 Cave room was Barbara D'Arcy's favorite. Its curved molded ceilings and free-form design created enormous attention.

The 1972 Frank Gehry room was the first room done entirely of cardboard: walls, floor, and furniture. Gehry fell out with his backers and the collection was discontinued after a year, making each piece a collector's item.

The Trellis room, or treillage, as this Edwardian architectural style is called, was the featured room of our centennial celebration and combined white lacquer furniture with French steel garden furniture.

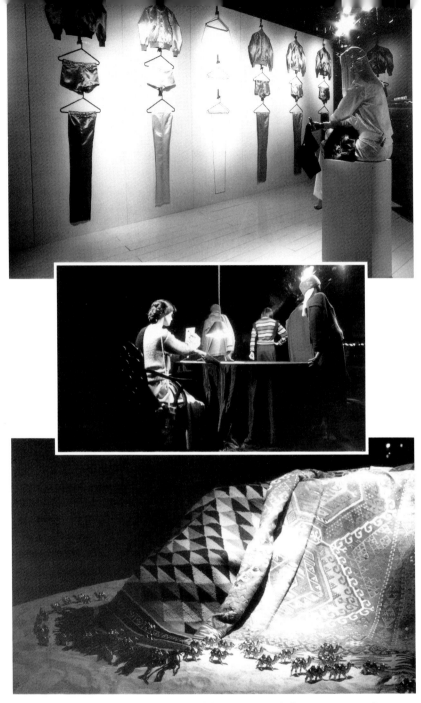

Candy Pratts' famous windows always told a story. *Top*: A designer reviews her collection of silk sportswear as it might be displayed in a showroom (1975). *Middle*: A group of mannequins in the latest Sonya Rykiel knits. According to Candy, "Their backs are turned from the card reader, who is reading their destiny" (1976). *Bottom*: A group of tribal handknit rugs from North Africa on a sand-covered floor are transformed into the Atlas Mountains for a herd of miniature camels. (1977).

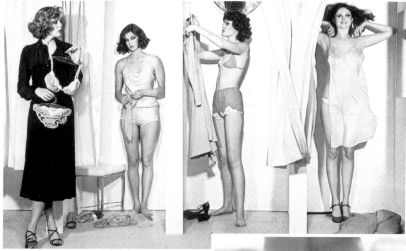

Guy Bourdin's controversial photos for the Sighs and Whispers catalog provided a voyeuristic display long before Victoria's Secret.

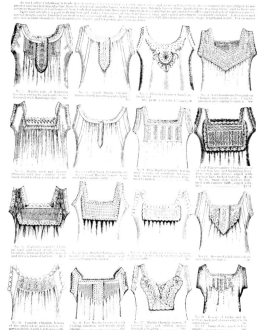

924 TO 928 THIRD AVE., AND 160 TO 104 EAST 59th STREET, NEW YO

LADIES' UNDERWEAR.

In the mid-seventies we introduced Bloomie's panties and sold more than 300,000 the first year. That taught us how valuable our name was as a brand. We added a world of Bloomingdale's products, including sweat shirts, T-shirts, towels, and caps. By 1990 our Bloomie's shops were a $20 million business.

In 1886 ladies' underwear was considerably more demure. The 1886 catalog featured nightgowns for 78¢, men's shirts for 48¢, and men's suits and overcoats for $9.98, as well as hoop skirts for 50¢ and bustles for $1.25.

Bloomingdale's award-winning advertising played a major role in building our image. Here are four of John Jay's favorite ads: 1982's "Chariots of Fire" campaign used the film's star Ben Cross photographed by Snowdon. 1988's "Intimacies" was photographed by Deborah Turbeville for the launch of our new intimate apparel department.

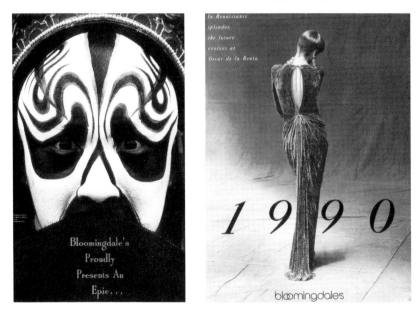

For "Year of the Dragon" in 1988 Herb Ritts photographed a star of the Beijing Opera at the Palace Museum—this was the first of a three-page spread in *The New York Times Magazine*. To launch our "1990" campaign, highlighting fashions for the new decade, Steven Meisel photographed Linda Evangelista in a dress by Oscar De la Renta.

The seventies were the decade when Bloomingdale's came into its own. It began in 1972 with "The Party of the Century" as we celebrated the store's hundredth anniversary. Janus was our symbol, looking back over the past hundred years and forward into the future. We honored prominent New Yorkers such as our dashing Mayor John Lindsay and the beloved Terence Cardinal Cooke, captured here with Joan Glynn.

In November 1975 we made the cover of *Time*; the next year, Bloomingdale's was the subject of a "60 Minutes" feature and the Queen of England came to pay a visit. Not bad for a store that had closed its basement store only nine years before.

Bloomingdale's rising stars of the 1970s, the new team building the business, *from left to right*, were Carl Levine, Barbara D'Arcy, Lester Gribetz, Katie Murphy, and Gordon Cooke. In the '70s Gordon sported a beard.

July 9, 1976. Her Majesty the Queen of England visits Bloomingdale's. A very young Donna Karan (pictured here) was presented to the Queen, along with Ralph Lauren and Calvin Klein.

Prime Minister Indira Gandhi visited the store in 1968, two years after my initial visit to her country. With my growing interest in India, I was very pleased to greet her. I am wearing one of the new Ralph Lauren wide ties.

"Israel: The Dream" was one of our most exciting promotions. Prime Minister Menachem Begin invited the Bloomingdale's team to his home to celebrate his being awarded the Nobel Peace Prize. *Left to right*: Candy Pratts Price, Peggy Healey, Menachem Begin, Peggy Traub, me, Lee Traub.

Our first buying trip to India in 1966 led to our "Colors of Asia" promotion the following year. In 1978 for "India: The Ultimate Fantasy," Barbara D'Arcy and Candy Pratts Price transformed the entire store, and had twenty-foot high *pichwais* (banners) created for the Lexington Avenue Arcade (before we built our balcony).

Of our twenty-one Country promotions, China in 1980 created the most excitement and attracted the most attention.

We photographed this ad for children's knitwear in a school for gifted children in Shanghai, using the students as models. Our Chinese hosts insisted on checking the camera's viewfinder to make sure that we did not crop the photos of Mao and Chou En-lai in the background. To do so, according to Chinese superstition, would sever their spirits.

The priceless Imperial Robes of the Forbidden City, worn by the Emperors of the Ming and Qing dynasties, were our greatest attraction, loaned to us by Mr. Peng, the director of the Palace Museum.

July 14, 1979. In Beijing, I signed a six-page trade agreement with Chia-Shih, the vice-minister of foreign trade.

Bloomingdale's, when written phonetically in Chinese, used symbols that translated as "Heralding the Dawn of a New Era," which became the slogan for our poster developed by the Number One Advertising agency, in Shanghai

Receiving the Legion d'Honneur from President Mitterrand in 1986 at the Elysée Palace was a great honor. As is the French custom, the president then kissed me on both cheeks.

The Carters did not shop at Bloomingdale's during their term in the White House. We were told Bloomingdale's image was "too trendy." In November 1980, shortly after President Carter lost the election, Rosalynn Carter opened an account in our White Flint store. A few weeks later at a White House reception I remarked to the President: "Who knows what would have happened if Mrs. Carter had shopped at Bloomingdale's all along?" President Carter then sent me this photo of him leaving to board the presidential helicopter, Bloomingdale's shopping bag in hand.

Lee's close and enduring friendship with Martha Graham grew out of a lifelong passion for dance starting when she studied at the Graham school. For many years Lee was chairman of the Martha Graham Dance Company. Here Lee, Martha and Mikhail Baryshnikov at an opening night gala for the company.

A week after acquiring Federated, Bob Campeau came to Bloomingdale's to attend our "Hooray for Hollywood" promotion. Bob was all smiles and basked in the glow of the media attention brought on by his new acquisition.

According to Bob Campeau, when he visited our Boca Raton store in November 1987, he felt it was the best-looking store he'd ever seen, and determined on the spot that he had to own Bloomingdale's and Federated.

The disastrous press conference in Tokyo on November 29, 1989. Unable to secure Japanese financing to purchase Bloomingdale's, Jeff Sherman and I try to put a positive face on our trip. I'm afraid we were unconvincing.

For our fall 1981 promotion of "Ireland, That Special Place," Waterford's finest craftsmen created a champagne cooler bearing the Great Seal of the United States, for Lee and me to present to President Reagan, whose ancestors hail from Balleyporeen. Ten days before the presentation we discovered the stem was cracked. Waterford's master cutters then worked day and night to create another, and flew it to New York in its own seat aboard Aer Lingus. The damaged original, now repaired, resides in my home.

Lee and I in Utah on the terrace of
our ski house in Deer Valley. *Below*:
The Traub family photographed at a
party our close friends Harry and
Barbara Fields gave in their home
the day after I left Bloomingdale's.
Left to right: Jimmy, Buffy, Lee, me,
Peggy, Andy, Phyllis, Lois.

Bloomingdale's main floor
November 15, 1991.
The enthusiastic rally by
Bloomingdale's associates
with cheerleaders, pom-poms,
and a marching band made
for a rousing and emotional
farewell.

November 11, 1991. At the Waldorf-Astoria, Leonard Lauder and Ralph Lauren
hosted a dinner in my honor. Fourteen hundred friends and associates attended a
benefit for the Lee and Marvin Traub scholarships at Harvard. *Left to right*: Leonard
Lauder, Ricky and Ralph Lauren, Lee, me, Alan Questrom, Ed Finkelstein.

who knew what was happening in New York, the man who was watching what was happening in Europe—would shop at Bloomingdale's. And Ralph saw it before many others did—even those who worked at the store.

In those days, the Bloomingdale's men's department was still cut very much in the Brooks Brothers mold. If Brooks carried shetland sweaters in four colors, we did, too. We had no designer names. When Bloomingdale's first began to carry Pierre Cardin, it was in the basement. Our buyers dealt, for the most part, only with people with whom they had long-standing relationships.

Ralph tried to sell Bloomingdale's his ties, but he wasn't a member of the club yet. He had a champion, though, in Joe Aezen, a tie salesman for Rooster neckwear. Joe was in his thirties and had great credibility among neckwear buyers throughout the industry. Joe knew ties, and loved the business.

Joe was very vocal in his enthusiasm for Ralph's ties. He would come in and tell Frank Simon, our menswear vice president, that he had to try on a Polo tie, and then he would give Frank one. He would tell Jack Shultz, our men's merchandise manager, about them, and he'd give Jack a tie. He gave one to Gary Shafer, the tie buyer as well. They were very flamboyant shapes. You put one on, and it made you smile. Wearing one of Ralph's wide ties made you feel that, within traditional boundaries, you were more with-it than the next guy.

Gary, who knew Ralph from his Rivetz days, had very good taste, and should have been the first to buy Ralph's ties. But Gary had his own design sensibilities. He believed that Ralph should modify his designs for Bloomingdale's. Gary offered to buy Ralph's ties if they were a touch narrower, and if Ralph would put a Bloomingdale's label in them. Ralph just closed his sample bag and said, "No. I can't do that."

It was a very gutsy move. Ralph wanted to be in Bloomingdale's very badly. Many people in Ralph's position would have accepted—many had, many would in years to come. But to his credit, Ralph said no.

At the same time, he was starting to attract other stores. Outside of New York, Neiman-Marcus started to carry his line. He turned down Wallach's and Macy's. He was fixated on Bloomingdale's.

Ralph's first break came several months later when Steve

Krauss, the tie department manager for the Bloomingdale's Fresh Meadow store, bought a few. They did very well. Joe Aezen kept coming in to 59th Street, saying, "How come you guys aren't carrying Ralph's ties yet? People are talking about them."

In the meantime, Gary had been to Europe and seen the new suit styles the Europeans were showing. Upon his return, he felt the time was right for Ralph and ordered a rack of the ties.

Ralph was ecstatic. I think the day we agreed to carry his ties at 59th Street was one of the happiest in his life. Now that he was in the store, he was leaving nothing to chance. Ralph would come in Monday and Thursday nights to make sure everything was all right. In those days, Ralph delivered the ties himself, leaving his car parked at the curb, running in dressed in a bomber jacket and jeans. On Saturday mornings, he would come in to straighten his cases. Even then Ralph was steadfast in how his designs should be displayed. He would give demonstrations on how his ties should be knotted, how he wanted them with a dimple, just so.

The ties were an immediate success, and at an average of $10 a tie, it was a very good business. More important, for the first time, we were starting a major trend in men's fashion. I was wearing traditional suits then but quickly became perfectly comfortable wearing a wide tie. That tie was the beginning of an explosion in America. Until then, menswear had little in the way of a fashion business. There had not been a major fashion change in a decade. Once you had a wide tie, however, all your old ties were dated. And you needed a new shirt, and a new suit to go with it. Ralph's ties, we realized, were the beginning of a change in American menswear.

For Father's Day, we did a full-page ad of a female model wearing nothing but a Ralph Lauren wide tie. It received tremendous attention.

The ties became a very important business, but the day came when Ralph had to move on. He remembers the day—or more specifically, the night—clearly. Ralph came in one Thursday evening, a few months after his ties had been selling like crazy, only to find another rack of wide ties next to his.

Ralph's first reaction was, "Oh God! They've knocked me off!" He turned to one of our merchandise managers, Joe Checkeon, and said, "What'll I do?"

Joe told him not to worry. "You know the difference between your ties and those?" Joe asked.

Ralph was still a little stunned.

"Well, I'll tell you," Joe explained, "it's love. The others are just cashing in on a fad; you love what you do."

It was true and Ralph never forgot that. He had poured his heart and soul into those ties, attending to every detail. But they were only the first part of a larger vision. He now had to move on to the next step.

b

Ralph was becoming a problem for Beau Brummel. They didn't know what to do with all his energy. Ralph wanted to do shirts and suits; he wanted his own line. Beau Brummel decided it was best to let Ralph leave. They agreed that if he would buy out his stock, they would let him take his tie division and keep the name Polo.

In 1968, he formed his own menswear company, Polo Fashions, Inc., with backing from Norman Hilton, a successful clothing manufacturer. Norman gave him $50,000 in credit and agreed to make Ralph's clothes, and that's how Polo started. Ralph decided to do shirts first and brought them to Bloomingdale's. We loved them. They were very unusual and exciting, very different—button-down oxfords in bold, colorful stripes. Ralph's shirts were all-cotton before all-cotton was in fashion; shoppers then still looked for new miracle "wrinkle free" fabric. He also took great care in how the shirt fronts were made; the cuffs were more tapered than most American shirts. They were distinctive and became a big hit.

Suits came next. Men's suits at that time were all big and baggy Brooks Brothers–type sack suits. Ralph's taste has always been more Anglophile. He wanted to take the Ivy League look and put shape into the classic dark suits to create a more European look. He wanted to use softer European fabrics and bring some of the elements of custom tailoring to his collection.

It took Ralph a while to have his vision of the English "university" executed. He also tried a line of "unconstructed" jackets that failed—they were about two decades ahead of their time. Finally, he found a way to create Polo suits that were shaped and followed the form of the body, with soft shoulders, flared at the back.

When I think of Ralph's first few men's collections and the image he was creating I think of Steve McQueen in *The Thomas Crown Affair*. The movie, written by Alan Trustman, was released around the same time as Ralph's first men's collection. In the movie, McQueen portrayed a jaded, thirty-six-year-old businessman who commits crimes just for the intellectual challenge. Faye Dunaway is the investigator pursuing him and his love interest in the film.

I have always thought of McQueen in that movie as the Ralph Lauren hero: a rugged, sophisticated loner who drives expensive cars. There is even a scene where Faye Dunaway watches McQueen playing polo. The movie demonstrated the extent to which Ralph was in tune with the culture, and the culture with Ralph. The movie was an acknowledged influence for some shots in Ralph's spring 1977 catalog.

In Ralph we had our first exclusive, our first home-grown designer. In 1969, the Coty awards were created to be the Oscars of the fashion industry, with the first being awarded to Bill Blass; Ralph won the second. It was about that time that Ralph told Franklin Simon, our general merchandise manager for menswear, that he needed his own shop. He wanted Bloomingdale's to create a men's club for him, his ties, sportswear, suits, all in one environment. There were no men's designer boutiques then.

Frank was concerned that it would hurt Polo's sales in other parts of the store. Ralph's suits were sold in the men's clothing department, and his shirts in the shirt department. In Ralph's case, however, selling the various lines together made particular sense because the wide tie demanded a certain collar, and the suits had wide lapels and were shaped in a way that complemented the shirts and ties. Ralph was selling an image, a life-style, and he needed a showcase for it. And, true to his uncompromising standards, he threatened to walk if he didn't get his own shop.

That fall, Ralph got his Polo shop, located on the 60th Street side of our main-floor men's store. He had very firm notions about everything in the shop, including the furniture. Ralph's Polo shop was fitted with paneling of distressed wormy chestnut in a beige finish. There was a stained parquet floor and an oriental rug giving the shop an elegant continental feeling. It was the most expensive shop we had ever built, but it was a great success. We had made a commitment to Ralph. He was our designer, and our men's business would rise or fall with him.

b

By 1970, Bloomingdale's was having tremendous success with women's sportswear. It was evident to Katie Murphy, Dick Hauser, and me that Ralph should apply his talent to the women's field. He had been thinking along the same lines.

Ralph said that he wanted to design a women's collection. At the time the women's fashion press was promoting the midi, but that was not a look that appealed to Ralph's wife, Ricki, and the other young women he knew. They were buying riding jackets and boy's blazers. Ralph had always liked the look of a Garbo or a Dietrich, a man-tailored look.

A whole collection would take time. So Katie asked him, "What could you do right away?"

Ralph said he could do a line of shirts.

In the 1970s there was a very large business in women's blouses. Anne Klein was the important designer. She was, in fact, *the* American sportswear designer, but she catered to an older woman with soft and feminine fashions.

Ralph, on the other hand, was thinking of the women of his generation. He loved the way his wife looked on the weekends, wearing one of his shirts. Ralph, who never went to fashion school, had no idea back then of how to design women's clothing. So he made a shirt and fitted it on his assistant. It was not a blouse, however. It was made like a man's shirt in every way, from the fabrics to the stitching. It may not have been the first time anyone had ever done a man-tailored shirt, but there were none popularly available in department stores.

A man-tailored shirt business did not exist, so Ralph's shirts represented a new direction and a great opportunity. The shirts were bold, in stripes or solid colors, with white collars and white cuffs, made with the best fabrics—fine cotton and wool blends. And they had two distinctive features worth mentioning. The first was that the shirt cuffs had a polo player insignia—the first time Ralph used the polo player as a symbol on his clothing. The other is that the shirt labels read "Polo by Ralph Lauren."

Designer names were important in women's clothes. In the European arena, Bloomingdale's was championing a whole new generation of sportswear designers. In the United States, the important
names were Bill Blass, Anne Klein, and Geoffrey Beene. So Ralph
thought it important to be identified not as a brand like Jantzen or
Gant, but as a designer.

We created a shop for Ralph's women's shirts on the third floor
across from the escalator. It was an instant success and we had
trouble keeping up with the demand. We then said to Ralph, "What
else do you want to do?" Ralph said he now wanted to do a full
women's collection. This was certain to stand out. There was a
classic element to his design that had a wide appeal. Women might
talk about Kenzo, but they were going to wear Ralph Lauren.

For his first women's collection, Ralph held a fashion show in
his offices. The clothes were tailored—he had scaled down the
men's line to a woman's proportions—the sleeves were slim, the
waists tapered but it was very feminine, very sexy. For the women's
collection there was a brown Harris tweed suit and a gray flannel
suit, with high-waisted cuffed pants, complete with three pleats and
a long zipper up the front.

In the early seventies there was something provocative yet completely establishment about a woman wearing a suit and tie. Just a
few years earlier, *Bonnie and Clyde* had given rise to gangster-chic
bold pinstripes, and women dressing like men was part of the spirit
of the day. At a time when youth were rebelling around the world, a
woman dressing in a man's suit was an acceptable way to express a
sophisticated brand of nonconformism. Once again, Ralph and the
culture were in tune. To prove that everything comes around again,
for his fall 1992 collection, representing his twenty-fifth year in
the business, Ralph designed a whole new group of women's man-
tailored clothes.

We were so confident of Ralph's success that we decided to
launch his women's line with its own shop, as one of the third-floor
boutiques we created for our centennial celebration. Ralph was the
only American along with Missoni, Sonia Rykiel, and the first Saint
Laurent Rive Gauche boutique in any American store. Ralph's shop
was directly across from Saint Laurent's. At that time Ralph was an
unproven designer of women's apparel, and locating his shop adja-

cent to YSL was both a risk for us and a vote of confidence that Ralph took as a great compliment.

Ralph had found the whole process of designing a women's collection, in his words, "scary." Having succeeded, and having a shop across from Saint Laurent, Ralph wanted to quit right there and then. How could he top that? Despite his success, Ralph still has the same fears each time he does a ready-to-wear collection. Designing a new women's collection every season does not come easy for Ralph. Men's apparel is second nature for him—he has always lived with menswear—but to come up with new ideas, new concepts, and new fashion directions for ready-to-wear is very challenging. His collections have influenced the way women dress all over the world. Over the years, I've noticed that many designers are prepared for failure, but few are prepared to succeed. And Ralph's success began to cause problems for his business.

His men's clothes continued to prosper, but the situation with his women's line was more complicated. Ralph was both designing and manufacturing his women's wear. His business was expanding, but he couldn't deliver on time. Although they looked perfect, his clothes did not always fit right. Ralph was designing his man-tailored women's clothes as if all women were built like boys. Women found the shirts too tight across the bust, or his pants too tight in the seat. He had to learn to make some adjustments. For example, Ralph liked to use actual men's zippers in his women's clothes, but he had to learn that to fit a woman's body, he had to shorten them.

Ralph's problem wasn't sales; it was logistics. He was not running an efficient business, and he was having cash-flow problems. Ralph had just bought out his partner, Norman Hilton. Since Norman did not need to sell, the price was high. As a result, Ralph was financially strapped. To add to that, he had started a Chaps pants line. They were selling, but the line was causing additional cash-flow problems.

In June 1971, the contrast between Ralph's success as a designer and as a businessman became more apparent. He won his second Coty award for his men's line, but at the same time he could no longer meet his payroll. Ralph came to see me to ask if Bloomingdale's might advance him the payment for what it ordered for fall.

"I'll see what I can do," I said. This was a highly unusual arrangement, yet, I understood how serious the situation was for him. I went immediately to Larry Lachman, who was Bloomingdale's chairman at that time.

"We have to do something unusual for him," I said. "We have to pay him in advance when we give him the orders, because he doesn't have enough money to make the goods." I knew it was unusual, but Ralph was the American designer the store had bet on, and we had to support him. To his credit, Larry agreed immediately. Over lunch the following Friday, I told Ralph that Bloomingdale's would give him an advance based on his fall orders. Today, when I read that Ralph Lauren is a $3 billion business, I think of the time when we had to send him the checks in advance so he could pay his bills and make his women's collection.

We were only a stop-gap solution. Ralph's financial problems continued to grow over the next year. By 1973, Ralph stood to lose everything. The big drain continued to be manufacturing the women's line. What he needed to do was pump cash into the business and license the manufacture of his women's line. However, Ralph had never licensed anything, and was afraid of losing control of his name.

Designers were then just starting to license. Bill Blass had licensed a menswear collection. Hardie Amies had done licenses in Europe, and Missoni had a licensee in the United States. Pierre Cardin was putting his name on anything that didn't move. To Ralph, however, there was an important difference. Most designers were licensing their names for markets, or products, that were separate from the arena in which they had made their reputations. Ralph was a working designer. For him to license women's wear in the United States was, he thought, very dangerous.

Ralph decided that although he would license the women's line, he would continue to design it. His vision of Polo/Ralph Lauren was so strong that he felt that, even under license, he could maintain the right image and the proper quality. He had to decide: license or go under. So he agreed to license the right to make Polo women's wear to Stuart Kreisler.

Kreisler was a bright, aggressive, twenty-seven-year-old then. In 1972, he had opened the Kreisler Group and was making clothes for such names as Clovis Ruffin and John Kloss. He knew Ralph and was willing to back him to the fullest. He gave personal guarantees to see that Polo remained above water.

The other important addition to Ralph's company was Peter Strom. As Norman Hilton's executive vice president, Peter had taken a leadership role in developing the Ralph Lauren business. The year after Ralph bought out Hilton, Peter joined Ralph's company as president and partner and has been a strong support ever since. Over the next few years, Ralph made a license agreement in Japan with Seibu, and another to open a shop in Beverly Hills. Doing so put his company on solid financial ground. Over the years, the prestige of Ralph's licenses has only increased, due to the fact that he sets high standards in his contracts and runs herd over the quality.

The Kreisler Group had its own financial tribulations and, ultimately, filed for Chapter 11 protection. Maurice Bidermann, a French industrialist, close friend and chairman of Bidermann Industries, took over the license with my encouragement. At Ralph's insistence, and with Maurice's agreement, Stuart Kreisler remained as president of Ralph Lauren women's wear.* Maurice dismissed almost everyone else explaining that, in his French, "they were all schmucks."

In 1979, as I recall, the women's business was doing $12 or $13 million and losing over a million dollars a year. Maurice immediately took the basic women's cotton knit shirt, had it made in Hong Kong for substantially less, and raised the price. On the success of that one cotton knit shirt, Maurice turned around the entire Ralph Lauren women's business, making it profitable in one year.

b

A funny thing happened when Ralph became a women's designer: He discovered the world of fashion shows, press, and publicity. But the fashion press, for the longest time, took no notice of Ralph Lauren. It didn't matter that he won his third Coty award in 1974, this time for women's wear, and that three years later he was in-

---

* Stuart Kreisler left Ralph Lauren in 1987 and became a principal in Sam & Libby, a growing West Coast shoe company. In 1993 he rejoined the Bidermann organization to work on building the Ralph Lauren women's business.

ducted into the Coty Hall of Fame. It was always the other designers, Halston and Calvin Klein, whom the fashion press wrote about
—not Ralph.

To read the fashion press, Ralph was barely a blip on the screen.
I know it bothered him. The fashion press is important: They are
engines in creating "word of mouth." They can be valuable partners
in creating an image for a designer.

The reason the fashion press initially ignored Ralph was obvious: Ralph was more interested in style than fashion, and the press
did not deem his designs newsworthy. Further, Ralph was not out
there making copy. While other designers were dancing the night
away at Studio 54, Ralph was at home with Ricki and their three
children. I sometimes feel the press held it against him. Ralph had
found a niche in the market, but no way to get the exposure he
wanted. He had not found the way to flesh out his image on a larger
screen.

The answer came from the movies. Instead of the movies inspir-
ing Ralph, they now called on him to be inspired. In 1973, Ralph
was asked to make some of the men's clothes for *The Great Gatsby*,
starring Robert Redford, a Ralph Lauren guy if ever there was one.
The notion of creating Gatsby's suits and shirts—the beautiful shirts
that made Daisy cry—was a dream assignment. Ralph loved to look
back to the clothes of the jazz age for the details he cared most
about: the length and spread of the collars, how the ties were knotted, the suits without vents. He couldn't have been more challenged,
or more inspired.

As a result, Ralph received the sort of national coverage that
had eluded him. There were articles in publications like *Daily News
Record* and *GQ* that focused as much, if not more, on Ralph's clothes
than the movie. And in many ways they were right: The clothes were
the star of the film.

Ralph, however, was not the Gatsby costume designer, Theoni
Aldredge was. Ralph was paid only to make the clothes; he was not
even paid a design fee. Nonetheless, he got most of the press attention. This must have irritated Ms. Aldredge no end, because when
she accepted her Oscar for costuming *The Great Gatsby*, she was
conspicuous in not mentioning Ralph. But no matter, he was
launched in the press.

In 1977, Ralph received tremendous attention when Woody Allen and Diane Keaton wore his clothes in *Annie Hall*, establishing a look for women that quickly passed into the popular culture. Ralph, too, was entering the mainstream. *Women's Wear* started to give him the recognition he deserved. But there was another reason for that: By then he had ventured into the image-conscious cosmetics industry.

b

Cosmetics was, in many ways, the conduit through which Ralph was finally able to communicate his vision to a mass public. Although he had been approached several times over the years about lending his name to a scent, Ralph was not interested in being just one line of a company; he wanted to be a whole brand unto himself. So when George Friedman, who had worked at Estée Lauder, approached him about a joint venture with Warner's, Ralph was interested. Friedman told Ralph that a Polo men's fragrance was a natural because Ralph had built such a strong following, and that his name, Lauren, was also perfect for a women's fragrance.

In 1976, Ralph entered into a partnership with Warner Communications to market and sell women's and men's fragrances. It was to be a license agreement, so he would have none of the problems he had had to date with manufacturing. Ralph was enthusiastic about the venture, having met Steve Ross, Warner's chief executive, with whom he had become friends. Ralph and George Friedman were joined by Bob Ruttenberg, who had worked with Friedman at Estée Lauder. Together they formed Warner/Lauren Limited, a division of Warner.

In 1978, Polo for men and Lauren for women were both launched at Bloomingdale's.* The following year they launched

---

* One side anecdote: As Bloomingdale's was preparing to launch Polo, I had a meeting at Warner with Lester Gribetz, George, Bob, and Steve Ross, who was also a friend of mine. We were discussing promotional ideas for the launch of the men's fragrance. I mentioned that I had just seen a new item the week before. It was a video game called Atari, and it was great. I thought that if we could have an Atari giveaway with the launch of Polo, that would be terrific. Steve's group said they would look into it. It turned out to be too late to use it for the launch, but a few months later Warner acquired Atari. Ultimately, Atari was a very big business for Warner and then a very big loss.

Chaps for men, an attempt at a more commercial fragrance like Revlon's Chaz. In 1983, Warner launched the Ralph Lauren Cosmetics Collection. Bloomingdale's gave it a prime location in the middle of the department, but it flopped. Warner's was struggling with the business, and it never fully got off the ground. Ultimately, Warner's sold the whole company to Cosmair, who made it into a very successful venture. Cosmair turned around the business by creating a separate Ralph Lauren fragrance division within the company, developing new lines such as Polo Crest and Safari for men and women and spending extensively for advertising and new Polo cosmetics outposts. In 1991, according to *WWD*, worldwide wholesale volume of all Ralph Lauren fragrances amounted to $150 million, Ralph's royalties, according to another source, were $7.5 million—for that year alone. With the successful launches of Safari and Safari for Men, the 1993 sales figures may approach $200 million.

Cosmetics allowed Ralph to support his entire business by investing many additional advertising dollars. He was able to project what he saw in his head and the mood he felt when he created the clothes. With the extra advertising budget for newspapers, magazines, and television, he could merchandise his clothes and products as no store could. At last the fashion press caught on.

Ralph's great strength is that he doesn't do things tentatively; he goes all out. Having a single page of advertising in *The New York Times Magazine* was a big deal then. Ralph, however, decided to do an eighteen-page spread. No one had ever taken that many ads in a single issue. The impact was tremendous. Today, "block advertising" is commonplace, but Ralph started it. The ads overwhelmed the magazine, telling the story of his collections directly to consumers. The ads themselves, one following another, with a perceived story line, had a cinematic effect like the early nickelodeons, where single images were flipped to produce moving pictures. Ralph was making movies, which I believe is what he has always wanted to do.

Ralph understood that fashion is all about one question: Who am I? When you close your eyes what sort of person do you see yourself as? Uptown or downtown? Banker, gangster, cowboy, or Indian chief? Over the years, Ralph has created distinct looks for each in both men's and women's wear. His talent was that he realized, early on, that no individual adopts one style all the time. You may be a business executive during the week and a cowboy on the weekend. Women may want to wear more lace in the evening than they do at the office, or vice versa. For whatever look you want, Ralph began to produce the elements. And Polo always offered marvelous colors and the finest fabrics. Take Fair Isle sweaters, for example. Ralph makes a softer one in more colors than anyone in the United States or Scotland.

Over the years, Ralph introduced designs inspired by Hopi Indian blankets and calico-dressed women in covered wagons. There were black velvet gowns and cashmere dresses. He went Country, Out of Africa, and On Safari. He's done the 1920s, 1930s, and 1940s, each time expanding the range and vision of his clothes.

At the same time, Ralph kept expanding into new areas. In 1978, when he couldn't find clothes he liked for his own sons, he launched a boy's line. Bloomingdale's created a separate shop for Ralph Lauren Boy's—fashioning a whole new business.

Meanwhile Ralph and I had been discussing, for some time over many lunches, his entry into the home furnishings field. Over the years, Ralph had been approached by several sheet companies to license a Ralph Lauren sheet. Many designers were doing it. Missoni had been very successful, Dior was a big best-seller. But that was not Ralph. If he went into what we call "domestics," he wasn't going to design just a sheet, he was going to create a whole concept for the home.

Ralph was very concerned that he have the right partners. Finally, he set up a joint venture with J. P. Stevens, then headed by Dave Tracy, a friend who had also gone to Harvard Business School, and was creative in his domestics marketing strategies.

The Ralph Lauren Home Collection was launched in 1983 at Bloomingdale's. This was the first time that a major modern apparel designer offered an all-encompassing program of home furnishings. The first collection was magnificent. There were $400 and $500 Irish linen sheets, $200 Italian printed sheets of magnificent fabrics, blankets, throws. Bloomingdale's built a shop for them on our domestics floor, an incredible home environment that Ralph and his team helped to create. Typical of Ralph's approach, he designed with lifestyles in mind.

The collection was beautiful but not merchandised like any other sheet line. There was no white sale, no irregulars. There were, however, Ralph's usual growing pains, particularly with delivery problems. So, beautiful as the collection was, it struggled to get off the ground.

Initially Stevens was calling the shots, but when the sheet collection was not succeeding well enough, the Ralph Lauren organization took over the marketing and management as well as the design. As we had suggested, they went to a strategy that included white sales and promotional merchandise. In no time, Ralph Lauren became Bloomingdale's largest single resource for sheets and domestics, with a taste level far superior to any other.

In his Home Collection, Ralph took the same life-style approach he had in his first men's collection. He introduced color and new ideas—all designed within classic boundaries. Most manufacturers start with a white sheet but Ralph's first was a button-down sheet in oxford blue, with actual buttons on the sheet. As he has done with apparel, Ralph's created a variety of different looks: New England, contemporary, American traditional, and an English country look. It was a unique collection for the home. From day one, Ralph had the best designs in the industry, which, when marketed properly, became a great success.

Having established that business, he turned next to towels. The distinguishing elements among towels are weight, heft, and color. Ralph immediately went into what he personally enjoys, a heavier towel in great colors. Although Polo towels were successful from the start, Ralph wasn't satisfied.

"You'll never have a towel business," he told me, "if you show the towels with the sheets." Ralph wanted a separate Polo towel shop. We worked together to design and build one. Ralph was right —once we installed Ralph's towel display, the business shot ahead and became one of Bloomingdale's best-selling towel collections. That is as much a testament to Ralph's consummate marketing and merchandising skills as it is to his design sense.

In 1986, the Home Collection expanded to include furniture, a rattan and wicker collection in the spring, and an upholstered collection in the fall. Over the following years, Ralph began to segment several different furniture looks, just as he had done for sheets, introducing styles with such names as Country Manor, Western, New England, and Thoroughbred. Today Ralph Lauren Home Furnishings has a dominant position in the sheet and towel industry. The challenge for Ralph is to gain the same position in the balance of home furnishings—particularly furniture and tabletop.

Ralph was well aware that no one store could merchandise his goods as well as he could. Several times over the years he had considered opening his own store. Each time I talked him out of it, and together we found ways to execute his vision at Bloomingdale's. By the early 1980s, Ralph's business had grown so much, in so many areas, that Bloomingdale's did not have the real estate to display all of his merchandise together in one environment, as he desired.

One day after one of our Four Seasons lunches Ralph asked if I would accompany him uptown. "There's something I want to show you," he said. Ralph took me to the corner of 72nd Street and Madison Avenue. Pointing to the ornate turn-of-the-century mansion on the corner, he said, "Marvin, I've just leased this building for what will be the ultimate Ralph Lauren Shop."

I admit I was nervous about having such major competition only twelve blocks north of Bloomingdale's. But I knew that Ralph's goal was not to lose his Bloomingdale's business. I promised to support him enthusiastically if he would work with us to build our Bloomingdale's business as well. I suspected that Ralph's own store would not only increase his prestige and reputation, but could also support our own Polo business. As Ralph was preparing his store on 72nd Street, I met with Peter Strom to plan the expansion and renovation of our own Ralph Lauren shops at 59th Street.

Most retailers have a violent negative reaction when a designer plans to open a shop in their area. Bergdorf's, for example, dropped Chanel when Chanel opened on 57th Street. I have found that response is mostly emotional. Retailers usually buy only a small portion of a designer's collection—one third or less. The designer wants a shop that can present the entire collection. Over the years the opening of Ralph Lauren, Chanel, Armani, Sonia Rykiel, and other designer stores did not significantly impact our business.

In 1986, Ralph opened his twenty-thousand-square-foot flagship store in the Rhinelander Mansion at Madison Avenue and East 72nd Street. The cost for renovating the mansion has been estimated at

$30 million—and Ralph does not own it, he has a long-term lease. So his investment in the store, in every sense of the word, was great.

The day the store opened Ralph invited Lee and me to see it. He led us on a tour of every room and every department. It was fantastic. This was Gatsby's mansion. Every detail was perfectly executed. Vintage tennis racquets and lacrosse sticks rested in rooms as if they'd just been left there a moment ago. When a book was on a shelf, it was a book, not just a fake binding, and was appropriate to that room, or the person one imagined inhabiting it. It was as if the images in Ralph's head had finally become three-dimensional.

As Ralph walked us down the main staircase we passed an old-world English portrait. We stopped to admire it. I thought that the gentleman must be of royal lineage.

"That," Ralph said jokingly," is Grandpa Lifschitz."

Lee's and my presence there meant a lot to Ralph. There were other retailers who were not as supportive, and there were some in the fashion press who would secretly have liked Ralph to fail, to self-destruct like Fitzgerald's Gatsby. But Ralph's store was a success. The first year sales volume was more than $30 million—and our Polo business went up that year as well.

Ralph understood Bloomingdale's, and I did my best to show that I understood Ralph. My function as president or chairman of Bloomingdale's was to be as supportive of Ralph as I could be. I stood by him: Whatever new venture he was interested in, I gave him the full benefit of my experience, resources, and advice. I was enthusiastic about each venture; and when at first they stumbled, I didn't pull back. I understood that Ralph's success lay in the breadth of his vision.

For example: Why is it that so many people who wore Lacoste alligator shirts ten years ago now wear Polo? And why do some people who wore Polo shirts five years ago now wear shirts from the Gap? If you are Ralph Lauren, the answer is clear.

When Lacoste first introduced their shirts, they had a certain cachet. They were European and worn by golf pros and tennis players. Vin Draddy, the personable president of David Crystal, Lacoste's American licensee, sent the shirts to President Eisenhower and the best-known golf and tennis pros, who started to wear them. Soon after, the alligator shirts started to turn up at country clubs all over the country. People who wore them were saying they had a certain sophistication. Lacoste became very successful. Then General Mills took it over, broadened the distribution, the quality suffered and much of the cachet was lost.

One day, Ralph tried one on, and was not pleased with it. He looked at the label and saw that it was not all cotton; and the cotton felt rough. He didn't like the collar, or the buttons. So he decided to make his own version of the shirt.

When Ralph made his shirt, it was 100 percent cotton, and he used a softer cotton. He made the shirt in several different weights and weaves, from a pebble grain to a knit. Where Lacoste offered a somewhat limited selection of colors, Ralph made them in thirty bold colors. Almost instantly they became Bloomingdale's best-selling knits, and in no time Polo knits became the standard.

There will always be a small group, perhaps 10 percent of consumers, whose self-image is as fashion leaders or nonconformists; they may move on from Polo to the Gap, and will soon shop elsewhere. But most consumers, even if they buy at the Gap, still buy Ralph Lauren shirts and clothes as part of their wardrobe mix. A Polo knit and Gap or Levi jeans is one of the most popular outfits in America. Consequently, in 1993, when many retailers' sales are flat, Ralph Lauren's mens' sales are up substantially.

When Ralph decided to do his own store I knew it would have tremendous impact. Suddenly, a whole other group "got" Ralph's display. The total image of what it meant to wear Ralph Lauren was apparent. Ralph's store explained to our store managers and salespeople how best to sell Ralph Lauren products.

In many ways Ralph is the most Bloomingdale's-like of the designers. The merchandising approach that revolutionized our home furnishings department, and that we extended to every department of the store, of displaying goods from different departments together as they fit a life-style is the same philosophy that inspires Ralph Lauren. Just as we targeted our core customer, and then gave them a multiplicity of choices, all congruent with their self-image, Ralph Lauren has done the same thing. Over the last two decades Bloomingdale's and Polo/Ralph Lauren have grown to be national brands. What we accomplished with publicity, Ralph has done with advertising. Over the years, I have stood by Ralph, and he has stood by Bloomingdale's.

I don't want to get ahead of my story, but it is important to say that when Bloomingdale's went into Chapter 11 in 1990, Ralph stood by us. He understood that the problems we faced had nothing to do with the store, but with the debt our parent company had assumed; and he believed it was important that Bloomingdale's survive.

Ralph is a life-style designer, and the trend is with him. As the suit business declines, more and more options become available for dressing for the workplace, the home, the weekend, the evening, for vacation, and for sports. As dressing has become more informal, many shoppers are less sure of what—or whom—to buy, but they feel comfortable buying Ralph Lauren.

б

To give some idea of the extent of Ralph's success, in 1991, according to *Women's Wear*, Polo/Ralph Lauren generated $3.1 billion in retail volume. Of that, *WWD* estimated that Polo's men's business accounts for $475 million in wholesale volume (and I think that number is low); the women's line, which includes Classics, Roughwear, Activewear, and the Collection, generates $120 to $130 million in wholesale volume, of which the Collection business is estimated at $10 to $15 million. Royalties on fragrance are also a profit center with a reported $150 million wholesale volume under a licensing arrangement with Cosmair, Inc., including Safari, Polo Crest, and Safari for Men. Home furnishings is estimated at $100 million; and the balance comes from such licenses as boy's wear, hosiery, belts, sunglasses, and small leather goods. There were, as of 1991, 145 Polo stores around the world, sixty-six of them in the United States and fifteen freestanding stores in Japan licensed thorough the Seibu Corp.

In 1992 Ralph received a Lifetime Achievement award from the Council of Fashion Designers of America. He had been in business for twenty-five years, no mean feat in the apparel business. I was honored on that same occasion, and it meant a great deal to me to share that special evening with Ralph.

Ralph's award was presented to him by Audrey Hepburn. Just a year before, Ralph had introduced her at a Lincoln Center gala in her honor. Audrey was the embodiment of the style that inspires Ralph. His vision is cinematic in its own way. To stand next to Audrey Hepburn, Ralph said in his acceptance speech, made him want to tell all his childhood friends with whom he went to the movies, "that you could get the girl," that you could make your dreams come true.

Ralph's dreams are not limited to fashion and furnishings. He has one of the world's great collection of classic cars, which he keeps at his various homes. When he was still a Rivetz tie salesman he drove a Morgan. He had to sell that car, but a decade later was able to buy himself a Porsche 911 Turbo. He now has a collection of racing cars including such classics as a 1947 Alpha Romeo Monza, an Alfa 2900B, a Porsche Spyder 1500Rs, a Mercedes SSK, and several Ferraris.

Ralph continues to be very ambitious: He has expressed interest in creating a magazine, a hotel, a spa, a ranch, and even a resort. He might still make a movie. He has even at times talked of going into the beef business. His ranch produces superb steaks that he sends to friends as Christmas gifts.

Ralph has not changed that much in the more than twenty-five years that I've known him. He is as driven today as he was when he was selling his first ties. Ralph has a tremendous drive to prove himself and he is his own toughest critic. He wants to be the best in anything he undertakes. At the same time, he embodies the very life-style he is selling. Even his corporate organization reflects his personal style. But no significant decision is made without him.

Ralph Lauren's enormous contribution to fashion is that he has become a designer for a total life-style, an individual who has changed the way men and women dress and furnish their homes throughout the world. Most consumers understand the Ralph Lauren look and visualize it instantly. Ralph launched a fashion direction in the sixties that spawned a whole sportswear generation from the Gap to Tommy Hilfiger, from Nautica to Banana Republic, among others.

There is something else that needs saying. Success has not changed Ralph Lauren. Other than some gray hairs and greater self-assurance, he and Ricki are very much the same couple Lee and I visited with in East Hampton twenty years ago, very much parents who took pride in their three children and still do.

This is not to say that Ralph doesn't enjoy his success. He has a 6,000-acre ranch in Rifle, Colorado, the Double RL; a home in

Round Hill, Jamaica, the former Douglas Dillon estate. He has a beautiful Fifth Avenue apartment overlooking Central Park, an oceanfront home in Montauk, and a manor house on a spectacular 200-acre property in Bedford. He enjoys them and is proud of them. He enjoys his family, and although Lee and I have gone out on occasion with Ralph and Ricki, they would sooner entertain at home.

I think one of the more poignant stories about Ralph that's not been in print involves a lunch we had in early 1987. Just a few months before Ralph had been on the cover of *Time*. We sat down to lunch in the middle booth at La Caravelle, but I immediately sensed that something was wrong.

"Ralph, you don't look very happy." I said.

"I've just had this cover story in *Time*," Ralph said. "I'm worth millions, I have all this success. Most people think I should be very happy. But this is a very difficult time for me. My father is in the hospital, I've just been up to see him. My brother had a stroke, and six months ago I was told that I have a brain tumor that's probably benign but needs to be operated on, and I haven't told anyone." Ralph then told me that although he was having headaches, he wanted to finish his next collection before the operation.

I told Ralph that my daughter, Peggy, had had a brain tumor. I told him about her symptoms, and how she was treated by the chief of neurology at New York Hospital.

"New York Hospital is where I am being treated," Ralph confided. (Ralph's tumor was later treated by several physicians at New York Hospital, including neurologist Frank Petito and neurosurgeon Richard Fraser.) And then before he could continue, he grabbed my arm and said, "I'm having a terrible headache right now."

"Let's leave the restaurant," I said. We had ordered, but the food had not arrived. So we rushed back to Ralph's office.

"Ralph, your health is more important than anything. Everyone thinks you're on top of the world. Only you and I know that you're not. But you have to attend to this right now. I'll call New York Hospital and I'll go up there with you."

Ralph truly must have been feeling ill, because he agreed. I called the doctor and told him what had happened to Ralph at lunch, called a car immediately and took Ralph to New York Hospital. It was a very intense time.

Ralph scheduled the operation. He told no one about it. It was important for him to finish that season's collection, which he did, appearing at the show. It was not terribly well received, but no one knew the strain he was under. He felt he would be letting down his whole organization and all the stores if he did not do a show. He then had the operation and the tumor was indeed benign.*

I've always remembered the few weeks when he was King Ralph to the public and facing his own mortality in private. He had dealt with it and kept it secret from everyone but his family and a few friends. That is a different side of Ralph Lauren. The Ralph Lauren no one knows.

---

* The extraordinary irony is that many months after writing this chapter, Lee was diagnosed with a tumor that was virtually the same as Ralph's. It was operated on successfully at New York Hospital by the same surgeon. Today, Lee can joke that she had the "Polo Ralph Lauren" tumor; but it is a harrowing experience to go through.

"*Whenever someone scoffs at dreaming the impossible dream, I tell them to think of Bloomingdale's—the way it was long, long ago, and the way it is now.*"

Drawing by W. Miller; © 1989 The New Yorker Magazine, Inc.

CHAPTER 10

Taking Bloomingdale's to the Top

By the 1970s, the transformation of Bloomingdale's was complete. Having succeeded at making Bloomingdale's a brand name, the next step was to take it national—something no department store had ever done before. The process of expanding from a downtown store with suburban branches to a chain of fifteen stores with locations as far afield as Dallas, Miami, and Chicago occurred over a sixteen-year period, and is ongoing. The results, though largely successful, were occasionally disappointing. Yet at the same time we broadened the recognition, reach, and value of Bloomingdale's through our renewed efforts in direct mail and public relations. By the late 1980s, we had introduced a new generation of foreign and American fashion designers. Each element—branch stores, a full-blown mail-order business, the success of such designers as Armani, Karl Lagerfeld, and Donna Karan—combined with the spending fever of the 1980s and the explosion of the bridge apparel business was alone an important chapter in Bloomingdale's evolution; taken together, they took Bloomingdale's to the top.

b

Shortly after I became president in 1969, our friends Jim and Helen Marcus invited Lee and me to join them aboard their new yacht for a vacation in the Caribbean. Most days were spent anchored off one island or another, frequently going ashore to golf, but halfway into our trip Jim decided that we should spend the day fishing. The fish, however, had other plans, and after some time without a bite, I became bored—not my sport, anyway. I decided instead to focus my attention on the future of Bloomingdale's. We had succeeded in building an exceptional store at 59th Street, one with an international reputation for fashion and style. We were successful and growing. What could we do now to maintain the momentum and expand?

The only way for Bloomingdale's to grow, I decided, was for the store to expand in a major way beyond the metropolitan area. At that time our business consisted of 59th Street and four suburban stores—Fresh Meadows, Stamford, Bergen County, and Short Hills. Bloomingdale's had become a name that meant something to people all over the country; the taste level and the life-style we catered to was no longer exclusive to New York. The Bloomingdale's couple could be found in Washington, D.C., Chicago, Florida, Texas— wherever there was a concentration of shoppers to whom our unique mix of merchandise would appeal.

Until now shoppers had traveled to 59th Street, making that store a priority destination and tourist attraction. But I concluded there were significant opportunities for Bloomingdale's branches in major cities that possessed a base of sophisticated, affluent consumers. If we opened Bloomingdale's in their communities, the excitement we created would draw the novice and the initiated, the curious and the jaded.

Selling the concept to Federated would not be easy. Sitting on the boat, I took out a yellow legal pad and wrote down a detailed plan for taking Bloomingdale's national. I then wrote what the critical issues would be for our corporate parent:

1. **Capital.** Building new stores would require substantial expense and investment.
2. **Would fashion sell?** There would be some concern, I knew, that the trendy fashions of Bloomingdale's would not sell across the country.
3. **Competition within Federated.** Since expansion would require the investment of Federated capital, there was an issue as to the willingness of the corporation to permit us to compete with other Federated divisions in some of the markets most appropriate for Bloomingdale's, such as Atlanta, Los Angeles, Houston, Dallas, Miami, and Boston.
4. **Management.** The more stores we opened, and the farther away from New York they were, the more difficulty we could have managing them.

5. **Transfer costs.** Warehousing and shipping bulky furniture and home furnishings for stores in distant locations could be very costly, making branch stores economically unfeasible.
6. **Advertising and promotional costs.** Entering new markets where we would not have critical mass would incur greater advertising and promotional costs than in our existing stores.

Then I wrote, in capital letters, what I thought was the greatest obstacle: NO ONE HAS EVER DONE IT BEFORE.

At the time no major department store had made itself a national chain. Department stores were, for the most part, still anchored to the downtown area of their home cities. A number had branches in nearby suburbs, but none had been able to grow their stores nationally.

I knew it would be a hard sell. But I saw an intermediate step. As Bloomingdale's strength and uniqueness was in home furnishings —our merchandise was very different from our competition's—I felt we could open a home furnishings chain at a considerably smaller investment than the cost of full branches. We would choose markets surrounding metropolitan New York in an ever-expanding circle. If the home furnishings stores were successful, we would have the leverage to either build a national home furnishings chain or eventually open complete stores across the country.

Upon my return, I made a presentation first to Larry Lachman, my partner, and then to Harold Krensky and Ralph Lazarus, the group president and chairman of Federated. After considerable review, the Federated board approved the plan and we began to seek locations for home furnishings stores. By 1973 we had four stores in four different markets with more than 250,000 square feet of space. We opened our first separate Bloomingdale's home furnishings stores in Manhasset, Long Island, in 1971; in Scarsdale, Westchester, in 1972; in Jenkintown near Philadelphia, also in 1972; and in Boston, in late 1973.

There was some concern that Philadelphia's conservative Main Line would not go for our trendy home furnishing fashions. To the contrary, modern furniture was the big seller in Jenkintown—precisely because Bloomingdale's was the best place to buy contemporary home furnishings in the Philadelphia area. The home furnishings stores were a success from day one.

More important, our surveys showed that the greatest complaint with our home furnishings stores was that they weren't full-line stores. The demand was there. So, armed with the research and our success in the early seventies, we convinced Federated that Bloomingdale's could prosper in communities filled with our customers. Our newest stores were still in the greater metropolitan New York area. We opened our Garden City, Long Island, branch in 1972. In 1975 we opened White Plains, which to this day is one of our most successful stores.

Garden City overlapped with the Manhasset home furnishings store, as did White Plains with our Eastchester store. Consumers will travel for furniture, so when we opened the new branches, we closed the furniture stores. Similarly, we closed Jenkintown when we opened Willow Grove in 1982.

Nonetheless, you could say we still served for the most part a group of people who all read *The New York Times* every morning. But we were determined to take Bloomingdale's in new directions. We initiated an ambitious program of nationwide expansion that had us opening almost a store a year in such places as Tyson's Corner, Virginia (1976), and White Flint, Maryland (1977) in the Washington, D.C., area; Chestnut Hill, Boston (1978)—an apparel store that complemented our adjacent home furnishings store; King of Prussia (1981) and Willow Grove (1982), outside Philadelphia; Dallas (1983); The Falls, near Miami (1984); Boca Raton (1986); and North Michigan Avenue in Chicago (1988). By 1989, the nine national stores added almost $500 million to the Bloomingdale's sales volume.*

b

A Bloomingdale's opening outside the New York metropolitan area was a major event. The day we opened our first full store in Washington at Tyson's Corner, 230,000 square feet on three levels, more than a thousand people showed up and traffic came to a complete halt on the Beltway.

---

* I was also involved in our Palm Beach store, which opened in 1991, and the planning of the Bloomingdale's Mall of America branch that opened in August 1992 in the suburbs of Minneapolis.

For the Washington opening, we wanted to position ourselves as distinct from the other Washington stores, so I asked our marketing group in consultation with Grey Advertising to devise a new store motto for the occasion. After a number of ideas were reviewed, I was handed a piece of paper with a number of phrases about the store. One leaped off the page: "Bloomingdale's, it's like no other store in the world."

"That's it," I said. "That's our slogan." First used for the Tyson's Center opening, "like no other store in the world" came to define the Bloomingdale's state of mind, and struck such a chord with our shoppers that it became the tag-line for all of Bloomingdale's, even to this day.

To open the Tyson's Corner store we asked Betty Ford to cut the ribbon. Lee and I had gotten to know President and Mrs. Ford through Betty and Lee's shared interest in the Martha Graham Company. Both had studied with Martha and were on the Graham board.* Over three thousand people showed up in black tie for the opening. The event was covered nationally on television and was later part of a major "60 Minutes" story on Bloomingdale's. Washington had come of age, many believed, because it had a Bloomingdale's.

The following year we opened a second Washington store in White Flint, adjacent to Bethesda, then the nation's most affluent market in terms of per capita income. We honored the Kennedy Center for the Arts and created model rooms inspired by famous personalities, including Mike Nichols and Elizabeth Taylor.

Elizabeth Taylor was then married to Senator John Warner, husband number seven. Warner was running for reelection and a Bloomingdale's opening would make for a good public appearance. Carl Levine was assigned to escort Elizabeth, who came beautifully attired, wearing a jeweled turban.

"Ms. Taylor, it's so nice to greet you," Carl said. "Bloomingdale's has been waiting for years to do a model room for you, ever since you made *National Velvet*."

---

* President and Mrs. Ford invited us to the White House dinner at which Martha Graham was awarded the Medal of Freedom. At the end of the evening the Fords and the Traubs were the last two couples on the dance floor—and that led to the start of a warm friendship.

"Honey, if you've been waiting that long," Elizabeth said, "the room must be full of antiques." That was the lead quote in the Washington papers the next day.

b

The design of each branch store was also an opportunity to enhance the Bloomingdale's image. We selected such well-known architects or firms as Edward Durrell Stone, Gyo Obata, and Skidmore, Owings and Merrill to design our stores. We worked hard to give every store its own flair. Whenever a customer looks at a store, whether at the exterior or the interior, that flair contributes to the customer's concept of what the merchandise is like.

In the King of Prussia mall, for example, we were originally slated for the end of a huge monolithic structure that housed Bamberger's on one side, then A&S, then Bloomingdale's at the far end. I didn't like that arrangement and insisted we would only go in if we could be in the middle of the mall; the developers agreed. I then told our architect, Gyo Obata, that we had to do something that would set us apart from the other stores in that building. He designed a six-story high-glass atrium that dominated the entire structure. Inside the atrium was a stream, twenty-four-foot trees, and a stone flooring. I was standing on the site on the day of the atrium's completion when I overheard one of the construction workers say to another, "Look at that building, there will never be another one like it."

Bloomingdale's in the 1980s seemed to bound from one store opening to the next. Each event was planned to generate the utmost excitement and publicity and, at the same time, benefit a local charity and involve us in the community. It was very important that Bloomingdale's be identified at these openings with colorful, celebrated people in order to give us that extra cachet of theatrics and drama. At the same time, the benefits were a show of goodwill that no amount of money could purchase.

The King of Prussia opening was, without question, one of our most memorable. The Philadelphia Mummer's marching band played "That's Entertainment" as guests in black tie waited in the parking lot for the store to open. Suddenly, a fleet of helicopters appeared flying in formation toward the store.

In order to encourage the designers to appear, I had hired most of the available helicopters on the East Coast. Influenced by *Apocalypse Now*, I had twelve helicopters fly in formation over the store, then circle back; as each landed in front of the store, different designers alighted. There was Oscar de la Renta and his first wife, Francoise, Calvin Klein, Bill Blass, Louis Dell'Olio, Donna Karan, Michaele Volbracht. As each door opened up, another designer stepped out and walked to the front of the store and the evening began.

The crowd applauded each designer with gusto. But Calvin was the big star that night. Customers were wildly enthusiastic, trying to get his autograph and dragging him from one end of the store to the other. King of Prussia was our biggest star-studded opening. Until the next year . . . when we opened Willow Grove.

Willow Grove had been a nineteenth-century amusement park, and the mall and our building had been designed with that same feeling. In keeping with that theme, we brought the Big Apple Circus down from New York for the opening. Jugglers, clowns, and other circus performers paraded with our designers and guests. Diane Von Furstenberg led the pack, riding an elephant.

For the opening of our first store in Florida, The Falls, outside Miami, Peter Allen flew down to do a show. Karl Lagerfeld came from Paris as a special favor to me. He arrived the night before, participated in our show and the ribbon-cutting ceremony, and was extraordinarily warm and friendly with customers. He had just launched his own line, Karl Lagerfeld, and showed his first collection as part of our opening.

One of our more beautiful branches is the Chicago store. Located on North Michigan Avenue in downtown Chicago, it is part of a sixty-one-story building that includes luxury apartments, office space, and a hotel. We had a spectacular opening there, with more than three thousand black-tie guests and a benefit for the Chicago Symphony. In many ways this store, in the center of Chicago's most prestigious shopping district, epitomized our ultimate branch store. But the reality is that from opening day, each branch store has had its own road to success.

b

Every store is a great success on opening day, much like every fragrance launch. However, with time, problems arise, conditions change, and every store is tested. The Bloomingdale's branch stores have, on the whole, been successful, adding substantial revenue. However, some of our expansion ventures produced mixed results.

In Washington, for example, we could not foresee that over the next decade new malls would open, adding millions of feet of retailing space. Macy's and Nordstrom followed us into the Washington market and Saks, Hechts, Woodies, and Lord & Taylor expanded. We could never match the advertising and sales promotion budget for radio, TV, and print of the local stores. With the added competition and new malls, our growth slowed and, in the case of our White Flint store, declined.

Admittedly, it was difficult to have the same performance at all branch stores as we did at 59th Street. Valley View in Dallas, Texas, was our first store beyond the Northeast area, and I was anxious that it be a great success. There were three malls in north Dallas: North Park, a very upscale mall with a most successful Neiman-Marcus and a Lord & Taylor store; Galleria, a thriving mall with Saks Fifth Avenue, Marshall Field's, an ice skating rink, and many upscale stores; and Valley View, a more moderate mall with Sanger-Harris, Sears, and Dillard's.

Gerry Hines, the owner of the Galleria mall, was most anxious to have Bloomingdale's as one of its anchors and offered us a $9 million subsidy to move there. Howard Goldfeder, Federated's chairman, decided against Galleria in favor of Valley View. He was worried about the impact of Bloomingdale's on Sanger-Harris's business, and felt we would be the key to making Valley View a more upscale mall. Valley View's developer renovated the mall and gave us a $1 million subsidy.

Although the Valley View mall was renovated, it did not succeed in attracting other upscale stores. Bloomingdale's Valley View was successful in its first year, but in the second year Galleria opened Macy's in the location we had been offered and our sales performance never again reached that first-year level. Today, the Galleria has become an even more successful mall, with a new Nordstrom. After the Texas economy burst, it seemed unlikely that Bloomingdale's Valley View would achieve the profits we needed in the foreseeable future, and in 1990 we reluctantly decided to close the store. I believe that if we had opened in the Galleria with the $9 million subsidy, Bloomingdale's might still be in Dallas.

At the time of our initial expansion we could not foresee that the end of the 1980s would bring a recession, nor could we imagine that Bloomingdale's would ever be in bankruptcy. When the time came, in 1990, to review our financial situation, being in Chapter 11 gave Federated the opportunity to review each of our leases and consider store closings. At Bloomingdale's, store closings were decided by looking at the future profit potential rather than on past profit performance. We were looking for pretax earnings of 10 to 12 percent or more. Based on such analysis, we decided not only to close our store in Valley View, but also those in Stamford, Connecticut, and Fresh Meadows, Long Island, even though those stores were profitable.

Stamford had been in business since 1954 and was a highly successful store in the sixties and seventies. With the development of the Taubman-operated Stamford Town Center, which attracted many of the younger customers, and the development of Danbury Mall, which cut off customers from the north, the Stamford store consistently lost market share. When a customer was murdered by a drug addict in the store's garage, people became uncomfortable parking there. We decided to close Stamford as part of Federated's reorganization, feeling that many of the Stamford customers would be served just as well at our White Plains store.

Fresh Meadows opened in 1949, the year before I joined Bloomingdale's, and we had several of the original employees still there. The problems of Fresh Meadows were exacerbated by a change in the neighborhood that made it much more difficult to do the Bloomingdale's kind of business, even though we drew some customers from Long Island's North Shore.

When I left Bloomingdale's at the end of 1991, there were a total of fourteen branch stores. The store's total volume was $1.1 billion, of which 59th Street contributed about $400 million. Our branch stores, for which we had an initial target of about $50 million each, perform on average between $40 and $70 million, with most in the $50 million plus range—still a very good business. The Bloomingdale's branches represent a volume of more than $700 million. And at each store, merchandising, marketing, and customer service must be a priority for it to succeed. Bloomingdale's stores have received an enthusiastic reception in Washington, Philadelphia, Florida, Boston, and Chicago. Based on that, I am sure that Bloomingdale's will, over the years, continue to expand in new and existing markets.

b

There's been some criticism that the 59th Street store was given too much attention at the expense of the branch stores and that is the reason some branches did not perform as expected. I don't agree. The reality is that in order to strengthen the branch stores, we had to invest *more* in 59th Street, not less; I believed that at the same time as we worked to update and renovate our existing branch stores, it was critical that Bloomingdale's 59th Street continue to amaze and beguile our customers.

Not everyone understands that Bloomingdale's 59th Street was our lab, and our best advertisement. Kill that and you've killed the golden goose. The best analogy I can provide is that of the Broadway theater. If a play succeeds out-of-town and bombs in New York, it is considered a failure; but a successful Broadway, or even off-Broadway, play can have a long life on the road. New York is still the place where a play must prove itself. Tradition, real estate, and talent all converge to make plays happen in New York. The same is true of Bloomingdale's.

Bloomingdale's 59th Street has traffic unequaled anywhere else in the country. New York is where the talent converges: Seventh Avenue and the various markets are still headquartered there; New York is still the seat of the national news media. If we do something on 59th Street, the whole nation knows.

There was another reason we had to strengthen 59th Street: Our competition was getting stronger. For most of the sixties, we had the field to ourselves. By the mid-seventies, Bob Suslow, chairman of Saks Fifth Avenue, was pursuing the fashion business with renewed vigor.* Joe Brooks at Lord & Taylor was aggressively changing that store to have a more middle-of-the-road appeal, increasing its market share.

---

* Bob was a former Bloomingdale's merchandise manager. Saks would continue to benefit from a Bloomingdale's-trained chairman with Arnold Aronson in the 1970s, Mel Jacobs in the 1980s, and Phil Miller in the 1990s.

At the same time, over on 34th Street, Ed Finkelstein was waking the sleeping giant Macy's, overtly bringing the same concepts to their advertising and merchandising in the 1970s that had been successful at Bloomingdale's in the 1950s and 1960s. During the 1970s, Macy's looked for ways to compete with Bloomingdale's. They went after our cosmetics business, our housewares business, our food business. When Bloomingdale's received attention each spring, for example, for flying in the new *fraises du bois*—wild strawberries—from France, Macy's competed with us by trying to bring them in first.

Nationally, Neiman-Marcus, under the leadership of Dick Hauser and then Phil Miller, both of whom had been senior Bloomingdale's executives, was pursuing contemporary fashion while undertaking their own national expansion program.

When we began our expansion, we started an ambitious renovation program at 59th Street. Over the next decade we rebuilt, redesigned, and revived almost every department in the store. I was convinced that what we had to do in the eighties was return to what we did best, do it better, and on a much larger scale. What we had to do was continue the mystique.

b

The opening of our branch stores, together with a renovated 59th Street, increased public awareness of Bloomingdale's as a quality national brand. By the late seventies and early eighties, that was something we began to trade on.

Bloomingdale's has always had a close, almost intimate relationship with its hard-core fans. In the mid-seventies, we traded on this when we manufactured panties bearing the name "bloomie's" (in bloomingtype, of course) across the bottoms. Some thought it outrageous, some thought it vulgar, but many, many women felt they just had to own a pair. We sold more than 300,000 the first year.

The growth of the Bloomies panties business showed us how much the Bloomingdale's name had become a brand. With an enormous number of out-of-town visitors who wanted to bring home something saying Bloomingdale's, we developed sweatshirts, caps, baseball jackets, T-shirts, dresses with the motto "shop 'til you drop," robes, key chains—a whole world of Bloomies products. The outgrowth of this occurred in 1986 when we opened two Bloomies

Express shops at JFK Airport. The next year we licensed the shops to Host International, which opened shops in Phoenix, Baltimore, and Cleveland. By 1990, our Bloomies products had become a $20 million business.

At the same time, our public relations took us to another level. Where, in the sixties, movie stars shopped at Bloomingdale's, in the eighties we went out of our way to encourage filmmakers to use Bloomingdale's as a location. The store was featured prominently in such movies as *The Electric Horseman, Splash, Starting Over,* and *Manhattan.* When Paul Mazursky made *Moscow on the Hudson,* in which a Russian, played by Robin Williams, decides to defect in Bloomingdale's, we received tremendous attention. Most of the Bloomingdale's scenes were filmed on location; however, Mazursky reproduced B'Way on a soundstage in Harlem.

b

It was one thing to build branches, but what about those shoppers who couldn't get to the store? By 1978, we were well aware that with the growth of women in the workforce there was a concurrent increase in shopping by mail. What struck me was that the great growth opportunities were not so much in traditional catalogs but for an upscale company such as ours. The Bloomingdale's name was a natural, I thought, to benefit from this trend. But running a mail-order business was different from what we had been doing.

Another plus of direct-mail marketing was that we could take advantage of the talents of Gordon Cooke. Gordon was our executive vice president for sales promotion. He had worked at Bon Marche in Seattle and Burdine's in Miami before going to Macy's in New York to run its sales promotion department. In 1977, when Doris Shaw resigned to become editor of *House Beautiful,* I quickly recruited (a polite way of saying stole) Gordon from Macy's.

Gordon, who is tall with a full head of dark curly hair and used to sport a bushy beard, is a free spirit at heart. Before coming to Bloomingdale's he had never held a job at any one place for more than two years. His interests are far-ranging, and his range of talents wide. Although he started in sales promotion, when he worked at Burdine's, Mel Jacobs, who was its chairman then, had made him a sportswear buyer—unusual training for a sales promotion director but helpful if you are going to run a catalog.

At Bloomingdale's, Gordon had an outstanding partner, John Jay, who combined unique creativity and drive with administrative skills and great dedication to the store. Nothing made John happier than a creative challenge. John developed our award-winning TV commercials for our promotions of France, Italy, and Spain—he won the gold medal three years in a row at the National Retail Advertising Conference. As Gordon focused on Bloomingdale's By Mail, John was there to back him up.

At Bloomingdale's, one of Gordon's first coups was our "conviction ads," as they came to be known. Our ready-wear buyers had committed to a new fall look in a major way, ordering substantial numbers of trousers that narrowed at the ankle; Kal Ruttenstein believed these would be worn with oversize tops. Just before Christmas, we decided to go out on a limb and took major full-page ads whose copy read, "We believe in peg trousers and big tops." John Jay hired a new artist, Antonio, to illustrate the ads. As we wanted to speak with authority, we left a great deal of white space on the page, giving our pronouncement even greater importance. The conviction ads generated tremendous attention and ran for several years, putting our fashion department in a class by itself.

Creating a successful mail-order business was, however, tantamount to creating a whole new company, and our president Jim Schoff, Gordon, and I sat down to discuss our plans. We agreed that, initially, we would start with a minimum of extra expense and not invest capital until we were sure it was a success. With that in mind, our priorities were, first, to hire an outside professional with direct-marketing expertise. Next, we had to make several changes in our long-established pattern of business to accommodate this new venture. For example, we could not run a mail-order business accepting only a Bloomingdale's credit card. After much negotiation with American Express and our parent, Federated, we arranged to accept the American Express card at our stores and for our mail-order business. We then set up an 800 number. That, plus our having access to the American Express data base, jump-started our entry into the mail-order business. Finally, we needed a place to warehouse and fulfill our catalog mail orders. Because the unionized Bloomingdale's warehouse was very high cost, we chose instead to use the basement of our closed New Rochelle store for our first fulfillment center.

Gordon and I learned quickly that our mail-order business was different from our department store business. First, some customers prefer to shop by mail—even if they live around the corner from the store. Our best mail-order market turned out to be the Upper East Side of New York. Second, mail-order buyers frequently are those who have trouble finding their size. Therefore our business in shoes, bras, or men's shirts was skewed to the very small or the very large. And finally, mail-order buyers tend to be middle-price customers.

Our volume in 1980, the first year, was a surprising $3 million, and we were amateurs. Two weeks before Christmas, at the end of our executive committee meeting at 59th Street, I explained to our senior merchants that there were thousands of orders that hadn't been filled and gave each person a stack of sales checks for their areas. (For example, Lester Gribetz was given the home furnishings checks.) With Christmas fast approaching, each one located the merchandise and had the orders filled—not exactly the way a major mail-order fulfillment should function. That night was a vivid reminder of the potential for the catalog.

The first requirement for building a sound catalog business is a great mailing list. We discovered that most of our charge customers were not mail-order buyers; we needed a list of people who liked to shop by mail. We hired Scali McCabe & Sloves to develop such a list, and they created the campaign "Bloomingdale's is no further away than your telephone." We ran a series of national ads showing, for example, two astronauts in space, a telephone, the slogan, and our 800 number. The response was terrific, and we rapidly began to build our list of mail-order buyers. It was an exciting time and we began to have almost geometric growth.

There are three pieces to a mail-order business. The first is "the list," having the right names to mail to, as just mentioned. The second is a strategy for marketing products by mail. As we grew more sophisticated, we found that cutting-edge fashions did not sell well in mail order. When the Bloomingdale's store was selling very short skirts, Bloomingdale's By Mail was not. On the other hand, we discovered that our mail-order customer tended to like something a little more exciting with a little more dash than we might have thought. "Glitzy" is what I mean, although there must be a better word for it. There was also tremendous demand for outsize merchandise.

We also refocused the home furnishings offerings in housewares, domestics, and tabletop. Bloomingdale's has such great strength in those areas, that we offered a wide array of unique merchandise. We discovered if an item was "first at Bloomingdale's," the response was very good.

We developed the practice of going to resources like Baccarat to launch new products in the catalog. We began to work with companies to offer items to our Bloomingdale's By Mail customer for a one-year exclusive before our stores carried it. We worked with many of the tabletop companies, such as Lenox and Orrefors, to develop a yearly special Christmas ornament that Bloomingdale's By Mail could launch.

At the same time, we discovered that there was no single Bloomingdale's By Mail customer. Rather, there were several very different kinds: There is the type who is very influenced by the country look of Ralph Lauren; another type, whom we call bedazzled, likes the glamorous, glitzy part of Bloomingdale's; a third customer is more traditional. We segmented those customers and did pages and model types with each of the various types in mind. Each page of copy was, in fact, specifically written to appeal to a customer type. Sometimes we created separate mailings for them; other times we mixed the pages all together in the same catalog. But once you know that, you can see exactly which customer type we were aiming at on each page of our catalogs.

The third part of an effective mail-order operation is logistics—taking calls, having the merchandise in stock, and promptly filling sales orders. After New Rochelle, we utilized a fulfillment center in West Virginia. A good way to begin, but not correct for building a large business. There was a problem with our mail-order associates and merchants having to commute to West Virginia. We learned from focus groups that Bloomingdale's By Mail customers didn't like hearing a Southern voice at the end of our 800 number; when they called the fulfillment center, they expected someone from New York.

In order to take us to the next level, we decided we needed to build our own state-of-the art fulfillment center. We found a beautiful industrial park in Cheshire, Connecticut, and obtained the $25 million investment to build it from the Federated board. This was the first recognition by Federated that Bloomingdale's By Mail was an inherent part of our future marketing strategy—until then, it had been considered an experiment. By the summer of 1987, when we moved in, our new facility had the latest in telephone answering system, data processing, and mechanical merchandise handling, and we hired the people to staff it.

During the 1980s, we assembled a talented team of mail-order merchants, some from our own organization and some experienced catalog professionals from companies such as Speigel's, Avon, and Talbot's. By 1991, it was clear Bloomingdale's By Mail was a potential $100 million business; sales at that time were exceeding $70 million. We knew that to achieve future growth we had to make Bloomingdale's By Mail a separate division with its own buying, merchandising, and creative staff. At the same time, it was clear that Gordon could no longer be responsible for both Bloomingdale's By Mail and sales promotion, so I offered him his choice. Gordon chose to give up his sales promotion responsibilities (and Bloomingdale's is considered the best sales promotion job in the United States). I was not surprised. Gordon is now a principal of Bloomingdale's By Mail, a $100 million plus very profitable company. John Jay then succeeded Gordon, becoming executive vice president for sales promotion.* The corporation is convinced, I believe, that Bloomingdale's By Mail has a bright future.

Although the 1980s saw an explosion of catalogs, today there is a shake-up going on with so many new competitors. I believe in catalogs for department stores with distinctive images, such as Bloomingdale's, Saks, or Neiman's. It is no longer the golden opportunity it was, but catalogs have great potential because there will always be people who prefer to shop by mail.

b

The late 1980s were the growth and glory days of Bloomingdale's. We had reached a peak in leadership, growth, and reputation. And

---

* In March 1993, John Jay left Bloomingdale's to become senior vice president and creative director of J. Crew.

we believed we would reach even greater heights. We were exploring opening Bloomingdale's at several California locations, both in Los Angeles and San Francisco, and we were discussing opening a store in Moscow. Bloomingdale's behaved as if we could do no wrong.

The 1980s were an era of extravagance. As Holly Brubach wrote in *The New Yorker:* "As society has grown more secular and materialistic, the connoisseurship that was once the rarified pastime of the Medicis has come to be an almost universal preoccupation. In our time, shopping has assumed unprecedented importance in the lives of many people, and the ability to find and recognize the finest clothes, cars, sheets and towels, kitchen equipment, luggage, light fixtures, gardening tools, cosmetics, food—the list is endless—is regarded as a form of self-expression. With the range of products available in every category wider than ever before, and every choice vested with greater personal significance, the role of the arbiter has, if anything, grown larger instead of smaller. . . . People are looking to the experts for a frame of reference, for suggestions, for ideas and images that they can use to portray themselves in the world." And for many, Bloomingdale's became the arbiter of the best.

During the Reagan years there was an enormous growth in earnings across the country. A feeling of affluence spread to more and more people. New money, from a variety of sources, permitted people to indulge in their fantasies. There was a feeling that prosperity would only grow greater with time.

Spending fever was occurring not only in New York but in Texas, California, and Kansas. It was easy to feel that the hunger for quality goods was spreading throughout the land and that could only mean more customers for Bloomingdale's.

In part because people were willing to pay more for the best, there was a virtual explosion in the price of designer clothes. In the ten years from 1978 to 1988, designer prices went up threefold, way ahead of increases in the cost of living or inflation. The $1,000 suit for women became an accepted fact of retailing. Designer dresses were being sold regularly for $4,000 to $6,000. Petrossian caviar became a million-dollar business at Bloomingdale's; in December alone we sold $500,000 worth of the world's most expensive caviar.

During those years, our personal shoppers had clients who spent $300,000 to $400,000 a year, or more, on clothes and accessories.

b

The 1980s were also a time when several new designers, from Paris, New York, and Milan, came into prominence. Bloomingdale's had built our fashion reputation throughout the sixties and early seventies, as Katie Murphy helped launch French ready-to-wear designers in the United States. Kal Ruttenstein, who joined Bloomingdale's in 1977 as our fashion director, took our reputation to the next level by introducing such important young designers as Claude Montana, Thierry Mugler, Romeo Gigli, and Jean Paul Gaultier, who are still fashion leaders today.

During Kal's first week at the store, Bloomingdale's held a Kenzo fashion show at Studio 54. It was a happening: Grace Jones performed, famous models walked the runway, there were paparazzi and TV cameras everywhere. It was an incredible hit. Kenzo loved it and so did Kal.

Another major fashion event that we organized was Thierry Mugler's first show in America on the occasion of the opening of Bond's discotheque in Times Square. Bond's was a former menswear store that was transformed into an enormous nightclub—it lasted for what seems like just a second, but on its opening night, it was the pinnacle of nightlife in New York. People stood on lines that stretched out to Broadway, waiting to get in. Mugler came in from Paris and put on a great show. French designers were the avant-garde then, and it was important for Bloomingdale's to carry the most forward fashions.

At the same time, Milan was making itself known as a fashion capital. When Kal came back from Italy in 1977, he was very impressed with the clothes of Giorgio Armani. Armani, born in 1935, first studied medicine at Milan University. After military service, however, he started the display department of La Rinascente, the Milan-based department store chain. In 1961 he joined Nino Cerruti as a designer. For the rest of the decade, he worked for a number of designers including Ungaro. When Kal first met him, Armani was doing a substantial men's business and very little women's. In the United States, his men's clothes were carried at the Jackie Rogers

Boutique on Madison Avenue and his women's wear was hardly carried at all. It wasn't a full-fledged collection. He did mostly jackets; very few pants or skirts.

The next time I went to Milan, Kal arranged for Giorgio to invite Lee, Peggy, and me for lunch. We went to his elegant apartment, which he and his partner, Sergio Galeotti, had decorated in varying shades of blue. We sat down for lunch. I was not sure why everyone was giggling as the main course was served. When I received mine I understood: Giorgio had prepared a blue risotto that matched his furnishings.

We had an immediate rapport and during the afternoon Giorgio and Sergio outlined their ambitions for the Armani business. They had set five-year goals for the next twenty years of exactly how they intended to expand and diversify the Armani business—the different lines, the different markets, the various businesses. It was very impressive. More impressive is that Giorgio stayed the course, and despite the death of his very talented partner he not only met his goals, he exceeded them.

We started carrying the Armani women's line first with one five-foot section, then two. By the time we had three sections, we had an Armani shop; when it became a full-fledged collection, we really got behind him. At the same time we started to carry the menswear. We learned early on that our core customer and the Armani target customer were one and the same. Bloomingdale's has always been a store for sportswear-oriented clothes, and Armani's casual elegance has always been perfect for our customers. To this day, the Armani business is Bloomingdale's biggest European designer business and our largest designer business after Ralph Lauren.

There are, in fact, some interesting similarities between the two. They both came to women's clothes from a menswear background. They are both more concerned with style than fashion. And they both have a very clear, unerring vision that has been, over the years, remarkably consistent.

b

Kal always found the Milanese and New York looks similar. I agree. Both feature casual, soft clothes where the woman is the star rather than the clothes. The Paris look is curvier, at times more innovative,

sometimes more gimmicky. That being said, however, the most conservative, yet most American of the French designers, and one of
the greatest successes of the 1980s, was Chanel.

Coco Chanel's fashions first became famous in the 1920s. She
closed her salon in 1939, only to reopen it in 1954, having sold her
business to Alain Wertheimer. The Chanel suit and handbag were
still mildly popular in the sixties, but by the late seventies Chanel
was a disaster. Phillipe Guibourgé was designing the couture collection then and it was unattractive. We carried it for years because I
felt the name was so strong that eventually it would return. Kal kept
wanting to drop it, but I refused.

In 1983 Kitty D'Alessio, then president of Chanel, hired Karl
Lagerfeld to design both the couture and the ready-to-wear. Chanel
took off, and they remembered our loyalty. We already had a very
good relationship with Karl from his days as Chloe's designer and as
a designer for Fendi. Chanel at Bloomingdale's, between their apparel and cosmetics, has grown to an almost $20 million business.

It would be appropriate to say a few words about Karl Lagerfeld,
who is one of the true geniuses of our industry. He is intense yet
always appears relaxed. He's opinionated about everything, reads
voraciously, and sleeps little. As busy as he is, he writes long letters
to his friends. He is like a character from another century—a Renaissance man, or the hero of a nineteenth-century novel.

Karl comes from a wealthy family in Germany that made an
enormous fortune in the dairy business. Karl and I developed a fast
friendship early on. It was most impressive to see him grow from
designing trendy furs for the Fendis and Chloe's ready-to-wear to
putting Chanel back on the map.

In the early 1980s, Fendi was Bloomingdale's most successful
and profitable accessories collection. We were the only major department store in New York that carried it. Carla Fendi asked that
we double the size of our Fendi boutique, which was at the Lexington Avenue corner of our main floor. To make the space more productive I suggested to Carla that Fendi go into the ready-to-wear
business—knowing that they could utilize Karl's talent. The
strength of Bloomingdale's was such that we could suggest that an
accessories company go into ready-to-wear just to fill a boutique—
and then help them succeed.

Subsequently, Karl launched his Karl Lagerfeld collection,

which was later sold to Maurice Bidermann. Karl is one of the few people who is both a designer and his own business manager. His talents extend far beyond designing: He is now serving as his own photographer for ads, and illustrating books. He has a great sense of interior design and did a model room for Bloomingdale's that was very successful. He even suggested new furniture resources for us. Karl is a man of many moods. At one point his home was furnished with exquisite Biedermeier furniture. Then he became bored; out it went, and he replaced it with Memphis modern. Karl moves as his mood directs him.

It was extraordinary to go to Paris and see on Saturday the Chloe collection, on Sunday the Lagerfeld collection, and on Monday the Chanel collection after having first seen, in Milan, the Fendi fur and ready-to-wear collections. Five collections in a season plus Chanel couture. Yet Karl is always backstage, smiling—usually waving his signature fan. He always has time to give Lee a warm greeting as he keeps track of everything going on.

b

Back in the United States, Kal and I worked closely with Donna Karan, one of the great success stories of the 1980s. She was born Donna Faske in Forest Hills, a well-to-do Queens community. Her father, a custom tailor, died when she was three. Her mother was a model and saleswoman. While Donna was attending the Parsons School of Design, Anne Klein gave her a summer job as a sketcher, and offered her a job upon graduation. Upon Klein's death in 1974, Tomio Taki, a Japanese textile manufacturer who had bought a 50 percent interest in the company, appointed her co-designer for the Anne Klein company with Louis Dell'Olio. She was twenty-six.

By 1984, Donna was no longer interested in being half of a design team and wanted to start her own label. Tomio Taki and his partner Frank Mori gave her six months to think about what her first collection would look like and made an initial investment of about $3 million to start the Donna Karan ready-to-wear company. Today, nine years later, the company has worldwide sales of more than $258 million, earnings of $29 million, and is getting ready to go public. After the offering, *Women's Wear* estimates Donna and her husband Steve Weiss will have stock worth $140 million.

Bloomingdale's proposed to create a new shop for Donna when

we opened our renovated designer floor, Boulevard 4. Donna believed her clothes should be merchandised in a stark, simple atmosphere with most of the clothes in a back stockroom and only a few pieces out on the floor, as in the old couture days.

As a merchant, I felt Donna would do better having more merchandise displayed. We argued and compromised somewhere between our two positions. Over time, more and more clothes turned up on the selling floor. Eventually we built a bigger shop for her on the fourth floor right at the top of the escalators.

Donna has said that she designs her collection by looking into her closet at the beginning of every season to see what's missing. Donna's success owes much to the fact that she is her own customer. She has an advantage over many designers in that she can try on all her clothes to see how they look and feel. Donna, like most women, does not have the figure of a runway supermodel, so she designs clothes that complement most women's figures.

Donna was the first to bring sex to the boardroom. At a time when most corporate women were basically wearing a man-tailored suit—it was the years of Alcott and Andrews—she understood power dressing for women. Donna's concept for clothes starts with layers, beginning with a black body suit, and everything that follows is flowing and draped. A sensuous attitude pervades, even in accessories such as the gold Robert Lee Morris jewelry she introduced. It was a very strong point of view that she has followed to this day.

b

At the same time as the designer business was growing, there was an increasing popular demand for fashion and taste. The middle class, bombarded with images of the life-styles of the rich and famous, also wanted designer clothes. I had been concerned for many years that designers not raise their prices too high; I have always felt there would come a point where some customers would walk away from their clothes. But designers wanted to maintain their image. That's when secondary lines started to appear. This was not unlike the sixties, when couture designers began their ready-to-wear lines, only today some ready-to-wear designers are creating what we now call "bridge." These collections are one price point below designer prices—generally 25 to 50 percent less. Ralph was one of the first to do this when he created Ralph Classification and Ralph Activewear. At the time, Ralph decided to have his secondary lines surround his collection all in one shop.

Many other designers had trouble deciding whether to show the collections together or separately. We helped them sort it through. Calvin Klein had a secondary line called Calvin Classifications. It wasn't successful for Calvin, although we did well with it. Recently he successfully relaunched it in a separate space as CK Sport. Over the years there was also Calvin Klein Sport, and for a brief moment his secondary line was also called Calvin Klein.

Donna single-handedly revolutionized the bridge designer business with her introduction of DKNY. When Donna first contemplated DKNY she was not sure whether it should be shown with her collection or separately. We felt very strongly that this could be the backbone of an emerging separate business because Donna Karan at lower price points would have tremendous appeal. She agreed and we treated DKNY as a separate business with its own buyer, and housed the clothes in a DKNY boutique. We gave her the best location on the third floor, opposite the up escalator.

Donna hired Arnell/Bickford to create a contemporary New York shop for DKNY, with subway doors as the entrance to the fitting rooms, subway tokens as the knobs for hanging garments, and graphics of movie theaters and memorable New York scenes all in black and white. It was an instant success and the following year she added DKNY denim as an offshoot—and added an additional 50 percent to the business. In 1992, at 59th Street, DKNY is more than a $7 million business—one of the largest in the store.

The creation of secondary lines at price points below designer forced us to examine how to classify other sportswear designers we carried. Where should we carry Adrienne Vittadini, for example? It was too expensive for our better sportswear department, which we call Sutton, but the look wasn't designer. Ellen Tracy got too expensive for YES, where it was originally carried, and certainly did not have the look or the price point of designer. We placed a few of these designers adjacent to each other and suddenly we had created a new bridge division.

When bridge first came along, we thought it unlikely that the designer customer would wear bridge clothes. DKNY revolutionized all that. Once designers started spending more time designing their bridge lines and the quality was there, the customer responded. A woman who might spend $1,000 on a Donna Karan jacket, but buy only one a year, would now shop DKNY year-round. And at $500 here, $200 there, it added up to a significant total—often more than she had spent on Donna Karan.

Today, the bridge business has evolved to the point where it is most successfully done by stores who have a large designer business and this becomes one price point down. Therefore it is no surprise that Neiman-Marcus, Saks, and Bloomingdale's all have major bridge businesses.

The future of the designer business in America is undoubtedly limited. With the possible exception of Saks, Neiman's, Bergdorf's, and Barney's, it is likely to decline as a percentage of most stores' total business. Expensive designer clothes do not generally fit in with the less extravagant life-styles of the nineties. Even among those who have the money, it is no longer fashionable to spend $3,000 or more for a new dress. Under its new regime, Bloomingdale's appears to be deemphasizing the designer business outside of 59th Street and limited branches but continues to have major focus on bridge.

b

For a young designer to become successful today, he or she needs three things: a good collection, press coverage, and an important store to support him or her. Kal Ruttenstein has always been the conscience of Bloomingdale's. He has a total underground network that keeps him in touch with any new and emerging talents. Kal gets enormous pleasure from developing new designers and made a practice of coming to me when he wanted support for one. Early on I got to know Christian Lacroix as well as Isaac Mizrahi. We had Dolce and Gabana exclusively for about three years in the eighties. When Kal had confidence in a new young designer, such as Byron Lars or Christian Francis Roth, we gave them a lunch in our boardroom. Usually between the main course and dessert, Kal would arrange to have a few models show the collection. While to an established designer that would be nothing special, to a designer who is struggling financially and seeking recognition, those lunches were a very important introduction to Bloomingdale's.

We sometimes came to very novel arrangements to support the designers we believed in. In 1967, Norma Kamali opened a boutique in New York with her husband selling highly original clothes. They divorced, and shortly thereafter Norma opened her own store called OMO (On My Own). Norma popularized long down coats, nylon jumpsuits, and a whole line of clothes made of sweat materials with cinched waists and padded shoulders. She also designed very successful one-piece bathing suits in bold colors.

Norma is both a difficult and talented woman. In the 1980s, she discontinued OMO as a supplier after a lengthy labor dispute, and Bloomingdale's entered into a rather unique arrangement with her. Norma had the idea of becoming a Bloomingdale's designer. After a series of luncheons with Kal and Russ Stravitz, our general merchandise manager, we came to an arrangement whereby Norma would do the designs and Bloomingdale's would manufacture the clothes. Norma Kamali became, in effect, our in-house designer.

Becoming a manufacturer was a new experience for Bloomingdale's. We had to hire production experts, a piece-goods buyer, and make commitments long in advance. We began with a very successful swimsuit collection and expanded into ready-to-wear, which grew into a reasonably successful business that was very good for our image. We began to expand Norma into other areas, developing our own exclusive Norma Kamali hosiery, which sold very well. When I left Bloomingdale's, we were working on lingerie and other products. Subsequent to my departure, however, Norma's arrangement with Bloomingdale's was discontinued.

b

Bloomingdale's had never been healthier. In the 1980s, the Japanese started to arrive in New York and Bloomingdale's became a mecca for them. As our reputation increased so did our percentage of overseas visitors—growing to 20 percent of our customer base at 59th Street. Our profits increased accordingly.

From 1977 to 1987, Bloomingdale's showed consistent increases in pretax income, growing in seven of those ten years. In the years 1977–80, the store's pretax income rose more than 50 percent, and it more than doubled between 1977 and 1987. In 1987, the year of the stock market crash, only two of the fourteen Federated divisions made their profit plan—Bloomingdale's and Bullock's—and they accounted for 30 percent of Federated department store profits.

There was growth in Bloomingdale's profits and a feeling within Federated that Bloomingdale's had great future potential as it expanded from the northeast to Texas and Florida. We had already planned the 1988 Chicago opening, and had begun to look at San Francisco and Los Angeles. We had plans to renovate and expand Bloomingdale's 59th Street. This was all part of the go-go atmosphere of the times.

The 1980s were also a great time for Lee and me on a personal level. Our three children had all graduated from Harvard College with honors and they were now all working and living in the metropolitan area. We moved to Greenwich to a new home we had built and built a ski house in Deer Valley, Utah, as well. Our first grandchildren were born.

Along with reaching a place of prominence in the retailing industry, as president and chairman of Bloomingdale's I was often called upon to speak at charity and industry events. It comes with the territory, I suppose. The luncheons and dinners, though, presented an opportunity. On very rare occasions I felt compelled, as a matter of conscience, to speak out on matters of national importance. It was personal rather than on behalf of the store. Three such incidents stand out in my memory.

On May 21, 1970, I traveled to Washington with a group of forty prominent New Yorkers concerned about the Vietnam War to meet with a congressional group. I felt the war was tearing our country apart and that it was time respectable businessmen spoke up in opposition to the war and what it was doing to the country. It was not a popular point of view at that time but it was a concern I felt very deeply. I got a number of rather vehement letters that I keep in my poison pen file to this day. A few people cut their charge cards in half as well, saying it was inappropriate for the president of Bloomingdale's to speak out on a political issue. I still think it was important and I would do it again.

In 1977, I received the Tommy Award from the American Printed Fabrics Council as Retailer of the Year and on that occasion addressed the annual dinner at the American Textile Institute. American textile manufacturers, I told the group, needed to update their marketing approach rather than trying to reduce imports by changing quotas or they would continue to lose business to Italy and the Orient. Not a popular point of view.

I was again compelled to speak out when the retail industry was slow in responding to the scourge of AIDS, even though there are few in our industry who have not seen friends and employees succumb. Bloomingdale's has lost some close friends, including Colin Birch our very talented vice president of visual merchandising—taken away in his mid-thirties. A consensus was growing that the fashion industry had to do something.

In the early 1980s, Elizabeth Taylor and Calvin Klein asked me to join them in chairing the first major fashion industry AIDS benefit at the Jacobs Javits Convention Center. At that time it was not a popular cause. They also asked if I would join them in taking an ad in *The New York Times* to raise funds for AIDS research and to mobilize our friends on Seventh Avenue. I agreed immediately. Of the three, I was probably regarded as the most conservative, and I believed it sent an important signal to the fashion industry.

b

By the end of the 1980s, I had received many honors and awards. In 1981, I was honored by the Parsons School of Design, which created the Marvin Traub Design Laboratory. The Fund for Higher Education awarded me the Flame of Truth award in 1985. At that time, a grant of $350,000 was given by the fund, the Federated Foundation, and by Lee and me to establish the Marvin and Lee Traub Flexible Financial Fund at Harvard College.

Each year five to seven students are selected for scholarship aid. The only requirement is that they be from middle-income families and in the top half of their class. Lee and I have an annual dinner for the students so that we can meet them and they can get to know each other. There are, to date, twenty-six Traub scholars who keep in touch with us, even after graduating; given how much I value my Harvard experience, this growing contribution gives me great satisfaction.

I received several international awards as well. In 1983, I was the recipient of Israel's Jabotinsky medal. In 1985, the Italian government awarded me the Commandatore de la Republica, their highest civilian award. Over the years, I received a number of citations from France. In 1973, I received L'Epingle d'Or, and in 1978, the Order of Merit. But perhaps the greatest honor was in 1986 when I received the Legion D'Honneur.

The Legion D'Honneur was presented to me by President François Mitterand at the Elysée Palace, a very special honor for a foreigner. For the occasion, family and friends flew over and after the ceremony the American ambassador arranged a reception at the embassy in Paris.

President Mitterand had memorized the background of all five awardees, and without any notes went over much of my career. He singled me out for my contributions to France, saying that I had fought on French soil to defend France and had opened windows for French products so that they would become better known in the United States. After Mitterand read our citations, each of us stepped forward. The president grabbed my arms and kissed me on both cheeks, a typically French custom. Afterward, he walked around greeting our friends.

For the reception at the embassy, all of our good friends from France attended. Edith Cresson, later to become foreign minister, presided. The room was filled with warm feelings. Christian Petrossian did me the tremendous honor of giving me a key ring with a 1924 U.S. $20 gold piece his father had given him when the business was founded. Looking around the room, it was hard not to be conscious of all the strong ties we had to France.

b

All in all, life was good. I had no reason to know that the most stressful years of my life were about to begin. Today, looking back, it is easy to pinpoint the moment after which nothing was ever the same. At the time, however, I was hardly conscious that anything of consequence was occurring.

I was in Paris for the spring ready-to-wear collections. We were dining with our good friends Leon and Martine Cligman, Mike Steinberg, Bloomingdale's general merchandise manager for home, and Chantal Rousseau at Maxim's. I was enjoying an excellent dinner. My business thoughts were focused on the future. The next day I was to leave for China to scout the possibilities of a "return to China" promotion the following year.

Halfway through dinner the headwaiter politely came over to our table. "Mr. Traub," he said, "you have a phone call." I wondered who knew I was at Maxim's and why they were calling in the middle of dinner. I went to the phone booth to discover it was a reporter from *Women's Wear*.

"Mr. Traub," he said, "the market has just dropped five hundred points, what do you think the impact will be on the retail business?"

At first I thought he was kidding, but after a few more questions it was evident he was not. It was a little premature, I thought, to make any sweeping statements about the impact of such a drop, but I suspected one thing: It wasn't going to be good.

PART 4

Buying
Bloomingdale's

"*Your idea of bringing the two of us closer together always seems to be for me to go with you to Bloomingdale's.*"

Drawing by Weber; © 1973 The New Yorker Magazine, Inc.

CHAPTER 11

The Deal

As Bloomingdale's and retailing came to be perceived as a glamorous arena with star fashion designers and billion-dollar cosmetics companies, and as launches, store openings, and promotions became star-studded media events, retailing caught the eye of financiers hungry for glamorous acquisitions.

Much has been written about the period of the late 1980s, when corporate raiders and financiers seemed to be the heroes of a new age, only for some to be revealed as scavengers or, worse, criminals. Looking back on that time, you have to wonder how the corporate community engaged in such madness; it is difficult to understand how companies were bought, sold, and ruined, how bankers and lawyers became rich in one flimsily financed deal after another.

How was it possible that Robert Campeau was allowed to gain control of one of the greatest chains of department stores ever assembled, Federated, with no true equity and incurring such debt that it was impossible for the underlying stores to succeed?

With hindsight, I can say that everything happened because there was a grain of wisdom at the core of each crazy undertaking. The retail industry in general, and Federated Department Stores, including Bloomingdale's, were adrift and complacent in the late 1980s in the face of their success. Federated's management did need fresh thinking, and bringing in an outsider with a new perspective was not a totally bad idea.

Campeau has been described by some as crazy; I have heard others say that he has been diagnosed as clinically manic-depressive. What I saw in working with him was someone whose ideas were not all bad: Federated did need to shed some of its nonperforming assets. Bloomingdale's needed to improve its customer service, and would have benefited from further national and international expansion into such markets as Los Angeles, San Francisco, and Toronto. However, the pace at which Bob proceeded, and his reluctance to heed sound financial advice—his conviction of his own infallibility—were his, and ultimately Bloomingdale's, downfall.

Finally, heading a management-led buyout of Bloomingdale's was attractive for many reasons, and my inability to do so successfully was one of the great disappointments of my career. However, the story of recent events at Bloomingdale's and Federated are representative of the travails of many modern businesses. In the last century, Bloomingdale's and Federated, like so many other American businesses, grew from family businesses to family-run corporations dominated by their larger-than-life founders to public corporations; and the management of public corporations had to evolve to meet changing economic needs.

The following chapters recount only a small portion of time, some four years. I have gone into great detail because the events had a profound impact on Bloomingdale's, and because they symbolize what happened to retailing and related industries. Many of these facts have never been disclosed before.

To fully understand how Bloomingdale's was taken over, offered for sale, put into bankruptcy, and emerged, one first has to step back and understand some of the history of Federated Department Stores.

b

Federated Department Stores was founded as a holding company in November 1929 bringing together Abraham & Straus, with annual sales of $25 million; Filene's of Boston, including R. H. White, with annual sales of $46 million; and F. & R. Lazarus of Columbus, Ohio, with annual sales of $12 million (including Shillito's of Cincinnati). When Bloomingdale's joined Federated three months later, its sales of $24 million brought total sales of the new chain to $107 million.

Lehman Brothers promoted this merger as a way to strengthen all four stores and it helped them in dealing with the Great Depression. Fred Lazarus, Jr., became president of Federated in 1945, and his son Ralph Lazarus would later succeed him to become Federated's chairman. For thirty-six years, the Lazarus family, father and son, ran the company.

Over the years, Federated acquired quality stores: Burdine's became a division in 1956; Rike's and Goldsmith's, the largest department stores in Dayton, Ohio, and Memphis, Tennessee, respectively, were acquired; Bullock's was added in 1964. The company purchased Dallas's Sanger-Harris in 1961 and later merged it with Houston's Foley's, which Federated bought just after the war; and in 1976, Federated acquired Rich's, Atlanta's leading department store.

Howard Goldfeder, who became CEO in 1981 and chairman in 1982, was the first nonfounding family member selected to lead Federated. Howard took over what was widely regarded as the premier retailing corporation in the United States. Federated had the finest retailing franchises in the major markets and had shown consistent growth and good profit performance.

b

Howard Goldfeder grew up in New York City, graduated from Tufts University, and joined Bloomingdale's as a trainee in 1947. He rose through a variety of assignments in the apparel area and was one of the outstanding coat buyers in the country. He took over responsibility for the Downstairs Store and later became vice president and general merchandise manager for all ready-to-wear, reporting to me. He resigned in 1967 to join Famous Barr in St. Louis, a division of the May Company. Two years later he became president of the May Company, California. With my encouragement, Harold Krensky recruited him in 1971 to become president of Bullock's. Howard became a vice chairman of Federated in 1977, and president in 1980. The next year he became CEO—and my boss. Howard Goldfeder was chosen to take Federated into the modern corporate age.

Howard was quick, detail-minded, tough, and direct. In our early Bloomingdale's days, we had been close. We both lived in Scarsdale, often commuting together; our wives were friendly and our children classmates. Howard had a good sense of humor, and we golfed together at many AMC (Associated Merchandising Corporation) and Federated functions.

Shortly after Howard rejoined Federated, the company instituted a process called Vista to encourage review and discussion by the division principals of all the major issues facing the company.

Howard was very analytical and not afraid to speak his mind. His strong personality and sharp mind were always in evidence and he was never afraid to challenge the Federated principals—good qualities for a leader in the making.

When Howard first became chairman, he appointed several vice chairmen to whom most of the department stores reported. At first I reported directly to Howard. This was a major change for me, as until then I had reported to Harold Krensky. Krensky supported Bloomingdale's and me. But Howard was driven by a bottom-line philosophy and was unwilling to recognize Bloomingdale's as the premier division of Federated with a global reputation.

Howard had early on left New York, living in St. Louis, Los Angeles, and Cincinnati. Those elements of Bloomingdale's mystique—New York and its sense of glamour, excitement, and drama —held no particular appeal for him. As a result, we fought a great deal. Howard shouted at me, and I shouted back—frequently in front of our respective organizations. A meeting with Howard in the early 1980s was no fun for me. Some members of senior management felt Howard had a bug about Bloomingdale's. I was much happier when Howard increased the number of vice chairmen and asked me to report to Mel Jacobs, and later Don Stone, who were both more sympathetic to the objectives of Bloomingdale's.

Howard was not optimistic about the future of department stores and wanted to diversify into other businesses. This strategy was supported by many members of Federated's new management, some of whom even wanted to drop "Department" from Federated's corporate name so it would be perceived more as a consumer-driven retailing organization than an agglomeration of department stores.

In the 1970s, diversification was the popular business philosophy for department store retailing corporations. Associated Dry Goods added Caldor's; the May Company added Venture, a shoe chain; Dayton (Hudson) built up Target and acquired Mervyn's. Business schools were preaching that the demise of the department store was imminent just as they had in 1949. Again, the only question was not if, but when.

Howard pushed Federated to diversify, but the numbers were not with him. Non–department store ventures took up a great deal of Federated's time, energy, and most important, capital. The results were disappointing. Gold Triangle, an attempt to get into the discount home furnishings business, closed in 1980. Gold Circle, an off-price apparel chain, was just under a $1 billion business by 1987, but 1987 pretax earnings were $17 million, or 1.8 percent—a poor showing. Children's Place was acquired in 1982; from 1982 to 1987 its sales rose from $103 million to $159 million, but pretax profit went from $4 million, the year it was acquired, to a loss of almost $11 million. MainStreet, a start-up business that Federated visualized as an updated version of Mervyn's, was launched in 1984 and by 1987 sales grew to $157 million, but the results were a pretax loss of $28 million. Only one of all the new ventures was successful: Ralph's, a California supermarket chain acquired in 1967; sales grew to almost $2.3 billion and pretax profits in 1987 were $95 million, compared to $37 million five years earlier. The failure of these non–department store ventures depleted funds that could have been used to expand and renovate existing profitable department stores.

In Howard's six years as CEO, from 1981 to 1987, department store sales increased $2 billion, but department store pretax income grew only by $67 million—3.4 percent. Federated's department store division had only one really good year, 1983, and in the others earnings were flat or declined. During the same period, non–department store earnings declined from a $30 million profit in 1983 to a loss of $44 million in 1987. So, in a five-year period, department store earnings were flat and non–department store profits turned into a substantial loss. It is not surprising that our stock did not perform well.

When the new ventures did not produce the desired results, it made Howard more driven than ever about bottom-line performance at each division. As Howard became more and more frustrated with his inability to be successful, he became more and more indecisive. Mel Jacobs left in 1982 to become chairman of Saks and Don Stone, a personable retailer with a keen mind and a good sense of humor (he defined his job as the person who could say, "Howard you're full of shit"—and had to, on several occasions), resigned in frustration in 1988.

Despite this, in the 1980s, Federated was still widely regarded as the premier retailing organization in the country with a history of conservative management, little leverage, and, consequently, an

AAA credit rating throughout the sixties and seventies. In 1987 Federated was still an $11 billion retailing powerhouse producing $492 million in pretax profits.

b

You may wonder how Federated went from being a prestige company one day to preparing to be sold to the highest bidder the next. In the logic of the 1980s our stock was undervalued, and we became a target. We had warnings in 1986, when the Hafts, Herbert and his son Robert, who had been greenmailers, announced by means of a required SEC filing that they owned 5 percent of our stock. There were board meetings with advisers and attorneys who recommended a whole series of protective measures. But there was a downturn in the market, and the Hafts sold their stock back to Federated at a loss.

After this, two of our most important outside directors, Reg Jones of General Electric and Pete Peterson, met privately with Howard and urged him to restructure the company to make it less vulnerable. The incident should have been a warning, but management did nothing to take the recommended protective measures. The reasons aren't clear. Perhaps Howard did not want to make a decision. At that time Will Storey, Federated's chief financial officer, was convinced that a severe recession was imminent and that we would need all the cash we had. In a recession, Storey argued, the last thing we would need was to put debt on our balance sheets.

Then, on October 19, 1987, the stock market crashed. In a single day, Federated's stock fell from 42.50 to 38.75 a share, making the company all the more attractive to outsiders. Over the next few months the stock fell even further, to $33 a share. Again, there were warnings of what was to follow: Maurice Biedermann told me at lunch a few weeks later that he thought Federated was very vulnerable. Then Maurice broached a stunning proposition: He and Sir James Goldsmith were prepared to put up a billion dollars in cash toward a friendly management-supported buyout of Federated. Maurice asked me to approach Howard, and report that Jimmy Goldsmith wanted to meet with him to make this offer.

"Tell him [Howard]," Maurice said, "that if he doesn't take advantage of our offer, then I believe that in the next sixty days Federated will be in play."

"Marvin," Howard said sternly when I told him of Maurice's offer, "this is not something that either you or I should be involved in. I do not want to meet with Jimmy Goldsmith." Howard wanted to have nothing to do with this. "If he is serious," he said, "he should call our bankers and discuss it with them."

I reported back to Maurice, who said of Howard: "That [expletive deleted]! Then, Goldsmith will not do it," Maurice concluded.

Little did I know that Howard had just passed up the best chance Federated's management would ever have to own the company.

b

At the same time, management was having serious doubts that the stock would ever return to its previous high. Federated had a rule in place that gave the board a onetime opportunity to sell their stock at the high price of the previous sixty days. When the stock plummeted, Howard organized a conference call in early December to propose that all board members sell their stock at $49.50—it was now in the low thirties.

I was not in favor of selling our shares; to do so, I felt, made a statement that management did not believe the stock would return to previous levels in the foreseeable future. It was a vote of no confidence. Christmas sales, however, were weak and optimism was hard to come by. Almost everyone was in favor of selling. Howard and our legal counsel felt that any vote had to be unanimous. I felt that I was the sole hold out. I was uncomfortable agreeing to sell the stock, but I would have been more uncomfortable going it alone. Being part of management, I decided, meant sometimes going along with decisions one didn't agree with. We sold our stock at $49.50.* Clearly, Federated was ripe for a takeover.

b

On Sunday, January 24, 1988, Federated management was notified that Bob Campeau, a Canadian real estate developer who had acquired Allied Stores the year before in one of the largest hostile

---

* The irony was that when the Campeau takeover occurred, five months later, the stock sold for $73.50, so not only was our earlier decision imprudent but we lost money on it as well.

takeovers in corporate history, would be making a bid for Federated the next morning. Howard called our attorneys and quickly organized a board meeting at Federated's New York office at 1440 Broadway for Monday morning.

In attendance were the members of the distinguished board of directors Ralph Lazarus had put together. The board included such outside directors as Reg Jones of GE; Phil Caldwell of Ford; Bill Miller, former chairman of the Federal Reserve; Bob Charpie of Cabot; Jim Ferguson of General Foods; Pete Peterson of the Blackstone Group; Kathy Wriston of Citibank; Charlotte Beers of Beers, Tatham and Laird; Daniel Leblond, chairman of Leblond Makino Machine Tool Company; Cliff Wharton, chairman and CEO of Teachers Insurance and Annuity Association–College Retirement Equities Fund (today, President Clinton's deputy secretary of state); and Howard Johnson, chairman of the corporation of MIT. Other Federated directors were Howard Goldfeder, Norman Matthews, Alan Questrom (Questrom, who had run the Bullock's division, had recently been made a Federated executive), CFO Will Storey, John Burden, Byron Allenbaugh, and me. Our attorney, Joe Flom, of Skadden Arps Meagher and Flom, dean of the mergers and acquisition field, was present along with Federated's investment banker, J. Tomilson ("Tommy") Hill, from Shearson Lehman Hutton.

In an offer dated January 25, Campeau had proposed to buy Federated for $47 a share cash or $4.2 billion. The board did not take him seriously, thinking that Campeau was looking for greenmail and would go away soon. The Allied deal had put him so far in debt that it was impossible to believe he could finance a Federated takeover. We could not comprehend how he was bidding with a negative net worth.

b

Bob Campeau was a Canadian success story. Born in remote Sudbury, Ontario, a northern mining town, he dropped out of school at fourteen to train as a machinist. The youngest of seven children of French and Scottish stock, Campeau's parents were, in his own words, "poor as Job." Campeau was earning $5,000 a year (Canadian) working for Canadian International Paper when he decided to become a real estate developer. He bought a building lot in Ottawa's east end and built a house with his own hands, on nights, weekends, and vacation. Campeau sold the house for a $3,000 profit and never looked back. A decade later, Campeau had become Ottawa's largest and most successful home builder, becoming a millionaire in the process. He had bucked Toronto's English old-boy network to mark the Ottawa skyline with his buildings.

Campeau first came to attention in the United States with his $4.4 billion hostile takeover of Allied Department Stores in 1988, the third-largest department store corporation in America. Allied's assets included Bonwit Teller, Brooks Brothers, Ann Taylor, and half a dozen other major department stores. Campeau was a rags to real estate to retail success story. He was not, however, one to rest on his laurels.

Unbeknownst to us, Campeau had been eyeing Federated for some time. In August 1987, Campeau had his investment bankers at First Boston crunching Federated's numbers. He believed that there was hidden value in the enormous real estate holdings of department store groups, and that with his knowledge of real estate, he could capitalize on them. Given Federated's Cincinnati headquarters, Campeau's team called this newest venture "Project Rose" for the Cincinnati Red's Pete Rose. Federated, they concluded, was undervalued. The October 19 stock plunge made the price even more attractive.

A few weeks later, on November 15, Donald Trump announced that he intended to purchase a $15 million block of Federated's stock. Although Trump never really pursued Federated, Campeau became concerned that other bidders might surface. Alan Finkelson, a partner at Cravath Swaine & Moore and a former investment banker who had been critical in convincing Campeau to buy Allied, now urged Campeau to go after Federated. At the same time there was a rumor that a tough Delaware antitakeover law was about to be passed. Campeau decided to go ahead with a low-ball offer just to protect himself in case the Delaware legislation passed.

b

The board did not take Campeau's January 25 offer seriously; nonetheless, we understood that our stock was in play. Howard asked each Federated division to assemble the appropriate facts and figures so the board could value the company. We met often during the next month at Skadden's offices at 919 Third Avenue, a tall, sleek, black-sheathed building in which Skadden had gobbled up so many floors that it was referred to as "the black octopus." We always met in a large conference room and there were always platters of deli sandwiches and sodas. By the middle of February, Federated had determined that the company was worth a maximum of $55 a share.

Many on the board, including myself, felt that a hostile takeover and its attendant debt was not in our best interests. So we began to explore alternatives—mergers with other retailers such as Dayton Hudson, The Limited, May Company, Dillard's, and Macy's. None were successful. We could not come to terms with Dayton Hudson because Federated had a fundamental difference of opinion about who the surviving company should be: We did not think it should be Dayton Hudson. Les Wexner was anxious to explore a buyout and put one of his Limited stores in each of the Federated divisions, but as the deal became more and more costly he dropped the idea.

b

At the same time, Campeau was having to rein in his own team. On February 2, investment bankers Bruce Wasserstein and Joseph Perella announced plans to leave First Boston to form their own firm. Campeau was committed to First Boston but didn't want to lose Wasserstein's counsel, so he retained both, increasing his costs, not to mention the logistical issues. But this didn't slow Campeau down; he was only gaining more speed.

On February 3, Campeau had a new proposal: He set a February 6 deadline to accept a sweetened, $5.5 billion bid of $61 a share for a friendly takeover. On February 5, Federated rejected the original offer, and challenged Campeau to prove he could finance a $5.5 billion bid.

The board was convinced that the numbers spoke for themselves: As of September 30, Campeau had long-term debt of more than $4.5 billion, short-term debt of $1.6 billion, and stockholder equity of only $82 million. Federated stockholder equity as of October 31 was $2.5 billion. Its long-term debt was $97 million. Federated's profit was more than $313 million after taxes; Campeau's losses more than $430 million. Based on these figures it would have seemed inconceivable for Campeau to acquire Federated; on the contrary, the opposite made more sense.

By challenging Campeau to "put up or shut up," Federated hoped to dismiss his bid, but the effect was entirely the opposite. From Campeau's point of view, by challenging him Federated was admitting it was for sale, and the rest was a matter of price and due diligence—mere technicalities to his way of thinking.

On February 10, Campeau announced that he had arranged financing from shopping center owner Ed DeBartolo and development company Olympia & York—DeBartolo had agreed to provide a $400 million loan to Campeau US. This was startling. DeBartolo had been Campeau's rival in his pursuit of Allied; now he was an investor. And equally surprising was an investment from Olympia & York, a legendary real estate firm run by the secretive Reichmann brothers from Canada who were known as conservative investors. The participation of DeBartolo and the Reichmanns increased Campeau's credibility. The message was clear: Campeau was a serious player.

The pressure was now on Federated. Not only had Campeau exceeded their $55 a share estimate, but he had shown he had the financing to back it up. Worse yet, five days later, on February 15, Campeau offered to sweeten his bid to $65 a share, or $6.75 billion. And Federated's management, particularly Howard, came under increasing criticism for having left the company so vulnerable.*

Wherever I went during the next few weeks, the possible deal was never far away. Everything was rushing forward. With every passing moment, Campeau's takeover of Federated was becoming more real. I was concerned that if Federated was going to change hands, I wanted to do my utmost to see that a group who understood retailing in general, and Bloomingdale's in particular, came aboard. Better yet, I wanted to be part of that management team. I envisioned a scenario in which a group purchased Federated and sold off Bloomingdale's to a management group I assembled. I called

---

* *Women's Wear Daily* put it this way at the time: "Federated's vulnerability to a takeover increased dramatically when the price of its stock plummeted in the Oct. 19 stock market crash, making the firm much cheaper to buy. But that turning point was preceded by years in which management's lack of decisiveness and central control over its strong-willed divisions made it difficult to generate the profit gains to drive the stock price up and put the company out of reach of raiders."

Todd Lang, a good friend and law partner at the firm of Weil, Gotschal, to ask whether as a director I could initiate such a plan.

"Under the law, you certainly have the right to do so," Todd said, "but first you have to go to Howard Goldfeder."

After the next meeting, I approached Howard with the idea of a management buyout, and asked whether he would be interested, personally, in participating. He said he had no interest whatsoever. "Do you mind if I try?" I asked. He had no objection. "Feel free to talk to Norman Matthews [Federated's president]," Howard said, explaining that Norman was the only other management executive anxious to back such a plan. I called Norman immediately and it was clear that he, too, was anxious to develop a strategy.

That weekend I went skiing. From Deer Valley, Utah, I called Henry Kravis, who was spending his weekend skiing in Aspen, Colorado, to ask if he would be interested in trying to participate in a buyout of Federated that would ultimately spin off Bloomingdale's. We spoke that Saturday morning and he suggested we get together at his New York apartment Sunday evening to discuss it.

When we met at his magnificent Fifth Avenue apartment, I was greeted warmly by Henry and his wife, Carolyne Roehm, whom I've known since she was Oscar de la Renta's assistant. The three of us sat down for a drink and then Carolyne excused herself to supervise dinner. We ate together, but before we finished, Carolyne left Henry and me alone to talk. I took Henry back through what I considered the opportunities in Federated, and the chances for a buyout. Henry was interested and promised to call Howard.

A week later the principals of each Federated division were asked to appear at the Kohlberg Kravis Roberts (KKR) offices. Henry and his associates wanted to go over the numbers in more detail to make their own assessment of the value and potential of the company. KKR was looking for a 40 percent return on investment, which, I later learned, was their usual criteria.

Having all division principals there at the same time, each waiting his turn, made for a funny scene. It was a little like getting called into the dean's office, except that my fellow "students" included Mike Steinberg, Hy Edelstein, and Howard Sokol—the chairmen of Foley's, A&S, and Burdine's.

After going over all the numbers, Henry decided that KKR was comfortable making a bid beyond the $55 estimate Federated itself had come up with. They were prepared to bid, Henry said, in the neighborhood of $61, and wanted to move forward. We also had reports that the May Company was examining the company.

Our board meeting on February 12 was critical because we expected bids from any interested party that morning. We sat in the Skadden Arps boardroom with our bankers and lawyers. We expected bids from Campeau, KKR, May Company, and possibly others. Each represented a different direction for the company and we sat there filled with excitement and concern. There was some question as to what KKR was going to bid, and they made an offer in the low sixties.

We waited to hear from the May Company, whose board had met the previous day. When no answer came, we asked Tommy Hill to call the May Company's CEO, Dave Farrell. The word came back that the May Company was not interested in bidding; we were all shocked.

From what I had understood, the May Company thought the price had gotten too high. They would be better off, they decided, letting Campeau buy the company and then trying to buy appropriate divisions from him. Ultimately this turned out to be a very sound strategy.

KKR's bid didn't stop Campeau, though. Amid a steady barrage of letters, press releases, motions in courts, and legal notices, he kept bumping up the price. Having heard that KKR was bidding somewhere in the low sixties, he announced a $65 cash offer. And on February 16, he issued a press release with an offer of $66 a share. Campeau also listed his financial backing as follows: the Reichmanns' Olympia & York, $260 million; DeBartolo $480 million; Bank Paribas and the Bank of Montreal, $500 million. In addition, First Boston announced that it was "prepared to commit" $1 billion.

It didn't matter that Campeau was offering no true equity—his funds were all O.P.M., other people's money. At the end of the day, Campeau's offer remained the best bid on the table. With a deal within striking distance, Campeau flew to London to sell Brooks Brothers, a move that would be a key step toward the Campeau era at Federated.

b

Lord Rayner, then chairman of Marks & Spencer, had long had his
eye on Brooks Brothers, the standard-bearer of classic American
menswear. Twice he had approached Campeau about selling the
store, and twice Campeau refused—price was not even discussed.
But Lord Rayner was not deterred. Early in January he flew to
Toronto and toured Campeau's Scotia Bank Plaza, only to be re-
buffed by the developer again.

Soon after, however, Campeau, with his debt increasing and
needing cash for the Federated deal, proposed that Lord Rayner
invest in Campeau Corp. This time, Rayner said no. A few months
later Campeau called Lord Rayner and said he would be in London.
Might they meet at the Ritz?

Over dinner Campeau did what he said he would not do—he
agreed to sell Brooks Brothers to Lord Rayner. Then they set about
hammering out a deal. When it was all over, Brooks Brothers was
Lord Rayner's, but he had paid a startling $750 million.

That Campeau had received so much for Brooks Brothers had a
dazzling effect. It caused many at Federated to think that maybe
Campeau's assets were worth what he claimed and that he was a
visionary, a magician who could make money out of thin air. The
effect was dramatic. Suddenly everyone at Federated and Shearson
became convinced that Campeau could raise the funds to buy Federated.

b

By February 25, Campeau's bid was at $67, though Howard was
looking for $68. Once again we met to open the bids. KKR's final
offer was a $65 combination of cash and paper. Dillard's had been
planning to submit an offer, but our lawyer informed us that "they
did not get their act together." Bill Dillard told me he didn't bid
because he felt he was running around between investment bankers
and was not ready to pay the kind of commitment money they
wanted. This was a new experience for him, and he was uncomfortable. Macy's had expressed some interest but did not bid. The
expression our lawyers used was that Macy's was "loosey-goosey,"
meaning they were only vaguely interested.

Acknowledging that no one seemed willing to bid higher than

Campeau, we invited Campeau's advisers to address us face-to-face
for the first time—if they raised their bid to $68 a share. We later
asked to meet Campeau himself.

On the evening of February 25, the Campeau team, led by Bruce
Wasserstein, filed into the large conference room at Skadden Arps.
Jim Maher and Mike Rothfeld represented First Boston. Finkelson
and Sam Butler came from Cravath. Bob Morosky, Allied's CEO,
who looked like a middle linebacker for the Giants and radiated
aggressiveness, hovered silently behind it all. There was one
woman, Carolyn Buck Luce, and at the time I wondered who she
was. Campeau himself, we were told, was in Austria and could not
make it.

Wasserstein made an impassioned speech about how this was a
great moment in our lives if only we had the courage to close the
deal. He struck me as a very articulate breed of high-pressure salesman. Finkelson spoke as well, trying to reassure us about Campeau's financing, or lack thereof. Campeau did not yet have the
backing of a commercial bank, but Finkelson said, "Who needs a
bank?"

Campeau's last bid was at $67 a share. We had asked for $68. I
believe Howard would have closed at $69 that evening. Wasserstein,
however, announced that he wasn't authorized to raise the bid at all:
Only Bob could do that, he said. We suggested he try to contact Mr.
Campeau, and adjourned for dinner. When we got back, everyone
was waiting for the meeting to be reconvened. We waited, and
waited. Many of the Federated directors were becoming angry and
wanted to leave. Wasserstein finally reached Campeau at the pay
phone of a local Austrian restaurant, and was authorized to raise the
bid to $68 a share, or $7 billion.

Wasserstein urged us to work all night on an agreement and sign
it the next morning. I now believe that some of the directors wanted
to make Campeau pay more just for having made them stay at Skadden so late. Howard was convinced we would need the weekend to
work out all the details and, to his credit, would not sign until we
had.

"I will not be stampeded," Howard said. We could reconvene
Monday, he said, and review the offer. Wasserstein expressed great
disappointment but assented.

Throughout the weekend our attorneys haggled with Campeau's

at their Wall Street offices. Campeau's attorneys agreed that Campeau would forfeit $200 million if he did not line up his financing in ninety days. Cravath then sent over sixty clean copies of an agreement for the Federated Board members to sign at their morning meeting on February 29. As far as Campeau, Wasserstein, and Finkelson were concerned, the company was theirs. They were in for a surprise.

b

That Friday night, many of us left the meeting at close to midnight thinking the Campeau takeover a done deal. I was unhappy about that, and as the deal had not yet closed, I felt I should do all I could to push for another, and in my opinion better, outcome. So I called a friend, Larry Tisch.

Larry and I had known each other for many years. We joke that I played a very small part in introducing him to retailing in the early 1960s. One night a few days after we had opened a major country promotion, Larry and his wife, Billie, and Lee and I had dinner together. Billie spent the evening talking about the promotion. I asked the Tisches if they would like to have the chance to see what the store looked like after hours. We walked over to the store; I turned on the lights and gave them a private tour of several floors. We visited the model rooms, the street of shops, the ready-to-wear floors, and the displays; the Tisches were intrigued.

Shortly after that, Larry took a major position in the stock of the Gimbel Corporation, which then owned Saks Fifth Avenue and the New York, Pittsburgh, and Philadelphia Gimbels. He had a brilliant strategy to sell off Gimbels for the real estate and build up Saks Fifth Avenue. However, in a few months British American Tobacco came in and bought Larry out at a handsome profit. That was one of Larry's first experiences in retailing. Subsequently, in 1986, in the course of the Macy's leveraged buyout, Larry acquired a 19 percent share of Macy's as a personal investment and went on the board, where he became one of the most influential directors.

During the negotiations, Larry and I had some conversations about the general status of Campeau and what was happening as Macy's and Larry studied whether they should have a role in the negotiations.

A few weeks earlier Ed Finkelstein had invited me over to his town house for breakfast. Ed and I had been classmates at college, and were a year apart at the business school. We had been tough competitors over the years but shared a healthy respect for each other. Now the world was changing and Ed wanted to discuss what would happen in the event Federated was acquired by Macy's. At seven in the morning on a Saturday, I drove up to his double town house on 77th Street where Ed and one of his large and friendly dogs, a Labrador, greeted me.

Ed wanted me to understand that he saw Bloomingdale's as a particularly fine opportunity, and it was one of the reasons he was interested in acquiring Federated. He wanted me to know that if he purchased Federated, the other divisions would report to Mark Handler, Macy's president, but I would report to him so we would work together to increase Bloomingdale's productivity in our existing branches and add new stores in the future.

Now, on Friday evening, as it seemed almost certain that Campeau would buy Federated, I called Larry Tisch. Without going into details, I left Larry with the feeling that unless they did something over the weekend, Campeau was going to get the company. I thought this was a great opportunity for Macy's.

The Macy's board met on Sunday. I had no idea what decision, if any, they made.

b

Monday morning I went to work with the very real possibility that I would soon be a Campeau employee. It seemed as if it was all over.

Jim Freund, one of our attorneys, had spent the weekend with Finkelson at his office on closing documents for the Campeau deal, working late into Sunday night. Freund had just left the Cravath offices when he received a midnight call to join Macy's advisers and Federated officials at Macy's law firm Weil, Gotshal & Manges. Macy's was going to bid.

The next morning there was a mid-morning conference call to announce the Macy's offer. A special meeting of Federated's board was called for February 29 to compare the Macy's and Campeau bids. Each side was trying to win us over. Campeau had informed our attorneys that if he acquired the company he would not spin off

Ralph's and we pondered that. We were also informed that Ed Finkelstein had asked to meet with our board. This was in marked contrast to Campeau, whom no one had as yet met. We agreed to hear Ed that very afternoon.

Ed made a powerful appeal to the board on the value of the merger. Today, as Macy's struggles to emerge from its own bankruptcy, you may wonder why I was so interested in having them acquire Federated. But this was the spring of 1988 and Ed Finkelstein was speaking from strength. Macy's had done their own buyout and appeared to be very successful. At the time, they had outstanding same store growth and their performance was improving.

Ed believed that a Federated-Macy's merger would produce the dominant American department store corporation. He predicted a $100 million savings in 1988 by consolidating Federated Merchandise Services with Macy's and creating one corporate office with a narrow overhead. He forecast an additional $40 million profit through the expansion of private label goods.

Altogether Ed felt a Macy's merger would improve earnings before interest and taxes by 1.5 percent. Bloomingdale's growth rate, he predicted, could be increased by 1.5 percent by improving growth in the branches, and that of Burdine's by 4 to 6 percent, Filene's by 5 percent, Foley's by 2 to 3 percent above the projection, and Magnin's by 20 percent. These were optimistic projections, but Ed argued that his track record showed they were achievable.

Ed said that he felt Macy's would do better than Campeau on social issues, meaning personnel questions, such as severance, layoffs, and retirement. Macy's agreed there would be full severance benefits for the seven senior executives, including full tax payments, paid at the time of the transaction. (Campeau had actually agreed to the same package.) Ed also said that the chairman, meaning Howard, would continue until the tender offer was closed. It was an impressive presentation and made a great impact on the Federated Board, particularly given the additional appeal that Ed, unlike Campeau, was a retailer.

As soon as Ed left, Howard gave his assessment. He thought there was only a 35 to 40 percent probability that Ed could deliver the things he promised. I spoke up to say that I thought those were not bad odds. The synergy between Macy's and Federated would create a unique department store organization. Macy's had a proven track record, and I expressed my opinion that Federated principals would fit more comfortably with those of Macy's than they would with the Campeau Corporation.

Howard, it was clear, was eager to retire, even before the buyout began. He saw his role as trying to maximize shareholder value and then stepping down. Howard and I had dinner around that time. He and I had totally different points of view. Howard had always looked forward to retiring to California and building a home near a golf course. I was looking forward to staying on. Accordingly we looked at the negotiations differently. Howard was most concerned with shareholder value; I wondered which arrangement would be best for Bloomingdale's.

With reflection, as I write this, I realize something I couldn't have known then, At that time, I thought Howard's viewpoint and mine mattered. Now I know better: They didn't, because a deal has a life of its own. And following Ed Finkelstein's presentation, matters rushed forward of their own volition. On March 2, in a 7:30 A.M. conference call, the Federated board voted to accept Macy's bid of a cash tender offer for approximately 70.5 million shares of Federated common stock, representing approximately 80 percent of the shares outstanding, at $74.50 per share. The agreement also provided that those Federated shares not purchased would be exchanged, tax free, for a number of newly issued Macy's Federated shares. Analysts and arbitragers valued the new stock at about $10 a share, according to *The Wall Street Journal*, making the Macy's offer worth $6.1 billion. We had, in effect, doubled the price of the stock in little more than a month.

The Macy's-Federated agreement also provided that Federated would pay Macy's as much as $45 million for expenses connected with the negotiations if the deal fell apart through no fault of their own. In addition, Macy's would be entitled to a topping fee of 25 percent of any competing bid in excess of $74.50 that Federated might accept. In other words, it was going to be expensive to walk away from a deal with Macy's.

Time magazine dubbed Macy's last-minute appearance as a white knight as "a new miracle on 34th Street."

b

As soon as the Macy's bid was accepted I called Ed to congratulate him and said that I looked forward to working together. I then sent champagne and caviar in Bloomingdale's gift baskets to him and Mark Handler with Bloomingdale's gold credit cards. On March 8, I got a note back from Mark saying he hoped the caviar didn't spoil before the deal went through. I had no idea how prophetic that would be.

When Federated announced that they had accepted the Macy's bid, Wasserstein went wild. Campeau claimed that he had been shut out of the deal and announced that he was going to raise his bid. Although we thought that we had sold the company to Ed Finkelstein and Macy's, the shareholders had not ratified that decision by voting their shares. Campeau raised his offer to $73 all cash and sent a tender offer to the shareholders with his new offer.

Campeau's strategy was to offer to buy the first 75 percent of the stock at a high price—the portion he needed to control the company—and the rest at a much lower price, about $40 a share. This was a very clever technique because it created the feeling that if you did not tender your stock to Campeau quickly you would lose out. And that put enormous pressure on Federated's employees to sell. My coworkers kept turning to me for advice as to whether they should tender their stock to Campeau. Our lawyer, Joe Flom, had told the division principals we could not advise anyone, but we could explain what it was we ourselves were doing.

Our decision as directors wasn't easy. We were constantly reminded by counsel that our sole objective was to maximize shareholder value. That concerned me. What if the highest price created a result that would be bad for the employees?

Campeau concerned me from day one. At Allied, thousands of employees had been fired and it had not been a benefit to the company, which was performing poorly. Maurice Bidermann had met with Campeau, who was trying to raise $300 million for the Federated deal. Campeau could have the money, Maurice said, if he'd agree to spin off Bloomingdale's. Campeau refused. "Bloomingdale's is the jewel in the crown," he said. There negotiations ended. That Campeau refused to spin off Bloomingdale's was not so strange, but Maurice found something odd about Campeau. "Marvin," he told me upon his return, "try to get Bloomingdale's out of this mess." Maurice paused and said of Campeau: "He's crazy."

As Macy's and Campeau kept bidding, they were in court suing each other. Nonetheless the judge let the bidding proceed, as he thought it was in the best interest of the shareholders. The prices continued to jump. Campeau went to $77.00 a share, Macy's went to $77.50 and then $78.00 a share.

The board met soon after and Joe Flom, with our approval, agreed to deliver instructions for final auction procedures to both Macy's and Campeau's advisers. Macy's had agreed to be bound by the procedures; Campeau did not. Nonetheless, we heard out both sides. Howard then revealed that the company had retained a valuation consultant who had determined that the company resulting from a merger with Campeau Corporation would be solvent (so much for valuations consultants). Federated's financial advisers were then asked to restate their analysis of the offers. We went over each detail of both proposals. Both the outside directors and the management directors agreed that Campeau's proposal was financially superior to Macy's.

However, the next morning, March 31, 1988, Macy's upped its offer to $78.92 per share for approximately 80 percent of the stock. In a conference call, Ed Finkelstein made an impassioned speech that we should accept his offer "in the interests of American industry." By the end of the day we were ready to accept; however, Joe Flom informed us that we would have to notify Campeau. The board agreed to meet the following morning, and once again I went home believing the company had been sold.

But there were major problems: Ed Finkelstein's offer was a verbal one and Larry Tisch was having serious doubts. He calculated that if Macy's went ahead with the deal, the first twelve cents of every sales dollar would go for debt service. Joe Flom knew of Larry's concern and was also aware that if Macy's withdrew their offer, Campeau would drop his price substantially. Therefore, Flom felt that the time had come to close the bidding.

Campeau had just returned from Europe and was in New York, having stopped to see his advisers on his way from Toronto to Florida. Flom invited Campeau and Finkelstein to meet at Ed Finkelstein's brownstone on East 77th Street.

That night, the town house began to fill with lawyers and advisers. Finkelstein had his team of lawyers, led by Ira Millstein. Campeau had his advisers, including Alan Finkelson. Proposed agreements were shuttled among the floors for each side to review. Ed, after discussion with Larry Tisch, had decided to purchase part of Federated rather than the whole. His first choice was to buy Bloomingdale's and Bullock's. Campeau was unwilling to sell Bloomingdale's but he was willing to part with Bullock's and I. Magnin. They argued about what the right price should be.

Finally, Flom proposed a settlement: Campeau would purchase the company for $73.50 a share all cash, a discount from the high bid. A thirty-seven-cent dividend was due but Federated agreed to suspend it. Macy's, for its part, would be allowed to purchase three Federated divisions: Bullock's, Bullock's/Wilshire, and I. Magnin—giving it additional West Coast outlets—for $1.1 billion. In addition, Macy's would be entitled to the fees Federated had promised in the event they did not win the merger—that is, their costs plus the topping fee, an estimated $60 million.

By 10:30 P.M., they had popped the cork on a bottle of Dom Perignon and clinked glasses. Bob Campeau had just become the largest retailer in North America.

Ten weeks after Campeau's original January 25 bid, it was all over. Tommy Hill told the *Los Angeles Times* that "Ultimately what the transaction boiled down to was simply a test of will over a two and a half month period." An expensive one.

I had a sinking feeling in my stomach that morning as I thought about what it would be like to work for Bob Campeau and what the future atmosphere would be like at Bloomingdale's and Federated. I really did not know how right I was. Although the stock price was $6.6 billion, the total cost to Campeau with his fees was closer to $8.8 billion. At the time, the Federated takeover was the largest successful hostile bid ever, and the largest takeover outside the oil industry. The transaction meant fat fees: advisers and bankers on the Campeau takeover took home a reported $350 million in fees; and, accordingly, hefty bonuses for the many individual players. For years Federated had retained Skadden Arps and Shearson to prevent a takeover, but in the end they were the facilitators.

The takeover announcement was made April 1, 1988—April Fools' Day no less. There was no small irony in that. *Fortune* would later characterize it as "the looniest deal ever."

b

It wasn't until several years later, in the Time Warner case, that a judge finally ruled that directors need not take the highest bid if doing so is not in the long-term interest of the company. But the Federated takeover was a victim of its times: There was a soaring belief in ever-inflating prices. The sky-high prices were, we thought, self-fulfilling prophecies. Each takeover seemed crazy—until the next one. Each deal validated the one before. We went ahead, naive, optimistic, hoping that somehow it would all work. We did not know we were building a house of cards. We were now eager to move forward, and curious to see what life would be like for Federated and for Bloomingdale's with Bob Campeau.

Courtesy of the Washington Post Writers Group

CHAPTER 12

Life with Campeau

ampeau was now in charge. Until that moment, I had been against a Campeau takeover; that morning, however, I decided to call Bob Campeau to congratulate him. The best way to protect our staff and store, I decided, was to woo him. I found out that Campeau was at his Florida home, north of Palm Beach, so on the morning Campeau's purchase of Federated was announced, I directed our Boca Raton store to send him a gift basket of champagne and caviar.

I had never met Campeau and so when I called, I was pleasantly surprised to find him exuberant and friendly. He insisted immediately that I call him Bob. He told me how anxious he was to meet me and tour Bloomingdale's 59th Street and said that he thought our Boca Raton store was the most beautiful in the world. He then told me that he had first seen our Boca store last November while visiting Allied's Jordan Marsh store in the same mall. He so fell in love with the design of our store, the merchandise, the presentation, and its atrium—I was to learn later that Bob had a thing for atriums—that he decided then and there to buy Bloomingdale's and Federated.

As a result, Bob wanted to hold a press conference that evening at our Boca store to announce his plans for Federated. I agreed to arrange it for him. A few hours later, he fielded phone calls in our store manager's office, including those from *The New York Times* and *The Wall Street Journal*. Campeau used the occasion to announce that he was not going to sell off Ralph's. This was not known by the chairman of Ralph's, who had been spending his time planning to take the supermarket chain private. I called Byron Allenbaugh, the chairman, and gave him the news.

That same afternoon Ralph Lazarus came to see me. He had just arrived in New York from London. I had known Ralph and his father, Fred, for many years and was very fond of both of them. I knew that Ralph had great pride in Federated and particularly Bloomingdale's. "Marvin, what's happened?" he asked. He had been completely left out of the loop. I brought him up to date. No one had told him that the company his father had founded had been sold that day to a Canadian developer with a negative net worth and no track record in retailing. Ralph was shaken. "Where did I go wrong? I entrusted the business to Howard and now. . . . Did I make a mistake?" I made no attempt to answer Ralph. That brief visit remains one of my saddest memories of that difficult era.

b

Bloomingdale's was launching a major promotion that week, "Hooray for Hollywood." The opening night was a black-tie AIDS benefit underwritten, in part, by Revlon. We were expecting over a thousand friends, vendors, and celebrities. I invited Mr. and Mrs. Campeau, along with Sue and Alan Finkelson and Bob Morosky and his wife, to be our guests and to join us for a drink in the executive offices before the party. I wanted to show off Bloomingdale's at its best.

There were klieg lights outside, and people waited on the sidewalk to stare at the celebrities entering the store, including Cher, Lauren Hutton, Douglas Fairbanks, Jr., Jaclyn Smith, Frank Gifford, and Jane Seymour. Bob Campeau and his wife, Ilse, arrived late and made a grand entrance. He was surrounded by reporters and movie stars. Many came up to congratulate him. Bob and Ilse came directly to our executive office where we met them for the first time. We toasted Bob on his acquisition with champagne. Bob made a good first impression; he had charisma. Ilse was more aloof, and Bob Morosky seemed downright grim.

As we toured the store, Campeau was enthusiastic about every detail, but Morosky still seemed gloomy. The swimwear department, Morosky said, was too big. I explained that it was one of our most profitable areas. Morosky made a few other comments that made me wonder how much he knew or understood our business.

I gave a speech welcoming the Campeaus to Bloomingdale's. Bob Campeau was clearly enjoying himself. He was the new kid on the block, and he owned the candy store to boot. All attention was on him. The TV cameras hovered nearby, and I introduced him to

Calvin Klein, Norma Kamali, Ron Perelman and his wife, Claudia Cohen. My main purpose was to let Bob bask in the Bloomingdale's mystique.

Within the week, Campeau summoned all the Federated principals to a meeting in Cincinnati. There were cocktails and hors d'oeuvres, followed by a rambling speech in which he told us how lucky we were to have been purchased by Campeau Corporation. There was $1.4 billion equity in the deal, he said, more equity than anyone else would have offered. He told us how he would cut costs and raise profits. Campeau Corp. stock, he predicted, would go from 15 to 80, or even 100. We would all be rich. This was, I discovered, a typical Bob Campeau speech.

That was the first time I met Campeau's talented management team, which was the main reason he succeeded for as long as he did. There was Ron Tysoe, a sharp young Canadian who was very creative in buying and selling companies; Jim Roddy, a top-flight financial adviser with sound judgment; Carolyn Buck Luce, a bright woman he had hired from First Boston; and Alan Finkelson, the Cravath lawyer. I was to get to know all of them much better in the ensuing months. Campeau was known to be an eccentric, but I was reassured by the fact that they seemed to get along well with him.

For dinner we took over the banquet room of the Cincinattian Hotel. Campeau asked me to join him at his table. Howard Goldfeder was sitting there as well, and I could tell he couldn't wait to get out of there. The May 4 closing couldn't come a moment too soon for him. I was the only former Federated board member staying on; the others, including John Burden, Alan Questrom, and Norman Matthews, were leaving.

I was staying on because I believed that continuity of management was essential to Bloomingdale's surviving Campeau. The other directors also had incentives to leave, including generous golden parachutes (Howard's was said to be $8 to $10 million). I was the only insider board member who was not provided for. The reason Howard gave at the time was that I was the only director who still ran a division, so it did not apply to me. This is not to say that I did not profit from the sale of Federated. As an employee since 1950, I had accumulated a large amount of stock and options, including funds set aside for my retirement.

b

The next morning Campeau's people gave Bloomingdale's president Bob Tammaro* and me the goal of cutting $50 to $60 million of expense—about 15 percent of the total—within thirty days. That would be particularly difficult, I said, as Bloomingdale's had some of the highest fixed costs of any store in the country, but we would try to cut $40 million.

When we returned to New York we called a meeting of the executive committee and asked each division head to assume their share of the burden with what we called our "U.J.A." approach: Bob Tammaro and I decided how much in savings we would ask each division head to pledge. We then turned to them and challenged them to meet the number by cuts in their own organization. We went to advertising, for example, and asked Gordon Cooke to save $5 million.

We got our $40 million savings, but not without some hardship. I had explained to the union in advance that we were trying to save as many jobs as we could and they were supportive. There were seven hundred jobs open in the company that spring that we had not filled. That allowed us, in the end, to only lay off 245 people out of a work force of fourteen thousand. Though the percentage of people fired was not great, it was nonetheless painful. I was sensitive to that fact, and our personnel division did their utmost to be compassionate and set up attractive severance packages and an outplacement program.

We presented our cuts and savings to Bob Campeau at a meeting attended by Bob Tammaro and Ron Tysoe. Campeau had also invited Dick van Pelt of Jordan Marsh, whose cost cutting Bob was particularly proud of. (As a result of those cuts, Jordan Marsh went from a reasonable profit to a loss in three years.) Campeau was pleased when we announced that we had saved $40 million, and we explained how we had done it. Bob Tammaro then told Campeau he was concerned: "Marvin may have gone too far in cutting the mer-

---

* In 1978, Larry Lachman retired and I became chairman. Jim Schoff, Jr., whom I had worked with for almost twenty years, then became president. Jim resigned in 1984 and was succeeded briefly by Jim Guinan of Gold Circle before being replaced by Bob Tammaro, the former president of A&S, in 1985. Bob brought to Bloomingdale's an extensive background in finance, operations, and data processing.

chandise organization." (In truth that was the part of the business we were most anxious to preserve.)

"I hope not," Bob Campeau said.

Bob Tammaro leaned over and whispered to me, "Marvin, you owe me one."

We cut down the number of executives and broadened the areas and departments each supervised. This created an immediate savings on paper, but in the short run it cut down on our effectiveness. With the changes in the buying organization, for fall 1988 many buyers and department managers were supervising departments they were not familiar with. No question it affected our 1988–89 performance, and consequently hurt our business. We lost sales and that lessened the impact of the savings we had made through consolidating jobs.

Sweeping changes were occurring throughout the former Federated organization. We met often during Campeau's first few weeks, and frequently he asked me to come to his suite at the Waldorf Towers to review different issues concerning Bloomingdale's and the corporation. I sensed Bob was anxious to have someone who could talk about the history and the background of Federated without any particular ax to grind. One day he asked me, in addition to running Bloomingdale's, to become vice chairman of Federated/Allied and serve on the Campeau Corporation board. All principals sat on the Federated/Allied board, but the parent corporation board was largely Canadian and met in Toronto. I accepted immediately, since I believed being on the board could ensure support for Bloomingdale's and for Federated.

Campeau's immediate concern was improving the profits and cutting expense. He explained how well it had been done at Jordan Marsh and at Allied. "Bob Morosky is an expert in that," Bob said.

I did not disagree. I had just one meeting with Morosky, but clearly he knew about cutting expenses. However, he did not seem to know much about merchandising. Morosky had been successful at The Limited, but he was different in style and approach from the people at Federated. Campeau then told me that he was having trouble finding a replacement for Howard Goldfeder, and was concerned because Goldfeder, Questrom, and Matthews had all left. I explained to Bob that it would be very difficult to find a chief merchant who would be willing to report to Bob Morosky.

Campeau was leaving for two weeks in Europe and said he would think it over. While Campeau was away, both Bob Tamaro and I noticed a change in Morosky. He seemed to become more conciliatory and we assumed he was anxious to get along with us better. But on the first day of Campeau's return, Bob called to say, "Morosky's gone." And I never saw Bob Morosky again. Campeau had paid off Morosky's contract, a reported $3 million for his six months at the helm of Federated/Allied, plus an estimated $200,000 in options in Campeau stock.

Campeau told me that he was going to make Jim Zimmerman of Rich's president of the company, and asked my opinion of him. Jim was an extraordinarily capable, dedicated operating executive, I said, and told Bob that I heartily agreed with his choice. Campeau was still very anxious to find a chairman of the board who would both pull the divisions together and give strong merchandising leadership. He was torn between John Burden and Alan Questrom and spoke to me at length about both. The major difference between the two, however, was that Alan had no interest in the job.

Alan had taken his golden parachute and wanted no part of Campeau Corp. "I'm sitting *shivah*," he told reporters. (For those not understanding business English, sitting *shivah* is a Hebrew phrase for mourning the dead.) John Burden, for his part, was at Sanibel Island, having retired with his $3 million parachute. He had recently stopped by my office to tell me how beautiful Sanibel was. He told me how much he was enjoying retirement, and how much I would enjoy it, too. I had always liked John and felt he had a genuine concern for people. I encouraged Bob to hire him, reporting that John was well liked at Federated and the division heads would support him. Bob offered him a generous contract of $1 million a year plus a $250,000 living allowance. He also told John he could run the company from New York and Sanibel rather than Cincinnati. On May 31, he came aboard.*

---

* At the same time, in early fall Bob Campeau invited me to the Waldorf Towers to help convince Frank Doroff, who had been president of Bullock's, to join Federated as head of Federated Allied Merchandising Services (FAMS). What Frank really wanted, however, was to succeed me as chairman of Bloomingdale's. I liked Frank, and I thought he had done a good job at Bullock's. That evening, I told him that if he did a good job as head of FAMS, he would be a candidate to succeed me at Bloomingdale's. Since then I have read that Campeau promised Frank my job. If so, Campeau never told me.

John Burden was one of several people who asked me why I was staying on. The answer was that Bloomingdale's had been my life for forty years. I had put too much effort into making Bloomingdale's what it was to leave. I felt I would be running out on too many people I loved and respected when they needed me most. I also believed that I was the best person to handle Bloomingdale's during this crisis and that my staying was critical to keeping the management team together.

Once John Burden joined the company, we had to face up to the very large problem of financing the debt. In order to secure the backing for Campeau's takeover, Ron Tysoe and First Boston had developed their own projections for each of the divisions to justify the $73.50-a-share purchase price.

I saw those numbers for the first time about a month after the purchase and they were wild. They showed Bloomingdale's, which had earnings before interest, tax, and depreciation of $128 million in 1987, going to $178 million in two years. This improvement was based on substantially increasing our rate of sales growth and raising gross margins while making major expense cuts. It was utterly unrealistic to assume we could make such drastic cuts in our organization and at the same time achieve major gains in sales and gross margin. I told Jim Zimmerman immediately that the numbers were impossible.

"They may be," he said. "I had no part in developing them, but they have been given to the banks. Now do your best to achieve them."

I then realized that all of the Campeau projections, not just for Bloomingdale's but for Federated, had been totally done within First Boston and the Campeau organization. They had been given to the bankers and lawyers to raise billions of dollars through the sale of junk bonds and to borrow money. No banker ever—and I repeat that, ever—came to Bloomingdale's to ask if I thought we could deliver those numbers. It was clear to me that Bob Campeau was not the only culprit in the financial problems that were to fall on us. It's extraordinary in hindsight that the banks loaned billions of dollars without ever checking the projections with the principals of the individual divisions.

So in the first three months, Campeau hired a new president and a new CEO, Bloomingdale's fired more than two hundred employees, and I realized that we were sinking in debt. Things were moving quickly. I still hoped they would be for the better, but my doubts were growing.

There were two Bob Campeaus, I discovered. One could be charming and charismatic, a man who liked to laugh and enjoyed a good time. This Campeau was a futurist who believed in ideas and innovation and above all in his own infallibility. The other Campeau could be mean, bigoted, impulsive, and quick to form opinions not necessarily based on facts. On any given occasion you never knew which Bob Campeau you were going to encounter.

In his first month at Federated, Campeau personally fired Herb Ross, the president of Lazarus and a very capable division president, because he was unimpressed with Herb's comments during the course of a plane trip they took together. Campeau also made the sudden decision to combine Rich's and Goldsmith's during a trip to visit those divisions. He summoned the management of Goldsmith's to Atlanta and then forgot he had called them. They waited in the hotel lobby until 11:30 at night, when they called Jim Zimmerman. Jim called Bob, who then invited them upstairs. They found Campeau in his pajamas, but he wasted no time in informing them that he was closing their division and terminating their jobs.

Shortly after Campeau took over, it occurred to me that, since so much had been said about him, Bob might like to address our merchants to create his own impression. He seized on the idea and we set an 8:30 A.M. morning meeting in the Showtime Cafe at Bloomingdale's 59th Street.

On the prearranged morning there were more than two hundred buyers, merchandise managers, and associates assembled waiting for Bob. However, by 8:30, he had not yet appeared. I called the Waldorf, only to find that Bob had not left. He assured me he would be there in fifteen minutes. Twenty minutes later I called again. He assured me he had just a few more things to take care of. He finally arrived an hour late. By then, he had already upset most of our merchandise organization. Bob Campeau, I learned, was almost never on time for an appointment. He believed people should wait for him.

Bob began the meeting by saying how much he believed in

Bloomingdale's and in Marvin Traub and how I was to become a vice chairman of Federated/Allied. He then gave a little history of the Campeau company, painting it in the most exaggerated terms. He spoke of his own background, his thoughts on Federated's expansion, and rambled on about Bloomingdale's. Many of my coworkers left the meeting wondering about Campeau and what was ahead for Federated.

The only reassurance we had was that it was very clear Bob Campeau loved everything that Bloomingdale's stood for. He had a particular fondness for Le Train Bleu. He loved eating or entertaining friends there. One day he called to say that Ilse's birthday was in two days and he wanted to give a romantic surprise party for her by taking over the restaurant for four couples. We created a candle-lit romantic mood, filled the room with beautiful flowers, and hired the same strolling violinists Estée Lauder used at her most elegant parties. Everyone enjoyed the superb food, wines, and champagne. At one point in the evening, Bob asked them to play romantic music from old Vienna and it wasn't too long before Bob himself was singing along with the musicians, serenading Ilse.

Bob called me frequently throughout the summer, often at home in the evening. I would call him at his home on the weekend as well. He was ebullient about his purchase of Federated and asked if I would plan a victory party for him so that he could entertain the right people in New York. At the time of his purchase of Allied, he had held a party in the Metropolitan Museum, but it was principally attended by First Boston and Allied employees. I was anxious to do everything I could to make our partnership a successful one and proposed that Lee and I host a black-tie dinner for him at the Metropolitan Museum. I told him we would have the party in September when everyone was back in New York and would begin planning for it right away.

b

In early May, Campeau hired Frank Doroff to head Federated Allied Merchandising Services (FAMS). A few weeks later, Bob had a brainstorm. He suggested that, as preferred customers, each of our major vendors should give us a 5 percent rebate. Apparently, this was customary in real estate. Bob had calculated that with purchases of $4 or $5 billion, the 5 percent rebate would go a long way toward improving our profit performance.

This was not an idea that would work in the retail arena, I told him. John Burden and Frank Doroff also tried to explain that the vendors would not respond well to this suggestion. Some people would consider it blackmail. Bob stuck with his idea and joined with Frank Doroff and John Burden in several presentations including West Point Pepperel and Fieldcrest Cannon. When he had no success, he turned the responsibility over to Frank.

Frank made a few more calls. In some cases, he was able to have discussions about improved terms, advertising or display, all of which were appropriate. But nothing ever came of the rebate idea that management wasted a great deal of time pursuing.

In June, Bob expressed a desire to meet New York's mayor Ed Koch. Bob had major plans for renovating downtown Brooklyn, including the creation of a new shopping center with an A&S, that he wanted to discuss with the mayor.

Ed Koch and I had been friends for many years. I supported him for mayor and he regarded Bloomingdale's as an important institution in the city and came to many of our events. For many years, we had a running discussion about his father, who had been a Bloomingdale's employee in our fur storage area. So when I called Ed and said I thought Bob Campeau could be helpful to the city, the mayor invited him to Gracie Mansion for a cookout. The other guests that evening were Alair Townsend, the director of development for the city, Lee and I, *The New York Times's* Max Frankel and his wife, *Times* reporter Joyce Purnick, and Sid Davidoff.

It was a very pleasant, warm evening, perfect for a barbecue. We sat on the terrace and watched the sun set. Campeau talked about his ambitious plans for Bloomingdale's and A&S in particular and made a date to have the development commissioner meet with him and A&S's management. The mayor talked about some of the problems New York was facing, and Bob gave Ed his thoughts on managing the city, which were not particularly appropriate.

Several days later, Bob invited me to his suite at the Waldorf to tell me that *The New York Times Magazine* was planning an article on him. He had just fired one public relations firm, and told me he had just turned down *Life* magazine for a story because they would not commit to putting him on the cover. The *Times Magazine* piece concerned him and he asked me to call Max Frankel, whom I had just introduced him to, to see what I could do to make the article favorable.

"I have two families, you know," Bob said for the first time. I didn't quite understand what he meant, but I was to learn later that while Bob had a wife and family in Sudsbury, he was living with his former secretary Ilse in Toronto. He had two children with Ilse, keeping it secret from his first family for many years while commuting between Sudbury and Toronto. In 1969 he divorced his first wife, and then married Ilse who bore him another child soon after.

"But I'm not worried about that," he said. "The facts are the facts, as long as they report it accurately. I'm concerned that they don't present me badly as a businessman." I told Bob that I could not influence the *Times*, but I would try and make sure the story was fair and accurate.

I called Jimmy Greenfield, the deputy managing editor with responsibility for the Sunday *Times Magazine*. I had known Jim from college, ever since he worked on the *Harvard Service News* while I was at the *Crimson*. I told him that Bob was concerned that he be portrayed fairly. Greenfield responded that the reporter was anxious to interview Campeau, who so far had been unwilling to meet with him, and that the reporter would be more than glad to check his facts against Campeau's. I reported back to Bob and encouraged him to meet with the *Times*, which he did.

On July 17, the cover story on Campeau, "The Man Who Bought Bloomingdale's" by Phil Patton, appeared. I received a copy a few days in advance of its general publication. I found it very favorable to Campeau. Campeau was portrayed as a hands-on, self-made financial success who had often beaten the odds. The article did mention, however, for the first time, that Campeau had suffered two bouts of severe depression and at one point maintained two families. It spoke of his "volatile" personality. But his advisers and associates spoke well of him, and his ambition to grow his businesses and his self-confidence were apparent. In particular, there was an extraordinary picture of Bob and Ilse on the cover, the two of them sitting in white wicker chairs with their dogs in their laps, and their 25,000-square-foot Norman-style Toronto mansion behind them.

Campeau called me very upset about the article. He was livid.

"Bob, what are you so upset about?" I asked.

"The *Times* reported that Morosky resigned," Bob said, fuming. "I fired the son of a bitch."

Bob wanted a correction, or a retraction. It took a while but I talked him out of it.

b

In July we had our first board meeting in Canada. Bob was exuberant. He told his shareholders: "No one can stop us but ourselves." While appearing on a Canadian TV program, Bob expressed great interest in Bloomingdale's expanding into Canada, with stores in Toronto and Montreal. He suggested we either put up a new store or acquire Simpson's, which had a major property in downtown Toronto. He left the unmistakable impression that Campeau Corporation was a thriving, growing concern.

Bob Campeau referred to his executives as "the family," which I found a rather nice gesture. He felt that the family should get together once a year, so he invited all of the principals and their wives for a combination meeting and entertainment visit at the Southampton Princess in Bermuda, August 27–29.

A *Fortune* article about Bob had implied that he cheated at golf. That disturbed me when I read it, but I had forgotten about it until we all arrived in Bermuda. Bob held a golf tournament, and arranged it so players were not teamed with their spouses. Bob was playing in the foursome ahead of me with Jim Zimmerman and Ronnie Allenbaugh, the wife of Ralph's chairman. Bob, from what I observed, is a genuinely good golfer who had perfected his game over the years, but he cannot stand losing.

On the tenth hole, a 250-yard dogleg over some woods, Campeau hit a drive that Jim and I thought went into the woods. Jim was looking in the woods for Bob's ball when Bob reached the green, looked into the cup and announced to Jim and his foursome, "I have a hole-in-one." There was some skepticism, but by the end of that day no one was surprised that Campeau won first prize. He was a gracious winner, buying champagne to celebrate his hole-in-one. Jim was shaking his head in dubious pleasure.

The following year, it was my turn to play with Campeau at

Quebec's Shadowfront Lake resort. I'm not a bad player; my handicap is twenty-one, but Bob is a far better and more serious player. Bob and I, each paired with an executive's wife, were playing "Best Ball," a game in which each player drives, then selects the best ball for each team, after which you hit alternate shots.

"Marvin, it's up to you to keep him honest," my associates said. On the first hole we finished, I said, "Bob you had a seven."

"No Marvin," he said. "I had a six."

"I thought it was a seven," I insisted.

"No, it was a six," he concluded. So I wrote down a six. On the second hole Bob got in trouble on the second shot. I said, "Bob, I think you had a six."

"No, Marvin," he said, "I had a five. In fact," he said, "I think it would be easier if I kept my score and you kept your score." And that's how the afternoon went, with Bob winning the tournament again. My associates were disappointed but not surprised.

b

Bob continued to amaze me. During 1988, I was working with Ambassador Lucky Roosevelt and John Hanes on the renovation of Blair House, the president's official guest house. Bloomingdale's had agreed to redo and restock the kitchen. We went to our suppliers and raised almost $100,000 to furnish Blair House with the right pots, cookware, china, and glassware.

Knowing how much Bob Campeau and Ilse enjoyed Bloomingdale's events, I invited them to the August reception for the refurbished Blair House. Bob was very comfortable among politicians. I introduced him to Secretary of State George Shultz. He and Bob Strauss hit it off as well. They were kindred spirits, talking about real estate development.

We went out to the garden with Lucky Roosevelt and I had a chance to present Bob and Ilse to President Reagan. Bob immediately started to tell the president what he was doing for the United States, Boston, and Bloomingdale's. Reagan clearly got a kick out of Bob. For his part, Campeau evidently felt a certain kinship with the former actor, because as they talked Bob started to pat Reagan on the shoulder, as was Bob's habit. I was sure that the Secret Service was going to come flying out of the woodwork. But the president seemed to enjoy it and in no time was clapping Bob on the back as well. Reagan and Campeau were an unusual couple: No matter what you think of each, both had a definite impact on the American economy.

b

Bob liked to visit the stores and speak to the employees. He often waxed enthusiastic about Bloomingdale's. When I took him to our Bergen County store that September, for example, he announced: "At this point, Marvin doesn't know it yet," he said, "but we are planning to open fifteen to twenty new stores over the next five years." The *Bergen Record* had a major story the next day about Bloomingdale's national expansion program. *Women's Wear* and *The New York Times* called me asking why I let the *Bergen Record* scoop them. "That's Campeau for you" was all I could say.

In fact, this was nothing new. When Bob visited Los Angeles he announced that he was going to bring a Bloomingdale's to California; in Atlanta, he said he was going to bring a Bloomingdale's to Georgia. He found that it made for a major story about Campeau Corporation in each market.

b

In September we held the big coming out party we had been planning since June to introduce Bob to "*le tout* New York" at the Metropolitan's Temple of Dendur. At my suggestion, Bob hired George Trescher, a well-known party planner. We set a budget of $300 a person but Bob was willing to spare no expense for this particular evening. We invited bankers, businessmen, media, and theater personalities. Almost everyone said yes. They were as anxious to meet Bob as he was to mingle with them.

For this black-tie event George Trescher provided superb champagne, white wine, hors d'oeuvres, and dinner. Bob and Ilse, Bill and Wendy Luers, the director of the Met and his wife, and Lee and I greeted guests as they followed a red carpet into the garden courtyard of the American wing. I introduced Bob to many of our friends, and the group went into a candlelit Temple of Dendur for dinner, dancing, entertainment, and speeches.

Bob had insisted that a friend of his, a Canadian singer, perform as part of the entertainment. She sang somewhat off key but people survived. I made a brief, and I hoped gracious, speech welcoming Bob to New York and said how pleased we were to have his support in the activities of the city and in helping to build Bloomingdale's.

Bob then took the microphone. He talked about how happy he was; how great the future of Bloomingdale's was; how much he appreciated Lee and me. He then told the assembled group, "but I am going to teach Marvin how to make a profit." My friends cringed. So did I. The irony, of course, is that sixteen months later, Campeau, for all his self-proclaimed business acumen, would file the largest bankruptcy in retailing history.

Bloomingdale's itself seemed unchanged. It was fall, and that meant a country promotion. The theme for 1988 was the "Year of the Dragon," a promotion of Hong Kong, China, and Macau. We continued to maintain our standard high level of excitement. For the opening event, we flew in the governor of Macau and converted Bloomingdale's 59th Street into a gambling casino with all proceeds going to charity. Macau chartered a 747 and flew in the entire casino, including seventy-five croupiers, gambling tables, and chips.

At least on the surface Bloomingdale's was not being inhibited by Campeau Corporation. In fact, Campeau needed us to keep a high profile. John Burden was trying to sell bonds and Campeau thought the better Bloomingdale's looked the more likely he was to sell them. Campeau was facing a time clock, and if he couldn't raise money fast, we would all be in trouble.

The vendors were still confident. In 1988, everyone, including myself, still felt that somehow it would all work out. In the eighties anything seemed possible: Maybe this crazy guy would pull it off. The expense cuts had given us some credibility. And after all, he had been able to sell Brooks Brothers for $750 million, and people were still impressed by that.

To show Bob the glamour of a Bloomingdale's store opening, I proposed that we have our September Campeau Corp. board meeting in Chicago to tie in with the launch of the Bloomingdale's North Michigan Avenue store.

The elegant Four Seasons Hotel was part of the skyscraper that held Bloomingdale's, luxury apartments, and office space. Since the Four Seasons is a Canadian company, Bob approved, and we reserved suites for all the board members. The omens were good: We had invited Bloomingdale's charge customers in the Chicago area and Bloomingdale's By Mail customers to come preview the store the day before it opened. In just five hours we did $600,000—that was spectacular.

That evening we held a black tie gala for 3,400 people, a glamorous benefit for the Chicago Symphony with an elegant Karl Lagerfeld couture fashion show. Many expected Bob to introduce me, but he wanted me to introduce him instead. Bob took the podium and began a meandering speech in which he recounted the history of Chicago in some detail, including a description of the famous radio personalities Fibber McGee and Molly, whom he called "fiber" McGee. Apparently Bob had found a book on the history of Chicago in his hotel room, and thinking it interesting, decided to incorporate major portions of it, verbatim, into his comments. If that were not embarrassing enough, Bob sounded the same note he had sounded so ungraciously in September, "Marvin, you may be a great merchant," he said, "but I'm going to teach you how to turn a profit." I tried to hide behind a column. Karl Lagerfeld, caught my eye and shook his head sadly. Later someone asked me, "Who was that little boor?"

b

The next day we had the best opening in our history. That was a high point for the Bloomingdale's organization, and during the last months of 1988 Bloomingdale's continued to be on an upswing. We were looking at three locations in California—South Coast Plaza, Beverly Hills, and San Francisco. I was traveling all over the country at Bob's behest, believing that he had the money to accomplish these projects. In November we did a Kansas promotion with Governor Mike Hayden, who invited us to consider a store in Kansas City. Bob assured us he would. On November 6, Tyson's Corner opened a Petrossian caviar shop with Mr. Petrossian in attendance as well as the Soviet ambassador Yuri Dubinin and his twin daughters. Bob told me he was interested in opening a Bloomingdale's in Moscow.

The reality, however, was that our business was softer. We attributed it to our reorganization, and hoped things would pick up.

Officially the store was up $11 million over the previous year, but that was misleading. Same store sales were still down from three years ago. Furthermore, we were behind plan 4.5 percent, trying to live up to Campeau's projection. We were struggling under the weight of the debt.

Campeau remained positive. Bob invited Lee and me to his December 9 Christmas party at his Toronto home. There were only fifty or so guests. Bob's acquisition of Federated and Bloomingdale's had made him an even more prominent figure in Canada, and this party was Bob in all his glory.

Bob led Lee and me on a tour of his magnificent 25,000-square-foot house, furnished with fine antiques acquired with the help of Jacques Grange, a leading French decorator. His bedroom had a spiral staircase that led down to his own private indoor Olympic-size pool. He had built it, Bob confided, because he liked to swim laps in the nude.

We had cocktails in a library with chinoiserie paneling and beautiful carpets and then went in to dinner. Lee was surprised to discover herself seated next to Cardinal Carter of Canada in his glamorous red robes and red skull cap. I was seated next to Bob, and on my left was one of Canada's Supreme Court justices. The table was filled with a cross section of Canada's top political and businesspeople. I have to believe that this evening was one of the high points for Bob, coming off the acquisition and the glamour and excitement of the Chicago opening.

On the surface it was a very positive Christmas. Bob was planning a major shopping center in downtown Boston, a total redevelopment including a Bloomingdale's, and was talking of our expanding across the country and into Canada. He was also building his new house in Salzburg and appeared to be on top of the world.

Actually, things had been going sour for some time. It was true that Bob's selling Brooks Brothers for $750 million was the coup that made possible his winning Federated. But that decision came back to haunt his financial officers. Bob had told his Allied bondholders he would never sell Brooks Brothers. When he did, they were angry, but they became furious when they found out he applied $200 million from the sale to the Federated purchase. They viewed that money as coverage for the Allied bonds.

The sale of Federated junk bonds was a nightmare. First Boston had hoped to sell $1.15 billion worth. Everywhere that Roddy and Luce went they found investment managers enraged about Allied. Campeau had destroyed a trust that was already tenuous. After several false starts, Campeau managed to unload $750 million worth, but only by offering interest rates as high as 17¾ percent, leaving First Boston stuck with $400 million of Campeau paper.

Bob, however, kept saying "don't worry, no problem." With the best of intentions, John Burden started on a campaign of increasing inventory of basic merchandise so we would never be out of stock on such essential commodities as men's shirts, men's and women's underwear, and hosiery. Federated increased its stock by $400 million. This would have been good policy if we had had a commensurate increase in business. But in a slow economy, the net result was that we tied up more than $200 million in capital, which made it even more difficult to create the cash flow to pay down our debt.

The lease on Bloomingdale's 59th Street was set to expire in 2006, and the building had air rights that had not been exploited. Campeau decided the lease was both a problem and an opportunity. Although we could by right build more stories on our present building, the foundation would need to be reinforced to sustain the added weight.

Several years earlier, I had met with a developer named Sheldon Gordon who had a plan to take over Alexander's 59th Street, across the street from Bloomingdale's. Sheldon wanted to expand Bloomingdale's by using that space, add a shopping center connected either underground or by a bridge above 59th Street, and add a hotel and an apartment or office structure, one at 58th and Lexington, the other at 60th Street and Third Avenue, taking advantage of both properties. Sheldon never got his plan off the ground but the concept intrigued both Bob Campeau and me.

I had estimated the cost at between $350 and $500 million. The Alexander property was owned by several investors, including Donald Trump and Steve Roth, each of whom owned 27 percent. Together they made up the majority but they did not like each other. Bob, who always talked as if the money were available, was eager to sit down with Trump and Roth and discuss it. In June 1988, I set up a luncheon for Donald Trump and Bob Campeau. I had originally chosen the Four Seasons, but Donald promptly moved it to the Plaza's Edwardian Room where he had the corner table.

The Donald had two large security men who hovered in the background. Bob began the lunch conversation by telling Donald about all the wonderful deals he'd done, which only prompted Donald to regale us with his tremendous accomplishments. I felt as if I were watching a Ping-Pong match between two giant egos. Each tried to one-up the other.

Donald's main agenda, I quickly realized, was not only Bloomingdale's or Alexander's but to sell Bob an apartment in the Plaza, which he hoped to transform into condos. After lunch, Donald had Ivana join us and she then led us on a tour of several suites that Bob could take in the Plaza for his personal use. Bob and Donald promised to discuss the lease situation in the future, but of course they never did.

There is, however, one follow-up. Donald did sell Bob an apartment in Trump Tower. It was one of the most ornate apartments I have ever seen, decorated with tens of thousands of dollars of black mirror. Richard Knapple was given the job of decorating it for the Campeaus. Richard took out all the mirrors, and furnished the apartment down to the last detail, including lining the drawers with jewelry compartments for Ilse. The cost of furnishing the apartment was more than $500,000. When the day came to move Bob from the Warldorf Towers, he informed Richard that he had changed his mind. Then we had to go back and remove all the furnishings from the apartment and dispose of them.

b

Despite our problems, in January 1989, Bob was still talking aggressively about expansion. Campeau always believed that with the Bloomingdale's name, mall owners would simply invite us in and pick up all of the expenses. I had several meetings that month on the subject of preparing Bloomingdale's to add fifteen to twenty stores over the next five years. We discussed at length the changes that would have to occur in the management organization and data processing and reviewed opportunities in California and Canada. We reviewed stores in Palm Beach Gardens, in Old Orchard Chicago, Rego Park, South Coast Plaza, Mall of America, Beverly Hills,

Boston Crossing, San Francisco, Perimeter in Atlanta, Palo Alto, Sherman Oaks, Toronto, Walnut Creek, and Montreal. The plan called for Bloomingdale's to have a total business of $2.9 billion by 1995. I expressed skepticism as to what seemed to me an overly ambitious plan. Campeau told me to support it anyway because it was appealing to our shareholders and creditors.

That spring it was still business as usual for Bloomingdale's. On April 14 I met with Norma Kamali to work on our exclusive program. On May 4 we gave a party for Claude Montana at the Royalton Hotel to launch his new fragrance. Campeau Corp., however, was getting desperate.

Campeau had boasted that he would sell Ann Taylor for $700 to $800 million. The ultimate price was only $430 million. Jim Roddy, Carolyn Buck Luce, and his bankers kept telling him that he was facing a cash crunch. Campeau believed they were wrong. He continued to have faith in himself—and in Bloomingdale's. Bob explained to me that he had sold Ann Taylor because he needed to raise money for the future expansion of Bloomingdale's and other things. The reality that the sale of Ann Taylor was going to be used to pay off some of the Federated bonds and that investment in Federated was treated rather parenthetically at the board meeting.

Campeau was always looking for the Big Idea. Throughout his career he had always saved the day at the last moment, so he had grown to trust his own instincts. In the spring of 1988, Campeau came up with a way to save his company: a $4 billion supermortgage collateralized by all his property. Campeau was even willing to trade equity for low interest and debt reduction. That would help him with his cash flow problems and his debt.

Campeau's advisers Jim Roddy and Carolyn Buck Luce tried to talk him out of it. He had a lot of Allied debt due in 1990. They had even arranged for $1.1 billion in long-term loans with Citibank to replace the debt that was coming due. The Citibank deal was a good one, Roddy and Buck Luce said. At least it would buy him time, but Campeau refused. He believed he could get the supermortgage and cure his problems in one fell swoop. He notified Citibank that he was declining their loan offer. Roddy and Buck Luce decided to leave the company, leaving the finances in Ron Tysoe's hands.

One of Bob's most memorable performances occurred on May 16, 1989. Bob had been asked by John Levy, president of the Gillian

Group, to host the annual United Jewish Appeal fund-raising event
for the dress industry. Bob had accepted on two conditions: one,
that he not be required to make a donation, and two, that he not
have to speak. Levy told Bob that he would just have to say thanks.
Bob, in turn, asked me to host it with him at Le Train Bleu. Everyone was curious to meet Bob, and the event was oversubscribed.
We began with a reception and then the actual fund-raising took
place. The contributions were generous, some in Bob's honor. Bob's
secretary had called John Levy a dozen times to confirm that he
would not have to give a speech. But Bob could not resist—he
wanted to make a contribution and asked me if he could say a few
words. So it was a surprise to everyone when, at Bob's request, I
introduced him and he went to the podium to speak.

Bob began by announcing a generous pledge of $50,000. "As a
French Canadian Catholic, I have known prejudice firsthand," Bob
told the predominantly Jewish audience. He continued: "And some
of my best friends are Jews"—he really said that—and mentioned
his association with the Reichmanns. From there Bob free-associ-
ated to his thoughts about the Holocaust and Hitler's role in it, which
seemed, given Bob's little knowledge of the subject, inappropriate.
"When he first came to power there were those who said that Hitler
would make Germany great, as Napoleon had done for France . . ."
I remember little else of what Bob Campeau said except that I, like
the rest of the audience, was too stunned to react.

b

On Monday, August 28, I was to return to work after a few days'
vacation. That morning, Bob called me at home in the city at
6:30 A.M.

"Marvin," he said, "could we meet for dinner Tuesday evening."

"Certainly," I said. "Where should we meet?"

"London," Bob said. "I'm calling from London."

"Is it that important that I fly to London for dinner?"

"Yes, it is," he said and asked that I meet him in the restaurant
of the Ritz Hotel in London at 8:00 P.M. the following evening. I
canceled my next day's appointments and booked a seat on the
Concorde.

The Ritz is a typical, old English hotel. The dark mahogany

dining room has tall windows looking out on the street. The service is excellent but not ostentatious. Ron Tysoe was with us. Bob wasted no time in coming to the point.

"Marvin," he said, "we have been studying our financial position and we have decided that our best course of action is to sell Bloomingdale's. We know that when Federated was for sale, you were very anxious to buy it. So we wanted you to be the first to know. We wanted to give you this opportunity to buy the company."

Bloomingdale's was for sale? Bloomingdale's was for sale! I told Bob and Ron that I was very excited at the prospect, but it would take substantial funds to mount an effort to buy it. "I've thought about that," Campeau said. He informed me that he and Ron had agreed to pay up to $1 million in fees for bankers and lawyers for me to mount a campaign to find a buyer, which struck me as more than fair.

"What do you think Bloomingdale's is worth?" I asked.

"Two billion dollars," Bob said. I looked at him. He was serious.

"That seems a very high figure, based on our earnings and the uncertainties of our real estate," I said.

"Hear me out," Bob said. "I believe the store should fetch at least $1.8 billion." He did his figuring on the back of an envelope and walked me though his calculations. His figures still seemed outrageous, but now wasn't the time to argue.

I asked how we should proceed and he said that when I went back, I should start on it quietly and that he would announce it within the next week.

I went back up to my room at the Ritz very excited. I picked up the phone and called Pete Peterson, who had been a Federated director and who had formed the very successful Blackstone Group. Under pledge of absolute confidentiality, I told him of my conversation with Campeau and said he was one of the people I would be most anxious to interview as a potential banker in the transaction. Pete was very enthusiastic.

I also called Lee, and was just finishing my call when there was a knock at the door. It was Bob Campeau.

When Bob came in, he was not his usual ebullient self. He looked somewhat haggard and unhappy. It was clear he was under a good deal of pressure.

"I've been thinking about our conversation at dinner, Marvin." Bob said, "and I want you to know that I really hate to sell Bloomingdale's. Of all the divisions in the company, it's meant the most to me, but it is also the one that will bring the best price. I know you are very anxious to have your independence but I just wanted you to know how badly I felt about this."

That was the only time I ever felt sorry for Bob Campeau.

b

Campeau had told me that he would wait until September 7 to announce that Bloomingdale's was for sale, but I did not want to waste a minute. I called Jeff Sherman, who was vacationing on Fire Island. He had been president for only a short time, but I had great confidence in him* and thought he would make an ideal partner in this venture. He felt, as I did, that this was a once-in-a-lifetime opportunity. We agreed to meet the next morning in the office.

Jeff and I realized that we would have to engage bankers, lawyers, and find sources of funding. I called Ira Millstein, who had been Macy's attorney, to discuss representing us. We told him that we hoped to put together a bid of more than a billion dollars. Ira recommended we meet with Drexel Burnham, since it was obvious, in his opinion, that we would have to finance part of this deal with high-yield securities—junk bonds. I didn't like the idea, but felt we needed, at this point, to explore all financing opportunities.

Jeff and I went to see Pete Peterson at the Blackstone Group's offices at 345 Park Avenue. At the time of the Campeau takeover, Pete had expressed the hope that one day he would help me buy Bloomingdale's. That day had come.

Peterson was a well-regarded figure in financial circles. A for-

---

* Jeff Sherman was one of the most talented executives I trained at Bloomingdale's. Jeff joined Bloomingdale's in 1971 as a systems analyst fresh from NYU graduate school. I thought he would benefit from merchandising experience, so he worked for a year as a buyer of men's overcoats before returning to finance and administration. After managing the White Flint store and serving as regional manager for Washington, I moved Jeff to the merchandising organization as vice president for men's and women's designer apparel. The next year Jeff took over responsibility for 59th Street, and as managing director he restructured the store. In 1985 he became the store's chief financial officer, and three years later his responsibilities expanded to include construction and real estate. In 1989, when Bob Tammaro was promoted to a corporate post, Jeff succeeded him as president of Bloomingdale's. No one was ever more prepared for the job. Or had more to face.

mer U.S. secretary of commerce and former CEO of Lehman Brothers, he had started the Blackstone Group in 1985. They were well known as advisers to management-led buyouts and had achieved several notable successes, particularly in Japan. Blackstone was highly regarded and retaining them would, in and of itself, attract a certain attention.

Pete's partners joined us for lunch, including Steve Schwartzman, former Office of Management and Budget director David Stockman, and Roger Altman. All were eager to work with us and were very knowledgeable about Bloomingdale's. They emphasized their significant contacts in Japan. The Japanese were very interested in prestige brands and Bloomingdale's was well known there. Peterson argued that if we were interested in Japanese financing we should engage them. First, and foremost, Nikei Securities owned a 20 percent stake in Blackstone itself. Second, Blackstone had completed several recent transactions with Japanese firms, including Sony's acquisition of CBS Records. We said we would consider them.

Everyone appeared tremendously supportive. The banks and lawyers all wanted to represent us, and I had every confidence that we would succeed. However, as we neared September 7, the day that Campeau would announce that Bloomingdale's was for sale, I was concerned not with our future but with the health of my daughter Peggy. The day before, September 6, Peggy, who was a Bloomingdale's buyer then, was scheduled for brain surgery.

Peggy had first discovered that she had a brain tumor in 1976. For Lee and me, it was an enormously painful time. The notion that your child's whole future hangs in the balance is a terrifying prospect. My father's hair had turned gray during the one year I spent in the hospital recovering from my war wounds. So did mine the year Peggy had her first brain operation.

On February 16, 1976, Peggy underwent surgery. The operation was successful in every respect, and Peggy returned to Scarsdale High after five weeks of radiation therapy. Then in 1986 she had to have an operation to remove fluid that had accumulated in the cavity. We were told it was not serious, but we still worried. Fortunately, everything went well. And then, a few weeks before Campeau informed me that he was going to put Bloomingdale's up for sale, Peggy began to experience more headaches. Russell Patterson, the chief of neurosurgery at New York Hospital, determined that he would have to operate a third time.

I spent the evening before with Peggy at the hospital. The following morning, I went to be with her before she was taken into surgery. I don't know if there is anything harder than watching your child being wheeled away down a hospital corridor.

From the hospital I went to the store to meet with the executive committee to announce that Bloomingdale's was for sale, and that Jeff Sherman and I were trying to arrange a buyout. They were enthusiastic in backing us.

I rushed back to the hospital where the operation was just concluding, and had a chance to talk to Dr. Patterson, who said they had removed debris from the earlier operation. He said that Peggy was fine, and the operation had gone well, but it was too early to tell whether the operation would leave Peggy with any side effects. I stayed until Peggy came out of the recovery room.

One of her first questions was, "What's happening at Bloomingdale's?"

"That's my daughter," I told Lee. We all laughed. The first moment of relief in a very emotional day.*

Campeau made the official announcement as scheduled and I spent the greater part of the day fielding calls from the press. I also met that morning with Ida Torres and John O'Neil, the union's president and executive vice president. I told them about my plans for trying to buy back the store and they said they would support me. Later, they even offered union funds for the buyout. I was very grateful because in the 1960s relations between Bloomingdale's and the union had been acrimonious. There had even been a strike in 1965. However, I worked hard during my tenure to make clear the extent to which we were partners rather than adversaries. The union's support was important to me.

That afternoon Jeff and I went to Drexel Burnham where we

---

* Coming out of the operation Peggy experienced some loss of vision. Two weeks later, she still could not see the right side of her visual field. We began to consult a neurologist with optometric expertise. My concern was eating away at my concentration at every moment. With time, however, she learned to deal very well with her deficit. Today, she skis and plays tennis. But the weeks of uncertainty were a tremendous strain for all of us.

were introduced to Fred Joseph, Drexel's chairman; Leon Black; and Dean Kehler. They talked with great enthusiasm about the Macy's leveraged buyout. "No one can raise the kinds of funds we can," they told us.

"We are looking to raise $1.2 billion," I said. They didn't think that would be a problem. I informed them that we were talking to the Blackstone Group about trying to raise funds in Japan, and asked how they felt about working with them. They were not happy about it. They said, however, it was not an uncommon arrangement, and if that's what it would take to get the assignment, they would do it.

Once the news was public, we were approached by Donaldson, Lufkin and Jenrette; my friend Evan Galbraith, the former ambassador to France, called on behalf of Morgan Stanley. I received calls as well from Jerry Kohlberg of KKR, Eli Jacobs, Maurice Bidermann for Jimmy Goldsmith, Maurice Greenberg representing American International Group (AIG), and Paul Demetric for the London-based Investcorp, among others.

After two weeks of meetings and interviews we decided to go ahead with the combination of Blackstone and Drexel, as bankers, and Ira Millstein of Weil, Gotshal as our attorney. Once the decisions were made as to our team, the important questions we faced were the size of our bid, and how to structure it as to cash, paper, and high-yield securities, and above all, how we would raise the money.

We got a call from Joe Brooks, who had recently acquired Ann Taylor, and he told us that he had Merrill Lynch behind him. He made it plain that if we did not support his bid, he would not keep us on as management after he acquired Bloomingdale's. We even had a meeting with Donald Trump. Donald wanted us to join him in a management buyout. When we demurred, he reminded us that it was he who put Federated in play and warned us that he would buy Bloomingdale's without us. Then, in a joking manner that implied he had given it some thought, he assured me that even if he bought the store he would not call it "Trump's," or even "Trump's Bloomingdale." We thanked him.

Roz Jacobs, the wife of my former basement colleague Mel Jacobs, steered us to Hans Mautner of CPI, the real estate concern that owns the GM building, Lenox Square, and Roosevelt Field, and from them to IFINT, Gianni Agnelli's investment firm. We heard from our friend Alan Thomas on behalf of the Sumitomo Bank. I contacted some of our vendors who were interested in investing, but the amount of investment was never substantial enough.

At the same time Campeau was also actively searching for other buyers. He had engaged First Boston, his trusted bankers, to prepare the offering on Bloomingdale's, or "the book" as we called it. The book was a source of enormous friction among Campeau, Jim Zimmerman, and myself. Jim and the people in Cincinnati were preparing numbers that would show major increases in Bloomingdale's profits over the next few years. Those numbers improved on current plans and projections. There was, however, a wide gap between what Campeau wanted and what Jeff and I considered appropriate. I did not want to sign off on numbers that I personally was not convinced could be attained. I was already living with a set of optimistic projections that Campeau had prepared when he acquired the company.

Mark Gallogly, a young Blackstone associate, took the lead with Jeff Sherman in assembling the research and crunching the numbers to provide our own more realistic assessment. Soon we had two sets of figures, and they needed to be reconciled. Campeau needed inflated figures to support his high asking price; he accused me of low-balling the figures to get a better price for my group. We went back and forth on this, delaying the preparation of the offering until late October.

In the six weeks since the prospective sale had first been announced, much had changed. On October 16 the stock market had its largest single decline since the previous year's crash. It was clear that the economy in general, and retailing in particular, were in a decline. It looked as if the heady 1980s were grinding to a halt.

The Reichmanns had been partners with Campeau since early in his takeover of Federated. As Campeau Corporation's woes became more public, the Reichmanns stepped in to protect their investment—at a price. Within ten days of Bloomingdale's being put up for sale, Federated got an emergency loan of $250 million from the Reichmann's real estate company Olympia & York. To secure the loan Campeau pledged some of his prime real estate, and Bob and his family's ownership of Campeau Corp. was diluted to 43.2 percent (from over 50 percent). The Reichmanns also received convertible debentures that if exercised would further reduce Bob's stake. Essentially the Reichmanns and Campeau would each own 38.4 percent of the company, and in effect the Reichmanns were now as much the owners of Federated as Campeau.

In September, the Campeau board appointed a four-man management committee composed of Paul Reichmann and Lionel Dodd, representing Olympia & York, and Ron Tysoe and Bill Miller, representing Federated. The point was to send a signal to the community that Federated was in good hands. At that time the Reichmanns' reputation in financial circles was impeccable. If they were at the helm, the message said, all would turn out well. Campeau himself was no longer part of the group managing the company.

At the October Federated/Allied principals meeting in New York, Lionell Dodd assured us we were now part of Olympia & York and handed out their annual report. It was impressive and made us all, temporarily, feel better. But that was the last time we heard from Mr. Dodd.

At the same time, we were optimistic about being able to bid for Bloomingdale's. We were in touch with two small investment groups who specialized in retail acquisitions, Freeman Spogli and Tom Lee.

Brad Freeman and Ron Spogli headed a Los Angeles–based investment group that had worked with Byron Allenbaugh to take Ralph's private. However, when Campeau acquired Federated, he decided not to spin off the chain. Byron referred Freeman Spogli to us. They met with Jeff and me, reviewed our numbers, and assured us that they would be able to fund a substantial portion of the equity.

Tom Lee had worked on the sale of Hills Department Stores and other retail ventures; both Jeff and I found him and his team very knowledgeable and easy to work with. Normally Tom Lee and Freeman Spogli were competitors, but in this case the purchase was so large that neither one alone could finance the purchase. They agreed to be copartners in the deal, an unusual arrangement for them. Agnelli's group was also committed to investing. Our confidence increased that we could finance our bid.

Ira Millstein, sensing that Federated was deteriorating, suggested we make a preemptive bid. Accordingly, Ira, Ken Heitner, Jeff, and I flew to Toronto on a September Sunday to meet with Paul

Reichmann and Ron Tysoe. Ken Heitner was a bright young partner
of Ira Millstein's at Weil, Gotschal who also had represented the
Reichmanns' on another project. He later became my personal attorney.

We met at the Olympia & York offices, which were elegant and
austere. The conference room had mahogany paneling decorated
with nautical-themed prints suggesting an old and wealthy New England bank. Paul Reichmann dressed the part of a British banker in
a dark blue suit and white shirt. He was tall, severe-looking, with a
dark beard, and, as an orthodox Jew, a yarmulke. He spoke so softly
I had to lean over to hear him. He has such extraordinary dignity
and bearing that when he speaks you get the feeling you are getting
"the word from on high."

Paul Reichmann let loose a bombshell at that meeting. He told
us that he had been concerned for several months about the financial
deterioration of Federated and Allied. Three weeks ago in August,
he said, he had invited Bob Campeau to visit him in London. "For
your own sake and to preserve your fortune," he told Bob, "I would
suggest that you put Federated/Allied into Chapter Eleven today
before your financial position deteriorates even further." Bob, he
said, would hear none of it, but Paul suggested he talk it over with
Ilse and think about it. The fact that Paul Reichmann had asked
Bob Campeau to seek bankruptcy protection in early August had
never been reported. But I now understood why Campeau had suddenly summoned me to London to tell me that Bloomingdale's was
for sale. He had no other choice: It was that or bankruptcy.

b

We proposed a preemptive bid of $1.1 billion. We explained that we
had not fully fleshed out the terms of our financing, but we were
convinced we could raise the funds. In order to speed up the whole
process, we proposed to submit the bid in writing, and give Campeau Corporation thirty days to shop it around to see if anyone was
prepared to bid higher.

Paul said he would not circumvent the auction procedure. He
was concerned that it might appear unfair to other potential bidders.
I was under the distinct impression that if we had bid more his
objections would have disappeared.

In addition to investors, we called on the banks. Besides needing

equity financing, we also needed debt financing. Citibank was holding most of Campeau's debt and so we approached them first. Although they gave us no initial commitment, it was clear they would
work with us. Mitsubishi and Chemical also expressed interest. Our
confidence increased.

On October 17 I flew to Toronto for the opening of Bob's pride
and joy, Scotia Plaza. It was the second tallest building in Toronto
(Bob was smart enough not to make his building taller than the
Reichmanns'). It is a beautiful building, and that day Bob had a full
marching band that made one think of Buckingham Palace. Later
that evening he held a huge party in the Scotia Plaza penthouse, a
benefit for Covenant House, and a tribute to Father Bruce Ritter
(who would later have his own troubles). That night was Bob's gala
to end all galas. There was something very Campeau about such
extravagance as the company was heading down the tubes. His set-
backs, he was saying, were only momentary. What better proof of
his success was there than Scotia Plaza and this party? In many
ways that party was Bob's last hurrah.

b

By November, Blackstone's Mark Gallogly had taken charge of putting our numbers together; Drexel had just about disappeared. I
know now that they were more concerned about their own imminent
bankruptcy than Federated's, but they had helped to provide us with
the entree to our potential equity partners Freeman Spogli, Tom
Lee, and IFINT. By our estimates, we were still far from an equity
investment that we thought reasonable. We knew that we could no
longer rely on, or even hope for, Drexel's much touted ability to
create financing. What we needed was one more major player: a
long-term investor who wouldn't demand a quick return and
wouldn't interfere in management. There was only one place to go
for that: Japan. So Jeff and I asked Blackstone to schedule a trip to
Japan right after Thanksgiving.

On Saturday, November 25, Jeff, Mark Gallogly, and I left for
Japan in high spirits. Given Bloomingdale's reputation we were confident that we would find interest there. We went to Japan without
alerting any of the U.S. or Japanese media because we believed that
the Japanese liked to negotiate in secrecy. We arrived in Tokyo

Sunday night. We had the offering with us, as well as a video, both of which were in English- as well as Japanese-language versions.

The next day's meetings were not encouraging. First thing in the morning we had a preliminary meeting with Tokyu Department Stores and Mr. Kiyoshi Imba, who was in charge of their investments, and some of his associates, but we did not meet with the top person. We took them through the book, emphasizing the benefits of Bloomie's and Bloomie's Express. It was a very formal but warm meeting. They expressed great interest but made no commitment. At ten I met with Akio Morita of Sony, a longtime friend, who warned me to be careful; Japan, he said, was a very difficult place to work. Japanese politeness is such that he would not speak directly, but I believed his implication was that Nikei Securities, Blackstone's partner in Japan, were not the best people.

I had lunch with another old friend, Mr. Masatoshi Ito, the principal shareholder of Ito Yokado, one of Japan's major chain of off-price retail stores that also owned the 7–Eleven franchise in Japan. In 1985, Mr. Ito had been very anxious to make a deal with Bloomingdale's to license our name. At the time our representative had steered us away from him. Mr. Ito then chose Robinson's name instead of ours. Now, he told us he had no interest in buying Bloomingdale's. It didn't fit with his current strategies.

The Japanese newspapers were beginning to get wind of the fact we were there. The press was calling our hotel but I was avoiding them. I had been disappointed that neither Pete Peterson nor Steve Schwartzman had accompanied us, but they assured us we would have very high-level representation in Tokyo.

Blackstone's Japan office was run by John Colby, who had flown over to meet us in September. John's father, William, was the former head of the CIA. John was in his early thirties, very personable, but not a person of great influence in Japan. Nikei was the one calling the shots.

Monday night Nikei Securities held an elegant Western-style dinner at one of the hotels. During the course of the evening I was alarmed to learn that the head of Nikei Securities, Osamu Hanamura, who was supposed to be our man in Japan, was leaving the next day for Thailand. They told us not to worry. So why did that make me anxious?

Nikei made a date for us to meet with Sumitomo Insurance. We sat down with their executives, exchanged business cards, and, as is the tradition, exchanged pleasantries. Nikei then led them through the deal. At the conclusion of the presentation Sumitomo told us they did not take equity participation in *any* investments. So why had Nikei sent us there?

Tuesday wasn't much better. We had an appointment to visit Hankyu in Osaka. Hankyu was one of the largest Japanese stores, and we had been assured that they had enormous interest in Bloomingdale's. We were waiting to board the train when I suddenly noticed that the senior Nikei representative, Yasuo Kanzaki, who was supposed to make the presentation and conduct the negotiations, wasn't there.

"Where's Mr. Kanzaki?" I asked.

I was told that he wasn't feeling well and had gone to the hospital. When were they going to tell me? So now, not only was the number one man in Thailand, but number two-san was in the hospital. This did not bode well.

We arrived at Hankyu and after the usual rituals sat down at a long conference table with all the Hankyu executives on one side and ours on the other. John Colby made the presentation with some of the lesser Nikei executives. The meeting was very structured and very formal. It was obvious that Hankyu was less aware of Bloomingdale's reputation and were less prepared for the meeting than we had been given to understand. I began to sense that not enough advance work had been done. Whatever the reason, our reception was definitely chilly.

Hankyu's chief representative stood and said brusquely, "Not only do we have no interest in Bloomingdale's, we don't think it would be a good acquisition." Then they went a step further, saying, "We think you are wasting our time." It was an absolutely rude dismissal.

Now I was really worried. Did we make the wrong presentation? Was it something we said? Or did? Did we insult them? I could not, for the life of me, understand it.

Later I discovered that, like much in Japan, it was about saving face. The Japanese newspapers were running daily accounts of our trip to Japan. The matter was now too public. Hankyu did not want

to be in the position of bidding for the company and losing to someone else. They assumed our meeting would be leaked to reporters
and decided that the best course was to publicly turn us down. And
immediately after the meeting, they called the press to tell them
they had done so.

The following day we returned to Tokyu Department Stores to
meet with Mr. Muira, the chairman. Once again, we made our presentation. Mr. Muira was very pleasant but unwilling to commit.
The next day Tokyu refused us. Much later we would find out that
they were interested, but felt they could not publicly acknowledge
their interest. Once Hankyu had refused us, they later explained,
we were like tainted goods. We also contacted Matsuzukaya, who
had expressed interest, but couldn't work anything out. This was
turning into a fiasco.

b

Toshihiko Yamamoto, a Drexel contact, had come to the Nikei dinner Monday night. Tosh had worked at the Sumitomo bank for fourteen years and is frequently credited with having introduced the
concept of greenmail to Japan. He had left Sumitomo to attend
Stanford Business School and had then gone into business as Drexel's Japanese representative. Some of the Japanese banking establishment found him suspect, as being "too American." He and the
Nikei executives had maintained an icy cordiality. We had little
opportunity to talk, but I found him knowledgeable: He had a far
better grasp of our situation than any of his Japanese counterparts.
He mentioned that he had a friend in the real estate business who
was a potential investor and would take us to meet him.

The day after our disastrous trip to Osaka, we went quietly with
Mr. Yamamoto to meet Mr. Shigeru Kobayashi of Shuwa. Everything about the meeting was extraordinary. First of all, to reach Mr.
Kobayashi's office we drove into his office building, located in one
of Tokyo's most prestigious neighborhoods. Inside, rather than parking in the garage as might be expected, we drove into a private
elevator that took our car to the seventh floor. There a valet greeted
us and we walked to his office.

I have been to many impressive offices, but Kobayashi-san's was
one of the most memorable. We were told that Mr. Kobayashi had

come from humble surroundings to amass a great fortune in real estate. It was something he wanted no one else to forget. His office was at least fifty feet long, encased in glass. There were knights in armor at each end, pictures of his buildings all around, and enormous flags from each of the countries he worked in. The walls were covered with photographs of Mr. Kobayashi in the company of famous people. On a huge table were pictures of Bloomingdale's, and all of the information about the store.

He spoke no English but was exciting to listen to. He was like an admiral in the Japanese navy. Everyone jumped when he spoke. After the formalities we talked about Bloomingdale's while Tosh translated. Kobayashi-san asked a lot of direct questions, to which he seemed to already know the answers. After impressing us that he understood our business, he got to the bottom line. He had concluded, he told us, that Bloomingdale's was worth $800 million.

"I am prepared to join in a bid at that price," he said.

Clearly, he had done his homework—it was certainly fair value in the current economy.

"Campeau will never sell it for that price." I let him know that Campeau had refused a preemptive bid of $1.1 billion.

"Then Campeau will never sell Bloomingdale's," he concluded.

We left matters there. There would be no deal with Mr. Kobayashi or Shuwa. However, I was impressed with Tosh. Compared to Nikei, he had produced someone credible, who was ready to make a serious offer.

I had become completely frustrated by Blackstone's performance. I decided to make some calls myself. I met that morning with my friend Mr. Tsitsumi, who was then head of Seibu Department Stores. In 1985, at the time of our Japan promotion, I had met with several leading Japanese retailers interested in licensing Bloomingdale's in Japan. We had come to an agreement with Seibu and Mr. Tsitsumi rather than Ito Yokado, but at the last moment a blip in the Japanese economy had caused Seibu to call off the deal. At the time Mr. Tsitsumi and I had become friendly: He had given a dinner party at his home in our honor, with the young intellectuals of Tokyo as his guests. Now he seemed rather cold to me. With hindsight, after Hankyu and Tokyu turned us down, how could

Seibu, which is a more prestigious store, express any interest? The way Nikei had handled matters we had been totally shut out of the Japanese market.

That evening we had dinner at John Colby's home, trying to relax after two very trying days. Earlier someone at Nikei Securities told me they had scheduled a press conference for me at 2:30 the following day. We were leaving that day, and I told them it was crazy.

"Why on earth would we want to have a press conference? We have nothing good to report. Call if off," I said.

The next morning, however, Nikei Securities called to tell us they were sorry, but it was too late to call off the press conference. *Asahi-Shimbun*, Japan's leading financial paper, had been running daily stories about whom we were seeing. They wanted to know what we had accomplished. I then realized that we were being used by Nikei to bolster their image in the Japanese investment community. The whole purpose of the press conference was so Nikei could say, "See? Bloomingdale's chose us." Having the press conference was certainly a bad idea, but I decided that to call it off now would only engender worse press.

That afternoon's press conference was, as I feared, a disaster. We were asked if we had raised money in Japan. I was forced to say no. I implied that we were in negotiations, but I had to admit we had not received any commitments. I did my best to handle it gracefully. Our trip was viewed very negatively in the Japanese press, and worse yet our failure to receive any positive commitment was picked up by the American press.

On the long flight home, I replayed events in my head: Blackstone had really screwed up. It was not only that they had the wrong people there, their tactics were awful. Even after only a few days in Japan, it was obvious to me that the way business was done there was to focus on one candidate, and negotiate in secrecy. How come they didn't know that? They had set up several meetings, and allowed the whole dog and pony show to be made public. Further, the Japanese, like everyone else, want to deal with the top man. That neither of the principals of the Blackstone group nor of Nikei securities made the presentations sent the message that ours was not a serious effort, that meeting with us was a waste of time. The meetings had been an insult to the heads of the Japanese companies; and an insult to our group. I won't say that I was depressed after our trip to Japan. No. What I felt was anger. I was furious and I didn't intend to keep my feelings to myself.

b

Upon my return I immediately called a meeting at the Blackstone offices to tell them how very disappointed I was with their performance in Japan. "Nikei securities' strategy was absolutely wrong," I told both Pete Peterson and Steve Schwartzman.

"All we did was stir the pot and create negative publicity. Worse still, we raised no money in Japan." I was concerned about our ability to buy the company. What was Blackstone doing?

"Marvin, I hear you," Pete said. "You are probably right. I don't think you quite understand the difficulty of the situation in Japan. But I'm now going to involve myself in Bloomingdale's situation and try to come up with additional financing."

It was a political speech. Peterson promised that we would now have Blackstone's full attention, but nothing very much happened after that. Pete had disappointed me tremendously.

I also held a meeting with Drexel's Fred Joseph about my displeasure with their performance. There, too, I got a speech.

I had put my dream of owning Bloomingdale's in the hands of Drexel and Blackstone. Drexel had done little, and Blackstone had handled it poorly. To them, this was just another deal. I couldn't believe that the fate of the store at which I had worked for forty years and all the employees who worked for it was coming down to this.

"Why Bloomie's?"

Drawing by Frascino; © 1990 The New Yorker Magazine, Inc.

CHAPTER 13

The Price of Campeau

ederated, too, was suffering from neglect. The Reichmann-dominated management committee had instilled confidence that Federated's financial woes would be dealt with. Instead, the Reichmanns did next to nothing. In December, after months of inaction, they met twice with Citibank officials. They had no solutions for refinancing. Rather, they reportedly chose to emphasize how little their actual stake in the company was.

To make everything worse, Federated and Bloomingdale's business was slowly unwinding. Many of our suppliers remained loyal, but more and more became suspicious and some stopped shipping. Although in theory we had a big inventory, the lifeblood of any store is reorders and fresh new merchandise. For example, Bloomingdale's did almost a million dollars in November and December with Krups, in coffeemakers, espresso machines, and other small electrics. That year Krups's sales executive told Lester Gribetz, "We're not going to ship Bloomingdale's." We tried to lean on them every way we could, but they were absolutely firm. Not having that merchandise meant substantial lost sales for the Christmas period. As vendors throughout the store, great and small, stopped shipping, we began to see that we were in the grip of a self-fulfilling downward spiral.

Federated was put on credit warnings in October and November by some of the apparel suppliers' credit guarantors, "the factors." This served to further dry up the flow of apparel. By December the factors announced that they would be guaranteeing Bloomingdale's shipments at only a 50 percent rate; half the risk then went back to the supplier. That put big pressure on many smaller firms with limited financial resources. Confidence in our ability to do business slipped by an equal amount. I urged Bob Campeau to have Ron

Tysoe meet with the factors, particularly the two largest, CIT and Heller. Campeau kept saying that everything was fine, but the factors complained that Campeau's people wouldn't give them any information.

In the midst of this debacle, I came to understand why Campeau was asking such a ridiculously high price for Bloomingdale's. Apparently, when he bought Federated, he paid no tax on the acquisition of the assets. However, were he to sell a piece of Federated, he would have to pay a capital gain. Therefore, if Bloomingdale's were sold for a billion dollars, the government would get $300 million and Campeau would get to keep only $700 million. So that meant that Bloomingdale's had to bring a price more than 30 percent higher than its objective. For example, to raise $1 billion, Bloomingdale's would have to be sold for $1.43 billion. That was not made clear when Campeau told me that the company was going to be for sale. Using this analysis, it's hard to come up with a number high enough for Campeau. And suddenly I had to wonder if Campeau was ever serious about selling the company in the first place. Part of Campeau's hope for saving Federated was selling off Bloomingdale's. We were still going to bid on it, as were others, but I began to doubt Campeau would get his price. We spent months researching ways to avoid these taxes but never came up with a satisfactory solution.

At the same time, we heard that Federated, in an attempt to begin to solve their financial problems, offered the bondholders a settlement of X cents on the dollar (the number was rumored to be sixty or seventy cents), taking the balance in future equity. The bondholders, however, weren't fully apprised of Federated's dire financial circumstances and were suspicious of the offer. They assumed that the Reichmanns were trying to buy the company at a discount. With hindsight, it could have been a generous offer—many bondholders ended up getting substantially less.

In retrospect, the whole process of trying to buy Bloomingdale's ran counter to our initial assumptions. I had thought Drexel would raise funds domestically, and Blackstone would lead to Japanese financing. In fact, it was Drexel's contact, Tosh Yamamoto, who brought us our most serious potential Japanese investor. Similarly, the soundest advice I received during the whole process came from the source I least expected: Mike Milken.

Diane Levbarg, who was one of our outstanding fashion buyers in the early seventies, was married to Martin Klein, a partner in the law firm of Dreyer & Traub (no relation). Diane and Martin kept in touch while I was trying to buy Bloomingdale's, and wanted to be helpful in any way they could. One day soon after I got back from Japan, Martin called: "Marvin, I know you're struggling to buy the company. I've been talking to Mike Milken and because he's a friend of mine and you're a friend of mine, if you'd like, Mike would be pleased to sit down with you, pro bono, and tell you how he would approach this transaction. But it has to be secret."

In fact, anyone using Drexel had been asked to refrain from speaking to Mike Milken. But it was the end of November, I thought, and we're nowhere. I don't see what I've got to lose, so I asked Martin to set the appointment.

Milken was in New York on trial for securities fraud. Apparently he had some time on his hands. Nonetheless, I wanted to be sure I was committing no wrong by seeing him. To double-check, I called Ira Millstein, and asked his opinion. "If you meet with him," Ira advised, "don't offer up any information, just hear what he has to say. And don't mention it to Drexel."

On Friday, December 1, Jeff Sherman and I went to the Carlyle Hotel at four o'clock. We met in Mike's suite; Martin was also there. Milken struck me as friendly, affable, sympathetic. More than anything, I was impressed by his encyclopedic knowledge and his grasp of details. Of all the investment bankers I met, and of all I have ever dealt with, he was the most brilliant by a wide margin. He is a walking computer of every deal ever done, down to its smallest terms.

Milken knew Bloomingdale's and Federated inside and out, and as he went through the problems we faced, he spun out alternatives and ideas. I cannot speak to his moral character, but given his extraordinary abilities, what happened to him is a waste, all the more so if it was his own fault.

In looking at Federated's problems, and our attempt to buy Bloomingdale's, he suggested that we were going about the financing the wrong way.

"The key to this," he said, "is the bank debt." Milken suggested we go to the banks and propose that they exchange their debt for equity in Bloomingdale's and give them a pay out based on Bloomingdale's earnings. The banks would then become our equity partner. There were advantages for the banks in this approach and clearly there were advantages for Bloomingdale's. Citibank, the lead bank, would then become our principal owner.

"Everybody needs this deal," Mike explained. His assessment of the deal was that Campeau was choking in the grip of debt and Citibank was on the line, as were so many other creditors and suppliers. It was in all their interest to renegotiate. "This is a very important transaction that has to take place if Campeau wants to save itself," Mike said.

Milken, by the way, asked no fee or participation for his advice. He just wanted to help because we were good friends of Martin Klein's. He looked at our attempt to buy Bloomingdale's as a case study. There was a problem and he wanted to keep his mind sharp by solving it.

Jeff and I both felt Milken had provided us with a solid, workable approach. The more we thought about it, the more surprised we were that none of our bankers had approached the problem the same way. We told them about our new idea, not explaining how we came up with it. They could find no flaw in it.

We called Larry Small at Citibank and made a date to see him. We presented him with the idea. He liked it but said our timing was off.

"This could have worked in September or October," Larry said. "But now it's too late."

I left the meeting feeling that, in spite of everything, if I had it to do all over again, I would have liked to work with Mike Milken from the beginning. Of all the investment bankers we dealt with, he was the only one who delivered something solid and had a fresh approach to the problems we faced.

b

Time was running out to buy Bloomingdale's. First Boston was delaying the auction again. December 8, however, was the date set in the offering memorandum for preliminary bids. All that was required was a letter stating the bid. We decided, in order to move the process forward, to put together a bid that would at least get us into the second round.

This was not an auction in the traditional sense—at least not from our point of view. For us the major challenge was to come up with a number that we could finance, and that would be sufficiently high to satisfy Campeau Corporation's needs. Our strategy was to offer an amount we felt comfortable with. Campeau would then tell us the number they had in mind. We would negotiate, and somehow, by a stretch and a miracle, we would agree.

Tom Lee and Freeman Spogli were our major equity partners. They continued to plug numbers into their computer models to determine the level they felt comfortable bidding. IFINT had also signed on to invest at a more subordinate level. We had no actual commitment from a bank. Then, after much negotiation, Citibank agreed to be our lead banker, and agreed to back us to the point where we were comfortable submitting a bid just shy of $1 billion.

Although I was not privy to the bids submitted on the eighth, my understanding was that Investcorp bid $800 million and the high bid was $1 billion from Merrill Lynch for Joe Brooks. We had expected bids from Tokyu, Shuwa, and JMB Realty, but they did not materialize.

That was no great surprise. By December, the outlook for both Campeau Corporation and Federated was grim. The estimates of the store's value in the offering were based on numbers that reflected a great Christmas and an even better performance the following year. With a weak Christmas based on poor deliveries, it was even harder to justify the price Campeau was asking.

At the same time, the Batus Corporation had put Saks Fifth Avenue, Marshall Field's, and Ivy on the block. Investors now had a choice of retailing investments. Saks had a lot to recommend it over Bloomingdale's. Like Bloomingdale's, they were a quality retailer with an international reputation, but they had a distinct advantage: Saks owned their building on Fifth Avenue. Bloomingdale's leased theirs from the Bloomingdale family, and the lease was to expire in 2006—not that far away if you are making a major long-term investment. Campeau, for all his real estate expertise, never addressed the lease issue.

We knew that, as management, we would have to be accepted

into the second round. George Weiksner was running the show for First Boston. He wanted an orderly auction but was having trouble getting the other bids going and having considerable trouble communicating with Campeau.

At the same time it seemed obvious that the company was heading for Chapter 11. Our concern became whether we could close a deal before Federated filed for bankruptcy; and then, if we did arrive at a deal, whether the bankruptcy court would void it if Federated subsequently filed. We also decided that it would be better to purchase Bloomingdale's from Campeau than from a creditor's committee, so we went ahead preparing our offer to move the process along.

George Weiksner told us that Merrill Lynch and Joe Brooks were part of the second round. He implied there were others, but he would not say who. Investcorp had bid high enough to be in the second round. Before bidding in the second round, they told First Boston that they would only go forward if they were indemnified for the cost of their due diligence in the event Bloomingdale's was taken off the market. First Boston refused. Accordingly Investcorp dropped out, only to later purchase Saks Fifth Avenue.

At the same time, you could detect a noticeable change of mood at Campeau Corporation. At our December principal's meeting, Jim Zimmerman and Tom Cody had begun to discuss the implications of bankruptcy. More and more, our suppliers were talking about that. And we were having terrible problems being shipped in the month of December.

In November we encouraged everyone to ship us. But by mid-December, when it was less clear what would happen to the company, people like Ralph Lauren, Anne Klein, and Donna Karan were still shipping, but less. I urged our merchants not to advise suppliers at all, to simply say it was their decision. Of course, this was like saying "don't ship." It was an enormously confusing time. The corporation lacked direction. The restructuring committee's efforts to solve Federated's financial crisis by both selling Bloomingdale's and settling with the bondholders was not working. I now assumed they had already decided that the company was beyond saving and that it should file for Chapter 11. Jim Zimmerman and John Burden were trying to struggle with the problems of the department store division. But the corporation's fiscal problems were really beyond their authority. They had no role in restructuring the company. So the Campeau Corporation had no leadership when it desperately needed it.

I was against bankruptcy for Bloomingdale's and wrote a white paper spelling out my arguments. Even if Federated filed, I felt, Bloomingdale's should be spared. Bankruptcy would be particularly difficult for a luxury retailer. Much of our image was tied to exclusives, special events, special orders, or special services, and I imagined a dangerous drop in these, as well as in how customers perceived the store, if we were under the constraints of bankruptcy.

In December, the thought that our bid might be accepted and that we might still own the company seemed more like a dream than a reality. But I still had to do everything in my power to try to make it happen. I spoke with our financial and legal advisers. I concluded that the only possibility was to try to start an auction for Bloomingdale's. We informed Ron Tysoe that we were submitting our second round bid.

The first round of bidding for Bloomingdale's had taken place in early December. Normally, a second round would have followed in thirty to sixty days. But to speed up the process, we decided to submit a firm, fully fleshed-out bid and give First Boston thirty days to shop it around, hoping that would at least bring us into a final negotiation to purchase Bloomingdale's—just as we had earlier attempted with our preemptive bid.

With Federated's blessing, we hired the accounting firm of Coopers & Lybrand to go over the numbers for our "due diligence." We were very anxious to submit the bid right after Christmas. Our partners, Freeman Spogli, Tom Lee, and IFINT stretched their numbers as far as they could and were solidly with us. We could see business was worsening and we knew that Merrill Lynch had made a soft bid of a billion dollars.

After much discussion, we decided that it would be enough to get the bidding process going if we bid $875 million. We were prepared to go as high as $1.1 billion, and possibly higher, but first we needed to get a sense of what number the other side needed to make a deal. We made a date with Ron Tysoe and Paul Reichmann for December 27 to submit our bid.

Bob Campeau had no part in the restructuring committee. He was off in his own world. He would still come to Bloomingdale's to shop and talk to me and Jeff. Campeau had lunch with us in mid-December at Le Train Bleu, and it's worth commenting on because it's one of those moments when Campeau's essential nature came through. On the one hand he talked about the sale. "On the other hand," Bob said, "Chapter Eleven is a good thing because you can lay off all the people you want, pay reduced salaries with greater incentives, and stop paying pensions." Bob concluded: "And that's how we'll rebuild the company."

I think my jaw dropped. It was a speech devoid of any compassion for all the people who worked at Federated.

b

We worked hard through Christmas to have our bid ready. On December 27, Ken Heitner, Ira Millstein, Jeff Sherman, and I met at the New York offices of Olympia & York on the twelfth floor of 466 Lexington Avenue at two o'clock. Tysoe proceeded to take us through what had happened that fall. When Bloomingdale's was put up for sale, he said, it was with the idea of helping to solve Federated's financial problem. Maybe Bloomingdale's was not worth the $1.8 billion or $2 billion they were seeking. However, unless Campeau Corp. received $1.4 to $1.5 billion—or $1 to $1.1 billion net after taxes—there was no point in selling it. It was better to keep Bloomingdale's than to sell it, even if the company was going into Chapter 11.

Accordingly, our bid of $875 million, Ron said, was totally inadequate for solving the company's problems.

"Even if Chapter Eleven makes sense for Federated," I said, "it is destructive for Bloomingdale's. You should sell off Bloomingdale's outside of Chapter Eleven."

"It's too late for that," Ron said. "Everything we've done has included Bloomingdale's."

And that was how the meeting ended. I left feeling that nothing was going to happen. Tysoe implied that other people were still interested in Bloomingdale's, but nothing more specific than that. I was discouraged.

I decided to see if I could help find another buyer, and contacted both Bill Dillard of Dillard's and Dave Farrell of the May Company. Although both said they had considered the investment, on balance Bloomingdale's was not a good fit for either.

At the same time, another serious problem arose. In talking with Jim Zimmerman and Ron Tysoe, one of the issues that was beginning to loom large was that vendor checks were due to be mailed on January 10 for all December shipments. Sending out all the December checks would lower our cash balance to a dangerous level.

With Zimmerman's encouragement I called ten of our most important vendors, and asked if they would be willing to extend the payments for fifteen or twenty days to get us through this cash crunch. I got mixed answers. Most said they would, if the others agreed as well. However, the story was leaked to the press and I was criticized for what was thought to be a wild idea. Two years later, almost to the day, Macy's would do the same thing with the vendors' support. By then no one thought it was so crazy—in the long run, it may have made little difference, as Macy's nonetheless went into bankruptcy.

While we were trying to buy time with vendors, we were seeking yet another way to stave off our problems, and that was by coming to some agreement with our bondholders, who were getting very nervous. The bondholders were ready to negotiate but no one from Federated appeared at the meeting to negotiate with them. After that meeting I got a call from Peter Solomon, the son of A&S's distinguished former chairman Sidney Solomon. An investment banker, he represented Eddie DeBartolo, Campeau's largest bondholder. Peter was frustrated that there was no one to negotiate with at Federated, and felt that an opportunity for settlement was slipping by. We agreed that Bill Miller, who was on the restructuring committee, was the logical person to lead the negotiations. So I called Bill, who said he'd be pleased to help but didn't have the authority to do so. A series of phone calls ensued, at the end of which Paul Reichmann agreed to let Bill negotiate with the bondholders.*

However, the situation at Campeau Corp. had reached a critical state and a meeting of the Campeau board was called for January 8, 1990, to decide the fate of the company. At the time of the Septem-

---

* In addition to my discussions with Peter Solomon, I found it very useful during this period to talk with Nate Thorn, a McKinsey consultant Federated hired to work on the restructuring and provide Campeau Corporation with some fiscal alternatives. Nate kept me informed of what was happening with the restructuring and I kept him apprised of the situation from my perspective.

ber 15 restructuring, the Campeau board had been reduced from twenty-four to ten, eliminating most of the inside directors—I left the board earlier when Bloomingdale's was offered for sale. Few of the remaining directors knew very much about American retailing.

On Sunday, January 7, Bill Miller was on his way to Washington's National Airport for his flight to Toronto for the crucial board meeting when he fell ill. A few hours later he called from Georgetown Hospital to say, "It's all right. I'll be fine, but I'm going to participate in the board meeting by telephone from the hospital bed."

Bill, reporting from his hospital bed, kept me informed. On the first day of meetings, two representatives from a Canadian bank appeared as new board members. They had financed a large purchase of Federated stock by Campeau and when the stock fell and he could no longer meet his obligations, they took control and were awarded two board seats. Bill told me that the board had to decide whether there were any alternatives left other than to file for Chapter 11. They also discussed the future of Bloomingdale's: Whether to sell at all and how to proceed. There was some discussion of whether Bloomingdale's could be kept out of Chapter 11. It was agreed that Bloomingdale's should not be separated out. But the proposed debtor-in-financing possession could continue to keep Bloomingdale's on the market. The other main item on the agenda was to remove Bob Campeau as CEO. The outside directors asked Jim Zimmerman if he thought the company would be better off without Campeau; he said it would. Bill was supposed to be the one to broach this in person with Bob. Clearly he could no longer do so.

Campeau attended the meeting in his capacity as CEO, though he was very down. At the end of Monday, the first day, Byron Allenbaugh of Ralph's went to dinner with him and asked, in the best interest of the company, that he step down. Campeau refused. "If they ask me to step down," he reportedly said, "I'll sue."

The next day, Jim Zimmerman, as a representative of Federated, addressed the board. Jim had a terrible cold, he almost lost his voice, but for hours he made an impassioned plea for Federated to pay its vendors in full: Regardless of what Federated did, Chapter 11 or not, we would have to live with the vendors for a very long time.

The board decided to send out the December checks Friday January 12. At Bloomingdale's we had one day to physically process the checks. At that time no one gave any thought to the fact that Monday, January 15, was Martin Luther King Day and a bank holiday, which meant that if a check was not cashed on Friday, it could not be processed until Tuesday, January 16. Rumors were rampant about our imminent bankruptcy and our suppliers understood that the sooner they deposited the check, the better. We were not supposed to favor one vendor over another, but Jeff and I knew that people would long remember how they were treated in this situation. We decided to do something exceptional. We had our buyers call every vendor and offer them the chance to pick up their checks on Friday in person, rather than wait for them to arrive in the mail.

On Friday there was, understandably, a long line waiting for checks. We took over our customer charge offices and set up that area alphabetically by vendor so the vendors could pick up their checks as easily as possible. Some vendors, fearing the worst, made a point of making sure the checks would clear, sometimes going to extraordinary lengths. Leonard Lauder, for example, had his check flown to Delaware the same day because the Federated checks were drawn on a Delaware account. Although I knew bankruptcy was an imminent possibility, I never imagined Federated would not honor the checks.

The Campeau Corporation board meetings were still going on in Canada. Bob was still trying to come up with new ideas and had spent Tuesday in New York trying, without success, to raise more funds. There was pressure from both the American and Canadian directors for Bob to resign, led by Bob's longtime friend and associate Bob Despres, but he continued to resist. At Thursday's two-and-a-half-hour meeting Bob Campeau finally resigned from Campeau U.S. There was a last-minute discussion between Tysoe and Citibank about an infusion of capital that fell through. The Reichmanns were conspicuously silent. The board agreed to hold a final meeting to decide the fate of Federated on Sunday, January 14, at 4:00 P.M.

Sunday afternoon, January 14, 1990, I was at home in Connecticut watching a football game when I got word that there would be a conference call that evening at nine between corporate management and the division principals. I feared the worst.

That night Lee and I were scheduled to attend the fiftieth anniversary of American Ballet Theatre at Lincoln Center. I decided that there was no reason to forgo attending. On the contrary, to do so would send a signal to the other retailers and vendors who would be attending. I made arrangements to take the conference call at Lincoln Center in the office of the manager of the Metropolitan Opera.

That black-tie gala was New York at its most glamorous. Limousines pulled up to Lincoln Center and the beautiful and powerful made their way to the Metropolitan Opera House to celebrate ABT. For me, a dark cloud hovered over the event.

We were the guests of Mr. and Mrs. Efraim Grinberg, the chairman of Movado, the evening's sponsor. Former ambassador to France Evan Galbraith and his wife, Bootsie, were sitting with us, along with Hamish Maxwell, chairman of Philip Morris, the corporate chairman for the evening, and his wife, and Mr. and Mrs. George Weisman, the chairman of Lincoln Center and his wife. We were seated in the center box and I deliberately sat in the back so I could leave without disturbing the others.

For this one night, the greatest dancers of American Ballet Theatre had gathered to perform their signature works supported by the very talented corps de ballet. But I was distracted. A few minutes before nine, as the room was held rapt by the music of Copeland and the lively choreography of Agnes de Mille's classic *Rodeo*, I made my way to the manager's office.

A staff member was waiting to let me inside. I passed through a large outer office to a smaller, cluttered one where I sat down alone, thinking of the incongruity of being in this office in black tie. The phone rang a few minutes later. The operator said, "Mr. Traub, are you there?" She listed the twenty-five other persons on the line, among whom were the chairman of each of the divisions including Hy Edelstein of A&S, Howard Sokol of Burdine's, and Jeff Sherman, as well as Jim Zimmerman, John Burden, and Tom Cody. Assorted bankers and lawyers were on the line, as well as Ron Tysoe, though Campeau himself was not.

Jim Zimmerman's voice was still hoarse. "Tomorrow," he said, "we will serve papers in Cincinnati seeking the protection of the courts under Chapter Eleven." He asked that each of us inform our own people at the stores before anyone else knew. Although by now bankruptcy was no surprise, I was still upset. Many people had worked very long and hard to avoid this; now that effort was over. The impact of bankruptcy on an upscale store like Bloomingdale's concerned me, as did the problem of trying to hold the organization together under what had to be very trying circumstances for everyone.

How would I tell the management and employees of Bloomingdale's? First I would have to tell them that we had not been successful in acquiring the company; worse yet, Federated would be filing for Chapter 11 protection. After the conference call, I immediately called Jeff Sherman to plan what we should do the next morning. I had left my seat just before intermission but by the time I returned the second act had begun, so I sat down without having to talk to anyone. As I sat in the dark I could only focus on the next morning.

At the next intermission I was able to whisper to Lee the news. I would have left then and there, but we were expected at dinner. So I sat through the main course, we danced a little, and then made our excuses. It was difficult to sit there, smiling. By the time we got home it was one in the morning. I did not get much sleep that night.

The bankruptcy was a terrible disappointment on several fronts. I was concerned with how our various groups—our salespeople, our executives, our customers, and our suppliers—would respond. In recent months there was a shortage of credit and that created severe problems, straining the good faith and credibility we had built up over the years. Recently, Grey, our advertising agency, told us that they couldn't place our television advertising. At one point, *The New York Times* said they could no longer accept any advertising from us because they weren't sure they'd be paid.

And then there was the unavoidable fact that Bloomingdale's was more than a business to me. I had spent almost my entire adult life working there. To watch what I, along with so many trusted colleagues, had worked so hard to create be transformed into an "asset," something to be taken over, only to crumble under the weight of some third party's debt, was very painful. Bankruptcy was the final indignity.

We were now just beginning to see the impact of what Bob Campeau had wrought. Federated's bankruptcy was just the first domino. Many would lose their jobs in the months to come, many more over the next few years. Federated's cutbacks would be followed by cutbacks in retail advertising, in shopping mall development, and commercial real estate. As a consequence, several other industries would contract, from magazine and newspaper publishing to cosmetics and manufacturing. Eventually, as the 1980s deal mania died with the decade, law firms and investment banks would also have massive layoffs, further imperiling the luxury goods market. Finally, in 1992, as a direct delayed consequence of Campeau's folly, Macy's would file for bankruptcy. All that was ahead of us.

Tomorrow, our staff and our suppliers would hear the news. I didn't know how they would react. It was a very sad moment for me, but I knew one thing: better they hear it from me than anyone else.

b

I stood on the balcony overlooking Bloomingdale's 59th Street's main floor filled with the anxious faces of my coworkers. A conference call had been set up that would broadcast my words to all fifteen branch stores plus our warehouses and offices. Over the years I had delivered many messages to my associates from this spot. However, having to tell the organization that today we were filing for bankruptcy was one of the hardest things I've ever done.

"Bloomingdale's is not going to be sold," I explained. "But that doesn't mean the end of the world, or the end of Bloomingdale's." My attitude was that bankruptcy would permit us to move forward. The struggle of the past few months to have merchandise shipped, to deal with the demands of Campeau Corp., were now resolved. We would operate under Chapter 11 much as we had before the takeover. Our attitude was business as usual. We would now have the opportunity to reorganize the company, I said, and would re-emerge a healthy store again. Despite my optimism, it was a very somber meeting.

Going into bankruptcy demanded a strategy for dealing with each one of our three constituencies: our vendors, our coworkers, and our customers. After beginning the morning by speaking to our coworkers, I intended to speak personally with as many of our most important suppliers as I could. There was an organized corporate effort to have each store principal call at least ten of our top suppliers. I called Leonard Lauder, Guy Peyrelongue of Lancôme, Frank Mori of Donna Karan, Peter Strom of Ralph Lauren, as well as Ralph himself. I told them that we were filing for bankruptcy and explained the details, reassuring them that I would answer any questions they had.

At that time, no major store had gone into Chapter 11 and ever emerged. Altman's, Korvette's, Bonwit Teller had all failed. In my conversations I emphasized that those were not healthy stores. The only problem Bloomingdale's had was its parent's debt. Accordingly, I hoped they would continue to ship us. Most said they would, but some took a wait-and-see attitude.

That was understandable. When Federated went into bankruptcy many vendors took a major hit. Crystal Brands, for example, was stuck with a $5.6 million debt, Liz Claiborne $5 million, Chanel $3.8 million, American Greetings $2.8 million, Sara Lee $2.9 million, Reebok $2 million, Polo $2.5 million. I made a point to get out to the market. I tried to visit all of our suppliers and assure them that I felt good about where we were. I was sorry we couldn't buy Bloomingdale's but I was convinced that we were going to get out of Chapter 11. I assured them that I was personally committed to the Bloomingdale's organization, and to seeing it come out of Chapter 11. I think my assurance was helpful.

I felt it was very important that our coworkers understand how we were working with our suppliers. I explained it to the executive committee and our salespeople and held a conference call to the stores. I then spoke with many of our buyers to make sure they understood our position.

I was most concerned about our customers. We ran a newspaper ad the first Sunday in *The New York Times* and other publications that treated Chapter 11 as a new beginning. I then asked Ann Stock and Carol Geist from public relations to develop and conduct a survey. Within thirty days they spoke to thousands of customers, both inside and outside our stores in every market, asking: (1) Did they know about the Chapter 11? (97 percent knew about it); (2) How did they feel about it?; and (3) Would it change their shopping habits? About 15 percent implied it might change their shopping habits, but 85 percent said it would not.

People were most concerned about their special orders. Would their furniture arrive? What about their bridal registry? Many no longer felt secure placing orders for long-term deliveries, or even sending gifts. There was also a perception among customers that a bankruptcy means bargains. So we went out of our way to try to explain to customers that bankruptcy does not mean a fire sale and over time people understood that.

b

On the corporate front, decisions critical to our surviving bankruptcy were being made. The first and most important occurred the day we filed. Federated was very fortunate in selecting Cincinnati, the corporate headquarters, as the venue in which to file Chapter 11. The bankruptcy judge hearing the case was familiar with Federated and was committed to our working out a plan that would see us emerge as a healthy retailing organization.

At the same time, as soon as the decision to file was made, I urged Bill Miller to take over the chairmanship. He had been offered it but had not yet accepted. He was the right man to lead us out of Chapter 11, I said. He had links to both the old Federated, having served on the board for many years, and to Campeau Corp., having been part of the reorganization committee, and he had been secretary of commerce during the Chrysler bankruptcy. Having Bill as chairman would communicate our commitment to coming out of Chapter 11, and send the right signal to our creditors, suppliers, and the bankruptcy court. After discussing the position with me and several other people, he became enthusiastic about the challenge ahead and accepted the chairmanship.

I urged Bill to get rid of the Campeau name as quickly as possible. I suggested that we return to using Federated Department Stores, which eighteen months earlier had stood for the finest in quality retailing. That became one of his first acts as chairman.

Bill's first priority was recruiting a new Federated CEO. His main responsibility was to deal with our creditors, including the banks, to arrange a settlement of our debts and restructure them so that we could emerge from Chapter 11. The immediate need however, was for a new chief merchant. When Campeau recruited him, John Burden had only agreed to stay on for eighteen months. He had no desire to stay on through the bankruptcy. The choice of a new

CEO was important because we needed to send a signal of strong leadership. Bill and I were in agreement that Alan Questrom was the leading candidate.

Alan, then fifty, was Brooklyn born and had started his career in retailing as part of the A&S training program. He became president of Rich's in 1978 and its chairman and CEO two years later. Having achieved the goals he had set for Rich's, Alan resigned in 1984 to take a ten-month sabbatical, at the end of which he returned to Federated as chairman and CEO of Bullock's/Bullock's Wilshire. During his tenure, Bullock's was one of the most profitable of Federated's divisions. In mid-1987, he also joined Federated's corporate management as executive vice president, and in January he became Federated's vice chairman with Filene's, Filene's Basement, Bullock's, Bullock's-Wilshire, and Bloomingdale's reporting to him. At the time he was generally thought to be a leading candidate to succeed Howard Goldfeder. Many Federated executives looked forward to that day, because during the 1980s, when Howard diversified into new businesses, Alan was a very vocal opponent. He was a strong believer in the department store, its strengths and potential, and its ability to compete and succeed in the marketplace. When Campeau took over, however, Alan fled, telling reporters that he found nothing positive about the change. Instead, he became chairman of Neiman-Marcus, and from that vantage point watched as Federated sank under the weight of Bob Campeau's ego.

That didn't stop Bob from continuing to try and recruit Alan. At Bob's request, I brought them together one weekend in March 1989 on the slopes of the Deer Valley ski resort. Alan and his wife, Kelli, were staying at our house. Bob took a suite in the Stein Erickson Lodge. (Lee had put down her foot. *"That man* is not staying with us," she said.) We skied together, but Alan was not to be swayed. It probably didn't help that Bob insisted on giving us all ski lessons as we made our way down the mountain.

Bill confided that Paul Reichmann had been pursuing Alan Questrom since fall, with no success. I didn't tell Bill, but when I was in the midst of trying to buy Bloomingdale's I invited Alan to breakfast at the Crillon in Paris. At that time Alan was CEO of Neiman-Marcus. I told him about our interest in buying Bloomingdale's and said that if we were successful, I would like him to join us. I thought he was the logical person to be my successor. I also believed that running Bloomingdale's was a job that he would enjoy.

"I have a contract with Neiman-Marcus," Alan had said. However, if we acquired Bloomingdale's, we should resume the conversation. I didn't take that as a yes or a no.

Becoming CEO of the new Federated Department Stores would, I felt, be an entirely different proposition for Alan. He would now have the freedom he never would have had under Bob Campeau. He would no longer be dealing with a company struggling under the weight of an overleveraged buyout: His mandate would be to take Federated out of bankruptcy and return it to a leadership role in department store retailing.

Bill held several conversations with Alan together with the Reichmanns. Alan was enjoying Neiman-Marcus, but Federated was offering an extremely attractive financial package. I can no longer recall how many phone calls I had with Alan and Kelli during this period. I worked very hard to convince him to return to Federated. By the end of January, Alan was ready to join the company at a compensation of $2 million a year for five years, with a $2 million bonus—$12 million.* This was substantially more than he would have earned running the healthy pre-Campeau Federated. He was also promised very substantial incentives for the performance of the Federated stock if and when the company came out of Chapter 11. But at the last minute, there was a hitch.

Alan was concerned that once he told Neiman-Marcus he was leaving, or if word got out and he didn't get confirmed by the bankruptcy court or the creditors, he would have no job and not be able to join Federated. So Paul Reichmann agreed to put $7 million in escrow by Friday, January 27, at 5:00 P.M. If for any reason his deal with Federated didn't go through, the $7 million was Alan's as damages. At the same time, there were a great number of other negotiations going on. Friday, January 27, came, and at 5:00 P.M. the money was not there. The Reichmanns' representatives assured Alan that the money would be there Monday morning. They explained that it

---

* In addition to the salary and bonus, Alan's proposed contract called for an equity appreciation payment based on the increase in the market value of Federated's common stock. That can pay Alan an additional $21 to $41 million at the conclusion of his contract.

was already sundown and, as observant Jews, they could no longer transact business.

"You committed to Friday," Alan said, and walked out of the negotiations. "A commitment is a commitment," Alan told me later. "They had three weeks."

I was skiing in Utah that weekend when I heard this from Bill Miller. I called Alan from Silver Lake Lodge at Deer Valley. "I can not work with people I can't trust," he said. I knew how much he was being paid, and how much the company needed him. I told him he was foolish not to wait until Monday.

"You really ought to give them a chance to come up with the money," I said.

"I'll think about it," he promised. Alan had subsequent talks with Bill Miller and Jim Zimmerman over the next two weeks. At the end of February, Alan Questrom was announced as Federated's new CEO and John Burden retired.

When you file for Chapter 11, it means all current bills are suspended in order to preserve cash for the company. Thus anyone Federated owed money to on January 15 became a creditor. On the other hand, Chapter 11 provides for debtor in possession financing by which banks provide new money to pay future bills and suppliers are virtually guaranteed payment on new shipments.

Many suppliers said they would ship us only if they were paid in advance or on special terms. At the conference call announcing our intention to file, Jim Zimmerman and the merchants, including me, agreed that from day one we would place orders with suppliers only on our regular terms. We would refuse to place any orders where the supplier expected to be paid in advance; to do so would have created a serious cash drain and would have made it difficult to emerge from Chapter 11. When Altman's and Bonwit Teller had gone into Chapter 11, they had made special payment deals in order to get shipped and it had not served them well. In fact, it may be one reason why they never recovered. So instead, Federated took the stand that we would have no special terms with any vendors. The first day when the principals called the vendors, we explained how important this policy was to our coming out of bankruptcy.

At first there was some confusion. We placed our orders. Some vendors, Mikasa, Krups, and Sony, for example, would not ship immediately. But we kept placing orders on our terms. Once it became apparent that we were very serious about our policy, we got almost everyone to agree. That was one of the milestones that separated this Chapter 11 from others.

On the other hand, many of Bloomingdale's regular suppliers, large and small, immediately resumed shipping without limitation. We were grateful. So we scrambled, and did our best to get business back on an even keel. In order to keep key employees we quickly put in a retention bonus. And to strengthen the impression that Bloomingdale's was back to business as usual, I felt it was important that we go forward with our spring and fall 1990 promotions. As we had limited time and effort to mount a full-blown country promotion, we came up with a local theme: the Broadway theater—"Broadway Ninety." Ann Stock and I met with a group of Broadway producers. Because theater attendance had been down the year before, they were anxious to cooperate. We received their total support to do model rooms and shops tied in with plays. It brought in people, it got us a good deal of press, and our business was stronger in April. Of course, we had less new merchandise than we would have had under ordinary circumstances. Nonetheless, we did hit one home run: We sold thousands of our *Miss Saigon* beach towel, making it an all-time best-seller.

By April, three months into the Chapter 11, a second survey of our customers showed they were remaining loyal. We still had major losses in such areas as interior design, bridal registry, and special order china, but we began to be more optimistic.

Economic issues sometimes take strange turns. There was some irony in the fact that the architect of Bob Campeau's takeover of Allied and then Federated, Ron Tysoe, the man who, as Campeau's representative, would not sell us Bloomingdale's and preferred instead to take it into bankruptcy along with Federated, was the person who led us back to financial recovery. Ron became Chief Financial Officer and made real progress in finding compromises and solutions with the four creditor groups, including converting much of Federated's debt into equity. Today he is vice chairman of Federated and a member of the board.

Questrom and Zimmerman refocused Federated, returning to its traditional strength, department stores, and made several innovations. Federated extended the use of SABRE, a computerized data processing system. They began a program of team buying to take advantage of the merchandising strength and buying power of Federated. Team buying brings together the best merchants from each store to serve on committees to cover specific commodities such as women's sportswear, menswear, cosmetics, and housewares. These teams are responsible for selecting merchandise that represents as much as 70 percent of the assortment for all stores. Since the other divisions had similar price points and customers it made sense. On the other hand, because Bloomingdale's had higher price points and a different merchandise emphasis, it was not part of the team buying process.

Bankruptcy provided several opportunities for reorganization. Chapter 11 meant that the contracts of every executive in the company were voided, and it was an opportunity, if one chose, to drop people. Bloomingdale's could also, for example, have voided our union contract. However, early on I met with the union to say we needed their support to get out of Chapter 11.

Being in Chapter 11 gave Federated the opportunity to review each of its leases and close individual stores that were not performing well. If we had a store lease or, for that matter, a leased department in one of our stores that was unprofitable, we could submit to the courts that this stood in the way of our coming out of Chapter 11 and void that lease. That gave us great strength in returning Federated to profitability, and over the course of the year Federated closed forty-one unproductive stores. As I mentioned earlier, Bloomingdale's decided to close our stores in Valley View, Texas; Stamford, Connecticut; and Fresh Meadows, Long Island.

Closing stores is not an easy thing for anyone. In fact, as Lee and I had lived in Greenwich for many years, we considered Stamford our local store, and I knew many of the people working there, which made it particularly painful. I decided to visit the store with Jeff Sherman the day of the announcement to talk to our coworkers myself. There were employees of twenty or thirty years' standing who'd known me all that time. They were tearful but appreciated our taking the time to console them.

The night of the closing we held a party with the Stamford employees and gave gifts to those who would have joined the twenty-five-year club that year. We toasted them and they in turn gave me a gift. In 1957, the *Saturday Evening Post* had done an amusing cover based on the Stamford store. They obtained the original, had it framed, and presented it to me. It hangs today in my apartment in New York. If you can close a store under good circumstances, we did.

Closing Fresh Meadows the following year, 1991, was also very difficult for me. Bill Hearst, our store manager, did an outstanding job of maintaining the morale of that store through the closing party for the employees. That party was held with a disc jockey, dancing, drinking, and mutual love and affection. I think it speaks well for Bloomingdale's that even at such sad occasions, we rally.

The store closings were even more difficult for me than I let on. Fresh Meadows was our first new branch, and I had planned Stamford in 1952 with Jed Davidson. Little did I know, when I first began considering which stores to close, that my career at Bloomingdale's was also about to be terminated.

PART 5

Bloomingdale's and Beyond

"This is my wife, Katerina, formerly of Bloomingdale's."

CHAPTER 14

Leaving Bloomingdale's

I n my career at Bloomingdale's I had close and important relationships with retailers of strong vision. Jed Davidson was the key figure in my coming to Bloomingdale's; Alan Questrom was instrumental in my leaving the store.

When Alan was appointed chairman of Federated in the spring of 1990, almost forty years after I first joined Bloomingdale's, he had strong merchandising ideas that I believed would be good for Bloomingdale's. He appreciated the importance of luxury retailing and we had worked well together for over twenty-five years both as Federated principals and as board members. Pre-Campeau, Bullock's and Bloomingdale's were the two most independent divisions in Federated; Alan and I frequently held the same point of view on corporate issues. And for the last few months before Campeau acquired Federated I even reported to Alan. From the time he started as chairman, we held regular strategy sessions; we also continued to see each other socially.

One Sunday in April we played golf together at Sunningdale, my country club. It could not have been friendlier. The next morning we were scheduled to have another of our strategy sessions, and I looked forward to seeing him and Jim Zimmerman, Federated's president, who always participated in these sessions. Alan had been CEO for only two months, so there was still much to review. He and Jim came to my office, and we sat comfortably on the couches. After a few pleasantries, Jim Zimmerman turned to me.

"We think it's time to begin to look for someone to replace you," he said.

This came as a complete surprise.

I was particularly surprised in light of Bloomingdale's fiscal performance. In 1987, despite the market collapse, Bloomingdale's had been one of two old Federated divisions, out of fourteen, to make our pretax income plan (the other was Bullock's). That year, we earned $129 million under our new criteria of earnings before interest, tax, and depreciation, EBITDA. In 1988, our EBITDA of $131 million was the largest in Federated and the only one of the five divisions to exceed the previous year. The year 1989 was a horrendous year for all Federated as we were not being shipped, and Bloomingdale's had the additional complication of being up for sale. Nevertheless, our EBITDA of $85 million was again the largest in Federated. Bloomingdale's performance in 1987, 1988, and 1989 was not just good; considering the constraints we were under it was, at the least, extraordinary. Although I tried hard not to show it, I was stunned. I was more than a little upset because of how hard I had worked to bring Alan into this job, only to have him terminate me as one of his first orders of business.

"I committed to running Bloomingdale's until I'm sixty-eight," I said, "which is three years away," and informed Alan and Jim that I had signed an agreement with board support and approval to that effect several years earlier.

Jim and Alan looked at each other. They didn't know about that. I promised to send them a copy.

"There's no rush," Alan said.

As Alan saw it, he had five years to turn Federated around. He felt he needed someone at Bloomingdale's who would be with him throughout that period and continue on after that. He wanted to appoint a new Bloomingdale's chairman before the end of 1991.

I told them that I thought the ideal succession would be to hire someone to work with me for a year or two.

"No," Alan said. "I think to attract the proper person we don't need more than a short overlap."

When Alan said that, I realized his mind was made up to replace me as soon as possible. I had always run Bloomingdale's as a separate arm of Federated; I believed that was one of our strengths. I now saw that Alan was anxious to bring in his own team who would be responsive to him. I was concerned, however, about the store and all the employees and vendors who were loyal to me. Without a proper transition, Bloomingdale's could be hurt.

I was still more than a little stunned and angry, but rather than show it, I did what I do under stress: I focused on the problem. I took out a piece of paper and pen, and said we should start composing a list of possible successors. Alan and Jim had said they had no specific individual in mind.

Bloomingdale's was too large and complex, Alan said, to entrust to anyone who had not been a CEO or chairman of another company, so that ruled out hiring anyone from within. We also agreed to keep the process secret. We began to toss out names in no particular order.

Roger Farrah, Art Reiner (of Macy's), Phil Miller, Barbara Bass, Russ Stravitz (despite the fact that he had not been a principal) were some of the candidates I put forward. Jim Zimmerman suggested Marshall Hillsburg of Lord & Taylor. Mickey Drexler, Norman Axelrod, Arnie Aronson, Bobby Friedman (Macy's), Phil Schlein, Howard Sokol, Irwin Zazulia, and Dick Battram were other names mentioned. In all, fourteen names appeared on the original list.

The meeting lasted for half an hour. The search had begun, and we agreed that I would be consulted on the process and have input in the selection of my eventual replacement, which was, we agreed, to occur somewhere more than a year away.

For the rest of the day I thought about what had happened. That evening I told Lee. She was upset on my behalf, but thought the opportunities for a sixty-five-year-old CEO were exponentially greater than for a sixty-eight-year-old, and if I wanted to start a second career, the sooner the better.

The following day I went back to the task of leading Bloomingdale's out of bankruptcy and set the question of my succession aside. One thought did, however, continue to rankle me: Here was a company four months into bankruptcy depending on my relationships in the markets and with our vendors to bring us back to health; to ask me to consider leaving in fifteen to eighteen months was, in effect, to ask me to stay through the most difficult part and then give it up.

Two weeks later, I gave a cocktail party in our Connecticut home to welcome our new neighbors—the Questroms, who had just bought a house near ours in Greenwich. One of the guests was Reg Jones, the former chairman of GE. I had been very close to Reg and trusted him. He had been on the board of both the old and the new

Federated. I told Reg that I was troubled and we agreed to meet. About a month later, when we lunched together at the Four Seasons, I told Reg of my conversation with Alan and the way I was treated. I wondered whether I shouldn't chuck the whole thing and leave Bloomingdale's now. Reg, speaking both as a director and a friend, urged me to stay on. He talked about his experience in the transition at GE, and the need for me to continue to be loyal to the company and also to understand what Alan was trying to accomplish. I decided that leaving really accomplished very little except perhaps a show of independence. What would be best for Bloomingdale's, I decided, was to stay and try to create an orderly transition.

b

Looking back, I can now see that in many ways my termination marked the end of an era in the individuality of department stores and their leaders. When I first joined Bloomingdale's in 1950, Sam Bloomingdale was still alive, as were Adam Gimbel, Andrew Goodman, Stanley Marcus,* Dick Rich, Walter Hoving, Dorothy Shaver, and Bob Lazarus. What distinguished these people was their personal connection to their stores. In their case, as in mine, the store and principal were very closely tied together. But as their stores passed from their hands to corporate management, the focus became increasingly on the bottom line.

For a certain period of transition, department store corporations, much like other businesses, tried to expand their reach beyond their traditional boundaries; and most failed. Today, when I read that Federated is once again focusing on its core department store business, it does not sound so different from the business news at IBM, American Express, or any of half a dozen other companies. Retailing, like so many other American businesses, is dominated by a new generation of super-managers—well-educated, bottom-line, numbers-oriented executives. I can think of few store chairmen today who are so identified with their store that they could not be recruited elsewhere next week (and who wouldn't leave). As a consequence, stores are not so distinctive as they once were.

---

* Interestingly, Stanley Marcus fashioned a very strong second career as a consultant. Today, in his eighties, Stanley is still very active. A good role model.

Alan Questrom is, to my view, very much the corporate manager for the 1990s. He has a strong grip on the bottom line and a firm vision of the way things should be run. He is very competitive: He wants any store he works at to be number one; and he relishes the challenge of restoring Federated to preeminence. But he holds no emotional allegiance to any store. It would not surprise me if, in five years, Alan is doing something different from retailing. He represents a different way of approaching the world than I do. I am very passionate about Bloomingdale's and its coworkers. He is not as interested in relationships and the personality of a store as I am. He runs cold, rather than hot. It seemed to me that I did not fit with the culture Alan wanted to create.

b

Alan and I continued to have lunch over the next year. Whenever we did, I'd ask about his progress and he would say they were pursuing the search and from time to time he would tell me about candidates. We had agreed in principle that when one of the candidates was under serious consideration, I would meet with him or her as well. By the fall of 1990, I started to hear rumors that I was soon to be replaced. I suspect it came out of the Federated and Allied creditor committee meetings, although I couldn't track it down.

Then in November, columnist Jim Brady, who is a good friend, wrote an article in *Crain's* saying I was going to be out by year-end. I called him up and said that was just plain not true. I asked him where he got it from, but he wouldn't say. He did, however, print a retraction.

Early the following spring, Isador Barmash ran a story in *The New York Times* saying that I was leaving Bloomingdale's and that Roger Farrah, Mike Gould, and Mickey Drexler were among the leading candidates to replace me. That caused considerable concern at Bloomingdale's, because several people on my team had stayed at the store based on my commitment to be around until 1993.*

---

* Over the years, I had talked Gordon Cooke and John Jay out of leaving to open their own advertising agency. I talked Lester out of leaving twice, once at the time of the bankruptcy and later when my resignation was announced. I talked Carl Levine out of leaving. Kal Ruttenstein came to see me; he reminded me that the last time I had talked him out of leaving, I had promised I would stay until 1993. "Kal," I said, "I can't always control everything."

At my next lunch with Alan in spring 1991 I told him that I was concerned about a disturbing rumor I kept hearing in the market. "I've heard you've been meeting with Mike Gould," I said. Mike had not been on our original list of candidates. "Is that true? And what's the status of your discussions with him?"

Alan said that it was true that they were talking to Mike, but nothing was concluded. He did say that he hoped to have someone in place by the middle of the year, if not sooner. In prior discussions I had told both Jim and Alan that I wanted six months' notice before my successor came aboard. They had thought it unusual but had agreed. I thought it important for an orderly transition. I reminded Alan of his promise of a transition period and he was clearly aware of it.

Mike Gould was, like Alan, a product of the A&S training program. He had been a sheet buyer at A&S and rose to divisional merchandise manager of domestics. He moved to California, and became chairman of Robinson's, and turned it into a high-fashion store. Avon then recruited him to be CEO of Giorgio, which he developed, successfully launching Red and making it one of the most popular prestige fragrances. Despite his successes, though, he had his detractors and I was among them.

I did not particularly like Mike Gould. We had a major argument when he was running Giorgio. Mike accused Bloomingdale's of "diverting" their product—selling off a portion of goods to other retailers, such as discount drugstores. Mike fought with Arlene Friedman, our vice president, and then with Lester Gribetz. When he and Lester reached a state of total hostility, I stepped in and we had a meeting. I told Mike that Bloomingdale's was not diverting his product. There might be problems in the chain of distribution, but the problem was not with Bloomingdale's. Mike then started to shout and curse at me. We reached a total impasse. The next day, the story appeared in *Women's Wear*.

Later we discovered that someone was stealing Giorgio from Bloomingdale's trucks and selling it, and that accounted for Mike's claims. Eventually, because of our mutual business interests we called a truce. However, I did not like the way he did business, and wondered if he was an appropriate match for the Bloomingdale's culture, a store whose success was so dependent on long-standing personal relationships.

I was so concerned that I wrote a memo to Alan and Jim, detailing the qualities needed in a Bloomingdale's CEO, the opportunities facing Bloomingdale's, and the reasons why the choice of the proper successor was important. My major doubts had to do with personal style. "In the past forty-one years," I wrote, "Bloomingdale's has had only three chief merchants—Jed Davidson, Harold Krensky, and me. I am doubtful if this candidate should be perceived as an appropriate fourth." I then met with Alan and Jim in April to discuss my memo.

"In a year of looking for a candidate," Alan said, "I have learned that there is no perfect person to replace you." All the candidates had problems. Alan acknowledged that much of what I had said about Mike in my memo was true. On the other hand, he said, Mike had many positive attributes. He possessed a great sense of urgency, understood luxury goods, and had a strong marketing background. Alan and Jim promised to consider my objections, and they assured me they would keep the store's best interests foremost in their minds. With hindsight, I suspect that Mike had been Alan's leading candidate from day one, and that by the time of our meeting Mike had already been offered the job.

A little more than a month later Lee and I had dinner Sunday night at Alan and Kelli's house. We had a pleasant dinner and discussed the planned renovation of their new home. The following morning Alan asked if I could come to his office at 4:30. I assumed it had to do with the transition.

When Harold Krensky retired from active management of Federated he was given an office at the New York corporate offices. It was larger and more comfortable than Alan's and so it was there that we met that afternoon. Once again Jim Zimmerman was present. Again, it was Jim who broke the news.

"We've decided on Mike Gould and would like to announce his appointment as soon as possible."

So much for my having input in the decision.

Alan said that they were committed to a six-month transition. I would remain as chairman and CEO until November 15. As they saw it, Mike would come aboard the first week of August and would have the title chairman and CEO elect until November 15.

Alan and Jim were anxious that I stay on at Federated until the end of my contract in 1993 (they had drafted a revised one for me to sign). I would move to the corporate office sometime after November 15, and they had several important projects they were eager for me to work on. Jim named a few: evaluating our overseas buying offices; continuing to serve as chairman of Federated's cosmetics team; and exploring possible expansion of Bloomingdale's into Japan—negotiations that I had recently initiated. I asked if they really wanted me to stay on, because I had no need to remain if they didn't want me to. They insisted they did.

Alan and Jim were also concerned about the announcement. They wanted to announce my intention to retire, as we called it, and Mike Gould's selection as my successor that Friday. They were concerned it would leak to the press.

I was more concerned that I have time to tell all my people at Bloomingdale's properly. I was also concerned that if the announcement were made Friday, or even late Thursday, it would only be printed on Saturday, and that the trade papers who only publish weekdays would be scooped. We agreed to hold the announcement until the following Monday.

The next day, however, I got a call from *The New York Times*. They were preparing an article saying that my successor was about to be named. I would not comment.

The stories took on a life of their own and seemed to gather momentum. Wednesday's *Times* speculated that my replacement would be either Roger Farrah or Mike Gould. Thursday, *Women's Wear* announced on its front page that Mike Gould would replace me. *The Wall Street Journal* on Friday confirmed that Mike Gould was to be named as my successor, as did the *Times* on Saturday. By Monday, Federated was faced with the dilemma of making an announcement that was no longer news.

The week between the meeting with Alan and the official announcement was very difficult. That Monday night I told Lee and we decided to invite all our children for dinner on Friday to tell them. On Tuesday I started to tell my close friends and merchants. They had hoped that the rumors they heard were not true. Meeting with Lester, Carl, and Barbara, friends I'd worked with, in some cases for forty years, was very difficult. The thought that a time would come when we were not working together was hard to bear. Even telling executives I'd known for a shorter time, but still felt very close to, such as Jeff, Kal, Ann Stock, John Jay, Gordon Cooke, Sue Kronick, or Margaret Hofbeck (our senior vice president of human resources) was very emotional. I kept a supply of handkerchiefs handy in my office for them.

On Wednesday morning I had breakfast with Mike Gould at my home. As we were still trying to keep the appointment secret I thought a private breakfast appropriate. Lee wanted to meet my successor as well. It was the first time Mike and I had met since our argument several years earlier. The meeting went as well as could be expected. Mike was solicitous and concerned that the transition go smoothly, and I told him I would help in every way I could.

As I continued to focus on the projects before me, I felt, for lack of a better word, strange. Each meeting with a vendor, each appointment, each decision, each task took on another dimension, although I proceeded with business as usual. If anything I threw myself more into my work. I met with a new young designer, Byron Lars, worked on our fall "Tempo d'Italia" promotion, and planned the opening of our new Mall of America store in August 1992.

On May 20 the announcement that I was to retire was major news, reported in newspapers across the United States as well as in Europe and Japan. *The New York Times* announced the story on their front page.* Bloomingdale's was then on the road to having a good year. I had every reason to expect, based on my projections, that the next year would be even better. I wanted people to realize that I was the one who accomplished that. I took enormous pride in Bloomingdale's and wanted the store to continue to succeed. In my era, Bloomingdale's became something very different from what it was. And what concerned me most was that ten, twenty, or fifty years from now, people would recognize that in the thirty years that Marvin Traub ran it, Bloomingdale's became a worldwide, powerful retailing institution. Accordingly, it was all the more important that Bloomingdale's thrive and grow even stronger in the years to come. Despite our past problems, I wanted Mike Gould to succeed.

---

* Two days later, on May 22, 1991, the *Times* did something unique: an editorial about Bloomingdale's under my tenure becoming "to retailing what Barnum & Bailey is to circuses: The Greatest Show on Earth." The editorial is reprinted in full on page 358. I liked that.

♭

There was another strange aspect to the succession. This was the first time since graduating business school in 1949 that I had no idea of what I would be doing a year hence. A whole new world of concerns opened. I wondered how life would be different once I left my position.

Being chairman of Bloomingdale's is one of the more powerful jobs in worldwide retailing. If I wanted a table at a restaurant, my secretary could call up at the last minute. If we were late, they kept the table open for us. There are a lot of privileges that went with both Bloomingdale's and my very high profile position all over the

The New York Times

WEDNESDAY, MAY 22, 1991

Topics of The Times

The Best of Bloomies

During the 41 years that Marvin Traub worked at Bloomingdale's — first as a merchandising assistant, eventually as chairman and chief executive officer — the store became to retailing what Barnum & Bailey is to circuses: the Greatest Show on Earth.

Bloomingdale's shopping bags have been seen all over the world, as evocative of a trip to New York as miniatures of the Statue of Liberty and ashtrays from the Empire State Building.

Bloomingdale's buyers have been all over the world, too. So, in a sense, have Bloomingdale's customers, even those who never leave town. To buy a dress from France, a stool from Japan or a cooking utensil from Germany, after all, they need only travel to the corner of 59th Street and Lexington Avenue.

Which is as far as they have to travel to see a room in a Spanish hacienda, a Provencal mas or a French maison de ville. Bloomingdale's model rooms have enchanted two, maybe three generations of gawkers. Sometimes, during the store's famous "country" promotions, they're as far as one has to go to see Israel, or China.

Marvin Traub is stepping down as chairman of Bloomingdale's later this year. He deserves having had as much fun being ringmaster as the rest of us have had shopping in his marvelous circus.

world. I had become used to the perks of being Mr. Bloomingdale's. I wondered if I would still have them as Marvin Traub.

b

Mike came aboard the first week in August. He addressed our co-workers and gave a gracious speech about the respect he had for Bloomingdale's and for me; he said he wanted to spend the next few months learning and listening. Over the course of the next week I began to introduce Mike to many of our most important resources. I found Mike had his own style and was outspoken in his opinions. The transition went by very quickly.

I pondered what would be an appropriate way to wind up forty-one years at Bloomingdale's and a special career in department store retailing. As I had done for every other matter in my business career, I sat down to organize all that I had to get done. I wanted to say farewell to our suppliers and also introduce Mike Gould to them. Accordingly, I made a schedule to go into the market from August until the end of October. In terms of overseas, we planned special events to occur at the time of my final visit to the Prêt-à-Porter in Paris in October, as Paris and the Prêt had been an important part of my career. For the stores I made a plan to visit each of the branches. Each planned their own farewell. The last two days I would visit the buying organization, and my final day, I decided, would be spent at Bloomingdale's 59th Street.

Sue Kronick, our senior executive vice president of stores, accompanied me on my trips to most of the fifteen stores, each of which planned its own special event for my visit. One of the Florida stores dedicated a plaque in my honor at the main door; another had a time capsule embedded in the column next to the escalator; still a third had a marching band to greet me. One Washington store gave me an exclusive Waterford crystal jar in the shape of the Capitol filled with jellybeans. Philadelphia gave me an album going back to the opening-day event. Every branch store gave me a framed photo of the store signed with best wishes from all the associates. Each store visit was filled with emotion and affection.

b

The months preceding my last day at Bloomingdale's were a whirl-wind of events. That first week I received many calls from friends and associates, among them Mel Jacobs, Barbara Bass, Mike Steinberg, and Calvin Klein. Within a week, I also received a call from Leonard Lauder and Ralph Lauren, who wanted to organize a dinner on my behalf. We agreed to hold a benefit for the Marvin and Lee Traub scholarship fund at Harvard, and set the date of November 12 at the Waldorf-Astoria Hotel.

I am still moved by the enormous outpouring of affection I received. The number of events, parties, and celebrations in my honor was extraordinary. What struck me most was how many lives I had touched in my career at Bloomingdale's, whether it was kitchen employees at a branch store restaurant or famous French designers.

On September 30, *The New York Times* gave a party in my honor at the Rainbow Room, capped off with a chorus line of Rockettes dancing as the *Times* wheeled in a huge cake in the shape of the Bloomingdale's Big Brown Bag. They invited my friends and associates, including Donna Karan, Isaac Mizrahi, Ralph Lauren, Joe Ronchetti, Harold Krensky, and Jim Brady. And the Bloomingdale's management committee gave a memorable dinner at "21," with gifts, toasts, jokes, and speeches from the heart by my associates.

One of the most touching tributes occurred in Paris that October at the time of the Prêt-à-Porter. On October 21, the Chambre Syndicale, the governing body of the French textile and apparel industry, gave a party in my honor at the Hotel Crillon hosted by Pierre Bergé, Sonia Rykiel, and Jacques Mouclier, the president of the Chambre Syndicale. France had always been very special and important to me. It was great to see so many of my old friends there including Count René de Chambrun, the head of Baccarat, as well as Christian Lacroix, Carla Fendi, Jean-Pierre Dumas of Hermès, Didier Grumbach, Ira Neimark, Burt Tanksy, Leah Gottlieb of Gottex. Who else? Jacques and Louise Rouet of the House of Dior were also there, as well as Jean Taittinger, Henri Recamier, Maurice Bidermann and his famous half-sister Regine, Karl Lagerfeld, Nino Cerruti, Claude Montana, and our own Kal Ruttenstein, plus three hundred guests.

For the party in my honor Chantal Rousseau,* our European representative, undertook an enormous surprise. She asked more than one hundred top French and Italian designers and principals to each take one page of a special book and to make a sketch, a drawing, or a photograph recalling some special anecdote involving me. Carla Fendi, for example, had a drawing made commemorating my first visit to the Fendi shop in Rome in 1967; Karl Lagerfeld drew a cartoon of Lee and me with Lee saying, "Marvin where do I shop now?" Emanuel Ungaro did four pages of spectacular artwork with a lengthy description of our friendship. Yves Saint Laurent drew a red heart with a note about his affection for me. Franco Moschino drew a torn heart, writing "My heart is broken." All of this was bound in an extraordinary album specially created by Hermès for the occasion.†

One of the more extraordinary evenings in my life was the November 12 dinner Ralph Lauren and Leonard Lauder gave in my honor at the Waldorf-Astoria to benefit the Marvin and Lee Traub flexible scholarship fund at Harvard. Attended by fourteen hundred friends and associates, I was moved by the presence of everyone from Ralph and Leonard and Harvard's president, Neil Rudenstine, who spoke beautifully, to the Harvard Glee Club, who performed, to the designers who flew in from Europe; from my associates at Bloomingdale's to my friends in the industry and the people I worked with my whole career. That night a twelve-minute video was screened that had been produced especially for the event with interviews with Ralph, Leonard, Mel Jacobs, Donna Karan, Giorgio Armani, Isaac Mizrahi, Norma Kamali, Oscar de la Renta, and Lee—

---

* Chantal Rousseau was one of the special people who helped make Bloomingdale's the success it is. A vivacious, attractive Parisian, she and I have worked closely for over twenty years. Chantal, a Bloomingdale's vice president, was our representative for Paris and Europe. She reported directly to me. We talk almost every Sunday. She has always enjoyed the total confidence of the French designers. She kept me up to date on what was happening in Paris and Europe, while I kept her informed about the store's plans and activities. She is one of the reasons why Bloomingdale's was able to be first so many times in Europe.

† On a much less formal note, my very close friends the Demerys threw a private black-tie dinner party, taking over a wonderful restaurant in the seventh arrondissement. The theme and music were Provençal; the dancing and drinking were lively, going on until almost two in the morning. In the middle of the evening everyone suddenly donned special "Marvin" T-shirts designed by the Demerys.

it was at moments very funny and throughout deeply touching. It all meant a great deal to me; I was struck by all the relationships I had enjoyed.

b

Before I knew it, it was November 15, 1991. My last day started early, as most of them do. There was an 8:30 A.M. meeting at 59th Street with all our buyers and merchandise managers in the Show-time Cafe. Lee was there to enjoy it with me. Each division had worked out skits and songs about me, with each more amusing than the last. I spoke to the group from the heart and told them how much they meant to me and how much the success of Bloomingdale's came from the talent and creativity of the merchants.

Then we went down to the main floor, to the steps adjacent to what had been the fur department. I thought back to the many meetings I had held there announcing country promotions, introducing Valentino and Dr. Ruth, announcing that Bloomingdale's was for sale, announcing the bankruptcy, and, most recently, introducing Mike Gould. Now the main floor from Lexington to Third Avenue was filled with over fifteen hundred of my coworkers. They backed up to the escalators and sat on the stairs. Every inch of space was taken. I saw many faces I knew well, faces I had greeted every morning, faces I saw at night. These were people with whom we had created a special feeling, a sense of purpose, camaraderie, and fun.

Jim Gundel and Marion Goodman, the 59th Street's store manager and operating vice president, had made a video of many Bloomingdale's people saying goodbye to me. They presented me with a book with pictures of my coworkers, and with a pillow inscribed "Like no other store in the world." Then Marion announced a special surprise for me: I heard cymbals and drums echoing as a marching band paraded down the main aisle followed by a group of enthusiastic cheerleaders with pom-poms wearing black sweatshirts spelling out Marvin Traub. The cheerleaders were Bloomingdale's associates who had rehearsed conscientiously for the occasion; they sang a song they had written especially for me and cheered loudly. Their love and affection was heartfelt and the Bloomingdale's team know I love a marching band.

I am not one given to open displays of emotion, but I choked back some tears at that particular moment. Lee and I looked at each other—Peggy, a Bloomingdale's merchandise manager then, was there, too—and we hugged each other. The ladies came up the steps, spread across the balcony, and gave a great cheer for me. Then it was my turn to speak. I tried to thank them all and tell them how much each of them meant to me and how together we had created such a special institution. There was a kinship and a bond between me and each of the employees that I will long remember, and I'm sure they felt the same way.

There was also a final executive committee luncheon, at which time my portrait was unveiled. The portrait now hangs in the center of the boardroom alongside portraits of my esteemed predecessors, Lyman and Sam Bloomingdale, Harold Krensky, Jed Davidson, Jim Schoff, Sr., and Larry Lachman. The painting by Peter Egeli portrays me in a gray-flannel business suit, wearing a blue shirt with a white collar and a blue tie, standing relaxed, with my glasses in one hand, as I often do. It is meant to convey the closeness and intimacy I develop in my business relationships. The portrait does create a strong presence and I jokingly told the assembled group that I hoped that whenever they met in the boardroom in the future they would feel that I was still watching everything they did.

Afterward Jeff Sherman and Mike Gould both made thoughtful speeches. Jeff presented me with the gift I had given to some of our most distinguished retiring executives: a Bloomingdale's brass footprint, a reminder of the days when they were embedded in Third Avenue, leading to the El. The plaque was inscribed: "With respect and admiration to the man who has left an indelible influence on all of us. With love and affection." We toasted each other.

The rest of that day I walked through each of the departments of the store shaking hands individually with the coworkers, both on the selling floor and behind the scenes.

By 5:00 P.M. I had made my way through the store and said goodbye personally to many of the store's more than two thousand employees. I had just completed walking through the main-floor cosmetics area and was about to leave B'way when a white-haired gentleman in a raincoat stopped to greet me. He seemed a bit disheveled, and with his raincoat and big brown shopping bag, he looked like just another shopper frazzled by the week's work and commute. But I recognized him immediately. It was Lyman Bloomingdale, Sam's son, who by coincidence was doing some shopping in the store his grandfather founded. He shook my hand and wished me well. I will never forget that moment and I would like to believe it was no accident. I have always felt that running a great department store was something akin to a trust. And that night, at that moment, I felt as if the Bloomingdale family was thanking me for my years of stewardship.

Drawing by Modell; © 1976 The New Yorker Magazine, Inc.

CHAPTER 15

A Second Career

From the moment of the announcement that I would be retiring from Bloomingdale's, my phone started to ring with job offers. Norman Matthews, a close friend and former Federated president, invited me to lunch. He gave me very sound advice.

"Marvin," he said, "field all the phone calls. Hear out the proposals. Take the meetings that interest you. And then think about it. Before you know it, you'll be too busy to think about what to do." I would now give the same advice to anyone retiring or leaving a position. It worked for me.

In the first week alone I got calls from a group negotiating to buy a large cosmetics company who wanted me to manage the company; Jerry Speyer of Tishman Speyer called about a 250,000-square-foot store in Berlin they wanted me to consult on; Donna Karan wanted me to work with her; someone else called to see if I would be willing to take the helm of a billion-dollar company in the Midwest that was in financial trouble. My calendar started to fill with breakfasts, lunches, and dinners to talk about my future.

Over the next few months, as I went about my Bloomingdale's business and started to make my last farewells, I continued to hear about all sorts of opportunities. At lunch, Ralph Lauren wanted to explore my working with him on two new projects he was considering. I had breakfast with Jim Robinson of American Express, who expressed interest in retaining me as a consultant. When I visited Jones New York, a leading manufacturer of better sportswear, the CEO, Sidney Kimmel, pulled me aside to ask if I would be available to work with him. Elsa Perretti requested my help in negotiating her new contract with Tiffany's and asked me to consider becoming a consultant or participant in her business. Each day seemed to bring new offers.

At the same time, Federated was keen on my continued participation as vice chairman of the company through August 1993. The main item on their agenda for me was creating a Bloomingdale's in Japan, a top-secret project that began to take a great deal of my time. As Federated was still in bankruptcy, the company could not enter into agreements without court approval. Furthermore, news of a deal with Japan could upset negotiations with creditors.

Shortly after Federated filed for bankruptcy I asked Bill Miller, who was familiar with international markets, whether I should look into licensing Bloomingdale's in Japan. With Bill's approval, I had then contacted Tosh Yamamoto, who by discreet inquiries—I had learned my lesson about how to do business in Japan—ascertained that Tokyu Department Stores was very interested in a joint venture to develop Bloomingdale's stores at several key locations in Tokyo over the next decade. They saw this as a great opportunity and wanted to structure the deal basically as a license arrangement in which they would supply all the funding; Bloomingdale's would advise as to the merchandise, marketing, and store design and would receive a royalty based on sales, as well as 25 percent ownership. The financial estimate was that Federated would receive $125 million in income over five years, with no financial investment on its part. For a company coming out of bankruptcy, that would be quite a deal.

The Japanese insisted that I be part of the deal. They were anxious to pay my salary and have me serve as chairman of the joint venture. I would in return give the equivalent of one week a month of my time, including visits to Japan. Tokyu proposed generous compensation for me plus participation in the joint venture. Negotiations proceeded through the fall. The Japanese and I developed detailed financial plans to present to Federated. With the assistance of Nigel French, an international retail consultant knowledgeable about Japan, I advised the Japanese how to translate their plans so that they could be understood by an American company. We converted all numbers from yen to dollars, all space requirements from *tsubos* to square feet, and we redid the entire profit and loss statements along the lines of an American rather than a Japanese statement.

b

By the Monday after my last day at Bloomingdale's, all that was definite of my future plans was that Lee and I were leaving for a three-week vacation in the South Pacific. I was anxious to get as far away as possible from 59th Street, feeling this would make for an easier transition. Things had moved so fast that the twenty-hour plane ride to Australia was the first chance I had to think about all that had happened in the last few weeks, the past few months, the last year, the last few years in fact.

By the time I moved into Federated's corporate offices in December 1991, I had received so many diverse offers that I knew that I would not be spending full time on Federated matters. I did not enjoy going to my dark, modest office at Federated and could not imagine spending the next few years there. I had never signed the new contract Alan and Jim had proffered me, so we negotiated a deal by which I would give Federated a quarter of my time for half my former salary. I would be free to consult for other companies, but for no other American department store.

Once that agreement was in place, I finalized negotiations to consult for American Express and Jones New York. Although I did help Elsa Perretti, we never arrived at an arrangement to work further together. Similarly, although I had extensive discussions with Donna Karan, our talks fell through. Ralph Lauren, whom I very much wanted to work with, was concerned that my arrangement with Jones New York might conflict. Six months later, Ralph and I met again, and he changed his mind: He decided my current experience made me all the more valuable as a consultant, and I was hired.

I was quickly getting more offers than I could handle alone. At the same time, Lester Gribetz resigned from Bloomingdale's after a disagreement with Mike Gould. The next day, he became a partner in Marvin Traub Associates and we took handsome office space on the fortieth floor of Carnegie Hall Tower with a dramatic view of Central Park. *The New York Times* and *The Wall Street Journal* took note. So did the retailing community and more calls started to come in.

What I quickly discovered was how valuable our experience was. Our talent at creating excitement for new products and at bringing the right parties together in a deal, combined with the great number of relationships we had built, proved invaluable. In no time we were looking at more than a dozen different ventures. It soon became clear that we were most comfortable taking on only a limited number of large consulting clients on an annual retainer, while looking for challenging projects in which we could have equity. We also discovered that as each deal required its own experts, we were free to bring in other talented executives as partners. For example, we are now involved in several ventures with Joe Ronchetti and Joe Spellman, the former chairman and current executive vice president of Elizabeth Arden, two of the most gifted marketers Lester and I have ever worked with.

Marvin Traub Associates learns as it goes along. Our long-term corporate consulting projects have had various degrees of success. American Express, for example, turned out to be one of our most challenging consulting assignments. We joined AMEX at a tumultuous time when they were rethinking their position in the credit card world as well as examining their direct market strategies.

Working with Jones New York's Sidney Kimmel and Andy Grossman has been very stimulating. Jones is the dominant supplier of sportswear to department stores with a sound record of growth in career and casual sportswear, petite and large sizes, and dresses, growing from less than $300 million in 1990 to $500 million plus in 1993, in a difficult retailing climate.

Polo/Ralph Lauren is a business I know, understand and appreciate, and I have thoroughly enjoyed working with Ralph, Peter Strom, and the Ralph Lauren organization—I find them a very creative team and have been able to contribute to many of their different businesses.

Federated was more problematic. On February 5, 1992, Federated came out of bankruptcy. It was a great achievement, highlighted by the fact that Macy's filed for bankruptcy that same week. My first order of business for Federated was trying to work out the deal with Japan. I made some six visits to Tokyo in the course of a year and a half, meeting with Tokyu, a $3 billion department store that was a division of a $27 billion corporation. They had already selected five locations for Bloomingdale's and were prepared to invest almost $900 million. We had put together projections that showed our building a $2 billion business in Japan in a decade.

In March, one month after Federated emerged from bankruptcy,

Alan, Jim, Mike Gould, and I visited Japan together with Nigel French, our London-based consultant, and his American president Patty Coughlin. We were hosted by the Tokyu people and we in turn hosted a dinner for them. Alan was fascinated by Japanese retailing. Jim was intrigued by the way the stores were organized. My impression was that Mike was generally unhappy to be there; he appeared to have little interest in the project.

As the negotiations got more and more serious, a problem arose. In our discussions we had projected Bloomingdale's Japan to be treated almost as a separate division. Mike Gould objected to that. He thought that Bloomingdale's Japan should report to him. He felt strongly enough to imply that he might be willing to leave over the issue. More important, he did not want to go ahead with Bloomingdale's Japan. He thought it would distract him from Bloomingdale's core business, and he questioned whether Tokyu was the right partner for the deal—whether their image and reputation in Japan was consistent with that of Bloomingdale's.

In June Alan told the Japanese that they would not be going ahead with the deal. The Japanese asked that Federated not announce a formal decision for another month. They were afraid that the public announcement of a refusal by Federated would sully their image in Japan. The Japanese still hoped to convince Mike Gould and Alan Questrom. They met with them again. At one point Tokyu offered to purchase 25 percent of Federated's new stock issue (10 million out of the 40 million shares) if that would help. But Questrom said no.

At the same time the Japanese asked me to try and find a new partner. I immediately contacted Mel Jacobs at Saks Fifth Avenue, who expressed great interest. We then met with Paul Soldatis and Savio Tung, the Investcorp partners on the Saks board, who wanted to proceed. I then spoke to Federated and offered to drop out of my consulting arrangement with them, in favor of another client whom I described to Federated as another American retailer but with whom I would work on overseas operations. Federated agreed. I negotiated a termination to my Federated agreement as of July 18. The following day, Saks Fifth Avenue retained me. It was hard to believe that after all these years, I was working with Saks.

Three weeks after Saks retained me, Mel Jacobs, Phil Miller,

Savio Tung, Paul Soldatis, and I, along with Nigel French, were back in Japan meeting with Tokyu. The Saks group moved much faster than Federated and by the time we left Japan we had an offer on the table. The chemistry was good, but unfortunately in 1992–93 the Japanese economy rapidly fell apart, and the department store business was particularly hard hit. Expansion was almost totally set aside as the Japanese grappled with new economic problems. Saks Fifth Avenue Japan was put on hold. At a certain point, I set it aside as well, and began to focus on other projects.

b

By June, seven months after I had left Bloomingdale's, I was involved in a broad range of activities. I had acted as a consultant reviewing the Australian retailing situation on a two-day visit; as an investment adviser, aiding in the purchase of Lacoste from Crystal Brands for $31 million; and we were consulting to *Men's Health* magazine. At the same time I was learning about exciting new forms of retailing.

In February 1992, shortly after I left Federated, I went to West Chester, Pennsylvania, to visit the QVC ("Quality, Value, Convenience") network to learn about home shopping. Joe Spellman, Lester Gribetz, and I accompanied Diane Von Furstenberg to QVC to discuss her designing a line of ready-to-wear and home furnishings. QVC programs 168 hours a week and reaches 44 million cable TV viewers. I watched Susan Lucci demonstrate her hair care products and sell $550,000 in an hour and $1.2 million over a weekend. This was the first really effective new way to reach large numbers of shoppers that I had seen in many years. I was very impressed with what I saw and we quickly reached an agreement, and Diane created a line called Silk Assets for QVC. On November 7, 1992, in her first appearance on the program, she sold $1.3 million worth of clothes. On her second appearance she sold $800,000.* Diane had asked her good friend Barry Diller to advise her. We met with Barry several times. Barry did his own research and was so impressed with QVC's

---

* Diane later reintroduced the wrap-dress for which she was famous and sold $600,000 of dresses.

potential that in spring 1993 he invested $25 million in the company and is now its chairman and CEO. Since Barry became chairman, the perception of QVC has clearly changed. As more and more manufacturers seek to participate, QVC is regarded as a hot growth company.

Lester and I quickly became involved in a number of projects involving selling through television. We developed a home furnishings program with Diane as well. We raised almost $1 million to form a new company to sell foods from Thailand, packaged with a brass wok and Thai utensils, to be marketed through an infomercial with Lucie Arnaz, home shopping department stores and food stores as well as QVC.

I also brought Phil Miller and Mel Jacobs of Saks Fifth Avenue together with QVC. Saks became very enthusiastic and decided to market their Real Clothes collection and had sales of $570,000 the first hour. Saks is developing an ongoing strategy with several major programs in the future.

Many retailers viewed TV home shopping as a competitor, but I saw that the medium could offer support to a department store, broadening the store's reach and increasing its sales volume.

I found myself exploring more and more exciting new projects. Projects such as a private label spa cosmetic collection for QVC and stores, or a Scaasi special occasion jewelry collection for QVC developed with the well-known designer. I introduced the concept of selling books to QVC with an appearance by the author; and on April 27, 1993, Barbara Taylor Bradford, a Random House author, sold 4,500 autographed books in a half hour.

Leaving Bloomingdale's presented me with the opportunity to acquire equity in new or turnaround ventures. In November, my son Andy, then a Macy's merchandise manager, approached me about acquiring Block Industries, a $38 million manufacturer of large- and regular-sized men's sportswear and sent me a detailed business plan. I agreed that the company had great potential, particularly with regard to the growth of large-size men's apparel. Block was part of a $1.5 billion conglomerate, National Service Industries, which had not given the company the focus it needed. Over the next six months, I worked closely with Andy and his partner Ken Lazar in finding investors, structuring the acquisition, and closing the deal, which we did in June. Andy then resigned from Macy's to become president of Block Industries. Block grew 25 percent in its first year with a substantial profit improvement and is now creating a Nino Cerruti sportswear collection aimed at department stores, and an Izod big and tall collection.

Several months later, Vestar, an investment banking firm, spoke to Lester and me about analyzing Conran's Habitat, a home furnishings chain, as a possible acquisition for them. Conran's, we discovered, was losing $13 million on sales of $51 million a year, or more than $1 million a month. As we looked the company over, Lester and I believed this was an exciting turnaround situation.

Vestar, however, did not want to work with the management, and lost interest. Despite Conran's dismal record of having lost $40 million over the last three years, Lester and I saw an opportunity. Conran's was owned by Storehouse P.L.C., a $1.6 billion British corporation that had signed on three of the store's leases, which made them liable in case of a bankruptcy.

Lester and I proposed to David Simmons, chairman of Habitat, that we assume their liabilities and set an advantageous purchase price comparing our offer with what it would cost Storehouse to close the U.S. stores or file for Chapter 11 protection. Simmons agreed with the concept. Three months of intense negotiations followed. I brought in Andy's partner from Block Industries, Ken Lazar, to help with the negotiations. We were negotiating simultaneously with Storehouse, Sir Terence Conran (who owned the name Conran's), and Ikea, which was purchasing Habitat UK and Habitat France.

In early November 1992, after a week of all-night sessions and round-the-clock negotiations in New York, David Simmons set a deadline of Wednesday, November 18, at 4:00 P.M. to complete the negotiations; otherwise he would leave for London with a bankruptcy attorney. A meeting of Storehouse's board had been set for Thursday morning at 9:00 A.M. in London, at which time David would either present them with our deal or announce his decision to file for bankruptcy and close the stores.

By Wednesday, although we had arrived at attractive terms with Storehouse, we did not have all our financing in place. We were reluctant to commit, so David went back to London, lawyer in tow.

By 6:30 P.M. that evening we were convinced that we had made a mistake. We found a new financing opportunity and called David's associate Michael Fleming, who had stayed behind to file for Chapter 11. We brought him back to the offices of our attorney, Joel Yunis at Rosenman Colin. Michael contacted his attorneys who had already flown back to Washington, and they came right back.

We negotiated from 10:00 P.M. to 4:00 A.M. before completing the deal. Michael had David Simmons paged in Heathrow Airport when he got off the plane. He told him we had a deal and David could inform the board at their meeting that morning. The board approved. Lester, Ken, and I now owned the company. I was back in the home furnishings business.

In no time we were able to put together a team that reunited many of the people with whom I had built the Bloomingdale's home furnishings business. Lester became president and Carl Levine signed on to consult with us. Helene Suval, the Bloomingdale's senior vice president of tabletop and housewares, became our executive vice president and general merchandise manager. My daughter Peggy resigned as group manager of lamps, gifts, and pillows at Bloomingdale's to become merchandise manager of lamps and domestics; Eileen Sweeney, a former Bloomingdale's china and glass buyer, resigned as merchandise manager of tabletop for the Federated corporate office to join us as merchandise manager of tabletop and housewares; and Wei Fan Ho resigned as a Bloomingdale's furniture buyer to become merchandise manager of furniture and rugs. Dan Levy, a former Bloomingdale's cosmetics buyer and vice chairman of Montgomery Ward, joined us as chairman and CEO. I remained chairman of the executive committee.

Lester and I found our first meetings like a Bloomingdale's reunion. The old gang was saddling up to ride again.

Forty years ago Lester and I had met at Bloomingdale's. Now, at a time when many of our contemporaries were slowing down, we had taken on the difficult challenge of turning around a $50 million home furnishings chain that is in trouble.

In spring 1993 we began another exciting venture, creating a jewelry company with Elizabeth Taylor. Elizabeth has two incredibly successful fragrances, White Diamonds and Passion, that represent a $150 million sales volume for Elizabeth Arden. Joe Ronchetti, former chairman of Elizabeth Arden, and Joe Spellman, executive vice president of Arden, joined with me and Lester in the negotiations.

Elizabeth's own jewelry is world famous; she has a great interest in and knowledge of jewelry, very high standards, and is used to earning substantial royalties for her ventures. Our first sublicensee will be the world's largest manufacturer of costume jewelry—Avon, which looks forward to launching the collection in time for Christmas 1993. With Elizabeth's help they have created an exciting collection. We are currently negotiating with several other potential licensees as well.

We found Elizabeth easy to work with: She is lovely and has tremendous presence—she is very much a star. She is also very well represented by Chen Sam, her business manager, and Neil Papiano, her attorney. Neil is a very tough negotiator—it took us ten months to conclude an agreement—but in the end, we all arrived at a deal we are very happy with.

When I left Bloomingdale's I had no idea how challenging and exciting my new career would be. What I found was that I was immediately immersed in so many areas that it was as if I were running a new department store—a department store without walls.

To give some idea of the scope of my activities: With Conran's, I am involved in specialty retailing and building a national chain; with Block Industries, I am a manufacturer and exploring niche marketing of large-size men's apparel. I am very involved in selling through television whether by infomercials or on QVC. Almost every day brings in new opportunities to consult or acquire equity in a growing business. I am represented by the Washington Speakers Bureau and make several paid speeches each year.

Today I am earning substantially more than I did in my best years as chairman of Bloomingdale's. I am engaged in all the traditional businesses that I learned at Bloomingdale's—home furnishings, clothing, cosmetics—and am developing new products and new businesses in areas such as housewares and jewelry, much as I did throughout my career. But the methods of reaching the customers are varied, and each represents a different aspect in the ongoing revolution in retailing.

"My girlfriend over in Central Planning says if everything stays on track it's definitely Bloomie's and Saks by the mid-nineties!"

CHAPTER 16

The Future of Retailing

Since the end of World War II, retailing has grown from a downtown business to a multistoried one focused on lifestyles and family. Fashion and fashion change was once a movement that began with the couture and limited specialty stores in a few markets such as Paris and New York and trickled down over time to consumers across the nation. Today, fashion leadership is no longer dominated by New York but fans out across the country. With the advent of mass communication, fashion change can move rapidly—consumers everywhere are interested in the latest trends. And fashion is no longer the province of designer names but can be found at Liz Claiborne, Jones New York, or Ellen Tracy as well.

In the sixties and seventies, Bloomingdale's lead in fashion merchandising, exciting merchandise presentation and the development of boutiques was followed by Federated's other divisions and other department stores. The Bloomingdale's boutique concept has since spread from apparel designers to more moderate suppliers and has extended from apparel to other areas such as home furnishings, housewares, and cosmetics. Today, one sees boutiques for everything from Ralph Lauren Home Furnishings and Waterford Crystal to Guess, Esprit, and JH Collectibles.

Macy's remade their Herald Square store in the seventies, eliminating the basement, turning it into the Cellar for housewares and providing space throughout the store to emphasize cosmetics and fashions, open designer shops, and do themed promotions. At the same time, Macy's changed their advertising so it was almost indistinguishable from that of Bloomingdale's. At one point in the 1970s, I was convinced that if one week *The New York Times* ran one of our ads upside down by mistake then the next week Macy's would have an upside down ad as well.

Our competitors all shopped us regularly—we were flattered by the attention. Suppliers began to focus more on life-styles and launches. At the same time we promoted Saturday's Generation and the Upper East Side as Bloomingdale's country, our neighborhood bank began advertising that we were in "Dry Dock Country." Ten years after we launched "Like no other store in the world," Mercedes launched a new campaign "Like no other car in the world."

The idea that shopping could be fun gained credence in stores all across the country. Retailing was changing and Bloomingdale's stood for change. As life-styles shifted from formal to casual in the sixties and seventies, Bloomingdale's took a leadership role by emphasizing sportswear and capitalizing on that trend. We were not alone. So did the Gap, The Limited, and other specialty retailers. So did some department stores.

The revolution in marketing casual sportswear was illustrated dramatically in April 1992 when the cover of the hundreth anniversary issue of *Vogue*, the bastion of designers and couture, featured ten famous models photographed in the exact same outfit: Gap white denim jeans and a matching Gap woven shirt. The message was clear: Fashion, like retailing, is all about change.

b

I have gone, in my lifetime, from working in a basement to creating a store like no other to working with new technologies in order to fashion the department store without walls. Yet through all this, the principles and beliefs developed at Bloomingdale's remain true.

There are many important lessons to be drawn from the Bloomingdale's experience. Bloomingdale's became a legend based on a number of sound retailing principles. I have tried to list nineteen of the most significant ones, drawn from my experience, including some new ones I believe will be of particular importance in the future:

Retailing Principles for the Nineties

1.   To build a successful retail business, define your core customer and merchandise the store—its price points, its

assortments, presentation and sales promotion—for that target group. Bloomingdale's defined our customer as an affluent, upwardly mobile, image-conscious twenty-five- to fifty-five-year-old who enjoyed a high level of discretionary spending.

2.   There must be a consistency that extends to every merchandise area of the store. The same taste level and price points should be found in menswear, ready-to-wear, home furnishings, and children's.

3.   At times it is appropriate and even necessary to give up volume, even profitable volume, by eliminating departments or divisions inconsistent with a store's image.

4.   Most stores carry very similar assortments; it is the unique merchandise, be it 10, 20, or 30 percent of the assortment, that creates a distinctive reputation.

5.   Developing unique and exclusive merchandise must be a clearly thought out, widely understood goal of a store if it desires to differentiate itself from its competitors.

6.   Value is what the customer thinks is a fair price, and it is not necessarily related to markup or cost. Regardless of the cost of an item, the customer will have a sense of what price is appropriate—this was the basis of our profitable furniture import program.

7.   Great stores are created in the image and creativity of one individual who then moves that store to the next plateau. That is the role for the merchandising principal who aspires to create a unique retailing institution.

8.   Publicity creates an image far better than paid advertising because it is more credible.

9.   The image of a store is like a good restaurant: the food or merchandise is a major ingredient, but the sum total of

the shopping experience—the exterior, window display, presentation, service, gift wrapping, logo, shopping bags, delivery, return policy—all create the image.

10.   Designers can play a vital role in developing the character of a store and building volume and adding distinction.

11.   The definition of a destination store is one that customers go out of their way to shop at. There are few true destination retailers. To become a destination, a store must anticipate or create trends, be it in fashion or home furnishings. For example, Saturday's Generation recognized the new life-style of the seventies, a casual yet elegant look for the weekend in sharp contrast to the career clothes worn during the week.

12.   Convenience and service are priorities for consumers. It is not enough anymore to have merchandise distinction; the department store customer today looks for superior service as well.

13.   Enthusiastic participation of the organization based on understanding of a clearly defined goal or vision creates a great store. Every merchant in the store must speak the same language.

14.   Cosmetics can create excitement, profit, build traffic, and serve a role beyond being merely part of a store's assortment. Cosmetics can be a major differentiator for the department store.

15.   Great stores are built by people: Attracting, retaining, and developing an outstanding and talented management team that can enthusiastically work together to achieve the goals of a company is essential.

I would add some principles that, in addition to the Bloomingdale's approach, are of critical importance to the successful retailer of the nineties:

16.   Technology will be of ever-increasing importance in the nineties—technology that should speed reorders, improve turnover, monitor inventories, analyze the customer data base for effective marketing, speed communications, and reduce expense. The new generation of merchants will have grown up on computers from their preschool days and will see computers as a tool for all operations.

17.   The future of retailing for any type of store, even fine specialty stores, is learning how to be a low-cost operator, recognizing that the definition of low cost can be different for various forms of retailing, be it a Saks Fifth Avenue or a J. C. Penney.

18.   The strongest and most successful businesses for both the store and the supplier are those in which each perceives the other as a partner. They share in the risks, the rewards, and work together on selling, service, and presentation. The huge business Bloomingdale's built with Ralph Lauren, Estée Lauder, Chanel, Donna Karan, and Baccarat are but a few examples of succesful partnerships.

19.   Successful stores are built on two important foundations: carefully thought through strategies combined with good execution. Execution will be the key word of the nineties.

We will soon be starting a new century. Retailing has changed enormously in the last decade. The department store will survive, because department stores meet a legitimate need of consumers. The concept of one-stop shopping, a single store where a customer can put together his or her entire wardrobe or completely furnish a home, is as vital today as it was more than a hundred years ago. If it did not exist, it would be invented to meet the needs of today's consumer. Today's department store, however, has many challenges, and must face up to them.

The department store is a mature industry and stores without a strong, clearly defined focus, and image as well as well-executed strategies, may not make it.

For too long department stores thought they only had to compete among themselves. They did not recognize their new emerging competitors and were caught by surprise when their customers left them to shop at specialty retailers such as Victoria's Secret, Toys-R-Us, and the Gap. In the nineties, as we struggle to cut our deficit, limit tax increases, get our economy moving, and create new jobs, we face a period of slower growth for department stores. As a consequence, some fundamental changes are occurring in retailing.

Today, department stores are moving toward greater and greater centralization. The major retail corporations are eliminating some of their stores and creating larger stores with a more centralized management in order to leverage expenses. For example, by combining G. Fox and Filene's, the May Company immediately reduced the central cost of operating two chains to operating one. This is not an isolated instance. Such mergers are occurring across the country.

In the postwar period, most department store corporations regarded the autonomy of their individual divisions such as Rich's, Dayton's, or Marshall Field's as a strength. Dillard's, however, founded in 1938, was not bound by any such tradition. From day one Dillard's has had a different culture, focused on centralized operations. Today, Dillard's runs over two hundred department stores *centrally*, utilizing very sophisticated computer technology, and only delegates to individual stores reorders and some determination of basic stock levels.

In Florida, for example, Federated combined Maas Brothers into Jordan Marsh, and then both into Burdine's. Jordan Marsh/Boston has been combined with A&S; Goldsmith's was merged into Rich's. What had been eleven Federated divisions are now seven. In 1992, the $1.4 billion volume of A&S/Jordan Marsh was Federated's largest. Burdine's and Bloomingdale's each achieved $1.2 billion.

The merging of stores is an industry-wide trend. This produces economies of scale in buying, leverages purchasing to give greater strength in dealing with suppliers, and capitalizes on merchandising strengths by giving more responsibility to the best buyers. The May Company has combined G. Fox with Filene's, May D&F with Foley's (Foley's was combined earlier with Sanger-Harris, which itself was a combination of Sanger Brothers and A. Harris) and the May Company Los Angeles with Robinson's. Carter Hawley Hale combined the Emporium, formerly Emporium Capwell and Weinstock's, with the Broadway—what were four divisions are now one. Although such economies of scale make department stores better able to compete with other forms of retailing such as specialty retailers and mass market stores, many famous retailing names, such as G. Fox, Sanger's, and Jordan Marsh/Florida have disappeared in the process —and in the future so will others.

The savings achieved by combining stores is only the first step in the restructuring occurring at many department stores. The next step is the centralization of the merchandising function, such as Federated's team buying program. I am not fully convinced team buying produces superior merchandising. It has advantages and disadvantages; for example, it's harder for each store to maintain its local identity, and the process discourages the entrepreneurial spirit of great buyers. Yet it appears to be the wave of the future, and I believe team buying is the first step in the transformation of the department store.

The next step may well be to eliminate much of the separate buying organization. If a team of as few as three buyers and a merchandise manager can select almost 70 percent of the merchandise for a department, do you really need individual buyers and merchandise managers at each store to select the remaining 30 percent? With few exceptions, I think not. Federated, I have to believe, must be examining this.

Many people who know me, or are familiar with Bloomingdale's during my regime, will be surprised to hear me talk about the virtues of team buying—a process in which Bloomingdale's did not participate. I still believe that Bloomingdale's merchandising functions should remain apart because the image of Bloomingdale's is so important to its success and its price lines are different from the rest of Federated. Like Neiman's, it has to buy separately to retain its character, assortments, and place in the market. On the other hand, even for Bloomingdale's there are potential cost and productivity advantages to be realized in combining nonmerchandising functions.

In the next few years, many deparment stores will no doubt change the way they approach their nonmerchandising function. If buying can be centralized, why not accounting, credit, distribution, merchandise information, personnel, accounts payable? Much of this has been accomplished at Macy's, May Company, and Dillard's. Federated has made major strides in this area. It could well be that within the decade we will have a new form of retail chain in which individual stores are shells for a centralized organization. A&S and Rich's, for example, could have separate organizations to run their stores, but most other functions might be done centrally. It could be a far more efficient way to run a $7 billion department store group.

What will this mean for the consumer? With a more efficient organization, the store can work with more narrowly focused assortments, more timely fashion merchandise, and better values. But if centralizing so many functions cannot be done well, the stores, as well as the individual buyers, will lose touch with their customers.

The increasing strength and lower operating costs of this new centralized department store organization will make it more difficult for the smaller independent department store to compete, and we will continue to see a decline in the number of department stores. To survive, smaller stores will have to remain distinctive by developing a special niche, such as Parisian does in the South through extraordinary service and attention to customer needs.

The outlook for the department stores—strong, well-managed groups such as May Company and Dillard's and possibly Federated, whose primary focus is the department store, should continue to show gains in sales, profits, and market share in a mature industry that, over the next ten years, is likely to receive a somewhat smaller share of the total consumer's dollar.

This raises the question: Can Bloomingdale's survive and prosper? Of course it will survive, but it will be a different store. Major retailing institutions tend to reflect the interests, concepts, and direction of their merchandising principal. Bloomingdale's presented a different but successful image in the era of Jed Davidson than in the years I supervised the store. Mike Gould and I have very different ideas, approaches, and priorities, and it is certain that Bloomingdale's has changed and will change in the future. This is inevitable and appropriate—each new management must set the tone for his or her administration.

Bloomingdale's possesses an outstanding name and reputation

globally, and it is putting renewed emphasis on marketing. In the coming years, Bloomingdale's will, in all probability, open new stores. To succeed, Bloomingdale's must reflect the nineties—the yuppies are growing older and have other financial priorities. They are less conspicuous spenders—carefree spending is over—but there is still an affluent consumer.

Today, Bloomingdale's is focusing on bridge and better apparel, featuring designer apparel primarily in the 59th Street store and a few selected branch stores. Bloomingdale's is giving priority to customer service, reducing expense, improving turnover. There is a continued effort to sell exclusive merchandise, but the store is moving away from import buying and country promotions. There appears to be a diminished emphasis on risk taking, product development, and creativity. Bloomingdale's must maintain its magic and mystique to set itself apart; to succeed, it must continue to view itself, and be viewed, as the most exciting store in the world—and maintain and attract talented people to build business in the nineties. That is the challenge it faces.

There are still many opportunities for luxury retailers. With the growth of the bridge business, Saks and Neiman's have both come alive in recent years. Saks, for example, is defining itself in the nineties as the leading retailer of designer and bridge apparel for men as well as women. Saks's management is committed to offering extraordinary service, quality merchandise, and value for its customer. They see the luxury markets as a niche with few competitors. Saks has discontinued virtually all of its home furnishings and is deemphasizing the children's division to focus more on apparel, accessories, and cosmetics.

Saks is reviewing its Fifth Avenue store, floor by floor, featuring new and emerging designers, all with an eye to becoming a mecca for the upscale international consumer. Estimated annual sales at the Fifth Avenue store exceed $300 million, almost $1,000 a square foot. It is now one of the three largest retail stores in the United States, and it is the largest seller of luxury merchandise. At the same time, the chain's own collections, Real Clothes, the Works, and Saks Fifth Avenue Sportswear, are a solid base of well-defined private label merchandise.

Saks seems poised to become more innovative and experimental. They are planning to open five more, 35,000-square-foot stores in resort areas, restructuring their existing stores, and launching a major program of opening free-standing specialty stores such as Armani A-X, Nancy Heller, and Salon Z (a large-size women's apparel store), as well as venturing into television marketing. Saks is refining their direct-mail marketing approach with their "Saks First" program, a target mailing and user-reward program for frequent customers, and by expanding Folio, their catalog operation. All this will create a new form of specialty apparel retailer. Saks's ambitious plans, backed by funding from Investcorp, should take it to well over $2 billion in sales within the decade.

Saks is studying opening stores in new markets outside the continental United States as well. They have announced plans for Hawaii, and are studying Mexico, Europe, and Asia. As Saks's new management team takes over, this new entrepreneurial spirit can bring to Saks in the next decade some of the excitement that Bloomingdale's enjoyed earlier.

Neiman-Marcus, another destination chain of the nineties, has been moving from an entrepreneurially run store to one with more professional management. With this, the sixth management team since Stanley Marcus, Terry Lundgren, the current chairman, is building on the foundation developed by Alan Questrom, with whom Lundgren worked at Bullock's. Because Neiman's has maintained its very strong designer image, the store has also been able to focus on bridge apparel. Neiman's probably possesses the largest bridge volume in the country and is building a sound franchise as a fine-apparel specialty store that can enjoy a profitable billion-dollar business.

Nordstrom's has been a unique retailing phenomenon of the eighties. It enjoys a well-deserved reputation for the finest service in department stores, built on a unique and dedicated organization, the most professional men's, women's, and children's shoe departments in the country, and a very well developed traditional menswear business. Nordstrom's built this business maintaining great local strengths by having each of their buyers responsible for only three stores or less and having them serve as a department manager in one of the three—providing strong local service. That worked very well prior to Nordstrom's going national. Now, with a new generation of management taking over, and some growing pains as a result of going national, Nordstrom's is at a crossroads. I believe this is a time for them to reexamine their future strategy and possibly consider more regional buying.

b

At the same time, mass market operations such as Sears and J. C. Penney are becoming more like traditional department stores every day. The last decade saw a confused Sears rapidly losing market share and position. Sears Merchandising Group, is, nonetheless, a $25 billion business with seven hundred stores in some of the best malls in America. Sears's opportunity is to leverage that strength by becoming more like a moderate-priced department store in assortment and presentation with far greater emphasis on fashion, which today represents only 25 percent of Sear's business, and less emphasis on its traditional low-margin appliance and auto accessories departments. This is a necessary change if Sears is to survive. Almost one half of all American women shop at Sears each year, yet when I visited one of its newest stores the main floor consisted of electronics, auto accessories, and appliances—traditionally male-oriented goods—with no space for cosmetics.

New management is in the process of redefining Sears by investing money from the closed catalog operation and selling off nonretailing divisions to upgrade their existing locations and make them more like department stores. The combination of this new approach and utilizing the names from their mail-order list, some of whom now shop at Sears, for target marketing could create a new Sears over the next decade. It is Sears's challenge now to become an effective low-cost operator and the reduction of 100,000 jobs is a major step in that direction.

Similarly, J. C. Penney has gone through a transition to become more of a fashion and apparel department store with greater emphasis on developing its own brands of ready-to-wear, menswear, and children's apparel. Penney's has strengthened its role in traditional cosmetics marketing with the addition of Revlon's Ultima, Passion by Elizabeth Taylor, and other lines. With this new change Penney's has come alive and added almost $2 billion in 1992 to its sales. J. C. Penney is now an $18 billion company with an improved profit performance and steadily increasing comparable store sales and productivity.

Meanwhile, non–department store retailing has undergone vast change. K mart, with a projected volume of more than $40 billion in 1993, does three quarters of the total U.S. department store volume. It has redirected itself in recent years—changing from Kresge, a five and dime chain, to K mart, a specialty retailing chain in six major businesses: K mart Stores, the parent and basis of the business; Builders Square, home improvement supplies; Office Max, office supplies and equipment; Sports Authority, the new generation of sporting goods store; Pace Warehouse Clubs; and Waldenbooks and now Borders, book superstores. This strategic approach combines the strength of a major discounter with five retailing operations aimed at specific segments of the market.

K mart projects a 1995 volume of larger than all U.S. department stores combined. A substantial portion of this volume will come from the new K mart specialty retail group and today K mart is developing 400,000-square-foot centers including all six divisions. K mart is starting or acquiring businesses in Czechoslovakia, Hungary, Mexico, and now owns 21 percent of Australia's largest retailer. K mart could well be the prototype of the aggressive, diversified, well-developed, and entrepreneurial international retailer of the next decade if it learns to manage these diverse businesses and remains focused on its core K mart business—a major challenge.

During the same period, the growth of Wal*Mart has been extraordinary. (Wal*Mart changed the spelling of their name recently, adding the * in the middle, in memory of Sam Walton, whom they view as among the stars.) Wal*Mart started in the rural areas of the Southwest by moving into smaller and mid-size communities, becoming the dominant store and eliminating much of their competition. The number of suppliers beating a path to Wal*Mart's doors has increased dramatically. Today, the Bentonville, Arkansas, airport home of Wal*Mart is a busy place.

A great strength of Wal*Mart is its partnership program with major suppliers. The company utilizes highly developed technology that it shares with its suppliers so they can replenish over two thousand stores quickly, accurately, and with a minimum of items out of stock. This has fueled the company's extraordinary growth.

In 1984 Wal*Mart sales were $4.7 billion. Wal*Mart's projected 1993 volume of $69 billion is $15 billion greater than that of all the department stores in the United States, combined. Of this, $48 billion will be in the 2,030 Wal*Mart stores, the balance in the 321 Sam's Price Clubs.

The question for the future is, with such a substantial share of market, can Wal*Mart continue to grow at its current rate? This is a major challenge, but Wal*Mart continues to seek new opportunities. For example, Wal*Mart was the first to move into the price club business with the creation of Sam's. In nine years, Sam's has grown to a volume of $12.3 billion and is one of America's largest retail companies. Today Wal*Mart is expanding into the very competitive East Coast and metropolitan area, creating new challenges for themselves and their competition. To maintain its impressive growth rate, Wal*Mart is looking beyond our borders; they are already in Mexico and are projecting new stores for Canada and Europe. A remarkable performance in thirty years. Despite its impressive volume, or maybe as a result of it, Wal*Mart remains the dominant low-cost operator in the United States.

The future of membership warehouse clubs, such as the Price Club, on the other hand, seems more uncertain. The concept is very appealing: vast assortments of different types of products—food in bulk sizes and general merchandise—all sold at very low prices. And it appeared to be very successful: The retailer takes a very low 10–12 percent markup; many of the profits are generated through a nominal membership fee. Yet as markets become saturated and merchandise less diverse there appears to be a limitation to the early exponential growth.

What happened to the price clubs, whose future seemed so bright? They have suffered a dramatic decline: comparable store sales increases of price clubs have gone from 21 percent in 1986 to 16 percent in 1987 to 13 percent in 1989–1991, and 7 percent in 1992. The outlook for 1993 appears to be flat or a small drop.

There are several reasons for this. Heightened competition brought about the proliferation of new warehouse clubs growing from 212 in 1986 to 625 in 1992. Price clubs have a great geographic reach and many of the new stores cannibalized sales from themselves and their competitors. There was also an absence of new ideas—many stores lost focus and some became less aggressive in their pricing. At the same time supermarkets awoke to their new competition and began to offer bulk packaging and lower prices.

In addition, there seems to be a somewhat more limited customer base for warehouse clubs than originally projected. A shake-out in the industry has already begun, and there has been a major increase in business failures among price clubs.

Despite this, there still exists untapped markets for warehouse clubs, and the industry expects that sales from the top five companies that do the greater bulk of price club business will double in the next five years. Price Clubs have become a substantial factor in the retail industry and are here to stay.

b

Specialty retailing, including The Limited, The Limited Express, the Gap, Gap Kids, Victoria's Secret, Banana Republic, and new chains such as Structure, has been the other major retail growth area. Such stores combine ease of shopping, clarity of assortment, a clearly defined customer, a value image, rapid replenishment, and centralized procurement in a very appealing blend. With the growing practice of clustering many specialty stores in a single mall, they have become, in a sense, the department store of the nineties. You can now wander from store to store, much as you would from department to department in a department store.

Specialty retailers like The Limited learned to take advantage of the weakness of the department stores in procuring fashion merchandise. The Limited controls its own manufacturing and distribution processes—they design and distribute through high-speed technology and even utilize a weekly chartered airplane to fly Far Eastern goods directly into a distribution and import-clearing warehouse in Columbus, Ohio. This reduces the time of getting goods from the Far East into a store from five months, as in department stores, to four weeks—an enormous asset in fashion merchandising, one that represents sizable savings in expense of capital, improvement in turnover, and reduction of markdowns, probably adding 3 to 4 percent to the bottom line. Les Wexner expects sales of The Limited divisions, now $7 billion, to grow 50 percent by the mid-1990s and hit $20 billion in the next decade.

b

I've been fascinated by the significant crossover between specialty store customers and those of the department store. Specialty stores thrive in malls or in downtown locations near department stores. Shoppers appear equally comfortable shopping in both, and it is part of the relaxed life-style of the times to wear an Armani jacket with a GAP T-shirt and Levi jeans. Shoppers must choose where to assemble the elements of their wardrobe. The challenge for the specialty stores is to keep their narrow focus from being boring.

One cannot review retailing in the nineties without commenting on the flourishing outlet and off-price malls. Off-price shopping has grown from dingy, poorly lit factory buildings to over 300 outlet malls in the United States with attractive buildings, good landscaping, pleasant food operations, and stores such as Polo/Ralph Lauren, Donna Karan, Calvin Klein, Anne Klein, Jones, Hanes, Mikasa, and Barney's. Saks, Neiman's, Nordstrom's, and I. Magnin have all joined this new fast-growing form of retailing. Outlet malls meet a legitimate need of consumers to find brand-name and designer merchandise at sale prices and a willingness by some consumers to buy last season's styles to obtain bargain prices.

As for the newest forms of shopping, I have already described my feelings about the potential for home shopping via television. Infomercials are essentially twenty-eight-minute commercials that both entertain and aim at selling a product or an idea, ranging from Ross Perot's economic lessons to the Juiceman. At the same time, on home shopping networks such as QVC, consumers respond to the interaction with the announcer. Somehow they become part of the marketing process. I believe that people grow to feel that QVC is a friend they can welcome into their homes, twenty-four hours a day, seven days a week. Part of the success of QVC is the announcer who, in a low-key manner, convincingly demonstrates the value of their products. The salesmanship is more professional than in most department stores.

A year ago, home shopping and its cousin, the infomercial, regarded retailers as the enemy. Today I see infomercials, home shopping, and stores as different aspects of the same marketing strategy. More and more stores and manufacturers will, I believe, combine all three elements. That is why I have worked to introduce Saks to QVC and why our Thai foods are being marketed through both channels of distribution.

Infomercials in 1992 represented a $750 million business. With more people going into the field, and a two- to three-minute short-form infomercial on the horizon, that number can double in the coming years. At the same time, QVC is only six years old and today does substantially over a billion dollars. The planned merger with Home Shopping Network adds another billion dollars and gives Barry Diller a dominant position in this industry.

Home shopping is no mere fad. Four trends will, I believe, explode this business in the coming years: first, a technological change in the lines that carry cable, called compression (you will hear that word more often in the future), will increase the number of cable channels, possibly to five hundred, and permit much more focused marketing. There will be channels aimed at each type of customer —a Saks, a Macy's, or a Wal*Mart. Other channels will operate like specialty stores or divisions; there will be a home furnishings channel, a menswear channel, and one dedicated to sports-related products. Second, the development of high-definition television, which has now been approved, will provide magazinelike reproduction on the TV screen. This will make each product even more appealing to the viewer and be greater competition for magazines and catalogs.

The next step in home shopping clearly will be interactive catalog shopping. The technology exists today for the viewer to call up on command a catalog page of typewriters, bicycles, TV sets, or laptop computers and order accordingly. Costs are substantially less than a catalog—items can be added or dropped based on sales or availability. Finally, until now, home selling has prospered with very little entertainment—the entertainment consisted of an ongoing presentation of products with some interaction with the show's host. Making the shopping programs themselves more fun to watch could improve sales dramatically. These elements, taken together, make home shopping a formidable force for the future of retailing.

b

Implicit in the future of retailing is the continuing importance of fashion. In the 1950s, taste and style were limited to a few stores and a very select clientele. In my own years at Bloomingdale's we saw the elements of style become available to, and of great interest to, a much broader group of shoppers. Today, a further democratization of style as communicated through television and the media has occurred. Style today is available to anyone who can afford a $10.50 Gap pocket T-shirt or a baseball cap (worn backwards). This is a significant factor as we face the future of retailing.

ᑫ

This book began with a portrait of retailing sixty years ago and described how the Bloomingdale's legend led to the revolution in American marketing. Now, as we approach the millennium, we are witnessing the further progress of that revolution.

Throughout this book I have discussed many specifics of what Bloomingdale's accomplished. Today, while we are all party to retailing's continued growth and evolution, certain elements remain constant:

What I am perhaps best remembered for at Bloomingdale's is making shopping fun and creating excitement. Nothing happens without enthusiasm. Enthusiasm in a retailer must spread from the top down: people must be excited to come to work. That is the challenge that everyone faces: how to get others excited about what they do.

I have had tremendous fun these past forty years. I was fortunate to enter retailing at a time of great change that permitted me to execute the strategies I believed in. For me, the excitement is far from over, and my enthusiasm is undiminished. If I can offer any advice or draw any conclusion from my career thus far, it is this: Create the excitement, and share in the fun.

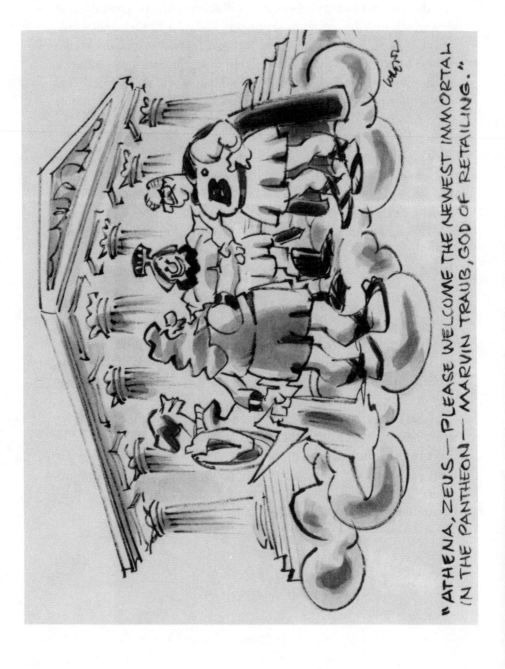

"ATHENA, ZEUS—PLEASE WELCOME THE NEWEST IMMORTAL IN THE PANTHEON— MARVIN TRAUB, GOD OF RETAILING."

A Personal Afterword

A life of intense activity, such as I lead, leaves little time for reflection. Writing this book has been a more challenging and demanding experience than I ever imagined, and it has led me to reflect on the various people who have played important roles in my life, and to consider what were the most meaningful experiences of a long and richly rewarding career.

I feel very blessed, not merely for my wife, my family, my career, my great friends all over the world, but for the good fortune that provided us with an extraordinary life. Above all, I owe much of my happiness in life to Lee and our children.

Lee has always been caring, capable, and decisive in her judgments, very willing to be the person who challenged me if she thought I was wrong; yet she contributed an atmosphere of love to our home that has made ours an extraordinary forty-five-year partnership.

It was Lee and then our children who made me look forward to coming home at night or on the weekend. It was Lee who added pleasure to all of my successes, because I had someone to share them with. She is truly a formidable person.

Early on in my career it became clear that I would have very full work days. Lee insisted we keep Sunday nights plus at least two nights a week for family dinners. Each child came to the dinner table with one event they wanted to discuss, be it something at school, in the news, or something they had seen on television, and the others would listen. Each one had a chance to participate and be heard. They knew they were expected to have something to add to the conversation. We could, and did, disagree strongly with each other, but these differences only created spirited dinner conversation. Our children look back very fondly on that kind of participation, and even today as adults, our meal time discussions are very lively.

Once every few months, I would spend an evening alone with each child; they chose the activity and selected the restaurant. The choice was completely theirs, whether we went to the theater, dance or a movie, baseball or football game. This may sound as if I were doing it for them, but those evenings were very special for me, and as soon as my grandchildren are old enough, I hope to start having nights out with them.

I would report to Lee and my children regularly about what was happening at work, and about all the personalities I dealt with. I made it a point that Lee meet the people with whom I worked.

When my work demanded that I travel a good deal I arranged for Lee to join me. She has played a very important role in the relationships I developed all over the world. My children, as an integral part of my life, are also part of my global friendships. Andy worked several summers at AMC's buying office in Florence, working on his Italian; Jimmy worked in Amsterdam and at the AMC office in Paris. Peggy worked in Paris and spent a vacation with the Missonis and their children at their summer home on an island off the coast of Yugoslavia. Peggy likes to recall that she knew she was fully accepted into the family when Tai and Rosita would shout at her the same way they did with their own children. And it created quite a stir a few years ago when, after receiving the Legion D'Honneur, I attended the Ungaro show in Paris with my three-year-old granddaughter Rebecca on my knee. She applauded loudly throughout the collection. Upon her return, her nursery school teachers wanted to know what it meant when she shouted: "Ingaro! Ingaro!"

By now, I believe my style has become evident: I'm open, curious, demanding, have high standards, a great interest in people, and a creative bent that makes new design, new products, and, above all, new ideas fascinating to me. I have a very high energy level and in a typical day will try to pack in all the events, projects, and meetings I can.

I have always had an enormous and unbridled enthusiasm for what I do. I look forward to coming to work each day, and regard business as a challenge and a game. My enthusiasm has carried over to my second career and is perhaps the most important factor in my energy level. There's nothing like loving what you do to give you great energy.

Just as Bloomingdale's was always committed to giving back to the community, Lee and I decided our family should be involved with helping others. In 1965, Lee and I told our children that for Christmas we were going to adopt a foster child in Hong Kong. Through Foster Parents we arranged to visit the family that we were going to help. We went to a tenement in Kowloon accompanied by the head of our Hong Kong office. We walked up six flights to find a family that had fled China living in a shack built on the roof. The shack was built by nailing large flattened-out tin cans together to create walls and a ceiling. Mother, father, and three children were living in a single room and sleeping in one bed. That was our introduction to Wei Ching Cheung, who was then fourteen years old.

We brought food to Wei Cheung and his family as well as a dictionary. Lee counseled him to learn to write in English. Our money for the next four years helped him attend a good school in Hong Kong and provided supplies and medical services for him and his family.

Some years later Wei Cheung, who had adopted the first name Thomas, arrived in New York with his new bride, Anna. We invited them to our house and helped him secure a job at Bloomingdale's, where he worked nights and Saturdays while studying Marine insurance at St. John's University. Today Thomas is a very successful vice president of Marine Insurance at Inchcape, a large British company with offices in Hong Kong. He travels the world and visits us whenever he comes to New York. He knows that we think of him as family and it means a good deal to us that he and Anna and their two children think of us in the same way.

When Lee and I last visited Thomas, he invited us to dinner at Hong Kong's exclusive Jockey Club. When dinner was over, I reached for the check, but he signed saying, "Dad, you're my guest. I'm a member now." We were very proud.

In 1970, at Expo in Osaka, we met Akiko Kawano, a young Japanese woman who had been assigned by the government to be our escort for our three days at the fair. At the end of our time together, she told us she was coming to the United States the next year to get a master's degree at Bucknell. We found her charming and invited her to our home in Scarsdale. Later she brought a tall friendly American named Ricky Jones for one of her weekend visits and asked what we thought of him. When we said we thought he was a fine young man, she told us she hoped to marry him. We were supportive and stayed in close touch. Akiko and Ricky got married, lived on a Sioux Indian reservation for two years, then moved to Bowling Green, Ohio, where Ricki is a full professor and Akiko teaches Japanese at Bowling Green University. They have two very bright, talented youngsters and the family visits us several times a year. Natalie, at eleven, is the youngest soloist ever to peform with the Toledo Symphony, and Nathaniel is an Ohio all-state swimmer. Both are outstanding students and they refer to Lee and me as Traub Mommy and Traub Daddy. They are very close to us and our children and have become an important part of the extended Traub family.

Over the years, we have built up a series of friends all over the world. We believed it was important that our children travel and be exposed to new cultures. When Jimmy graduated from Harvard, he spent a year teaching at a college in Aurangabad in central India. Jimmy loved India and wrote a book about the country. Peggy spent her junior year of college at the Hebrew University in Jerusalem. Andy spent a summer at the Scripps Institute in California studying oceanography and traveled extensively in Europe, staying with our friends the Villigers in Zurich.

In the 1960s one of our Indian friends in New York left her three-year-old boy with us for six weeks while she visited her family in New Delhi. The ladies of the Indian community in New York were scandalized and wagged their heads and clucked their tongues and wondered, "Why did you leave him with an Amedican?" Today that three-year-old is completing work for his doctorate at Columbia. At other times we've had exchange students from Colombia and Spain living with us.

Our travels have sometimes led to new interests. In the course of Bloomingdale's 1978 Israel promotion, I became friends with Michael Sela, the head of the Weizman Institute. The Institute's work so impressed Lee and me that three years later we raised money to endow a Marvin and Lee Traub laboratory there in the field of immunology to be used by Professor Sela.

I've always been a major supporter of the arts and of education. My activities in these areas have only made my life that much more interesting. I have served for many years on the development committee of Lincoln Center, the business committee of the Metropolitan Museum of Art, and recently I joined the development committee of the Whitney Museum of American Art. During President Carter's administration I served on the White House Preservation Fund. I served for the last five years as a member of the Visiting Committee of the Harvard School of Public Health and enjoyed very much working with the dean and the faculty. Harvard has been very important to me. I am very dedicated to it and take pride in our scholarship holders and my committee assignments. Lee has had a lifelong love of dance. As chairman of the Martha Graham board for many years, Lee was very close to Martha, who was one of the great geniuses of our age. And it was my pleasure along with Lee to be with Martha and her company on many occasions.

b

Lee and I place great value on having the family together. When we built our house in Greenwich it was planned with the children in mind. We included several guest bedrooms and had a pool and tennis court installed so that our home would become Camp Traub for our children and grandchildren. We found that skiing was a wonderful family vacation, and built a six-bedroom home in Utah that can bunk our whole troop. Having three generations of Traubs ski down the mountain together fills us with pride and gives a great sense of family.

This is not to say that over the years I haven't fought with my children. Each has gone through a rebellious phase, but considering that they grew up in the 1960s and 1970s, they rebelled amazingly little. And through it all we continued to talk to each other. Lee and I created an atmosphere where everyone could present their views. We could disagree about everything except that we were family and loved each other. As a consequence, I'm very proud of my children —not only of their accomplishments, which are considerable in their own right, but of the people they have become.

Andy chose to attend Harvard and Harvard Business School, as I did, and to enter the retailing field. He started at Neiman's, then worked for several years at Macy's where he rose to merchandise vice president, before becoming president of Block Industries. When Andy suggested the Block Industries deal, I was pleased to have the chance to work with him; seeing his success is tremendously gratifying.

Jimmy chose to become a journalist and author. He probably doesn't realize it, but by doing so he is fulfilling ambitions I nurtured while in high school and at the *Crimson* but never pursued. His work has appeared in such publications as *The New Yorker, Harper's, The New Republic, Vogue,* and *The New York Times Magazine,* and he is the author of a well-received book on the Wedtech scandal, *Too Good to Be True,* as well as a textbook on India, *India, the Challenge of Change.* Currently he is working on a book about City College that I have no doubt will be a great success.

Peggy chose perhaps the hardest route of all, following me not only into retailing but by working at Bloomingdale's, where she was the group manager of lamps, gifts, and pillows. She is now working with me at Conran's as merchandise manager for lighting and domestics. It is a pleasure to see how great her talent is, and to appreciate it by working with her. All in all, I am very fortunate.

One of the more difficult moments that Lee and I had as parents was when Peggy told us she was gay. I thought long about whether this subject had any place in this book. I decided that there are many parents of gay children who have gone through, or will go through, what we did. I thought that if anyone benefited from our experience it was worth including.

One evening in 1981, Peggy asked to come to dinner in Greenwich with Lee and me. At dinner she told the two of us that she was gay. I didn't quite know what to say. Like many parents, at first I thought there must be something wrong. Had Lee and I done something wrong as parents? Was there something wrong with Peggy?

A few years later, Peggy told us that she had met her life partner, Phyllis, and was very happy about it. As far as Peggy was concerned, this was the person she was committed to sharing the rest of her life with. Lee and I did not know Phyllis very well at that time.

This was very difficult for us. I wasn't quite sure how to deal with Phyllis and Peggy's relationship. The question then became:

What sort of relationship did *we* want to have with Peggy? The answer was clear: We wanted to continue to have a close and loving relationship with our daughter. We decided that we had to accept Peggy for who she was. Lee and I came to the conclusion that being gay was as much a part of who Peggy was as the color of her eyes, or her native intelligence. I don't say this was as easy as it sounds, but it was the right decision. We wanted Peggy to be a part of the family, and welcomed Phyllis into our hearts as we had Lois and Buffy (Andy's and Jimmy's wives). And we are happy to be able to say now that Peggy and Phyllis's relationship is every bit as harmonious and enduring as the best heterosexual marriages we have known.

Andy and Lois are parents of our three delightful granddaughters, Rebecca, Rachel, and Abigail. Jimmy and Buffy are parents of our ebullient grandson Alexander.

Many parents think their children should cater to their wishes. I believe you have to meet them halfway. They have their own lives; we have ours. It is important to find ways to include your children's lives, and life-styles, in your.

b

The period from 1987 to 1991 was the most stressful I had ever experienced: from the stock market crash through the sale of Federated, life under Campeau, Bloomingdale's being put up for sale, my failed attempt to buy the store, including our disastrous trip to Japan, the bankruptcy itself, to Alan's decision to seek my replacement and my last day at Bloomingdale's, life had been a series of difficult shocks. There is no other way to describe that period. However, during that time I was fortunate enough to have the support of Lee, Andy, Lois, Jimmy, Buffy, Peggy, Phyllis, and the distraction of our grandchildren. I could not have dealt with it as well as I did without them.

Further Acknowledgments

Over the years, many people have suggested that I write a book, but I was always too busy to do so. However, one morning three years ago, I found myself seated at breakfast with Bob Barnett and Ann Stock. Bob is a partner in the prestigious Washington law firm of Williams & Connolly—Edward Bennet Williams's firm—and has represented a variety of prominent figures in business and government in their book contracts; Ann, at that time, was in charge of public relations for Bloomingdale's. Both Bob and Ann strongly urged me to write a book, and this time, because of all that had transpired during the Campeau regime, and a realization that much in retailing had changed since my career began—and because of Ann's and Bob's persuasive abilities—I said yes.

Among the eight publishers Bob contacted, I was very impressed by Random House, their chairman Alberto Vitale, and Times Books' publisher Peter Osnos. I was even more delighted when their bid was the highest, and Peter was to be my editor.

To choose a collaborator, I interviewed more than a dozen writers and chose Tom Teicholz. Tom's talent and intelligence were sufficient reason, but in addition he was young enough to be in touch with contemporary trends and had grown up near Bloomingdale's, understanding the store and all it had come to represent. At our first meeting Tom told me, with some apprehension, that his father-in-law, Gene Rappeport, was a longtime Federated employee, the former chairman of Federated Marketing Services, with whom I had worked closely for more than twenty-five years. "That could be an asset—or a liability," Tom said. I decided it was a plus. Thanks, Gene.

To write and research this book, I dictated more than 2,200 pages and Tom conducted more than a hundred interviews both in the United States and in France. Tom accompanied me to the Prêt-à-Porter in Paris, on store and market visits, and during my final days at Bloomingdale's. We worked on weekends, early in the mornings, and very late at night. So I want to thank Tom here for all his hard work—I appreciated it and very much enjoyed our collaboration. I wish to apologize to his wife, Amy, for taking him away so often.

Getting to know Amy was also a benefit of working on the book. Amy's projects at American Express overlapped with my interests there and we enjoyed discussing American Express; Lee and I both enjoyed her company.

Nothing would have been accomplished without the help of my dedicated and trusted assistants. At Marvin Traub Associates, Cynthia Adler Luzon, who starts early and works very late, and Gloria Antinori, her partner, and thanks as well to a very dedicated David Rey; at Bloomingdale's, Patty Donohue; and at Federated, Ann Cossman. Special thanks to Ron Parham, who over the past fourteen years has become part of our extended family and who almost always managed to get me to my appointments on time.

Many of my closest friends do not appear in the book, but they are an important part of my life. They listened to me and counseled me on this book. I wish to acknowledge them here. Harry and Barbara Fields, our close friends of thirty-five years travel the world with us. Edythe and Mike Gladstein, for their continuing support as well as their friendship. Larry and Dalia Leeds, Barbara and Alan Thomas, Joan Easton, Marcia Rose and Jerry Shestack, Al and Joan Kronick, Sally and Martin Blumenthal, Ed and Sandy Meyer, Bob and Helen Bernstein, Steve Stevens, Beverly Sills and Peter Greenough, Dick and Edna Salomon, George and Jennifer Lang, Finn Berger and Lulu Christenson of Copenhagen, Rudi and Doris Villiger of Zurich, Philippe and Solange Mayer and Christianne Demery of Paris.

In writing this book I wish there was space enough to give credit to the thousands of Bloomingdale's coworkers who in the past forty years collaborated with me in making Bloomingdale's into the unique institution it became. A number of the key players are in this book—many are not. I felt it appropriate here to list some of the players, omitted so far, who made our team the pennant winner it became.

The woman in the fifties who headed executive training and recruitment and who brought to Bloomingdale's the talent that started to build our business: Martha Scudder. Our research director in the fifties—an excellent sounding board for Jed and later me—Alfred Guttman; my partner in building the home furnishings business in the fifties: Oliver Roberge. An ex-Gimbel's piece goods buyer who started in the basement the same day I did, later to become a star in the gourmet food business: Bob Gumport.

A host of talented executives who helped to create the Bloomingdale's legend in the fifties, sixties, and seventies: Jim Coe, Barbara Bass, Ron Grudberg, Joe Preminger, Arthur Fulgentiz, Heb Berman, Mort Huff, John Hardin, Tom Mayers, Mike Risavy, Bob Lee, Ron Ruskin, Murray Friedman, Dick Brenner, Phil Brous, Bob Silver, Phil Kelly, Jack Schultz, Peggy Healy, Rosalind Starkman, Norman Axelrod, Jerry Applebome.

To give credit to some of today's team who were part of my era as well: Margaret Hofbeck, my dedicated partner for personnel, who was usually at the store when I arrived at 7:00 A.M., Sue Kronick, Steve Spiro, Alan Kahn, Julie Taub, Stu Glasser, Wil Hellmeyer, Kathy Stanton, Barbara Kennedy, Dave Fischer, Marty Newman, Rob Goldfarb, Larry Schecterman, Jim Held, Marty Nealon, June Seelig, Nora Holley, Pat Chadwick. To all not mentioned—my thanks; I wish I could list everyone.

The Bloomingdale's import program was made possible by our AMC overseas offices and I want to acknowledge Lee Abraham, Renato Mosco, Steve Osterweiss, and Bill French who have led AMC these past thirty years.

For the last two years my golf partners have had to listen to me talk about the book; I thank Don Blum, Don Landis, Henry Graff, Wally Stern, and Peter Spitz for their indulgence.

On the manufacturing side many manufacturers and designers have been critical to our success—I cannot mention all of them here but I should include Guy Peyrelongue, the head of Lancôme L'Oreal USA who built an extraordinary business with us; Art Otenberg, Jerry Chazen, and Liz Claiborne—I started with them when Liz Claiborne was a struggling sportswear business; John and Laura Pomerantz; Linda Wachner of Warnaco (earlier of Max Factor) a tremendous success story of the nineties; Adrienne and Gigi Vittadini; Tommy Hilfiger; Eli Tahari; Steve Ruzow of Donna Karan; Herb Gallen of Ellen Tracy; Ken Ross of JH Collectibles; Sol Levine of Revlon; Fred and Gayle Hayman of Giorgio; Sam Farber of Copco; Reneede Chambrun and Francois de Montmorin of Baccarat; Earl de Voto of Orrefors; Sy Stewart; George and Maurice Marciano; Josie and Ken Natori; Albert Bouilhet of Christofle, and thousands of other suppliers large and small. Over the years there have been substantial numbers of suppliers who got their start because a Bloomingdale's buyer believed in them. I wish to thank those suppliers and those buyers.

b

I want also to thank the many people who cooperated and gave of their time for this book.

First, the many people Tom interviewed, in particular: Arthur Bruckman, May Levine, Harvey Pack, Joan Messinger, Steve Stevens, Stanley Marcus, Ella Wasserberg, Sue Kronick, Al Kronick, Janina Wilner, Sumner Feldberg, Wilbur Cowett, Vin Brennan, Barbara D'Arcy, Carl Levine, Dick Hauser, Mel Jacobs, Diane Levbarg, Tai and Rosita Missoni, Sonia Rykiel, Maurice Cau, Emanuel Ungaro, Dick Salomon, Chantal Rousseau, Christiane Demery, Christian Petrossian, Leah Gottlieb, Joan Glynn, Candy Pratts, Arthur Cohen, Steven J. Roth, Tony Michaels, Anne Lacombe, Matthew Rubel, Leonard Lauder, Charles Revson, Jr., William Lauder, Amy Fine Collins, Arie Kopelman, Lester Gribetz, Ralph Lauren, John Schultz, Larry Lachman, Carla Fendi, Steve Spiro, Ann Stock, David Enders, John Levy, Kal Ruttenstein, Didier Grumbach, Don Stone, Gene Rappeport, Brad Freeman, Ron Spogli, and Jeff Sherman.

The close readers of the manuscript who by their comments made it that much better: Walter Loeb, who shared his thoughts on the future of retailing; Jimmy Traub—my severest critic; Andy Traub; Peggy Traub; Lee Traub; Lester Gribetz; Amy Rappeport; Mike Gladstein; and Harry Fields.

The Times Books all-stars: Peter Osnos, who always kept the book on course, giving encouragement and helping us throughout the process; Ken Gellman, for his editorial attention; Peter Smith for his diligence; Robin Schiff, for her hard work in creating a great cover and Naomi Osnos and Kristen Bearse for making the book as interesting to look at as we hope it is to read; and Mary Beth Murphy, director of publicity who herself deserves all the attention that she gets her authors.

The research in this book was significantly aided by the resources of the New York and Beverly Hills public libraries as well as the libraries of New York's Harvard Club and of the National Retail Federation. In addition we would like to thank *The New York Times* for giving us access to their morgue; and *Women's Wear* for access to their archives. Ann Stock, David Enders, and Bloomingdale's public relations office were a great help as were the personnel offices' back issues of the "Tally" and Jeff Madoff's interviews on videotape. Dixie Barker at Federated was also very helpful—thank you for your cooperation.

Another great source of information that we wish to acknowledge was Maxine Brady's *bloomingdale's* book—we uncovered a great deal of research only to find she had been there first; and Barbara Darcy's *Bloomingdale's Book of Decorating*.

For the Campeau section, in addition to the original material at our disposal, the national coverage in *The New York Times* and *The Wall Street Journal* were consulted. On Campeau himself, Arthur Johnson's articles in *Report on Canadian Business* were very helpful; and the coverage of the Campeau deal in the *Los Angeles Times* was particularly informative, as was John Rothchild's *Going for Broke*. Walter Salmon's Harvard Business School case study was illuminating as well.

b

In addition to all of the above, Tom Teicholz would like to thank Nessa Rapoport, the queen of the acknowledgments—you earned this one for steering me to Bill and teaching me about "voice." Bill Novak, king of the ghosts, was my mentor on this journey and I thank him for his counsel. Peter Osnos, whose support helped me push that peanut up the hill. Ken Gellman and Peter Smith, for their hard work and friendship. Gene Rappeport, for encouraging me to take on this project. Scott Wetzler for his insightful comments on the text. To Marvin Traub, of course, for his generosity, warmth, and for making working hard seem like fun. To Lee Traub for her hospitality, friendship, and for those wonderful summer salads; and to Amy for all her love while I was writing.

b

An apology to any who should be mentioned but were not by error or omission.

Finally, we thank all of you for helping us make this "like no other book in the world."

The Bloomingdale's Alumni Club

Associates I Worked with Closely Who Became Principals *

ARNOLD ARONSON	CEO Bullock's, CEO Saks Fifth Avenue, CEO BATUS, CEO Woodward & Lothrop, CEO Wanamaker's
NORMAN AXELROD	CEO Linens 'N Things
BARBARA BASS	CEO I. Magnin, CEO Emporium, CEO Capwell-Weinstock's
ROBIN BURNS	CEO Estée Lauder U.S.A.
JIM COE	President, Meier & Frank
ARTHUR COHEN	President, Worldwide Marketing, President, Paramount
GORDON COOKE	CEO Bloomingdale's By Mail
MICKEY DREXLER	President, the Gap
WARREN FELDBERG	CEO Marshall's
HOWARD GOLDFEDER	CEO Bullock's, CEO Federated Department Stores
LESTER GRIBETZ	President, Conran's·Habitat
RON GRUDBERG	CEO Findlay Jewelers

* With apologies to anyone I omitted and to those who will become principals in the future.

RICHARD HAUSER	CEO Neiman-Marcus, CEO The Broadway, CEO Wanamaker's
MELVIN JACOBS	CEO Burdine's, Vice Chairman, Federated Department Stores, CEO Saks Fifth Avenue
PHIL KELLY	CEO Robinsons, CEO Marshall Field's, CEO Garfinckel's
SUE KRONICK	President, Rich's
DANIEL LEVY	President, Kauffman's, CEO Gimbels Pittsburgh Vice Chairman, Montgomery Ward, CEO Conran's Habitat
JACK LIPPMAN	CEO Drizzle Coats
PHILLIP MILLER	CEO Neiman-Marcus, CEO Marshall Field's, CEO Saks Fifth Avenue
RONALD RUSKIN	CEO Best & Co, CEO Gimbels, President, BATUS
JAMES SCHOFF, JR.	President, Bloomingdale's
JEFF SHERMAN	President, Bloomingdale's
MARK SHULMAN	CEO Ann Taylor, CEO Bendel's
JACK SHULTZ	CEO B. Altman
DENISE SIEGEL	President, DKNY
FRANKLIN SIMON	CEO Bullock's
MIKE STEINBERG	CEO Foley's, CEO Macy's West
CHERYL STERLING	President, Ralph Lauren
RUSSELL STRAVITZ	CEO Rich's
ROBERT SUSLOW	CEO Saks Fifth Avenue, CEO BATUS

Country Promotions, 1960–1991

1960 Casa Bella—Italia H.F.
1961 L'Esprit de France
1962 Romance Everlasting
1963 Tradition
1964 Johnny So Long at the Fair
1965 Symphony in B
1966 Colors of Asia
1967 All the World's a Stage
1968 New York, New York
1969 Art Beat
1970 The Creators

ხ

1978 India, the Ultimate Fantasy
1979 Israel, the Dream
1980 China: Heralding the Dawn of a New Era
1981 Ireland—That Special Place
1982 America the Beautiful
     The Philippines
1983 Fête de France
1984 Ecco l'Italia
1985 Japan
1986 The South China Seas
1987 Mediterranean Odyssey
1988 Year of the Dragon
1989 Vive la France
     Hooray for Hollywood
1990 Spain: Europe's Rising Star
     Broadway '90
1991 Tempo d'Italia

Index

About the Authors

MARVIN S. TRAUB is president of Marvin Traub Associates. He lives in New York and Greenwich, Connecticut.

TOM TEICHOLZ is a writer and an attorney. He lives in New York and Los Angeles.

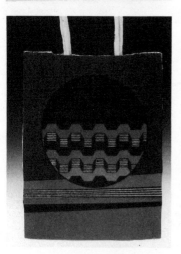

Fall 1961
L'Esprit de France, Jonah Kiningstein

Spring 1976
Michaele Vollbracht

Spring 1988
Neville Brody

Fall 1964
Johnny So Long at the Fair

Fall 1963
Tradition

Spring 1991
Malcolm Garrett

Spring 1971
Tai and Rosita Missoni

Fall 1989
Vive la France, Geoff Kern

Fall 1987
Mediterranean Odyssey, Ann

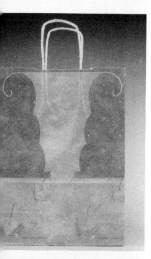

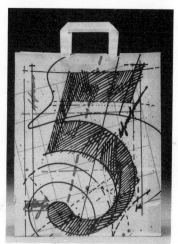

Spring 1984
Michael Graves

Fall 1984 Ecco L'Italia
Ettore Sottsass

Spring 1985
Scandinavia

Spring 1986
Mark Kostabi

Fall 1990
Palm Beach Store. Laurie Rosenwald

Spring 1985
Tim Girvin

Summer 1983
Susan Curtis

Fall 1982
America

Fall 1991, Tempo D'Italia
Franco Moschino (see last page)

This was the only shopping bag we ever pulled out
of our stores. We did so at the request of the Italian
government, who objected to Moschino's irreverent
phrase IN PIZZA WE TRUST. Today the shopping bags
have become a collector's item.